AFTER THE GDR

GERMAN MONITOR No. 54
General Editor: Ian Wallace

AFTER THE GDR

New Perspectives on the Old GDR and the Young *Länder*

Edited by

Laurence McFalls
and
Lothar Probst

Amsterdam - Atlanta, GA 2001

The paper on which this book is printed meets the requirements of "ISO 9706:1994, Information and documentation - Paper for documents - Requirements for permanence".

ISBN: 90-420-1336-2 (bound)
©Editions Rodopi B.V., Amsterdam - Atlanta, GA 2001
Printed in The Netherlands

Table of Contents

Introduction

The GDR is dead, long live the GDR! As the articles collected in this volume testify, the German Democratic Republic has enjoyed remarkable posthumous success not only as an object of study but as a community of experience. Indeed, in the decade since the GDR's formal dissolution, it has become a cliché to point out that unification achieved that which eluded the GDR for forty years, namely the forging of a strong sense of identity among its former citizens. Opinion polls regularly confirm the questionable stereotype according to which eastern Germans — allegedly suffering from the construction of a "wall in their heads" — understand themselves to be "former GDR-citizens" or second-class citizens of the Federal Republic and to define themselves in opposition to the overbearing western "Other". This stereotype, of course, exaggerates the bonds that do distinguish and partially unite eastern Germans: their memories of life under real-existing socialism and their need to adjust to a new social, economic, and political order. To be sure, eastern Germans' memories of the past and adjustments to the present vary greatly, and some eastern Germans may have more in common with some western Germans than with other eastern Germans. Still, their shared experiences of past and present, regardless of whether they are strong enough to constitute an enduring collective identity, define eastern Germans as a social group subject to monographic study.

This volume represents the efforts of a group of scholars from eastern and western Germany, Canada, the United States, France, and Norway to work through the complex and sometimes compromising past and the current struggles that together define eastern German identity ten years after unification. The following fifteen papers were selected from among the twenty-seven presented at the Sixth Triennial Congress of the Eastern German Studies Association held in Montréal, Québec, in November 1998. Most of them have been revised and brought up-to-date and none has been previously published. Between them, they offer an exemplary illustration of the variety of disciplinary methods and new source materials that established and younger scholars can draw on today to further our understanding of the old GDR and the young *Länder*.

Although readers will no doubt pick out the texts addressing their particular interests, the sequence of the papers does follow a thematic and chronological order. The opening essay, by *Wolfgang Emmerich*, transcends its ostensible topic — the social role of literary elites since 1989 — to raise the question of intellectuals' fascination with, even seduction by, socialism.

For anyone with an interest in the (former) GDR and its failed promises, this question is not merely historical: intellectuals' attraction to utopianism, no matter how perverted any effort to apply it may be, remains perhaps, as Emmerich concludes, a defining characteristic of an intellectual. The young historian *Marie-Elisabeth Räkel*'s paper offers a brilliant illustration of how intellectuals and politicians in the founding years of the GDR could sincerely believe in their utopian project and why they themselves had to succomb to the logic of the infernal machine they had created to re-educate the less enlightened.

Examining the same founding years of the GDR, *Gerhard Wettig* proposes an alternative explanation for the establishment of communist dictatorship in the GDR. He draws on previously unavailable Russian sources to show not only how Stalinization proceeded by Soviet command in their occupation zone but how a symbiosis developed between East German communists and their Soviet masters in which each used the other to justify policies with no popular support. Also relying on new archival sources, *Gary Bruce* examines five cases of popular resistance to the dictatorship of the 1950s and concludes that mass dissatisfaction lacked revolutionary potential precisely because political and intellectual leadership was absent — no doubt for the reasons Wettig, Räkel, and Emmerich suggest. Political scientist *Jeffrey Kopstein* picks up the question of the efficacy of diffuse popular resistance to dictatorship in his theoretically thought-provoking comparison of the GDR and Nazi Germany. He makes an important distinction between the two German dictatorships on the grounds that everyday resistance ultimately brought down the Honeckero-Brezhnevite GDR but could not have stopped the genocidal Nazi war machine. On a lighter note, *Randall Bytwerk* examines how published and cabaret humour offered limited outlets for the expression of everyday resistance to a regime that demanded an untenable universal public affirmation of its infallibility. By the end of the GDR's days, however, criticism was oozing out everywhere, even in allegedly indefectible bastions of support, as *David Harding* shows in his subtle and surprising analysis of *Nationale Volksarmee* military doctrine in the 1980s.

Whereas historians and political scientists debate the empirical facts and theoretical significance of authority structures and societal resistance in the GDR, practitioners of Cultural Studies know that the historical "reality" of the GDR is but a distant cousin to the individual and collective memories that define the GDR's past. As *Karen Kramer* argues in her contribution, the images from old films made in the GDR will probably displace actual memories and play at least as great a part in the construction of the GDR past as will the best archivally-informed historiography. *Bernd Lindner* similarly reflects on the roles of different media of memory construction, particularly as the GDR becomes the object of historicization and musealization. To be sure, intellectuals, i.e. the manipulators of words, will continue to play a leading role in the construction of GDR memories and of the resulting eastern German identity. *Roswitha Skare* thus goes about deconstructing how three intellectuals born, raised, and matured in the GDR construct their own and their readers' memories in retrospective texts.

Memory and identity are not just interesting in their own right, but also because they shape political culture and conflicts in united Germany today. Like Skare, *Lothar Probst* takes on the issue of alleged "Ostalgie", but with an aim to understanding whether loyalty to values and identities inherited from the GDR past hinders or helps their integration into (post)modern, democratic, globalized society. He argues that eastern communitarianism, in opposition to allegedly more modern western individualism, was not only the progressive historical product of resistance to authoritarianism but may be more adaptive to the contemporary context of globalization. Moving from the global to the local level, *Catherine Perron*, in a fruitful comparative study of eastern Germany and the Czech Republic, demonstrates how competitive politics at the municipal level have allowed the reconciliation between past practices and experiences and new democratic institutions and norms, especially in eastern Germany with its relatively high rate of local-level elite continuity. Former communists in particular have been well integrated into the new political system thanks to the PDS's dynamism at the local level. *Meredith Heiser-Duron* also raises the question of the PDS's role in the political integration of (former) communists and GDR loyalists. Her analysis of the PDS's recent *Landtag* election successes leads her to conclude that the communist successor-party effectively represents much more than old GDR milieux but real interests. Like Heiser-Duron, *Jennifer Yoder* considers the varying sources of PDS success in the different new *Länder* but does so as part of a broader analysis of the growing political differentiation between eastern German regions. Finally, *Astrid Segert* brings attention back to the fundamental question of distributive justice that binds eastern Germans despite their differences in opposition to western Germans. Looking at the underrepresentation of eastern Germans in various elite functions, Segert dismisses the overly simple arguments of socialization and colonialization theories, which posit respectively that easterners lack the experience or have been unilaterally excluded from elite functions. Instead, she argues that eastern Germans have different and perhaps more appropriate qualifications for elite roles but qualifications which exclude them from recruitment processes.

In short, the papers presented in this volume offer a differentiated view of the old GDR and the new *Länder*. They show how utopian ideals quickly degenerated into a dictatorship that provoked the everyday resistance at all levels of society that ultimately brought the regime to its demise. They also suggest how the GDR might live on in memory to shape the emerging varieties of postcommunist politics in the young states of the Federal Republic and how the GDR experience of community and resistance might inspire new practices and concepts for German society as a whole. Most importantly, the papers here testify to the multidisciplinary vitality of a field whose original object of enquiry disappeared a decade ago. The GDR is dead, long live GDR and Eastern German Studies!

Laurence McFalls

I. The Betrayal of the Intellectuals?

Wolfgang Emmerich

Deutsche Intellektuelle: was nun?
Zum Funktionswandel der (ostdeutschen) literarischen Intelligenz zwischen 1945 und 1998

This chapter addresses the dramatic change in the role and function of East German intellectuals since unification. Starting with a brief reconstruction of the problematic history of German intellectuals in the twentieth century, it turns to the social status and the ideological positions of the literary intelligentsia in the GDR. It highlights the pivotal role of antifascism as the founding myth of the GDR, which was – with a few exceptions – internalized by a whole generation of GDR writers and intellectuals, and finally demonstrates their long and painful farewell to the utopia of a better socialist GDR.

I

Kaum eine andere soziale Gruppe aus der untergegangenen DDR hat durch das Ende dieses Staates und mit ihm seines durch und durch gelenkten kulturellen Institutionengefüges so dramatische Veränderungen hinnehmen müssen, teilweise bis hin zur völligen Entwertung, wie die Intellektuellen, also die Schriftsteller und Künstler, im weiteren Sinne auch Publizisten, Geisteswissenschaftler, Literaturkritiker und andere 'Wortproduzenten'. Damit sind erhebliche Verluste und Verunsicherungen ökonomischer und sozialer Art gemeint. Verluste an Stellen, Ämtern, Verlagshonoraren, Tantiemen oder in manchen Fällen monatliche Zuweisungen z.B. durch die Akademie der Künste der DDR. Vor allem aber meine ich damit Verluste an Sozialprestige und moralischem Nimbus, die auf das "Desaster der interpretierenden Klasse" – so die Formel von Wolf Lepenies[1] – gefolgt sind. Was ich im folgenden versuchen will, ist eine historische Rekonstruktion der Standorte und Rollen der literarischen Intelligenz in vier Jahrzehnten DDR sowie in der 'Wende' 1989/90. Damit verbunden, versuche ich, die grundsätzlichen Optionen von uns (deutschen) Intellektuellen heute zu reflektieren. Das muß uns interessieren – schließlich sind wohl alle, die das folgende hören oder lesen, Intellektuelle, ob sie wollen oder auch nicht.

Bei alldem ist es nicht zu vermeiden, hier und da auch auf die problematische Geschichte der Intellektuellen im Deutschland der letzten einhundert Jahre – zwischen Verketzerung und Selbstüberhebung – Bezug zu nehmen. Ja, man muß erst einmal einige Merkmale aus der Phänomenologie 'des Intellektuellen' nennen, um klarzumachen, auf welche typologischen

Muster dieser soziokulturellen Rolle man sich bezieht, kurz, wie man 'den Intellektuellen' definiert.

'Der Intellektuelle', im Singular wie im Plural, bezeichnet weder eine soziale Schicht noch eine Berufsgruppe. Vielmehr ist er ein durch und durch *"diskursives Phänomen"*, das jeweils "aus den Elementen des Intellektuellen-Diskurses" in einer bestimmten historischen Situation "rekonstruiert werden muß."[2] Was ein Intellektueller ist, ergibt sich aus den je vorgenommenen *Zuschreibungen* der ihm zukommenden oder nicht zukommenden 'Sendung' oder 'Bestimmung'. Aus solchen Zuschreibungen resultiert nun freilich in der Regel auch eine *soziale Rolle,* die angenommen oder abgelehnt werden kann. Gleichwohl bleibt die *soziale Lage,* in der sich 'die Intellektuellen' befinden, diffus. Sie gehören, über eine größere Zahl von Berufsgruppen verteilt, zur "sozial freischwebenden Intelligenz" (so die Charakterisierung zuerst von Alfred Weber, dann, differenzierter, von Karl Mannheim), einer "relativ klassenlosen, nicht allzufest gelagerten Schicht im sozialen Raum".[3] Diese merkwürdige Schwebelage sensibilisiert sie sozial und schafft ein "homogenes Medium" für Vielstimmigkeit und dynamische Widersprüchlichkeit in der diskursiven Auseinandersetzung. Zugleich begünstigt sie Distanz, den vielberufenen intellektuellen "Zweifel" als Korrespondenz zur sozialen "Gebrochenheit".[4]

Diese allgemeinen (wissens-)soziologischen Bemerkungen lassen sich sinnvoll mit einigen historisch konkreten Überlegungen zum Intellektuellen-problem verknüpfen. Die diskursiv generierte Figur des modernen Intellektuellen als des Sprechers im Namen universeller Werte, als des 'Gewissens' (wahlweise der Nation, der Klasse, der Demokratie, der Menschheit usf.), des Sachwalters von "meinungs- und glaubenshaften Letztwerten"[5], der zuständig ist für die symbolische Ordnung der Dinge, tritt nicht zufällig gleichzeitig mit dem Verfall der Religiosität in der abendländischen Moderne im Zeichen durchgreifender Entzauberung, Rationalisierung und Säkularisierung auf. Moderne Intellektuelle, in der Regel freigestellt von unmittelbar zwanghaften Lebens- und Arbeits-verhältnissen und mit dem Privileg tendenziell unbehinderten, bestehende Grenzen überschreitenden Nachdenkens ausgestattet, sind gleichzeitig der Gefahr ausgesetzt, den Weltzustand der zivilisatorischen Moderne in seiner ganzen Heillosigkeit ungeschönt wahrnehmen und durchdenken zu müssen. Der Intellektuelle als eine Ausgeburt des Modernisierungsprozesses *par excellence* erfährt als erster und am bewußtesten die Pathologie der Moderne als Sinn- und Heilsentzug.[6]

Doch die menschliche Psyche ist nicht so beschaffen, daß sie dieser Erfahrung ohne weiteres standhält. Vielmehr sucht der Intellektuelle, mit immer wieder verfeinerten und anspruchsvolleren Argumenten, seiner Lebensführung wie seinem Lebenslauf einen durchgehenden 'Sinn' zu verleihen, sich als mit sich selbst, mit der Menschheit und mit dem Weltlauf in Übereinstimmung befindlich darzustellen. Er trachtet, als der dem Priester nachfolgende konstitutionelle Sinnsucher, die metaphysische Entzugs-erfahrung zu kompensieren und wird zum Sinnstifter und Heilslehrer auf der kalten, wüsten, von Gott verlassenen Stätte, der im Extremfall "die Heilsherrschaft über alle Wirklichkeit"[7] beansprucht.

Sehr verschiedene Philosophen, (Wissens-)Soziologen und Historiker von Karl Mannheim und Karl Löwith bis zu François Lyotard und François Furet haben die folgenschwere Tendenz des modernen Denkens, die säkularisierte "Weltgeschichte als Heilsgeschehen"[8] zu projektieren, so verständnisvoll wie kritisch beschrieben. Mannheim hat in *Ideologie und Utopie* (1929) als erster gezeigt, wie in der sozialistisch-kommunistischen Utopie die alte chiliastische Erwartung des Himmelreichs auf Erden erneuert und, mit dem Versprechen eines baldigen Untergangs des Kapitalismus, in die nahe Zukunft verlegt wird. Freilich, so Mannheim, versäumt es das marxistische Denken, sein gegen alle anderen Denkweisen als Ideologien gerichtetes kritisches Enthüllungsverfahren, "diese seinsrelativierende Methode", auch gegen sich selbst, gegen "die eigene Hypostasierung und Verabsolutierung" zu wenden.[9] Vielmehr ermächtigt die kommunistische Utopie ihre eigenen Ideen von einem Reich der Freiheit und Gleichheit zur materiellen Gewalt, deren Durchsetzung nicht aufzuhalten sei. Ideen wird in solchem Denken ein fragloser Realitätsstatus zugesprochen, eine die soziale Wirklichkeit gesetzmäßig und unaufhaltsam steuernde Macht, so daß man nicht zufällig an den in früheren Epochen dominanten Status religiöser Glaubensinhalte und speziell deren Zukunftsprojektionen erinnert ist. Eben diesen Zusammenhang hat Karl Löwith so materialreich wie überzeugend aufgewiesen: Die großen geschichtsphilosophischen Entwürfe der Neuzeit, und speziell die marxistischen, sind "ganz und gar abhängig von der Theologie, das heißt von der theologischen Ausdeutung der Geschichte als eines Heilsgeschehens." Sie säkularisieren ihr eschatologisches Vorbild durchgreifend, stellen nach dem "Leitfaden eines Prinzips" zwischen allen historischen Einzelereignissen einen Zusammenhang her und beziehen sie solchermaßen auf einen letzten Sinn.[10] Mittels einer solchen Deutung des Geschichtsprozesses als "Sinngebung des Sinnlosen", mit Theodor Lessing zu sprechen[11], gehört die marxistische Sinnstiftung namens Kommunismus mit ihrem "theologischen Glutkern" (Ernst Bloch) allemal zu den "verkappten Religionen"[12], wie sie zumal seit der Jahrhundertwende in Europa in vielen Arten blühten.

Es erscheint mir wichtig, den hier angedeuteten Zusammenhang zwischen der Entstehung des modernen Intellektuellen und der radikalen Sinnkrise der abendländischen Zivilisation, die den Hunger nach Sinn gewaltig anwachsen ließ, bei allen Untersuchungen zu den Selbstbildern und Rollen der Intellektuellen im Auge zu behalten, ja, zur leitenden Perspektive zu machen. Das ideologische Schwärmen, das das ältere religiöse Schwärmen ablöste, blieb – dies ist entscheidend – nicht bei sich selbst stehen. Vielmehr steckte in den neuen politischen Mythologien eine Kraft, die unweigerlich zur Praxis drängte: zur totalitären Ideokratie, in der die Ideen tatsächlich zur materiellen, ja, zur blutigen Gewalt wurden. Schon die "Ideen von 1914", also die radikal chauvinistischen, militant gewalttätigen Visionen deutscher Intellektueller – Schriftsteller, Philosophen, Historiker, Sozialwissenschaftler, Literaturwissenschaftler usw. (die meisten von ihnen wohlbestallte Professoren) – zeigen ein erstes Mal, welch grauenhafte Beiträge Intellektuelle als Herrscher über die symbolisch-kulturelle Ordnung, als selbsternanntes 'Gewissen der Nation' zur blutigen Realgeschichte leisten können.[13] Doch erst das Zeitalter der totalitären Regime von 1917/18 bis 1945 resp. 1989/90, das ohne die großen Systemutopien, die totalisierenden Metaerzählungen aus der Feder von Intellektuellen so nicht möglich gewesen wäre, hat auf erschreckende Weise deutlich gemacht, wie weit der "Verrat der Intellektuellen" gehen kann. Nota Bene: Ich rücke Julien Bendas immer wieder zitierten Titel *La Trahison des Clercs* hier in eine Perspektive, die nicht ganz die seine ist.[14] Er hatte seinerzeit als Hauptverräter des klassischen Intellektuellen im Sinne von Voltaire (in der Affäre Calas 1761-65) und Zola (in der Dreyfus-Affäre 1897) vor allem die Nationalchauvinisten und andere Irrationalisten auf dem Weg in den Faschismus hinein ausgemacht. Mir geht es hier um die Liaison utopischer Entwürfe von Intellektuellen mit rechten *und* linken Versionen des Totalitarismus. Vor allem im Blick auf den Marxismus bleibt es eine anhaltende Irritation, daß dieser Entwurf, in seiner ideellen Intention universeller und freiheitlicher selbst als das Christentum, sich in so massiver Weise mit totalitärer Praxis verbunden und einen erschreckenden "Hang zur Maßnahme"[15] entwickelt hat. Dies ist hier nicht mein Thema, aber ich will immerhin auf zwei prominente Beispiele verweisen. Zum einen auf den Intellektuellen Gottfried Benn, der dem NS-

Staat das *sacrificium intellectus* brachte, indem er in seiner Rede "Der neue Staat und die Intellektuellen" am 25. April 1933 unter anderem den "Verlust des Ichs an das Totale, den Staat, die Rasse" feierte"[16]; und zweitens auf den nicht weniger prominenten Heinrich Mann, der in seiner Autobiographie *Ein Zeitalter wird besichtigt* (Erstdruck Stockholm 1945) die Moskauer Prozesse unter Stalin als "klassische Auseinandersetzung", als Prozeß der "Selbst-reinigung" und "Entsündigung" rühmte.[17] Doch dies nur am Rande.

Mich soll die Frage beschäftigen, warum es noch nach 1945 – und über weitere Jahrzehnte hin – möglich war, daß sich so viele Angehörige der Intelligenz aufs neue dem sozialistischen Projekt mit Haut und Haaren verschrieben, wo sich doch die Irrtums- und Enttäuschungsgeschichte des Sozialismus schon über Jahrzehnte erstreckte und dementsprechend genügend Erfahrungsmaterial bereithielt, mit Hilfe dessen man die eigenen Wünsche und Projektionen hätte überprüfen können.

II

Als der Krieg zu Ende war, verfügten die am Leben gebliebenen Deutschen in allen vier Besatzungszonen über die gleiche Erbschaft an Trümmern und Zerstörung, an Wegsehen und Mitmachen, in selteneren Fällen auch an Mut und Solidarität. "In weniger als sechs Jahren", schrieb Hannah Arendt 1950, "zerstörte Deutschland das moralische Gefüge der westlichen Welt, und zwar durch Verbrechen, die niemand für möglich gehalten hätte [...]."[18] Doch was in der Folge aus dieser Erbschaft wurde, hing entscheidend von dem Einfluß der jeweiligen Besatzungsmacht ab sowie davon, auf welche Teile der Bevölkerung und auf welche Institutionen sie sich stützte und welche politischen und ideologischen Weichenstellungen sie beförderte.

Herfried Münkler hat in einem lesenswerten Aufsatz von 1996 über "Politische Mythen der DDR" überzeugend dargelegt, daß *die junge Bundesrepublik*, trotz Beihilfe der Westalliierten in Sachen *reeducation* und Demokratisierung, im Grunde keinen genuin politischen, ideellen Gründungsmythos hatte. Ihr Gründungsmythos war vielmehr ein *wirt-schaftlicher*, "denn die Identifikation der Bürger mit ihrer Gemeinschaft wurde gestiftet über die Narrationen und Synthetisierungen der Währungs-reform und des anschließenden Wirtschaftswunders."[19] Diese und "das Wunder von Bern" (der überraschende Gewinn der Fußballweltmeisterschaft 1954) legten den Grund für das neue (west-)deutsche Selbstverständnis – und keine wie immer geartete kulturelle resp. ideologische 'Gründung'.

Wie anders *die junge DDR*, die den *Antifaschismus* zu ihrem Gründungsmythos schlechthin machte und ihre eigene Existenz an den antifaschistischen Widerstand "ansippte", wie Münkler häßlich, aber treffend formuliert.[20] Bei diesem Prozeß der – wohlbemerkt: mythischen – kulturellen und moralischen 'Gründung' bzw. "Ansippung" der entstehenden DDR spielte die Intelligenz vor allem zweier Generationen eine ganz entscheidende Rolle. Ein entscheidender Unterschied zu den Westzonen liegt zunächst darin, daß die meisten Schriftsteller und auch einige Wissenschaftler, die als Kommunisten (oder Sozialisten) ins Exil gegangen waren, die Sowjetische Besatzungszone bzw. die junge DDR als neuen Lebensort und damit auch als Zentrum ihres literarischen und politischen Wirkens wählten. Einige, wie Bertolt Brecht, Ernst Bloch, Stephan Hermlin, Arnold Zweig, Erich Arendt, Rudolf Leonhard oder Stefan Heym, zögerten lange, nicht zuletzt, weil sie nicht völlig blind gegenüber dem stalinistischen Terror seit 1936 waren und einer KPD/SED unter Führung Walter Ulbrichts zumindest skeptisch gegenüberstanden. Dennoch taten sie wie vor ihnen viele andere den folgenreichen Schritt. Der Haß auf die Nazis und deren Verbrechen an den eigenen Leuten saß tief, und das Bedürfnis, so viele Jahre Lebenszeit, die nur aus Opfern und Entsagung bestanden, nun endlich hinter sich zu lassen, war groß. Hinzu kam wachsende Skepsis gegenüber der westdeutschen Entwicklung im Bündnis mit der kapitalistischen Führungsmacht USA. Doch den Ausschlag gab vermutlich die Versuchung, endlich einmal – zum erstenmal! – in einem deutschen Staat leben zu können, der auf der 'richtigen' Seite, nämlich der der Humanität, des Fortschritts und der sozialen Gerechtigkeit, zu stehen schien und zudem der Kultur und den Künsten einen hohen Stellenwert beimaß. So erschienen schon der *ersten*, vorwiegend aus Exilierten bestehenden Generation der literarischen Intelligenz der DDR die Chancen des Dafürseins größer als die Risiken.[21]

Um wieviel mehr galt das für die *zweite* Generation der in den 20er Jahren Geborenen. Eine große Zahl von ihnen band sich – für nachträgliche Beobachter zunächst überraschend – freiwillig, gläubig und affirmativ an das neue antifaschistisch-sozialistische Staatswesen – und fesselte sich damit selbst mit noch nicht absehbaren Folgen. Es geht gerade nicht um die erste weiträumige Generation der literarischen Intelligenz von Brecht, Becher, Seghers, Zweig und Bloch bis zu Hans Mayer und Stefan Heym, die eine durch ihre frühere Biographie im Exil beglaubigte antinazistische linke Identität hatten oder eine solche zumindest glaubhaft machen konnten. Vielmehr sind es die in den zwanziger Jahren geborenen Autoren – Autoren, die das NS-Regime und den Krieg als junge Männer und Frauen, oft noch als Kinder, als Soldaten, SA-Leute, Hitlerjungen und BdM-Mädel erlebt hatten, in der Regel als naiv Begeisterte oder als Mitläufer. Ich nenne stellvertretend die Namen Erwin Strittmatter, Franz Fühmann, Hermann Kant, Günter de Bruyn, Erich Loest, Christa Wolf, Heiner Müller, Dieter Noll und Erik Neutsch. Ihre Bekehrung erfuhren sie, sofern sie Soldaten gewesen waren, häufig in der Kriegsgefangenschaft oder dann zu Hause. Die Regel ist, daß ein Glaube, ein totales Weltbild durch einen neuen Glauben, ein neues totalisierendes, geschlossenes Weltbild ersetzt wurde, das des Marxismus. Günther Deicke (1922 geboren) hat das 1988 bestätigt: "Ein westdeutscher Publizist nannte uns 'Dichter im Dienst', und wir wollten das tatsächlich auch sein."[22] Eine der wenigen Ausnahmen markierte, schon aufgrund seiner zum Teil jüdischen Herkunft, Günter Kunert.

Bemerkenswert und folgenreich ist der psychologische Mechanismus, der diesem Vorgang zugrundeliegt. Am Anfang standen Verstörung, Scham, Erschütterung, Schuldbewußtsein auf seiten der ehemaligen Mitläufer des Nationalsozialismus – und ihnen gegenüber eine Sozialistische Einheitspartei (an ihrer Spitze antifaschistische Widerstandskämpfer und Exilierte, legitimiert durch entbehrungsreiche KZ- und Zuchthausaufenthalte oder den Verlust der Heimat), die die versöhnende Hand ausstreckte, Absolution erteilte und die 'Überläufer' gleich noch handstreichartig zu "Siegern der Geschichte" erklärte. Am (vorläufigen) Ende dieses Prozesses stand die freiwillig-unfreiwillige Selbstbindung des reuigen Sünders an den Anti-Faschismus als das Gegenteil dessen, dem er einst verfallen war: dem Faschismus, der auch Auschwitz hervorgebracht hatte. In diesem Kontext ist Franz Fühmanns vielzitiertes Wort "ich bin über Auschwitz in die andere Gesellschaftsordnung gekommen"[23] zu verstehen – und es gilt für fast alle Autoren dieser Generation. War "der Faschismus" (wie in der DDR das NS-Regime pauschalierend genannt wurde) das Böse schlechthin, so wurde "der Antifaschismus" (was immer das konkret meinte) als sein Gegenteil automatisch zum Guten und Wahren, zur ideologischen Klammer, die fast alles zusammenhielt. Zweifellos war der DDR-Antifaschismus "verordnet" (selbst Heiner Müller nannte ihn ohne Abstriche so[24]), aber im gleichen Atemzuge wurde er freiwillig als Anker der moralischen Selbstrettung und imaginativen Wiedergutmachung ergriffen. So promovierte "der Anti-faschismus", und auf seinem Rücken der Sozialismus gleich mit, automatisch zum *humanum* schlechthin, das zudem – nachdem die eine, die nazistische gerade in sich zusammengestürzt war – eine neue heilsgeschichtliche

Perspektive auf Erden eröffnete. Und das gilt bekanntlich nicht nur für die literarische Intelligenz, sondern für die Bevölkerung im ganzen. Jurek Becker pflegte das so zum Vorteil aller umgemodelte politische Selbstverständnis der DDR-Bevölkerung gern mit dem folgenden Bonmot zu erhellen: "In Nazi-Deutschland gab es circa 50 000 Antifaschisten. Davon lebten allein 16 Millionen in der DDR."

Daß man damals einem dergestalt dualistischen, prinzipalistischen Vorstellen und Denken verhaftet war, ist historisch plausibel. Gegenüber dem terroristischen NS-Regime gab es tatsächlich nur zwei Grundmöglichkeiten des Verhaltens: Anpassung und Unterwerfung oder Verweigerung und Widerstand. 'Abseits gestanden' oder ' nur mitgelaufen' zu sein, hatte sich im Nachhinein als moralische Illusion erwiesen. Die von den neuen Machthabern, den *founding fathers* der DDR, eröffnete Falle bestand darin, daß sie diesen Dualismus als unausweichlich andauernd dekretierten. Wer nicht "antifaschistisch" und für den Aufbau des Sozialismus war, wurde rasch dem unterstellten Gegenteil, dem "Faschismus" (später gemildert zu "feindlich-negativer Einstellung") zugeordnet. "Politische Traditionslinien jenseits der Entgegensetzung von Faschismus und seinem behaupteten Gegenteil treten damit erst gar nicht in den Blick", so hat Dan Diner treffend festgestellt.[25] Das Angebot an alle ehemaligen Mitläufer, ja sogar an die sogenannten "kleinen Täter" aus dem Dritten Reich, jetzt ins breite antifaschistische Bündnis eintreten zu dürfen und damit zu den "Siegern der Geschichte" zu gehören, war verlockend und beruhigend zugleich, sofern jemandem das schlechte Gewissen schlug. Zugleich aber erwies es sich als "Loyalitätsfalle" (ich übernehme Annette Simons hilfreichen Ausdruck[26]), der schwer wieder zu entkommen war. Denn wer das DDR-Regime unbeschönigt beschreiben wollte (z.B. als Schriftsteller) oder gar entsprechend seinen kritischen Einsichten zu handeln gedachte, der verließ automatisch den antifaschistischen Grundkonsens, nach dem Antifaschist-Sein und ein guter DDR-Bürger-Sein miteinander identisch waren und umgekehrt. "Man hätte bei uns [in der DDR, W.E.] Antifaschisten bekämpfen müssen, um den Stalinismus zu bekämpfen" – auf diese frappierende Formel hat es nach der Wende Wolfgang Kohlhaase gebracht.[27] Daraus entstand jene intime, kindliche, familiäre Loyalität, um nicht zu sagen Gefolgschaftstreue, der vom sozialistischen Übervater in Gnaden angenommenen gefallenen Kinder, die für lange Jahre die Texte dieser Autoren der zweiten Generation durchzieht und ihr Selbstverständnis und Handeln als 'Intellektuelle' prägt. Was Julien Benda 1927 prophetisch als "Verrat der Intellektuellen" stigmatisiert hatte, nämlich die Bereitschaft, das Amt eines Sprechers für universelle Werte, für Bürger- und Menschenrechte preiszugeben zugunsten eines Eintretens für partiale und ausschließende Werte, was zwischen 1933 und 1945 bereits in Nazi-Deutschland und in der Sowjetunion unter Stalin von Intellektuellen so schrecklich praktiziert worden war, vollzogen die meisten Angehörigen der literarischen Intelligenz in der DDR, und zumal die aus der zweiten Generation, auf paradoxe Weise freiwillig und gezwungenermaßen zugleich, gläubig und notgedrungen. Die von der SED-Führung durchaus geschickt (und bis zu einem gewissen Grad gleichfalls gläubig) vollzogene "Engführung des Politischen " (Dan Diner[28]) engte zugleich die Optionen von Intellektuellen in der DDR radikal ein. Außer Dafürsein blieb nur: Dagegensein, und eben das wollte man nicht.

Jorge Sempruns (Horkheimers berühmtes Kapitalismus-Faschismus-Diktum abwandelndes) Wort: "Wer vom Stalinismus nicht reden will, soll auch vom Faschismus schweigen" markiert das zentrale Tabu des verordneten DDR-Antifaschismus als Staatsdoktrin und Lebenslüge zugleich. Kaum einer hat das schon so (relativ) früh und so treffend durchschaut wie Uwe Johnson in seinem "Versuch, eine Mentalität zu erklären" von 1970. "Der Fall war", konstatierte Johnson, "daß hier mit der Vergangenheit gebrochen werden sollte" – was kein Wohlmeinender verweigern konnte. Und auch der "Annahme, daß nach dem abgetanen System der Faschisten diese neue Autorität von Haus aus die bessere war, weil anti-faschistisch", war kaum zu entgehen: "Die moralische Eindeutigkeit war verführerisch. Das saß." So konnte sich die DDR "als Lehrerin, so streng und wunderlich sie auftrat, [...] lange Zeit fast unbedenklich verlassen auf die beiden moralischen Wurzeln, die antifaschistische und die der sozialen Proportion [...]. Denn die Einladung zum neueren Leben, die Gebärde der weit geöffneten Arme, sie war zum Mißverstehen gewesen"[29] – so erkannte Johnson, und damit meinte er die Älteren, von Krieg und Nazismus Gebrannten, wie die Jüngeren, zu denen er selbst gehörte.

Die Belege für den skizzierten Sachverhalt aus der DDR-Belletristik wie aus autobiographischen Zeugnissen von DDR-Autoren sind ungemein zahlreich und haben sich seit der Wende noch einmal beträchtlich vermehrt. Hier sei nur ein einziger zitiert, und zwar gezielt von Christa Wolf. Er dokumentiert zugleich ihr prototypisches Befangensein (um nicht zu sagen Gefangensein) in der verordneten "Engführung des Politischen" – und ihr im Lauf der Jahre und Jahrzehnte zunehmend kritisches Bewußtsein von dieser Beengung. In einem öffentlichen Gespräch aus dem Jahre 1987 sagte sie u.a.

die folgenden Sätze: "Meine Generation hat früh eine Ideologie gegen eine andere ausgetauscht, sie ist erst spät, zögernd, teilweise gar nicht erwachsen geworden, will sagen, reif, autonom. Daher kommen ihre – unsere Schwierigkeiten mit den Jüngeren. Da ist eine große Unsicherheit, weil die eigene Ablösung von ideologischen Setzungen, intensiven Bindungen an festgelegte Strukturen so wenig gelungen ist, die Jungen so wenig selbständiges Denken und Handeln sehen und daher keine Leitfiguren finden, auf die sie sich verlassen können. So holt uns, im Verhältnis zu den Jungen, unsere nicht genügend verarbeitete Kindheit wieder ein."[30]

Was Christa Wolf hier selbstkritisch auf der Ebene von individueller psychischer Deformation und gestörtem Generationenverhältnis beschreibt, hatte auch konkrete politische Konsequenzen. Indem man sich bedingungslos mit "dem Antifaschismus" à la DDR identifizierte, übernahm man gleichsam huckepack die Zukunftsperspektive Sozialismus, ohne dessen bisherige von Terror gezeichnete Realgeschichte auch nur ansatzweise zur Kenntnis zu nehmen. Die Sehnsucht, nach dem zerstörten Sinnkonstrukt Nationalsozialismus einer neuen, scheinbar unbefleckten Glücksverheißung zu folgen, die Verlockung, endlich einmal ohne schlechtes Gewissen dafürsein zu können im guten neuen Staat, erstickte alle möglichen kritischen Vorbehalte schon im Keim. Daß dieses Dafürsein auch beträchtliche Risiken, ja, Aporien barg, dämmerte erst viel später. Und selbst dann hielt man in der Regel am zentralen Muster der Sinnfindung und -deutung des (nachgeholten oder imaginierten) Antifaschismus fest.

Man kann sich fragen, woher die Kräfte hätten kommen sollen, die frühe Zweifel, ja Distanz gegenüber dem angetragenen Projekt hätten wecken können, nunmehr zu den "Siegern der Geschichte" zu gehören und einen erkennbar undemokratischen Sozialismus aufzubauen. Es gab ja auch einige Kommunisten, alte und junge, wie Theodor Plivier oder Wolfgang Leonhard, die sich schon früh, 1947/48/49/50, der realsozialistischen Diktatur versagten und die DDR verließen. Doch gerade weil sie nicht frei, öffentlich wirken konnten, vielmehr aus der SBZ resp. DDR flüchten mußten, war ihr Einfluß auf die jungen potentiellen Intellektuellen, die Orientierung jenseits der offiziellen Doktrin hätten brauchen können, fast gleich Null. Am ehesten waren jene Angehörigen der Kriegsgeneration gegen die erörterte antifaschistisch-sozialistische Selbstbindung als Selbstfesselung gefeit, die Widerstandskraft aus einem intakten religiösen, bildungsbürgerlich-humanistischen oder auch sozialdemokratisch-konservativen Wertehorizont schöpften. Ich will hier nur auf das Beispiel Günter de Bruyn hinweisen, dessen beide Autobiographiebände *Zwischenbilanz* (1992) und *Vierzig Jahre* (1996) eindrucksvoll belegen, daß und wie die Prägung durch ein katholisches Familienmilieu sich als dauerhafte Imprägnierung gegen die heilsgeschichtlichen Versprechungen des "realen Sozialismus" bewähren konnte. Schließlich stehen noch Forschungen aus zu dem, was Günter Wirth für die Zeit bis ca. 1950 als "Gegenkultur aus bildungsbürgerlichem Geist" bezeichnet hat.[31] Immerhin gab es ja an den ostdeutschen Universitäten, neben den linken Remigranten wie Bloch, Hans Mayer, Werner Krauss, Ernst Engelberg oder Walter Markov, bedeutende bürgerliche Gelehrte wie Hans-Georg Gadamer, Hermann August Korff und Theodor Litt in Leipzig, Hans Leisegang oder Max Bense in Jena, Wilhelm Fraenger (den Volkskundler und Kunsthistoriker) in Dresden oder Eduard Spranger in Berlin. Es gab die Dresdener Künstlerszene um Josef Hegenbarth, Hans Theo Richter und Fritz Löffler, und es gab nicht zuletzt vom Nazismus weit entfernte bürgerliche Literaten im Umkreis von *Sinn und Form* wie Hermann Kasack, Werner E. Stichnote und Werner Wilk. Fast alle Genannten verließen, mehr oder weniger freiwillig, bis 1950 die SBZ/DDR. Damit wurde der in sich plurale antinazistische Grundkonsens des Anfangs, der alles andere als nur kommunistisch war, zerstört. Aus dem Antifaschismus als einem authentischen politischen und kulturellen Impuls zum Neubeginn wurde die künstlich homogenisierte "ideologische Existenzlüge" der DDR (mit Dan Diner zu sprechen[32]), und das für 45 Jahre. Friedrich Dieckmann, nicht als Schönredner der verblichenen DDR bekannt, hat einmal behauptet, in der SBZ sei der "Schnitt [zum NS-Regime, W.E.] [...] realiter und gewaltsam vollzogen" worden, "nicht von Nachgeborenen, die sich an die Stelle der Widerstandskämpfer setzten, sondern von diesen selbst, von Menschen, die aus den Lagern, den Gefängnissen, den Todeszellen des Hitlerstaats gekommen waren oder aus Exilländern zurückkehrten. Der Vorgang machte den Erfahrungsvorsprung jener Zone aus, die seit 1949 Deutsche Demokratische Republik hieß [...]."[33] Dem möchte ich widersprechen. Zum einen muß es mit dem Wissen von heute als fraglich gelten, ob die aus dem sowjetischen Exil zurückkehrenden Kommunisten (die mit Glück und Geschick überlebt hatten) oder die ehemaligen Lagerhäftlinge von Buchenwald (die auf ebensolche Weise überlebt hatten) wirklich den "Erfahrungsvorsprung" hatten, den Dieckmann ja im Sinne einer moralischen Qualität meint. Und zum andern wirkten auch in den Westzonen/der Bundesrepublik Widerständler und Exilierte, von Adenauer und Schumacher bis zu Heinemann und Brandt, denen ein "Erfahrungsvorsprung" nicht abzusprechen ist.

Eine in der Folgewirkung ganz erhebliche Begleiterscheinung des planen "Antifaschismus" war, daß der Sowjetunion als der Macht, die den Nazismus heroisch besiegt hatte (und das hatte sie unzweifelhaft und unter ungeheuren Opfern) ein "Nachkriegsbonus"[34] eingeräumt wurde, der auch auf ihr sozialistisches System übertragen wurde. Zumindest unter manchen Angehörigen der literarischen Intelligenz verbreitete sich ein vertrackter "Philosowjetismus"[35], dem es häufig weit über 1956 hinaus gelang, die Verbrechen des Stalinismus zu ignorieren oder schönzureden. Dies ist ein wichtiger und bisher eher vernachlässigter Aspekt der Selbstfesselung der DDR-Intelligenz, den ich hier nur erwähnen kann.

Überblickt man die ersten zwanzig Jahre der ostdeutschen Sonderexistenz von 1945 bis etwa 1965, dann muß man feststellen, daß die übergroße Mehrzahl der Schriftsteller, gerade aus der von mir so genannten *zweiten Generation*, die ihr angetragene Rolle als Erzieher der noch nachhinkenden Volksmassen auf dem Weg zum Endziel Sozialismus, als sozialistisches Gewissen willig annahm und sich ihrer volkspädagogischen, "ganz ausgesprochen sozialaktivistischen" Aufgabe (Uwe Johnson[36]) mit Hingabe widmete. Da die DDR sich den Autoren lange erfolgreich als "das bessere Deutschland" darstellte (noch Anfang der 60er Jahre fühlte sich Heinz Czechowski "in diesem besseren Land", und Adolf Endler und Karl Mickel wählten die Wendung 1966 als Titel einer bedeutenden Lyrikanthologie[37]), gingen diese bereitwillig auf das ihnen gemachte Angebot ein, an der Macht beteiligt zu sein, eben als Erzieher und Sprecher der sozialistischen Nation. Schon der Leninismus hatte die Vormachtstellung der Intelligenz gegenüber der Arbeiterklasse begründet und festgeschrieben. György Konrads Buch *Die Intelligenz auf dem Weg zur Klassenmacht* (deutsch 1978) hat gezeigt, daß unter anderem aufgrund dieser Privilegierung die Attraktivität des sozialistischen Modells für große Teile der Intelligenz so lange erhalten blieb. Das galt für keine Gruppierung mehr als für die literarische Intelligenz. Die Literatur sollte in der DDR als einem sozialistischem Land gerade keine autonome Wertsphäre im Sinne Max Webers sein, sondern als dem Gesamtsystem "sozialistische Gesellschaft" zugehörige eingreifende Kraft die Massen für den Sozialismus mobilisieren und "sozialistische Persönlichkeiten" heranbilden helfen. Diese Aufgabenzuschreibung band die Schriftsteller – und schmeichelte ihnen doch zugleich, weil sie sich selbst wichtig finden durften. In diesem Sinne hatte die Literatur einen tendenziell vormodernen Systemstatus, der noch dadurch befestigt wurde, daß die Gesamtkultur der DDR viel stärker als in vergleichbaren westlichen Ländern in der traditionellen Schriftkultur verharrte.[38]

Hier sind wohl die größten Unterschiede im prekären Verhältnis von Geist und Macht in Ost und West zu konstatieren. So geriet die Literatur in der Bundesrepublik viel früher und heftiger als im Osten in die Konkurrenz mit den audiovisuellen wie auch den anderen Printmedien und mußte (durfte) sich über Jahrzehnte hin schrittweise daran gewöhnen, kein wegweisendes Leitmedium mehr zu sein. Und sie hatte sich, ob ihre Urheber wollten oder nicht, als tendenziell autonome Wertsphäre in einer modernen pluralen Gesellschaft zu bewähren, der ein politischer Erziehungsauftrag allenfalls zeitweise von bestimmten konservativen, ab 1968 dann auch linken Gruppen auferlegt wurde. Selbst wenn die politische Führung in der Bundesrepublik den Intellektuellen und Schriftstellern angeboten hätte, sie in irgendeiner Weise an der Macht zu beteiligen, hätten diese sich grundsätzlich verweigert, eben weil sie gegenüber der konservativen, als restaurativ taxierten Mehrheits- und Regierungspartei 'nonkonform' waren und bleiben wollten. Diese Haltung radikalisierte sich sogar noch in der Phase der Großen Koalition und dauerte, verändert, fort in Zeiten der sozial-liberalen Regierung. Indem die Intellektuellen nicht oder allenfalls partiell 'dafür' sein konnten, entgingen ihnen die verführerischen, schmeichelhaften Optionen, die sich der literarischen Intelligenz der DDR boten, aber auch die damit verknüpften Risiken und Illusionen.

Vielen Angehörigen der literarischen Intelligenz in sozialistischen Ländern, zumal in der DDR, gelang – oder geschah? – im Lauf der späten 60er und 70er Jahre etwas ganz Erstaunliches: Auch als ihre Einstellung gegenüber dem "real existierenden Sozialismus" als dem falschen, miß-lungenen kritischer und kritischer wurde, hielten sie – nachweislich ungebrochen auf der Basis eines emphatischen Bekenntnisses zum "Antifaschismus" – an der vertrauten Zuschreibung fest, einer Elite mit aufklärerisch-erzieherischem Auftrag anzugehören. Diese beharrliche Selbst-zuschreibung wurde natürlich durch den tendenziell vormodernen System-status von Literatur in der DDR, durch ihr ideologisch verordnetes Verharren in der Schriftkultur und den ihr zugewachsenen Status einer 'Ersatz-öffentlichkeit' mangels einer genuin bürgerlich-liberalen Öffentlichkeit ermöglicht. Die besagte Selbstzuschreibung wurde überdies bestätigt und befestigt durch eine westdeutsche linke Kulturintelligenz, die mit dem schmeichelhaften sozialen Status der kritischen DDR-Literaten sympathi-sierte, gerade weil sie ihn längst nicht mehr innehatte. Diese systemischen

Bedingungen hielten mehr oder weniger bis zum Ende des Staates DDR an. Gewiß sind für die späten 70er und 80er Jahre gravierende Veränderungen und Verschiebungen auch in den Rollen-(Selbst-)Zuschreibungen der literarischen Intelligenz zu verzeichnen – aber ebenso bleibende Strukturen des weiterhin Dafürsein-Wollens, des Sich-nicht-lösen-Könnens. In diesem Sinne konnte Stefan Heym am 1. Dezember 1976, zwei Wochen nach der Biermann-Ausbürgerung, einem Korrespondenten von *Newsweek*, der nach den "Dissidenten" in der DDR fragte, zumindest partiell zutreffend antworten: "Es gibt keine Dissidenten bei uns in dem im Westen gebräuchlichen Sinne, selbst Biermann sei alles andere als ein Solschenizyn, und die Schriftsteller gar, die den Protestbrief unterzeichneten, seien sämtlich *für* die Republik, *für* den Sozialismus."[39] Heym hatte nur allzu recht mit dieser Bilanz. Als im Herbst/Winter 1889/90 "die Republik" fast binnen Wochen unterging, war die reformsozialistische Linke der DDR so heimatlos und haltlos geworden wie noch nie zuvor. Sie hatte noch ihr ideales Sozialismusmodell "für ihr Land" im Kopf, aber "ihr Land", d.h. die überwältigende Mehrheit der Bevölkerung, wollte es nicht haben. Die DDR wurde westlich-kapitalistisch, mit allem, was dazu gehört. Ich habe den nun eintretenden Zustand von Melancholie und Verlustangst, den *furor melancholicus*, mehrfach beschrieben[40] – er ist auch neun, bald zehn Jahre nach dem Eintreten dieser Situation noch nicht gänzlich abgeklungen. Texte wie Volker Brauns "Das Eigentum", Heiner Müllers "Mommsens Block" oder Christa Wolfs *Medea. Stimmen* stehen als bleibende literarische Dokumente dafür.

III

Wenigstens an einem signifikanten Beispiel sei gezeigt, wie diese dilemmatische Situation sich für den einzelnen Autor darstellte, wie schwer es war und ist, den erlittenen Verlust an Sozialprestige und moralischem Nimbus zu akzeptieren. Besonders aufschlußreich ist, immer wieder, der Fall Christa Wolf – ihr langer Weg zum späten, und in manchen Punkten nie vollzogenen Abschied vom Projekt Sozialismus und den damit verknüpften liebgewordenen Erinnerungen. Einige neuere Quelleneditionen, vor allem der Band *In Sachen Biermann. Protokolle, Berichte und Briefe zu den Folgen der Ausbürgerung* von 1994[41], der u.a. die Vorgänge in der Berliner (SED-) Parteigruppe im Schriftstellerverband seit Mitte November 1976 re- konstruiert, sind aufschlußreich. Dokumentiert sind vor allem die Parteiversammlungen vom 23.11. 1976 und vom 20.1. 1977 sowie Briefwechsel zwischen Autoren und Parteileitung.

Christa Wolfs Briefe zeigen eindrucksvoll ihre schon seit dem 11. Plenum des ZK der SED im Dezember 1965 bekannte protestantisch gefärbte Standhaftigkeit gegenüber einer Parteileitung, die sie zur Rücknahme ihrer Unterschrift und zur Reue schlechthin zwingen wollte. Sie tat weder das eine noch das andere – und beharrte doch gleichzeitig darauf, daß sie sich "immer als Genossin fühlen" werde "und auch versuchen [werde], so zu handeln". Wenn die Partei "nach einer Parteizugehörigkeit von siebenundzwanzig Jahren, die ich niemals formal aufgefaßt habe", ihre weitere Mitgliedschaft "von dem Eingeständnis eines Fehlers" abhängig mache, "was nicht aufrichtig wäre, dann muß eben auch ich mit dem höchsten Strafmaß rechnen und darauf bestehen."[42] Der Schritt, die 'Kirche' SED von sich aus zu verlassen, ist für Christa Wolf und manche andere ein noch zu großer zu diesem Zeitpunkt. Die Verkehrsformen des Strafens und Bestraftwerdens, von Reue und Buße gelten noch als normal, auch wenn Wolf sich im konkreten Fall strikt verweigert. Gewiß ging es damals, im Spätherbst/Winter 1976/77, "um einen Versuch intellektueller Emanzipierung", wie der in der Halbdistanz stehende, der sozialistischen Lehre immer fremd gebliebene Günter de Bruyn in seiner autobiographischen Bilanz *Vierzig Jahre* treffend festgestellt hat. Aber der Emanzipationsversuch war von vornherein gebremst dadurch, daß (so weiter de Bruyn) das, "was die Individualisten verband", die da protestiert hatten, "die Ablehnung des Ausbürgerungsaktes" war, "nicht des Regimes".[43] Ganz deutlich zeigt das auch eine Einlassung von Christa Wolf während des Gesprächs von einigen aufmüpfigen Autoren und Schauspielern mit dem SED-Politbüromitglied Werner Lamberz und zwei anderen Funktionären im Haus von Manfred Krug am 20. November 1976, das dieser 1996 in seinem Buch *Abgehauen* nach dem heimlich mitlaufenden Tonband dokumentiert hat. Dort gibt die Autorin ihrer Hoffnung Ausdruck, daß in der DDR eine "offene" Diskussion, eine wirklich kritische Öffentlichkeit entstehen werde. Käme sie, "dann wäre das natürlich eine ganz große Sache. Und ihr [im Politbüro, W.E.] hättet uns [die Protestanten, W.E.] alle wieder zu euren Verbündeten. Wir alle zusammen wären an diesem selben Zug, und das wollen wir auch."[44]

Fünfzehn Jahre später, im September 1991, hat Christa Wolf in einem Brief an Wolfgang Thierse die Einsicht formuliert, daß sie und andere "sich an *unlösbaren* [Kursivierung von mir, W.E.] Widersprüchen in einem Dauerkonflikt aufgerieben hätten. Gleichzeitig sieht sie noch 1991 keine authentische Alternative zu ihrer bis zum Staatsende durchgetragenen Haltung: "den [welchen?, W.E.] Widerspruch aufrecht[zu]erhalten und Leuten [zu] helfen".[45] In einem Brief an Günter Grass aus der gleichen Zeit erklärt sie sich deutlicher: "Ich habe dieses Land [DDR, W.E.] geliebt."[46] Und damit meint sie ja nicht nur die mecklenburgische Landschaft oder Klein-Machnow, sondern zu allererst das politische Versprechen des Staates DDR, wie es frühzeitig in seinen Gründungsmythen Antifaschismus und Sozialismus artikuliert wurde. Auch der Aufruf "Für unser Land" vom Dezember 1989 folgt dieser inneren Logik. Interessanterweise kehren solche und ähnliche Wendungen dann noch einmal in einer in freie Verse gekleideten "Rückäußerung. Auf den Brief eines Freundes" von Ende März 1993 aus Santa Monica, gerichtet an Volker Braun, auf. Hier zitiert und reflektiert die Autorin zunächst Brauns schon oft als Schlüsseltext der Aporien des Reformsozialismus erkanntes Gedicht "Das Eigentum". Später dann heißt es:

> Das Schlimme ist
>> Wir haben dieses Land geliebt
> (Regieanweisung: Tosendes Gelächter),

und kurz darauf:

>>> Daß das Andere
>>> nicht das Unsere war
>> daß wir es zu dem Unseren auch nicht machen konnten
>> das war und ist allerdings unser Problem
>>> Überanstrengte Leben
>>> Hatten wir keine Wahl
>
> Ich Volker hätte damals eine Wahl gehabt
>> Warum hab ich mich nicht verweigert
> Ich weiß es nicht mehr
>> Das Gedächtnis
>>> ist ein tückischer Filter
> Kaum wollte ich mir selber glauben daß ich das vergessen konnte
> Antwortversuche   Ich habe sie noch nicht als DIE ANDEREN gesehen
>> Ich traute meinen eigenen Gefühlen nicht
>> Ich glaubte ihnen Auskunft schuldig zu sein
>> Beklommen glaubte ich DER SACHE so zu nützen
>> Ich wußte mir nicht zu helfen
>> Ich hatte Angst
>> [...][47]

Der Text spielt natürlich auf die (vergessene) IM-Tätigkeit von Christa Wolf von 1959-62 an, aber das ist eigentlich sekundär. Entscheidend ist die Frage nach den Motiven dafür, warum die Autorin damals, zwischen 1945 und Anfang der 50er Jahre, der Option namens "Antifaschismus" und später "Deutsche Demokratische Republik" gefolgt ist und warum sie dieser Option so lange die Treue gehalten hat. Ihre eigenen "Antwortversuche" sind, denke ich, von meinen historisch-psychologischen Erklärungsversuchen nicht sehr weit entfernt.

Freilich, daß das Leben in der Nähe der Macht, Schikanen und Zensur zum Trotz gleichwohl mit beträchtlichen Privilegien ausgestattet, zu einer bemerkenswerten Entfernung vom 'Volk' – und zu dessen Verkennung – führen kann, zeigt das befremdlich verirrte Bild von der DDR-Bevölkerung und ihren Wünschen in der Wendezeit, vor allem in dem Aufruf "Für unser Land" vom November 1989, aber auch in manchen anderen persönlichen Texten von Christa Wolf, die in den Bänden *Im Dialog. Aktuelle Texte* von 1990 und *Auf dem Weg nach Tabou* von 1994 gesammelt sind. In ihnen wird immer noch der ewige Intellektuellentraum von der Erziehung der Massen und ihrem 'Anderswerden' geträumt, der doch nur die Kehrseite von der Arroganz der Intellektuellen gegenüber den Massen, zugespitzt, mit John Carey, vom "Haß auf die Massen" ist.[48]

Ein letzter Blick soll im Blick auf die Wendezeit Christa Wolfs literarischen Versuchen gewidmet sein. Auch in ihnen wird das erlittene Trauma, der zugemutete Verlust an öffentlicher Geltung, kaum in überzeugender Weise verarbeitet. So wird z.B. in "Nagelprobe" die eigene Künstler- und Intellektuellenexistenz mittels des christlichen Zentralmotivs der Kreuzigung als "eine fortlaufende Passion" allegorisch überhöht. Matthias Grünewalds Isenheimer Altar liefert die Folie dafür: "*Prinzip Hoffnung* // Genagelt / ans Kreuz der Vergangenheit. // Jede Bewegung / treibt / die Nägel / ins Fleisch."[49] Wolfgang Bergem hat mit Recht darauf hingewiesen, daß nirgends sonst in "der Nachwendeliteratur [...] das Motiv des Leidens so intensiv, so überhöht – und auch so geschmacklos – gestaltet worden" ist wie hier.[50] – Christa Wolfs Medeafigur aus dem Roman *Medea. Stimmen* von 1995/96 wurde dann vollends zur Allegorie der gestürzten, ihrer Rolle verlustig gegangenen Wahrsagerin und Zauberin, des Priester-Intellektuellen von einst. Die Autorin zeigt Medea, die über zwei Jahrtausende unangefochtene Version des Euripides bekanntlich umkehrend, nicht als Täterin, sondern als Opfer, das ein Passionsgeschehen durchläuft. Verbrechen, die *sie* zuerst aufdeckte, werden, groteske Verkehrung, *ihr* jetzt zur Last gelegt. In einer Deutlichkeit wie nie zuvor erscheinen in diesem Roman 'die Massen' so, wie die Autorin sie im Mai 1991 noch halb ironisch, sich des eigentlich "ungehörigen Vergleichs" bewußt, charakterisiert hatte: als "Ameisenvolk, [...] ruchlos seine Identität verleugnend".[51]

IV

Schon seit Ende 1989 wurde den ostdeutschen Intellektuellen gelegentlich vorgeworfen, sie schwiegen zu den großen Ereignissen, die im Gange seien. Nun stimmte dieser Vorwurf schon damals nicht, und erst recht nicht für die Jahre seither. Nicht wenige ostdeutsche Intellektuelle haben sich zu Wort gemeldet und um ihre eigenen Belange gekümmert: Einzelne, bewußt nur für sich Sprechende wie Günter de Bruyn, Friedrich Dieckmann oder auch Christoph Dieckmann, aber auch Vertreter des sog. Reformsozialismus, allen voran Christa Wolf, Christoph Hein und Heiner Müller, der sich nicht zu schade war, den größten Teil seiner verbliebenen Lebensenergie in den Erhalt und die Erneuerung zweier künstlerisch hochrangiger Institutionen der abgelebten DDR zu stecken, der Akademie der Künste und des Berliner Ensembles. Aber der gleiche Müller hat auch in "Mommsens Block" in aufschlußreicher Weise seine Schreibblockade formuliert – angesichts der, aus seiner Sicht, kapitalistischen Okkupation der DDR, die bei ihm nur tiefe Melancholie und Ekel auslöste (wie Neros wüste Verbrechen einst bei Theodor Mommsen). Etwas von dieser Sprech- und Schreibhemmung findet sich, überblickt man die vergangenen sechs, sieben Jahre, generell bei den *Älteren* aus der literarischen Intelligenz der DDR. Der Gründungsmythos der DDR wie ihres individuellen Lebens, der Antifaschismus, hat den Staat DDR überlebt. Um ihn kreisen sie, in hohem Maße selbstreflexiv, damit aber auch auf ihn fixiert, an ihn gefesselt.

Bei den wichtigsten Kontroversen der letzten Jahre waren, so hat Wolfgang Bergem richtig festgestellt, die Intellektuellen aus der ehemaligen DDR merklich unterrepräsentiert[52], sofern sie sich überhaupt beteiligten: so in der Goldhagen-Kontroverse (die doch auch mit "Faschismus" zu tun hatte!), so in den Diskussionen um den Status von Ausländern in Deutschland, so vor allem in den Debatten zwischen 'Pazifisten' und 'Bellizisten' im Golfkrieg und in den ersten Phasen der kriegerischen Auseinandersetzungen in Teilen des einstigen Jugoslawien. Daß Massenmord, Ethnozid vor unserer Haustür stattfand, nicht nur im fernen Ruanda, hätte ausreichender Anlaß sein können, vielleicht müssen, daß Intellektuelle und Künstler sich einmischen. Das geschah auch, freilich ohne relevante Beteiligung der literarischen Intelligenz aus den neuen Bundesländern. Vielleicht hat bei ihnen der abrupte Fall aus großer Höhe, die

Zurechtstutzung der einst hypertrophen politischen Rolle auf eine ganz bescheidene dazu geführt, daß, aus Enttäuschung wie Kränkung, nicht einmal diese bescheidene Rolle ausgefüllt wird. Immerhin, im Spätherbst des Jahres 1998 haben einige Dutzend wackere ältere Damen und Herren eine Sammlung der literarischen Intelligenz zuwegegebracht, an die man zeitweise nicht mehr recht zu glauben vermochte, die aber mittlerweile kaum noch jemanden interessiert: nämlich die friedliche Vereinigung der deutschen PEN-Zentren Ost und West. In der *Frankfurter Allgemeinen* erschien ein mäßig langer Zweispalter dazu, in der *ZEIT* nicht einmal das. Das Treiben der Intelligentsia wird offenbar, nachdem die Verteilungskämpfe weitgehend abgeschlossen und die kulturelle Definitionsmacht des Westens unangefochten zu sein scheint, nicht mehr als spannend taxiert – obwohl man doch einen würdigen Präsidenten (Christoph Hein) fand und dieser eine überzeugende Agenda aufstellte, indem er dem Einsatz für *writers in prison* eindeutig Priorität zusprach.

Auffällig war, daß beim PEN-Treffen (wie bei vergleichbaren anderen Gelegenheiten in den letzten Jahren) kaum jüngere Autoren präsent waren (wobei mit 'jünger' hier großzügig ein Lebensalter bis zu ca. vierzig Jahren gemeint ist). Christoph Hein räumte diesen Sachverhalt in einem Interview ein, aber er spielte ihn herunter. Was er damit ausblendete (und seine PEN-Brüder und -Schwestern mit ihm), ist, daß *jüngere Autorengenerationen* heranwachsen, deren Angehörige die alten Spiele nicht mehr mitspielen wollen; die die ihnen angebotenen Rollen – z.B. als Intellektuelle im großen Sinn, als Mahner und Rufer, als Sprecher im Namen von Letztwerten, als Wegweiser und Sinnproduzenten – ausschlagen. Sie tun dies entweder, weil sie solche Rollenmöglichkeiten gar nicht mehr wahrnehmen, oder, weil sie diese bewußt, reflektiert als unangemessen ablehnen. Einige der vieldiskutierten ostdeutschen Autoren der letzten Jahre, geboren Anfang bis Mitte der 60er Jahre, sind symptomatisch für diese Haltung. Ob Durs Grünbein, Ingo Schulze, Ingo Schramm oder Thomas Brussig – sie alle haben die DDR nicht, wie Christa Wolf oder Volker Braun, "geliebt", auch nicht haßgeliebt wie Heiner Müller, aber auch nicht wirklich gehaßt. Sie haben in ihr gelebt, sich mit ihr und ihren Lebensvorgaben mehr oder weniger arrangiert, abseits von geschichtsphilosophischem Pathos und jenseits jener tragisch-heroischen Weltanschauung, die Heinz Bude so treffend als DDR-typisch (und sie miterhaltend) diagnostiziert hat.[53] Keine Kreuzespassion, nirgends.

Einige Zitate mögen diese veränderte Haltung belegen. So bemerkte Ingo Schulze selbst, daß sein entspanntes Verhältnis zur einstmaligen DDR offenbar nur schwer vermittelbar war: "Die simple Tatsache, daß ich die DDR weder nachahmens- noch in ihrer real existierenden Gestalt erhaltenswert fand, aber dort nicht unglücklich war, läßt sich manchmal schwer begreiflich machen."[54] Ein Jahr später, im Oktober 1998, brachte er sein politisches und literarisches Selbstverständnis dann explizit auf den Begriff: "Ich bin sehr froh, daß die DDR zu Ende gegangen ist und empfinde keine Trauer. Ich spüre eine starke literarische Generationsgrenze zu den vorherigen Generationen, die viel mehr in der DDR drinsteckten. Wir hatten das Glück, daß wir einen Anfang hatten, ohne richtig involviert zu sein. [...] Unsere Generation ist eher gegen Utopien gefeit."[55]

Ebenso deutlich hat sich Durs Grünbein artikuliert – allergisch gegen alle geschichtsphilosophischen Konstrukte und eschatologischen Erwartungen. All die "kleinen Alltagsverrichtungen", so sagt er, sind "jetzt mein Schicksal, nicht mehr die geschichtlichen Determinanten." Und noch krasser, verstörend für ältere linke Intellektuelle: "Zukunft ist eine hysterische Kategorie." Grünbein nennt sein Verhältnis zur Wirklichkeit "Bejahungsironie". "Ich schaue interessiert in den Abgrund, gehe am Rande auf und ab und treffe ein paar Aussagen über den Abgrund. Und bin ein wenig gerettet. Während viele die Hände über dem Kopf zusammenschlagen. Die verwechseln das mit Pessimismus."[56]

Nun, so abgeklärt wie Grünbein sind nicht alle. Auch bei manchen Jüngeren klingt Trauer um Verluste – von Zukunft, von Utopie, von einem intakten Wertehorizont – durch, und Thomas Brussig macht deutlich, er habe sein Buch *Helden wie wir* "aus Wut und Enttäuschung über die nicht stattgefundene Vergangenheitsbewältigung geschrieben". Zwar ist ihm "Utopie [...] zu hoch gegriffen", aber: "Eine Sehnsucht nach Gerechtigkeit empfinde ich schon."[57] Hier klingt an, daß manche der jüngeren Autoren sich nicht mit der Null-Option bezüglich ihrer Rolle als Intellektuelle zufriedengeben werden und ihre Perspektive in für jedermann nachvollziehbaren, bescheidenen Sinnkonstrukten von mittlerer Reichweite suchen – wie eben "Gerechtigkeit", nicht im Lande Nirgendwo, sondern hier und jetzt. Zu bedauern wäre es langfristig jedenfalls, wenn die jüngere literarische Intelligenz durch völlige Abstinenz von der politischen Öffentlichkeit ihr geistiges Kapital einfach verschenkte. Daß diese Verweigerungshaltung entstehen konnte, ist freilich nicht nur dem Zusammenbruch der *grands récits*

weltweit zuzuschreiben, sondern auch jener hypertrophen, nicht mehr glaub-
würdigen Ausformung der Intellektuellenrolle, wie sie hier skizziert wurde.

So schließe ich mit einem ambivalenten Fazit. Zum einen scheint es mir,
mehr als bislang geschehen, notwendig, die Illusionen und Anmaßungen zu
reflektieren, in die unser eigenes Verständnis als Intellektuelle immer wieder
zu geraten droht – Illusionen und Anmaßungen, die in einer langen geschichtlichen Tradition des Intellektuellen als des besserwissenden Welt-
gewissens fundiert sind. Das sind Reste eines priesterlichen Machtverhaltens,
die im Zeitalter der Säkularisierung allzu lange und mit schlimmen Folgen
überlebt haben. Solche Selbsterkenntnis und Selbstbeschränkung vorausgesetzt, mögen Intellektuelle sich durchaus mit guten Ideen und Sinnkonstrukten von mittlerer Reichweite einschalten in die öffentliche Debatte,
und auch weiterhin für Erniedrigte und Beleidigte, wo auch immer auf der
Erde, ihre Stimme erheben. Warum? Vielleicht, mit Voltaire zu sprechen:
"weil kein anderer es tut".

Anmerkungen

[1] Wolf Lepenies, "Fall und Aufstieg der Intellektuellen in Europa", *Neue Rundschau* 102
(1991), Heft 1, 14.

[2] Georg Jäger, "Der Schriftsteller als Intellektueller. Diskussionsvorlage: Materialien,
Fragen und Thesen". Ungedrucktes Typoskript, München 1996, 1.

[3] Karl Mannheim, *Ideologie und Utopie*, Bonn: Cohen 1929, 123.

[4] Vgl. Martin Greiffenhagen, "Die Intellektuellen in der deutschen Politik", *Der Monat* 233
(1968), 33-43.

[5] Helmut Schelsky, *Die Arbeit tun die andern. Klassenkampf und Priesterherrschaft der
Intellektuellen*, Opladen: Westdeutscher Verlag 1975, 106.

[6] Vgl. Karl Löwith, *Weltgeschichte und Heilsgeschehen. Die theologischen
Voraussetzungen der Geschichtsphilosophie*, Stuttgart u.a.: Kohlhammer 10. Aufl. 1990,
sowie meinen Aufsatz "Heilsgeschehen und Geschichte – nach Karl Löwith", *Sinn und
Form* 46 (1994), Heft 6, 894-915.

[7] Schelsky, op.cit., 94.

[8] Vgl. Löwith, op.cit.

[9] Mannheim, op.cit., 215.

[10] Löwith, op.cit., 11.

[11] Vgl. Theodor Lessings einflußreiches Buch mit dem Titel *Geschichte als Sinngebung des Sinnlosen*, München: Beck 1919.

[12] Vgl. Carl Christian Bry, *Verkappte Religionen*, Gotha: Perthes 1924.

[13] Vgl. neben der umfangreichen älteren Literatur neuerdings Wolfgang Mommsen (Hg.), *Kultur und Krieg. Die Rolle der Intellektuellen, Künstler und Schriftsteller im Ersten Weltkrieg*, München: Oldenbourg 1996.

[14] Vgl. Julien Benda, *La Trahison des Clercs*, Paris: Grasset 1927. Eine auszugsweise deutsche Übersetzung erschien erst 1948 unter dem Titel "Der Verrat der Geistigen" in der *Literarischen Revue* 3, 1948.

[15] Ulrich Raulff, "Ende einer Parallelaktion. J'accuse...! Hundert Jahre Intellektuelle und Intelligenz", *Frankfurter Allgemeine Zeitung* vom 13. Januar 1998.

[16] Gottfried Benn, "Der neue Staat und die Intellektuellen", *Gesammelte Werke*, Bd. 1, Wiesbaden: Limes 1959, 440.

[17] Heinrich Mann, *Ein Zeitalter wird besichtigt*, Berlin: Aufbau 1947, 120f. und passim.

[18] Hannah Arendt, *Besuch in Deutschland. Die Nachwirkungen des Naziregimes* [1950], Berlin: Rotbuch 1993, 23.

[19] Herfried Münkler, "Politische Mythen der DDR", *Berlin-Brandenburgische Akademie der Wissenschaften. Jahrbuch 1996*, 123-156; hier 131.

[20] Münkler, op.cit., 128 und passim.

[21] Vgl. dazu jetzt, diesen Befund bestätigend und erhellend, Victor Klemperer, *So sitze ich denn zwischen allen Stühlen. Tagebücher 1945-1959*, Berlin: Aufbau 1999.

[22] Günther Deicke, "Die jungen Autoren der vierziger Jahre", *Sinn und Form* 39 (1987), Heft 3, 644. Deicke spielte damit auf das Buch *Dichter im Dienst. Der sozialistische Realismus in der deutschen Literatur* von Lothar Balluseck an, das zuerst Wiesbaden: Limes 1956, erweitert 1963, erschien.

[23] Franz Fühmann, "Zweiundzwanzig Tage oder die Hälfte des Lebens", in: F.F., *Das Judenauto* [u.a. Texte], Rostock: Hinstorff 1979, 478.

[24] Heiner Müller, *Krieg ohne Schlacht. Leben in zwei Diktaturen*, Köln: Kiepenheuer & Witsch 1992, 364.

[25] Dan Diner, "Kontraphobisch. Über Engführungen des Politischen", in: D.D.: *Kreisläufe. Nationalsozialismus und Gedächtnis*. Berlin: Rowohlt 1995, 102.

[26] Annette Simon, "Antifaschismus als Loyalitätsfalle", *Frankfurter Allgemeine Zeitung* vom 1. Februar 1993.

[27] Wolfgang Kohlhaase in einem Gespräch mit *die tageszeitung* (Ausgabe Bremen) vom 17. Juni 1990.

[28] Diner, op.cit., 95 und passim.

[29] Uwe Johnson, "Versuch, eine Mentalität zu erklären. Über eine Art DDR-Bürger in der Bundesrepublik Deutschland", in: U.J., *Berliner Sachen. Aufsätze*, Frankfurt a.M.: Suhrkamp 1975, 53f.

[30] "[Therese Hörnigk im] Gespräch mit Christa Wolf", in: T. Hörnigk, *Christa Wolf*, Berlin (Ost) : Aufbau 1989, 9.

[31] Günter Wirth, "Gegenkultur aus bildungsbürgerlichem Geist", *Frankfurter Allgemeine Zeitung* vom 1. April 1995.

[32] D. Diner, "Antifaschistische Weltanschauung", op.cit., 79.

[33] Friedrich Dieckmann, "Land unter Bomben. Vereint in der Zerstörung, im Aufbau gespalten", *Frankfurter Allgemeine Zeitung* vom 19. April 1995.

[34] Diner, "Antifaschistische Weltanschauung", op.cit., 82.

[35] Ibid., 84.

[36] Uwe Johnson in dem Gespräch "Sie sprechen verschiedene Sprachen. Schriftsteller diskutieren", *alternative* 7 (1964), Heft 38/39, 98.

[37] Heinz Czechowski, "Brief" [= Gedichttitel], in: *In diesem besseren Land. Gedichte der deutschen Demokratischen Republik seit 1945*, Halle a.d. S.: Mitteldeutscher Verlag 1966, 286.

[38] Vgl. hierzu meinen Aufsatz "Zwischen Hypertrophie und Melancholie. Die literarische Intelligenz der DDR im historischen Kontext", *Universitas* 1993, Heft 8, 778-792.

[39] Stefan Heym, *Der Winter unsers Mißvergnügens. Aus den Aufzeichnungen des OV Diversant*, München: Goldmann 1996, 123.

[40] Vgl. u.a. meinen Aufsatz "Status melancholicus. Zur Transformation der Utopie in der DDR-Literatur", *Literatur in der DDR. Rückblicke* (= *Text + Kritik*, Sonderband), München: edition text und kritik 1991, 232-245.

[41] Roland Berbig (Hg.), *In Sachen Biermann. Protokolle, Berichte und Briefe zu den Folgen einer Ausbürgerung*, Berlin: Ch. Links 1994.

[42] Christa Wolf, op.cit., 278f.

[43] Günter de Bruyn, *Vierzig Jahre. Ein Lebensbericht*, Frankfurt a.M.: S. Fischer 1996, 212.

[44] C. Wolf in Manfred Krug, *Abgehauen. Ein Mitschnitt und Ein Tagebuch*, Düsseldorf: Econ 1996, 79.

[45] C. Wolf, *Auf dem Weg nach Tabou. Texte 1990-1994*, Köln: Kiepenheuer & Witsch 1994, 81.

[46] Ibid., 262.

[47] C. Wolf, op.cit., 273f.

[48] John Carey, *Haß auf die Massen. Intellektuelle 1880-1939*, Göttingen: Steidl 1996 (englisch: *The Intellectuals and the Masses. Pride and Prejudice among the Literary Intelligentsia, 1880-1939*, London: Faber and Faber 1992). Careys Buch ist, wie immer überzogen er polemisieren mag, ein wichtiges Lehrstück über den elitär-verächtlichen Wahn der Intellektuellen, rechter wie linker, die unbedarften Massen erziehen, sprich: unterwerfen und notfalls sogar vernichten zu müssen.

[49] C. Wolf, "Nagelprobe", in: C.W., *Auf dem Weg nach Tabou*, 169.

[50] Wolfgang Bergem, "Ostdeutsche als Thema und als Teilnehmer intellektueller Diskurse seit der Vereinigung". Vortragsmanuskript für das 24th New Hampshire Symposium, Conway (NH) 1998, 14.

[51] C. Wolf, "Wo ist euer Lächeln geblieben? Brachland Berlin 1990", in: C.W., *Auf dem Weg nach Tabou*, 44.

[52] W. Bergem, op. cit., 14f.

[53] Heinz Bude, "Das Ende einer tragische Gesellschaft", in: Hans Joas / Martin Kohli (Hg.), *Der Zusammenbruch der DDR. Soziologische Analysen*, Frankfurt a.M.: Suhrkamp 1993, 267-281; komplementär dazu H. Budes Aufsatz zur Bundesrepublik "Die ironische Nation", *Mittelweg 36*, 1998, Heft 2, 3-11.

[54] Ingo Schulze, "Berlin ist eine unschuldige Stadt" [I. Schulze gemeinsam mit Richard Ford in Berlin], *DIE ZEIT magazin*, Nr. 41, vom 3. Oktober 1997, 34.

[55] "Gefeit vor Utopien". Thomas Brussig und Ingo Schulze im Gespräch mit Michael Neubauer, *die tageszeitung (taz)* vom 5. Oktober 1998.

[56] Zitiert in: Matthias Kamann, "Entfaltung in der Falle: Durs Grünbein", *DIE ZEIT magazin*, Nr. 44, vom 30. Oktober 1998, 16, 14 und 10f.

[57] Thomas Brussig in: "Gefeit vor Utopien", op.cit.

Marie-Elisabeth Räkel

**Der Nationalsozialismus im kulturpolitischen Diskurs der SED
1946-1956**⁎

As important as the "antifascist myth" which lay at the foundation of the GDR was the profound influence that the national-socialist past exerted on the mentality and behaviour of German communists and their sympathizers both right after the war and throughout the history of the GDR. The perception of national socialism as an absolute evil and a constant threat continually shaped the SED's political program. By analysing the impact of this perception on the official discourse of leading German communists in the field of cultural policy, this chapter shows that reference to the national-socialist past helped to stabilize the regime in the short term, because it justified an extremely orthodox interpretation of the communist ideology. In the long term, though, the leaders' obsession with the past distorted their vision of reality and contributed to the perversion of communists ideals.

1. Die besondere Aufgabe der Kulturpolitik

In seinen *Gedanken zur Kultur* fällt Otto Grotewohl im September 1948 ein radikales Urteil:

> Das deutsche Volk ist Gegenstand einer Katastrophe, wie sie furchtbarer, namenloser, grenzenloser noch kein großes Volk in der Geschichte getroffen hat. Nur in der Zerstörung Karthagos und Jerusalems und im Ausgang des Dreißigjährigen Krieges bieten sich uns vielleicht Vorgänge zum Vergleich an. Der Ertrag der ganzen deutschen Geschichte und des Hitler-Regimes erweist sich als ein schreckliches Nichts[1].

Für die nach Deutschland zurückgekehrten kommunistischen Funktionäre sind die Ruinen und die Trümmer der zerbombten deutschen Städte nicht nur Zeugen einer materiellen Vernichtung, sondern auch das Sinnbild eines viel schwerwiegenderen Verlustes. Obwohl es den meisten Deutschen noch nicht klar ist, so die Funktionäre, wird sich bald zeigen, dass die schlimmsten Folgen der nationalsozialistischen Herrschaft das geistige Leben betreffen. So beschreibt Johannes R. Becher den Anblick, der sich ihm nach seiner Rückkehr aus dem Moskauer Exil bietet: "Eine trümmerreiche chaotische Hinterlassenschaft begegnet uns auf Schritt und Tritt. Bis in das Innerste jedes Überlebenden hinein reichen Trümmerfelder, Gräber, Schlachtstätten. Wir treffen Verwüstungen an auf geistigem und moralischem Gebiet"[2]. Für Otto Grotewohl gibt es keinen Zweifel, dass "der geistige Lebensraum [des deutschen Volkes] den gleichen kümmerlichen Anblick eines Ruinenfeldes gewährt, wie ihn sein äußerlich umgebender Lebensraum darbietet"[3].

Die Vernichtung der geistigen und kulturellen Werte Deutschlands in Folge des Nationalsozialismus wird in den ersten Reden und Überlegungen der Kommunisten mit Hilfe einer Metapher ausgedrückt. Es wird von den "Ruinen der deutschen Kultur" gesprochen oder von den "Ruinenfeldern der Kultur", zuweilen auch von "Schutthaufen der Kultur" oder von "verschütteter Kultur". Das deutsche Volk ist, wie Becher es auszudrücken pflegt "geistig zusammengebrochen" und "moralisch ausgebombt". Zuweilen werden auch wirtschaftliche Bilder bemüht wie in den Ausdrücken "die Kultur ist entwertet" oder "Deutschland hat keinen politischen, keinen wirtschaftlichen und keinen kulturellen Groschen mehr". Man kann die Bilanz auch auf einfachere Weise ziehen, mit den Worten Otto Grotewohls: "alles ist dahin."[4]

Diese Feststellung kann als der Tenor der ersten kommunistischen Äußerungen zum Zustand Deutschlands nach dem Ende des Krieges betrachtet werden. Die Betonung wird erstens auf das Ausmaß und den Umfang der Katastrophe gelegt, auf ihre Totalität. Es wird auf die breite, durch alle Bevölkerungsschichten hindurchgehende Schuld oder Mittäterschaft des deutschen Volkes hingewiesen, aber auch auf die tiefe Verstrickung aller Gebiete des Wissens, der Moral und des kulturellen Lebens in die Verbrechen der Nationalsozialisten. Für Johannes R. Becher ist die deutsche Niederlage

> eine Niederlage der deutschen Philosophie, der deutschen Geschichtsschreibung, der deutschen Pädagogik, der deutschen Wissenschaft, eine Niederlage des deutschen Denkens und deutschen Gefühlslebens im tiefsten und breitesten Sinn. Jedes dieser Wissensgebiete ist in diese Totalniederlage mit einbezogen und hat aktiv zu dieser Totalniederlage mit beigetragen[5].

Wilhelm Pieck führt auf der ersten Kulturtagung der KPD im Februar 1946 aus, dass die deutsche Kultur in dieser Situation keinen Trost und keine Orientierung spenden kann, da sie es auch nicht vermocht hat, dem Nationalsozialismus Einhalt zu gebieten: "Der einst in alle Welt hinausleuchtende Ruhmeskranz, den die erhabensten Geistesgrößen durch ihre genialen Kulturschöpfungen dem deutschen Volk geflochten hatten, ist entblättert und mit Schmach und Schande bedeckt."[6]

Zweitens wird in den kulturpolitischen Überlegungen hervorgehoben, dass der Nationalsozialismus nicht ein plötzliches Ereignis war und nicht von außen über Deutschland hereingebrochen ist, sondern dass die Wurzeln des Phänomens weit in die deutsche Vergangenheit und Tradition reichen. Das deutsche Volk steht sozusagen vor dem kulturellen Nichts, weil keine Überlieferung als intakt angesehen werden kann. Die geistige Substanz ist angegriffen. Der Nationalsozialismus wird als Resultat einer "langwierigen geistigen Krise" beschrieben. Für Johannes R. Becher ist "die Hitler-katastrophe […] der Total- und endgültige Schlussbankrott unserer gesamten geschichtlichen Entwicklung"[7] und es war ein "sich hinziehender geistig-moralischer Auflösungs- und Fäulnisprozess"[8] der zur Hitlerherrschaft geführt hat.

Die offizielle marxistisch-leninistische Definition sieht in dem National-sozialismus eine Variante des Faschismus, der von Dimitroff auf dem XIII. Plenum des Exekutivkomitees der Kommunistischen Internationale 1933 als "die offene terroristische Diktatur der am meisten reaktionären, chauvi-nistischen und imperialistischen Elemente des Finanzkapitals" charakterisiert wurde.[9] Wenn man von dieser Definition ausgeht, die sich auf eine rein wirtschaftliche Analyse des Nationalsozialismus beschränkt, liegt die Rettung Deutschlands in der Bekämpfung des Großkapitals und des Junkertums, also in der Vernichtung der Fundamente des Imperialismus. Es genügt, diesen Kräften ihre wirtschaftliche Basis zu entziehen, so die gängige Interpretation, um ein völliges Verschwinden der nationalsozialistischen Ideologie herbeizu-führen und so das Problem ein für alle mal aus der Welt zu schaffen. Die Herbeiführung des Sozialismus stellt in sich selbst schon eine Bewältigung der Vergangenheit dar. Obwohl diese Theorie in der SBZ und später in der DDR vorherrschte und auch der Grund dafür war, dass die DDR jede Entschädigung an jüdische Opfer des nationalsozialistischen Terrors abgelehnt hat, entdeckt man in den Texten parallel zur offiziellen Inter-pretation auch andere Töne.

Viele Bemerkungen der SED-Funktionäre zeugen von dem Empfinden, im Nationalsozialismus ein völlig abnormes, einmaliges, aus jedem analytischen Rahmen fallendes Phänomen vor sich zu haben, dem nicht ausreichend mit einer klassischen marxistischen Analyse beizukommen ist. In ihren Formulierungen entfernen sich die Funktionäre von der offiziell vorgeschriebenen Sichtweise und bedienen sich anderer Kategorien, anderer Bilder, um ihrem Entsetzen Ausdruck zu geben. Der Nationalsozialismus wird so einerseits als geschichtlicher Rückfall in eine weitentfernte Epoche gesehen. Für Grotewohl zum Beispiel wurden im Nationalsozialismus "Die barbarischen und mörderischen Instinkte, die durch die Kultur unterdrückt und in jahrtausendelanger Entwicklung in menschliche Bahnen gelenkt wurden, [werden] bewusst reaktiviert."[10] Der NS wird andererseits aber auch als ein Aussteigen aus einem normalen geschichtlichen und menschlichen Rahmen geschildert: "Es geht um den Über- und Untergang in einen Zustand, den man, da der Begriff dafür noch fehlt, behelfsmäßig mit 'Barbarei' umschreiben kann."[11]

In dieser Situation geht es nicht mehr nur um eine Verrohung der Sitten, wie sie von einem kapitalistischen System erzeugt wird, und es erscheint den Kulturfunktionären fraglich, ob eine klassische Vorgehensweise nach dem Lehrbuch des Marxismus-Leninismus, d.h. eine Reform der wirtschaftlichen Verhältnisse begleitet von bewusstseinserweiternden Maßnahmen, die Lösung herbeiführen kann. Die geistige und kulturelle Verankerung der nationalsozialistischen Ideologie in der ganzen Bevölkerung, die Infrage-stellung der deutschen Tradition selbst erfordern besondere Methoden, die nicht nur wirtschaftlicher sondern auch und vor allem geistiger Natur sein müssen. In diesem Kontext rücken also Kultur und Kulturpolitik, der sogenannte Überbau, in den Vordergrund. Die Erneuerung der geistigen Grundlagen wird oft als Voraussetzung für das Gelingen von wirtschaftlichen und sozialen Veränderungen angeführt. So meint Becher:

> Es wäre ein Selbstbetrug ohnegleichen, wenn wir annehmen würden, der Aufbau Deutschlands wäre vorwiegend eine wirtschaftliche, eine technische Angelegenheit [...]. Die Ordnung unseres materiellen Lebens hängt weit mehr denn je davon ab, ob wir uns eine neue freiheitliche innere Ordnung geben, ob wir eine neue geistig-moralische Ordnung zu schaffen vermögen. Ohne Enttrümmerung, ohne eine Erneuerungsbewegung auf geistigem Gebiet, ohne eine moralische Neugeburt unseres Volkes muss jeder materielle Neuaufbau über kurz oder lang zum Scheitern verurteilt sein.[12]

Für Otto Grotewohl steht ebenfalls fest: "Ohne die geistige und seelische Erneuerung des deutschen Menschen hat Deutschland keine Zukunft."[13] Die Kulturpolitik muss also die dringende Aufgabe der "Enttrümmerung auf geistigem Gebiet" übernehmen. Den Kulturpolitikern und Kulturschaffenden wird so die Rolle von Trümmerfrauen des Geistes zugewiesen. Die Hauptmission der Kulturpolitik in der SBZ/DDR ist es, zuerst einmal die NS-Ideologie zu vernichten und dem besonders gefährlichen Angriff des NS auf die geistige Substanz Deutschlands und auf die menschliche Zivilisation überhaupt eine Antwort entgegenzusetzen. Wegen dieser Aufgabe nimmt die Kulturpolitik in der SBZ/DDR eine besondere und wichtige Rolle ein.

2. Eine dualistische Sicht von Kultur
Nun stellt sich aber für die Kulturfunktionäre und die SED-nahen Kulturschaffenden die Frage, welche Züge diese "Enttrümmerung auf

geistigem Gebiet" tragen wird und wie mit dem geistigen Erbe der Vergangenheit umgegangen werden soll. Otto Grotewohl fragt sich:

> Ist es erlaubt, in dieser Situation die suchenden Menschen in Deutschland an die Vergangenheit, an alte Traditionen zu verweisen? Sind die alten Traditionen nicht nur die bloßen Vorstufen jenes Zusammenbruchs, jener Katastrophe und jenes Chaos, in welches das deutsche Volk hineingeraten ist? Sind diese Traditionen nicht durch ihre Früchte, deren Tatsache das Dritte Reich und der Ausgang von 1945 gewesen sind, endgültig widerlegt?[14]

Seine unmittelbare Antwort auf diese Frage lautet: "Die Wieder-anknüpfung an Traditionen würde bedeuten, dass man in Deutschland den verfehlten Weg nochmals zu gehen gedenke, auf dem man so schauerlich gescheitert ist." Die Reden und Texte der SED-Funktionäre schwanken am Anfang zwischen zwei Optionen des Umgangs mit der Vergangenheit. Eine erste Variante besteht darin, den Ruinen des Nationalsozialismus das absolut neue entgegenzusetzen und der Vergangenheit den Rücken zu kehren. Die Reise in eine neue Zukunft soll ohne störendes kulturelles Gepäck angetreten werden. Bei der Neugeburt des deutschen Volkes soll die Nabelschnur alter Traditionen abgeschnitten werden. In den Texten drücken verschiedene Metaphern den Willen zu diesem radikalen Schnitt aus: die kulturelle Arbeit ist "Aufräumungsarbeit,"[15] es gilt "das bösartige Geschwür Nazismus aus dem Körper unseres Volkes herauszuschneiden,"[16] oder einen "radikalen Bruch" herbeizuführen. Alfred Kantorowicz ist darüber erleichtert, dass Deutschland im höchsten Grade verwüstet ist. So ist die Garantie gegeben, dass es unmöglich sein wird, Deutschland so aufzubauen, wie es vor dem Krieg war. Das ist in seinen Augen ein Vorteil, "denn wir wollen ja ein von Grund auf neues Deutschland bauen, das nichts mehr gemein haben wird mit jenem Deutschland, das schon den Keim der tödlichen sozialen Krankheit Nazismus in sich trug und sich den Tollwütigen auslieferte."[17]

Die zweite kulturpolitische Variante kann als mildere, realistischere, dem Zweck der Bündnispolitik und der Legitimation dienende Vorgehens-weise charakterisiert werden. In diesem Fall entscheidet man sich fürs Aussortieren der Kultur. Die Metapher der Ruinen der Kultur wird hier leicht umgewandelt, so dass ein Teil der Kultur "unter den Trümmern noch atmet", oder "unter den Trümmerbergen ewige Schätze ruhen."[18] Die Wieder-gewinnung der Kultur wird in diesem Kontext archäologischen Aus-grabungen gleichen, denn die Kultur muss "entdeckt" und "gehoben", aber auch von der bürgerlichen Staubschicht befreit werden, um im alten Glanz zu erstrahlen. In der Tat siegt diese zweite Variante, denn ein Neuanfang aus dem Nichts heraus erweist sich als unmöglich. Eine Orientierungshilfe ist in

der neuen Welt notwendig und willkommen. Becher führt aus: "So blicken
wir um uns und halten Umschau nach allem und jedem, was uns aus der
Niedergeschlagenheit und Gebeugtheit aufzurichten vermag."[19] Die SED
kann im Neuanfang auf die Stütze der Kultur und der nationalen Tradition
nicht verzichten.

Den beiden Entwürfen ist gemeinsam, dass sie erstens eine schnelle,
einmalige und vollständige Entsorgung der deutschen Vergangenheit für
möglich halten, und zweitens sich auf eine dualistische Sicht von Kultur
stützen. Im ersten Fall wird zwischen alter und neuer Kultur unterschieden:
der Wille, eine neue Welt zu schaffen, wird als Damm gegen alte Ideen
errichtet, so dass diese daran gehindert werden, in die neue Zeit hinüberzu-
schwappen. Alte und neue Kultur erscheinen als zwei hermetisch in sich
abgeschlossene Welten. Im zweiten Fall herrscht die Vorstellung einer nach
guten und schlechten Eigenschaften sortierbaren, trennbaren und wieder-
verwertbaren Kultur. Für Becher gilt es "das viele Gute [...], wie es zu
unserer Geschichte gehört in unsere Gegenwart hinüberzuretten [...]. Die
schädlichen Elemente des Vergangenen aus unserer Gegenwart und aus uns
selber gründlich auszuscheiden."[20] Das von der SED ausgesuchte Sortiment
enthält vor allem Werke der deutschen Klassik und des deutschen
Humanismus. Dieses Vorgehen rechtfertigt sich durch die Tatsache, so die
kulturpolitischen Funktionäre, dass die Geschichte insgesamt aus dem Kampf
zwischen reaktionären und fortschrittlichen Tendenzen besteht. Im Nachhinein, also nach der Erfahrung des Nationalsozialismus, lassen sich die
Fronten der Geschichte besser unterscheiden. Dieser Filter kann dafür
verwendet werden, das Erbe zu sichten und den kulturellen Dachboden
aufzuräumen.

Es scheint, dass die dualistische oder binäre Sicht der Welt, die schon
vor dem Nationalsozialismus der kommunistischen Ideologie inhärent war,
sich durch die Auseinandersetzung mit dem NS und dem Krieg noch weiter
entwickelt und verhärtet hat. Ein Grund dafür liegt sicherlich in der
herrschenden Wahrnehmung des Nationalsozialismus als Verkörperung des
Bösen schlechthin. In den Beschreibungen der Kommunisten wird gerne das
Totale, das Extreme, das Absolute, das Unmenschliche im Nationalsozialismus hervorgehoben. Diese Erfahrung fasst Becher in folgende Worte
zusammen:

> Jedes natürliche menschliche Gefühl wehrt und sträubt sich zunächst dagegen, dieses
> Grauen für wahr, für menschenmöglich zu halten: es ist zu ungeheuerlich, um wahr
> zu sein! Wehrlos, sprachlos stehen wir zunächst vor diesem Entsetzen. Wir
> versuchen uns in der Geschichte zu orientieren, aber Vergleiche fehlen. Durch eine

unübersteigbare Schranke an Tradition und Moral ist unser Menschenreich getrennt von dieser Umwelt, wo alle menschlichen Grenzen ins unmenschlich Grenzenlose überschritten sind.[21]

In diesem Kontext gewinnen die absoluten Kategorien von gut und schlecht einen neuen Sinn. Der NS verlangt nach einer totalen Verurteilung: jeder Relativismus, jedes Vergleichen und Abwägen erscheinen hier als unangebracht und moralisch unanständig. In diesem Sinn findet das manichäische Weltbild der Kommunisten eine Bestätigung in der Aufwertung der Moral und der Idee des Guten, die auch von einem bürgerlichen Schriftsteller wie Thomas Mann empfunden wird:

Ja, wir wissen wieder, was Gut und Böse ist. Das Böse hat sich uns in einer Nacktheit und Gemeinheit offenbart, dass uns die Augen aufgegangen sind für die Würde und schlichte Schönheit des Guten, dass wir uns ein Herz dazu gefasst haben und es für keinen Raub an unserer Finesse erachten, es zu bekennen.[22]

Die Aufrufe der SED zu einem Neubeginn, zu einer Einheit aller antifaschistischen Kräfte im Namen des Guten, zur Notwendigkeit einer geschlossenen Front gegen die Übermacht des Bösen gewinnen vor dem Hintergrund der Erfahrungen des NS an Berechtigung.

Die SED hebt die Notwendigkeit hervor, auf den NS etwas gänzlich "anderes" folgen zu lassen, sie verspricht eine noch nie dagewesene soziale und wirtschaftliche Ordnung. Die Parteinahme für den Sozialismus ergibt sich aus dem Anblick der Ruinen: "Aus unserer Mitte ist all dieses unsagbare Entsetzen über die Welt hereingebrochen. Nur ein unheilbar irrer, nur ein hoffnungslos verstockter Verbrecher kann sich da noch der Einsicht verschließen, dass es bei uns und dass es in uns anders, gründlich anders werden muss."[23] Wenn Hitler das eine Ende der moralischen Skala besetzt, so erhebt die SED den Anspruch auf das Andere, Entgegengesetzte, auf die Verkörperung des absolut Guten. Für Becher ist klar: "Eine freie Aussicht in die Zukunft winkt uns Deutschen nur auf dem Weg, der dem Hitlers ganz und gar entgegengerichtet ist."[24]

Der dualistische Gedanke manifestiert sich auch im Geschichtsbild der SED. Deutschland, so die Kommunisten, hat sich mit dem NS der normalen geschichtlichen Entwicklung widersetzt, hat sich auf Abwege und in Sackgassen der Geschichte begeben und ist so zum Verschwinden verurteilt. Für Becher steht fest:

Eine Nation, die nicht die ihr gestellten geschichtlichen Forderungen erfüllt, sondern ihnen verstockt und hartnäckig jahrzehntelang zuwiderhandelt, solch eine Nation muss blutiges Lehrgeld zahlen, bis sie endlich belehrt wird darüber, worin die geschichtlichen Forderungen bestehen, die ihr zu erfüllen zugewiesen sind.[25]

In den Darstellungen der SED bieten sich nur zwei geschichtliche Optionen für Deutschland. Entweder es findet eine absolute Kehrtwende, ein Neubeginn statt, in den Worten Bechers eine "Wiedergeburt", eine "Auferstehung", oder der alte Weg wird wieder begangen und somit die geschichtliche Existenz Deutschlands beendet. Zwischen dem alten Weg der Weimarer Republik, also dem erneuten Einreihen in die Kette der Ursachen des NS, und dem neuen Leben im Sozialismus ist keine andere Alternative vorhanden. Es geht in der Wahrnehmung der Funktionäre um Leben oder Tod Deutschlands. Becher erklärt: "Die Geschichte selbst stellt uns gebieterisch vor ein 'Entweder-Oder'. Die freiheitliche Lösung der deutschen Tragödie hat einen unerbittlichen Zwangscharakter angenommen."[26]

Das Weltbild der Kommunisten, das die Geschichte als Kampf zwischen Fortschritt und Reaktion auffasst und die Welt in zwei entgegengesetzte Kategorien einteilt, führt zu einem ausgeprägten Freund-Feind Schema. So bedeutet jede kleine Abweichung vom kommunistischen Projekt ein Zugehen auf den Feind. Da die SED den Pol des absolut Guten besetzt hat, ist jede Veränderung ein Aufgeben zugunsten des Feindes. Es besteht keine Möglichkeit für Unterscheidungen und Nuancen. Liberalismus, Kapitalismus, Imperialismus, Faschismus, oder Nationalsozialismus sind ein und derselbe Feind: "Das Reaktionäre kann nicht Maß halten, es gibt keine gemäßigte, vernünftige, liberale Reaktion, die Reaktion ist ihrem Wesen nach irreal, unvernünftig und maßlos und muss, selbst wenn sie eine Niederlage erlitten hat und entwaffnet ist, über kurz oder lang wieder aufrüsten."[27] Diese dualistische Weltsicht hat eine völlige Erstarrung des Landes zur Folge. Die Verabsolutierung der kommunistischen Ideologie im Kampf gegen das Böse lässt keinen Platz für Reformen, Anpassungen oder Kompromisse. Das manichäische Weltbild und das Alles-oder-nichts-Prinzip der SED blockiert jede realistische Einschätzung der Lage und hebt die Politik von der Wirklichkeit ab.

3. Die Kultur dem Volke?
Die SED sieht in der Demokratisierung der Kultur eines der Hauptziele ihrer Kulturpolitik. Die Kultur muss den Massen zugänglich gemacht werden. Wilhelm Pieck erklärt schon 1946: "Wir werden uns mit allen Kräften dafür einsetzen, dass die bisherige Fernhaltung der breiten Massen unseres Volkes von der kulturellen Betätigung und von dem Genuss der durch das kulturschöpferische Wirken erzeugten Werte beseitigt wird."[28] Andererseits heißt Demokratisierung auch, dass dem Volk nicht nur der Genuss der

Kulturgüter zusteht, sondern auch als rechtmäßigem Eigentümer der Kultur die Kompetenz über kulturelle Belange zu entscheiden. Anton Ackermann ist davon überzeugt, dass: "die kulturelle Erneuerung Deutschlands [...] nicht nur Sache einzelner Spezialisten auf dem Gebiete der Kultur, nicht nur einzelner Berufe sein kann, sondern dass sie Sache des ganzen schaffenden Volkes ist."[29]

Diese Willensbekundungen der SED werden aber auch von anderen Tönen begleitet. Für die SED ist klar, dass im Nachkriegsdeutschland keine revolutionäre Situation herrscht und dass das deutsche Volk die Niederlage Hitlers nicht als Befreiung und Chance einer demokratischen Umwandlung sieht. Becher schätzt die Situation so ein: "Wenn heute die meisten Deutschen, die gegen Hitler sind – seien wir offen –, nur deshalb gegen Hitler sind, weil er den Krieg verloren hat, so ist eine solche Gegnerschaft ganz und gar keine Gewähr dafür, dass Deutschland seinen Weg in die Zukunft findet."[30] Das deutsche Volk hat sich, so kann man in den Reden der ersten Nachkriegsjahre lesen, mitschuldig gemacht. Die nationalsozialistische Herrschaft ist nicht nur die Tat einer kleinen Gruppe, sondern wurde auch vom Volk unterstützt. Die Schuld, die das deutsche Volk trifft, ist eine zweifache. Erstens besteht bei dem Ausmaß der Judenvernichtung kein Zweifel, dass "[e]s [...] sich um Millionen [handelt], die wissentlich an diesem Mordhandel beteiligt waren."[31] Zweitens war das Volk nicht fähig, seinen Fehler zu erkennen und sich selbst zu befreien. So hat Deutschland eine "ungeheuerliche Schuld und Schmach" auf sich geladen, als "es sich außerstande zeigte, den Naziverbrechern rechtzeitig die Gefolgschaft aufzukündigen."[32] Diese Tatsachen lassen Becher "in Scham und Zorn erglühen."[33] Bei seiner Ankunft in Deutschland diagnostiziert er im deutschen Volk eine "tiefe moralische Zerrüttung und kriminelle Verwahrlosung, besonders unter der Jugend."[34]

Man kann aber feststellen, dass Bemerkungen zu der aktiven Täterschaft des Volkes bald von Ausdrücken überlagert oder ersetzt werden, die die passive Rolle und die Ohnmacht des Volkes betonen. Der Nationalsozialismus erscheint plötzlich wie eine unvermeidbare Naturkatastrophe. Für Ackermann wurde das Volk "in einen dunklen Abgrund geschleudert."[35] Grotewohl meint: "In diesen hundert Jahren ist die Entwicklung mit der Wucht eines elementaren Naturgesetzes über die Völker der Erde hereingebrochen. Wir aber stehen heute vor den Resultaten dieser Lawine des Kapitalismus."[36] Der NS wird auch gerne als "geistige Infizierung"[37] bezeichnet und es heißt der NS habe "Geistes- und Vorstellungswelt eines

Millionenvolkes in einen Zustand hoffnungsloser, krankhafter Verwirrung versetzt."[38] In dieser neuen Rollenverteilung ist das Volk zwar schuldig, aber diese Schuld ist eingeschränkt, weil das Volk sozusagen aus Unwissenheit oder Ohnmacht verführt wurde. Die SED ist gewillt, dem Volk zu erlauben, von der Rolle des Mittäters in die des unwissenden Opfers zu schlüpfen.

Dieses Modell entspricht auch eher den politischen Zwängen, da es für die SED schwierig wäre, eine Bevölkerung zu regieren, die sie als kriminell gebrandmarkt hätte. So findet zwischen Volk und Partei eine Art Pakt statt. Die Partei gewährt dem Volk die Gnade der Unmündigkeit und der Unzurechnungsfähigkeit und eignet sich im Gegenzug den Titel eines Vormunds des Volkes an und übernimmt die Aufsicht über seine Erziehung. Denn, so Grotewohl "[n]iemand hat die gründliche Erziehung zur Humanität nötiger als dieser deutsche Mensch."[39] Das Volk trägt nicht mehr die volle Last der Schuld, muss aber dafür die Partei als Erziehungsberechtigten dulden und ihren Anweisungen Folge leisten. Für die Kommunisten fällt der SED die Rolle des Erziehers selbstverständlich zu. Nach offizieller kommunistischer Sicht sind die Kommunisten die einzige politische Kraft, die den NS immer und systematisch bekämpft hat. Darüber hinaus stützt sich die SED als einzige Partei auf eine wissenschaftliche Gesellschaftstheorie, die, so die Partei, gerade ihre Bestätigung durch die geschichtlichen Ereignisse selbst erfahren hat, da der Verfall der alten Welt nun Wirklichkeit geworden ist. Für Grotewohl ist klar: "Wenn der Kapitalismus nach seinem Aufstieg und seiner Blüte den Niedergang und Zerfall erfährt, so bedeutet dies, dass die Menschheit auch an der Schwelle des Übergangs zu einer neuen Kulturepoche steht. Diese Epoche ist der Sozialismus."[40]

So findet in der SBZ das leninsche Motiv der notwendigen Führungsrolle der Partei, der Partei als Avantgarde der Arbeiterklasse eine zusätzliche Rechtfertigung. Da wo die Partei sonst der Arbeiterklasse Hilfestellung beim Erlangen des "sozialistischen Bewusstseins" leisten soll, ist beim deutschen Volk weit mehr zu leisten. Wer könnte leugnen, dass dieses deutsche Volk, das Hitler an die Macht gebracht hat, einer Führung und sogar einer Erziehung bedarf, bevor es in die komplizierte Welt der Demokratie entlassen wird? Der Gedanke einer Übergangsphase, die für eine Umerziehung und Demokratisierung des deutschen Volkes genutzt werden soll, ist auch in den westlichen Besatzungszonen präsent. Im Fall der SBZ und der DDR allerdings hat dieser Gedanke weitreichendere Folgen, da er dazu dienen wird, eine kommunistische Diktatur zu errichten und zu rechtfertigen.

Dem Volk kann also unmöglich die ausgemalte kulturelle Verant-wortung übergeben werden. Das erste Ziel der Kulturpolitik muss sein, das deutsche Volk für diese Tätigkeit vorzubereiten, es umzuerziehen und es einem Wandlungsprozess nach den Maßstäben der SED zu unterziehen. Es gilt, "eine Masse sturer Befehlsempfänger zu einem Volk werden zu lassen."[41] Das Volk ist zuerst reines Objekt der Politik und soll eine passive Rolle einnehmen. Der Kulturbund, zum Beispiel, sieht seine Aufgabe darin "unser Volk zu retten,"[42] Ackermann will das Volk "so rasch wie möglich an das Licht [...] eines neuen Tages [...] führen."[43] Demokratisierung der Kultur bedeutet in den ersten Jahren der SED-Herrschaft und der DDR ein Oktroyieren einer pädagogisch geprägten Kultur von oben und nicht eine Emanzipation des Volkes in kulturellen Fragen. Unter den Aufgaben der Kulturpolitik befinden sich der Kampf gegen die NS-Ideologie, aber auch die "Hebung des kulturellen Niveaus der Werktätigen"[44] und das Erwecken eines Bedürfnisses nach guter Kultur bei den Werktätigen.

Das deutsche Volk soll durch eine spezielle Umerziehung die Chance bekommen, sich in die normale Völkergemeinschaft einzugliedern. Wie Becher es auch betont, basiert diese pädagogische Herangehensweise auf dem humanistischen Glauben, auf dem Vertrauen in die "große Fähigkeit des Menschen, trotz des Gesetzes der Trägheit, wie es ihm innewohnt, umzu-lernen, sich eines Besseren belehren und sich zum Besseren bekehren zu lassen."[45] So kann der Staat DDR auch als überdimensionierte Besserungs-anstalt betrachtet werden. Wie in der Besserungsanstalt sind die Regeln ohne Zutun der Insassen definiert worden, weil der Insasse nicht dazu berechtigt sein kann, über die Maßnahmen, die zu seiner Besserung notwendig sind, selber zu entscheiden. In seiner Eigenschaft als Delinquent ist er auch nicht dazu berechtigt, an den Methoden seiner Erziehung etwas auszusetzen oder Kritik zu üben. Die Rollen sind also klar definiert. Jede Rebellion, jeder Fluchtversuch des Delinquenten wird in diesem Rahmen immer als Unwille, als Verweigerung zur Besserung interpretiert werden.

Der Besserungsprozess wird im Fall des deutschen Volkes von der SED als schwierig eingeschätzt. In einem Artikel der Zeitschrift *Aufbau* kann man im Jahr 1947 lesen:

> Der NS wurde nicht von innen her überwunden, sondern von außen her zerschlagen. Daraus folgt, dass die Genesung unseres Volkes von nationalsozialistischen Konzeptionen und Ideologien ein langer und komplizierter Prozess sein wird, und dass wir dabei mit schweren Rückschlägen zu rechnen haben.[46]

In dieser Bemerkung scheint der 17. Juni schon vorweggenommen und entsprechend kodiert zu sein, als erneutes Sich-beirren-lassen des Volkes von faschistischen Provokateuren. Die Furcht der Partei vor dem Volk, vor dem inneren Feind ist groß und die versprochene Entlassung in die Freiheit wird immer wieder verschoben. Die Mündigkeit wird dem Volk zeitlebens der DDR nicht attestiert.

Die SED wird aber von ihrem eigenen humanistischen Anspruch eingeholt, sobald klar wird, dass sie das Versprechen der "Erziehung zur Freiheit" nicht einhalten kann. Die Besserungsanstalt erfüllt nie ihren Zweck, trotzdem bleibt sie aber als Institution bestehen. Da die Emanzipation des Volkes immer wieder in die Zukunft verschoben wird, erleidet die Partei einen erheblichen Verlust an Legitimität. Die Kommunisten hatten verkündet, sich an die rationale, moralische Seite des Menschen wenden zu wollen und auf die Veränderbarkeit des Menschen zu bauen. Da der Pakt mit dem Volk nie eingelöst wird, muss die Anfangskonstellation immer brüchiger werden.

4. Kultur im Dienst der Politik

In den ersten Nachkriegsjahren beschäftigt sich die SED mit den möglichen Ursachen des Nationalsozialismus in Deutschland. Ein Faktor, der immer wieder erwähnt und zu einem Leitmotiv der Reden und Texte zur Kulturpolitik wird, ist der unpolitische Charakter der deutschen Intellektuellen und die daraus resultierende Trennung von Geist und Macht. Infolge der misslungenen Revolution von 1848, so die gängige Erklärung, haben sich die Intellektuellen aus der Politik zurückgezogen und sich in eine unpolitische Kultur geflüchtet. So sieht Alexander Abusch in den "geistigen Folgen der unvollendeten Revolution"[47] die Ursache der späteren Katastrophe: "Hundert Jahre lang hatten viele deutsche Intellektuelle sich daran gewöhnt, dass der Geist machtlos ist und die Macht geistlos."[48] Otto Grotewohl sieht in der Diskrepanz zwischen geistiger und politischer Entwicklung ein "Grundphänomen der Geschichte Deutschlands innerhalb der letzten eineinhalb Jahrhunderte."[49] Für Becher besteht in Deutschland ein "unheilvoller Widerspruch zwischen Geist und Macht."[50]

Die unpolitische Haltung der deutschen Intelligenz hat sich, so die SED, als fataler Fehler entpuppt. Während die Intellektuellen glaubten, ihre Unschuld zu bewahren, indem sie sich vom tagespolitischen Geschehen fernhielten, haben sie nur Hitlers Machtergreifung erleichtert. Die Intellektuellen sollten eine Lehre aus dieser Erfahrung ziehen und verstehen, dass eine Kultur, die keine politische Relevanz hat und keine politischen und gesellschaftlichen Folgen anstrebt, keine Berechtigung hat. Becher stellt klar: "Das Wissen bedarf, um zum Wissen für uns alle, um zu einem Wissen zu unser aller Nutzen zu werden: der Machtwerdung. Wille zur Wahrheit muss sich stets kundtun als Machtwille, um der Wahrheit Geltung zu verschaffen."[51] Kultur und Politik, Geist und Macht gehören zusammen, denn "Geist, der darauf verzichtet Macht zu werden, der Geist hat seinen Geist schon aufgegeben."[52]

So ist die Zeit gekommen, aus den Fehlern der Vergangenheit Lehren zu ziehen. Schon die erste Nummer des *Sonntags* (Zeitschrift des Kulturbundes) befasst sich mit dem Problem des "unpolitischen Menschen" und insbesondere der unpolitischen Intellektuellen.[53] Durch Nichtbeherrschung der politischen Regeln haben die Intellektuellen die Katastrophe nicht vorhersehen können und so nicht richtig reagiert. Immer noch, so der Autor, gibt es Intellektuelle, die dies nicht verstanden haben und die kein Interesse für politische Parteien zeigen und Tageszeitungen verschmähen. Die Gesellschaft kann aber keine Passivität dulden und kann verlangen, dass jeder an der Verantwortung teilnimmt. Die SED übt mit diesen Argumenten moralischen Druck auf die Intelligentsia aus. Für Becher kann die Intelligentsia so nicht weiter bestehen: "Wir müssen uns im klaren darüber sein, dass die deutsche Intelligenz nicht so fortbestehen kann, als wäre nichts geschehen, und dass sie sich von neuem den Anspruch erkämpfen muss, als die geistige Elite ihres Volkes zu gelten."[54]

Die Partei gibt aber gleichzeitig den Intellektuellen die Chance und die Möglichkeit ihre Schuld zu sühnen. Durch ihre Unterstützung für die SED, die einzige wahre antifaschistische Kraft, und durch ihr Mitwirken am Aufbau einer neuen Ordnung können die Kulturschaffenden zeigen, dass sie aus der Vergangenheit gelernt haben. Die Kultur soll jetzt der Sache der Partei und des Sozialismus dienen. Der Intellektuelle muss aus der Isolation treten und eine aktive politische und gesellschaftliche Rolle spielen. Die SED wird als die Partei der Versöhnung von Geist und Macht vorgestellt. Becher erklärt: "[die] marxistische Partei ist sowohl Erkenntnisorgan der objektiven Wahrheit als auch ein Vollzugsorgan der aus dieser objektiven Wahrheits-erkenntnis folgenden geschichtlichen Notwendigkeiten."[55]

So wird zum Beispiel schon 1946 die erste Wahl in der SBZ mit dem Thema der Schuld der Intellektuellen verknüpft. Im *Sonntag* wird die Wahl als Chance für die Intellektuellen gewertet, ihr "Wollen und Können in den Dienst des Volkes" zu stellen, indem sie für die SED stimmen.[56] Die Mit-arbeit der Intellektuellen wird von der SED gefordert, sei es im Kulturbund, in der Nationalen Front, durch ihre Schriften oder Kunstwerke, bei Unterschriftensammlungen für Frieden und Einheit, bei Wahlen und anderen propagandaträchtigen Aktionen. Diese Aktivitäten sind sozusagen die Ablassbriefe der Intelligentsia. Ein Entkommen aus den politischen Pflichten ist schwierig, da gerade die Passivität der Intellektuellen in der Vergangenheit verurteilt wird und die SED diese selbst als aktive Unterstützung des Feindes wertet.

Auch entspricht in der besonderen Nachkriegskonstellation die Politik der SED den Wünschen von linken Intellektuellen. Viele begrüßen den Neuanfang, sehen in der SED die einzige antifaschistische Kraft in Deutschland. Der Aufruf zu einer politischen Kunst trifft ein Bedürfnis bei den Kulturschaffenden, die nach dem Krieg eine politisch und sozial engagierte Kunst betreiben wollen. Die SED kann sich auch auf deren Schuldgefühle stützen. Becher bekennt für alle anderen linken Intellektuelle: "[d]ass wir solches mit uns geschehen ließen, diese Wehrlosigkeit des deutschen Geistes ist unsere Schuld, auf diese Weise sind auch wir mitverantwortlich geworden für die Katastrophe und sind mit einverstrickt in die deutsche Tragödie."[57] Die SED versucht mit Erfolg die Intellektuellen durch besondere Privilegien und Verantwortungsposten in der Gesellschaft für sich einzunehmen. In der Besserungsanstalt DDR beziehen die parteinahen Intellektuellen eine besondere Stellung zwischen SED und Volk. Als Bewährungshelfer des Volkes teilen sie das Misstrauen der Partei gegenüber ihren Schützlingen. Wie schon andere vor mir bemerkt haben, erklärt sich die besondere Loyalität der DDR-Intellektuellen zur Partei vor allem aus ihren Schuldgefühlen, aus dem Willen zum antifaschistischen Neuanfang und aus der Angst, jede Kritik gegenüber dem Stalinismus könne das Regime und so die Chance eines anderen Deutschland vernichten. Die vollständige Indienstnahme der Kultur durch die Partei erwächst also aus einer Konstellation, wo politisches Engagement in der Kultur als Lernprozess und Sühne gegenüber der Vergangenheit verstanden wurden.

Der kommunistische Diskurs gewinnt im Nachkriegsdeutschland, anders als in allen anderen Satellitenstaaten der Sowjetunion, auf der Grundlage der nationalsozialistischen Vergangenheit eine besondere Bedeutung. Der Sozialismus in Deutschland ist zuerst primär eine Antwort auf den Nationalsozialismus und weniger ein utopisches Zukunftsprojekt. Die SED bezieht ihre Identität und Legitimität vorwiegend aus dem antifaschistischen Kampf heraus. Diese spezifische historische Konstellation hat Folgen für die Entwicklung der DDR. Erstens kann man sagen, dass die nationalsozialistische Vergangenheit der SED eine Legitimitätschance gibt, weil die Lage den Prophezeiungen der Marxisten zu entsprechen scheint und das sozialistische

Programm eine erhöhte Berechtigung erhält. So wirkt sich der National-sozialismus wie eine Art Verstärker für die kommunistischen Thesen aus.

Andererseits bedeutet aber diese Konstellation in der längeren Sicht ein Defizit und eine Destabilisierungsgefahr für die DDR. Durch die Selbst-definition der SED als Gegenpol zum Nationalsozialismus wird das dualis-tische und polarisierende Weltbild der kommunistischen Ideologie weiter verstärkt. Die Wahrnehmung des Nationalsozialismus als des absolut Bösen nährt den Wunsch nach einem totalen Neuanfang bei linken Sympathisanten, verstärkt aber gleichzeitig das Freund-Feind Bild und verhindert so eine realistische Politik. So tritt eine Blockierung und Erstarrung der Politik ein. Mit der Zeit rückt die nationalsozialistische Vergangenheit in die Ferne, und mit ihr verschwindet auch die Legitimationsbasis und die anfängliche moralische Rechtfertigung, eine Diktatur über das deutsche Volk zu verhängen. Bei den linken Intellektuellen bewirken die Schuldgefühle einen lähmenden Effekt, da aus dieser Lage heraus keine richtige Kritik oder Dissidenz entstehen kann und so kein gradueller Reformprozess in Gang gesetzt werden kann.

Anmerkungen

* Diese Überlegungen basieren auf Ergebnisse meiner Dissertation (*La politique culturelle de la RDA de 1945 à 1956: l'échec d'un discours*, Université de Montréal), die vom CRSH und FCAR unterstützt wurde.

[1] Otto Grotewohl, *Gedanken zur Kultur*, Weimar: Verlag Werden und Wirken, 1948, S. 7.

[2] Johannes R. Becher, "Erziehung zur Freiheit", *Gesammelte Werke*, Bd. 16 (Publizistik 2), Berlin: Aufbau-Verlag, 1978, S. 527.

[3] Otto Grotewohl, *Gedanken zur Kultur*, S. 9.

[4] Ebda., S. 6.

[5] Johannes R. Becher, "Zur Frage der politisch-moralischen Vernichtung des Faschismus", *Gesammelte Werke*, Bd. 16 (Publizistik 2), S. 411.

[6] Wilhelm Pieck, "Um die Erneuerung der deutschen Kultur", *Um die Erneuerung der deutschen Kultur. Erste zentrale Kulturtagung der KPD*, Berlin: Verlag Neuer Weg, 1946, S. 13.

[7] Johannes R. Becher, "Zur Frage der politisch-moralischen Vernichtung des Faschismus", S. 411.

[8] Johannes R. Becher, "Deutsches Bekenntnis", *Gesammelte Werke*, Bd. 16 (Publizistik 2), S. 481.

[9] Rainer Eppelmann *et al.* (Hrsg.), *Lexikon des DDR-Sozialismus*, Paderborn: Verlag Ferdinand Schöningh, 1997, Bd. 1, S. 66.

[10] Otto Grotewohl, "Die geistige Situation der Gegenwart und der Marxismus", *Protokoll der Verhandlungen des I. Kulturtages der SED 1948*, Berlin: Dietz, 1948, S. 27.

[11] Johannes R. Becher, "Hitlers Gassumpf", *Gesammelte Werke*, Bd. 16 (Publizistik 2), S. 444.

[12] Johannes R. Becher, "Rede an München", *Gesammelte Werke*, Bd. 17 (Publizistik 3), Berlin: Aufbau-Verlag, 1979, S. 12.

[13] Otto Grotewohl, *Gedanken zur Kultur*, S. 35.

[14] Ebda., S. 9.

[15] Johannes R. Becher, "Zur Frage der politisch-moralischen Vernichtung des Faschismus", S. 403.

[16] Alfred Kantorowicz, "Vom moralischen Gewinn der Niederlage", *Sonntag*, 4. Mai 1947, S. 1.

[17] Ebda.

[18] Johannes R. Becher, "Versunkene Glocke", *Gesammelte Werke*, Bd. 16 (Publizistik 2), S. 499.

[19] Ebda., S. 499.

[20] Johannes R. Becher, "Rede an München", S. 13.

[21] Johannes R. Becher, "Hitlers Gassumpf", S. 444.

[22] Thomas Mann, "Kultur und Politik", 1939, *Gesammelte Werke*, Berlin: Aufbau-Verlag, 1955, Bd. 12, S. 835.

[23] Johannes R. Becher, "Auferstehen!", *Gesammelte Werke*, Bd. 16 (Publizistik 2), S. 461.

[24] Johannes R. Becher, "Erziehung zur Freiheit", S. 542.

[25] Johannes R. Becher, "Deutsches Bekenntnis", S. 482.

[26] Johannes R. Becher, "Erziehung zur Freiheit", S. 536.

[27] Johannes R. Becher, "Rede an München", S. 17.

[28] Wilhelm Pieck, "Um die Erneuerung der deutschen Kultur", S. 22.

[29] Anton Ackermann, "Unsere kulturpolitische Sendung", *Um die Erneuerung der deutschen Kultur*, S. 37.

[30] Johannes R. Becher, "Erziehung zur Freiheit", S. 542.

[31] Johannes R. Becher, "Hitlers Gassumpf", S. 441.

[32] Johannes R. Becher, "Der Sieg", *Gesammelte Werke*, Bd. 16 (Publizistik 2), S. 448.

[33] Johannes R. Becher, "Hitlers Gassumpf", S. 442.

[34] Johannes R. Becher, "Zur Frage der politisch-moralischen Vernichtung des Faschismus", S. 430.

[35] Anton Ackermann, "Unsere kulturpolitische Sendung", S. 36.

[36] Otto Grotewohl, "Amboss oder Hammer", *Über Politik, Geschichte und Kultur. Ausgewählte Reden und Schriften 1945-1961*, Berlin: Dietz Verlag, 1979, S. 111.

[37] "Eine Vertrauenskrise", *Sonntag*, 2. Februar 1947, S. 1.

[38] "Hygienische Volksbildung ist praktische Gesundheitspolitik", *Sonntag*, 13. Oktober 1946, S. 11.

[39] Otto Grotewohl, *Gedanken zur Kultur*, S. 10.

[40] Ebda., S. 37.

[41] Johannes R. Becher, "Zur Frage der politisch-moralischen Vernichtung des Faschismus", S. 411.

[42] "Der Kulturbund und die Berliner Wahlen. Aufruf der Stadtleitung Groß-Berlin", *Sonntag*, 13. Oktober 1946, S. 2.

[43] Anton Ackermann, "Unsere kulturpolitische Sendung", S. 36.

44 "Die Republik schützt die Kultur des Volkes. Verordnung zur Entwicklung einer fortschrittlichen demokratischen Kultur des deutschen Volkes und zur weiteren Verbesserung der Arbeits- und Lebensbedingungen der Intelligenz vom 16. März 1950", *Sonntag*, 2. April, 1950, S. 4.

45 Johannes R. Becher, "Erziehung zur Freiheit", S. 524.

46 "Gibt es eine besondere deutsche geistige Krise?", *Aufbau*, 1947, S. 316.

47 Alexander Abusch, "Geistige Folgen der unvollendeten Revolution", *Aufbau*, 1948, S. 275.

48 Ebda., S. 279.

49 Otto Grotewohl, "Die geistige Situation der Gegenwart und der Marxismus", S. 31.

50 Johannes R. Becher, "Auferstehen!", S. 461.

51 Johannes R. Becher, "Rede an München", S. 32.

52 Johannes R. Becher, "Erziehung zur Freiheit", S. 636.

53 "Vom unpolitischen Menschen", *Sonntag*, 7. Juli 1946, S. 1.

54 Johannes R. Becher, "Uns ist bange, aber wir verzagen nicht", *Gesammelte Werke*, S. 79.

55 Johannes R. Becher, "Erziehung zur Freiheit", S. 598.

56 "Die Intellektuellen und die Wahlen", *Sonntag*, 18. August 1946, S. 1.

57 Johannes R. Becher, "Rede an München", S. 31.

II. Dictatorship, Resistance and Autonomy in the GDR

Gerhard Wettig

Autonomy and Dependence:
The East German Regime's Relationship with the USSR, 1945-1949

In 1945, the USSR assumed supreme authority as an occupation power in defeated Germany and imposed an alien repressive regime and system. While a semblance of democratic self-government was created, the effort was actually directed at exerting Soviet power through German personnel, notably communist cadres who had been trained in Moscow but also others, including dependent non-communists. This allowed the Kremlin to make its policies on Germany appear as if they expressed the will of the indigenous people. As a result, it was able to act at the level not only of inter-allied relations but also of intra-German affairs as well.

The Soviet Occupation Regime

As a result of World War II, the four occupation powers assumed "supreme authority" in Germany.[1] The defeated country was subjected to allied government. Decisions on Germany as a whole were to be taken by the Allied Control Council, while the individual zones were under the respective military governor's authority. Delimitation between the two spheres of competence was left undefined. While the Control Council was largely paralyzed by dissent, the USSR pursued a unilateralist zonal policy and initiated socio-political transformation. It exercised excessive occupation authority in line with its systemic characteristics which did not allow for an autonomous society and did not respect any limit to the leadership's power. The Soviet claim to full control of any German activity was justified by an idea of "democracy" which held that the "true interests of the people" (as defined by Marxist-Leninist doctrine) had to be served with no regard for the people's actual will. Since Mosow thus claimed to represent the people's cause, it demanded absolute subservience. Accordingly, political parties were not accorded autonomy. The Soviet Military Administration of Germany (SMAG) subjected the non-communists both to general instructions and ex post censorship of their decisions and pronouncements. Control over the communists was even more rigorous: No statement was permitted which the SMAG had not previously approved or, in most cases, initiated. This was due to a pecular function assigned to the communist party (CP).

In its foreign policy, the Kremlin relied on both traditional diplomacy and the international communist network. When the Comintern was dissolved in 1943, its apparat was transferred to the Soviet Central Committee (CC).[2] A sizeable number of German communists were trained for employment in their native country. Under Stalin's and Dimitrov's guidance, their leaders devised a program for postwar development.[3] When the Red Army entered Germany, indigenous cadres were brought back from the USSR to serve as direct subordinates and to implement decisions taken by the CC. These "Moscow cadres" – a total of 200-400 persons – were put into key positions in the occupied territory and provided the nucleus of both administration and party.[4]

These people and the personnel they coopted under Soviet control were entrusted the "leading role" in the party system. An "antifascist-democratic bloc" served to prevent the non-communists from opting out of the consensus determined by the KPD to execute Soviet policy. In the Kremlin's view, this function required particularly strict control: While non-communist statements were of minor relevance and hence might contain mistakes to be corrected only afterwards, the party that was to provide intra-German leadership might not. The indigenous CP was to serve as a "transmission belt" which had to make the other parties fulfill orders which the Soviet side did not want to give directly so as to conceal the scope of intervention. Communist "proposals" to the bloc parties supposedly resulted from autonomous decision-making but actually were instructions by the occupation power.[5]

Stalin's USSR was not a monolith: The dictator's control was based, inter alia, on his subordinates' mutual rivalry which did not allow them to create their own power bases and made them dependent on the leader's permanent benevolence.[6] Much infighting resulted[7] which was reflected in the SMAG departments. Their differing affiliations put limits to their "supreme head's" authority. The competences of the departments were ill-defined and gave rise to frequent conflict; the security services and reparation committees were practically independent; their activities often interfered with occupation policies. Key functionaries were the head of the Propaganda, or Information, Department, Colonel Tiulpanov (who controlled notably party activities), and the SMAG Political Advisor, Vladimir Semionov (who played a crucial role in devising occupation policies).[8] Stalin, who took a particularly keen interest in Germany[9] and paid attention even to small details,[10] controlled German affairs to a full extent.[11]

While the USSR provided muscle, the indigenous CP was important in both implementing Soviet policies and creating the appearance of German initiative whenever this seemed appropriate to support and/or justify measures by the occupation power. Between leading SMAG officers and their indigenous communist counterparts special relations often developed, notably in the case of those "Moscow cadres" who had previously held important posts in the USSR. Also, the German communists had internalized the feeling that the Soviet Union was their political homeland to which they owed unconditional obedience: "Liberation of mankind" through socialism depended on its maintenance and victory. In any country, therefore, communist interest was seen to coincide with Moscow's goals. In postwar Germany, such ideological and political partisanship was reinforced by the awareness that Soviet support was indispensable for success. The higher a cadre's rank and "consciousness", the more he felt a need to prove his loyalty by obedience. Additionally, Stalin enjoyed incredibly high prestige. He was seen to personify a superhuman degree of political wisdom which did not allow doubt on any Moscow instruction. The Soviet party organization was seen to provide a model to guarantee power and victory.[12]

Such attitudes would have provided optimal preconditions for allowing the occupation regime to be based primarily on indirect exercise of authority. But Stalin was not prepared simply to rely on his followers' loyalty. He was pathologically suspicious – a phenomenon which may be at least partly attributed to the Soviet system.[13] Whoever had a responsible position was seen to require constant supervision and control. The mass of KPD members met with particular distrust given the fact that they had survived under Hitler. Even underground workers were deemed ideologically backward and hence prone to political error. On the basis of its "leading role", the KPD needed even more Soviet guidance and inspection than others.[14] Even the most reliable "Moscow cadres" were not permitted much leeway but kept under strict surveillance. All political, material, and juridical power (including all incentives and pressures) lay with the occupation authorities, who exploited their possibilities amply.[15] The logic of *divide et impera* was generally applied. When the Kremlin's most trusted person, Ulbricht, was put in charge of the central party apparat, a strong rival, Dahlem, was placed at his side.[16]

KPD/SED Decision-Making

From the very beginning, the KPD organizational structure, political program and composition of leading bodies was determined by the Kremlin. The basic instructions underlying the party's re-establishment on 11 June 1945 were issued by Stalin a week earlier and then jointly worked out by CPSU and KPD cadres under Dimitrov's supervision.[17] Until 1953, Soviet control of the German CP continued on a day-to-day basis. No decision on intraparty personnel and structure was taken without previous Soviet approval. SMAG officials were present at any relevant session and meeting; their initiative,[18] or consent, (which required clearance with Moscow, often with Stalin himself,[19] in any somehow important case) underlay all decisions, resolutions, and statements. The drafts submitted usually elicited detailed comment and correction.[20] No intraparty matter nor administrative affair was exempt from Soviet control.[21]

How the occupation power's "advice" was handled can be seen from an internal report by one of Tiulpanov's deputies. The SMAG official in charge would turn to his counterpart, saying that "we have an opinion". He would add that the latter's party "would be welcome" to explain its view with regard to the matter in question. The German would respond by indicating agreement and asking for additional information. The occupation officer would then insist that he was simply broaching his own ideas and not giving orders, pull out a pre-formulated text, hand it to his interlocutor, and add oral explanations on what a resulting regulation might look like. In doing so, he knew that the other side would instruct its staff to work out a draft on this basis. On a short deadline, the German communists would present the product of their effort, which would then undergo thorough scrutiny and correction. Naturally, all resulting comments were included in the final text. As Tiulpanov's man concluded, practically all SED decisions and statements were prepared in this manner. There was "no document [of the East German party] which we have not formulated and approved of in its entirety".[22]

All major KPD/SED measures were initiated by the Kremlin until early 1954. Indeed, the East German communists relied almost exclusively on Soviet support and protection. They depended on the "friends" both to get their regime started and to maintain it, as popular support failed to emerge. The party had no choice but to substitute domestic backing by the occupiers' power, which in turn was increasingly rejected by the "masses". A vicious circle resulted. The communists grew ever more dependent on the USSR and thus deprived themselves of any national image which, in the interests notably of their all-German ambition, they eagerly sought. This reinforced their reputation of being a "Russian party". To be sure, dissatisfaction with dismantling policies, ruthless intervention in economics, arbitrary arrests and soldiers' excesses was cautiously expressed[23] but the leaders knew they had to identify with Soviet policies unconditionally. The resulting lack of political credibility made even leading SMAG figures think about allowing for some leeway,[24] but nothing except short-lived marginal leeway resulted.

The occupation power was unwilling to dispense with justification by its German "friends" and continued to prevent any articulation of grievances.[25]

The indigenous communists' weakness at the domestic level reinforced Soviet inclination to treat them as occupied subordinates rather than "internationalist" partners. The SED was excluded even from the Cominform satellite network to indicate that it ranked below the CPs both in the "outer Soviet empire" and in Western Europe.[26] Unconditional subordination to, and staunch approval of, Soviet instructions was essential. The KPD/SED cadres knew that otherwise they were likely to be victimized by the occupation power's security *organy* or by intraparty cleansing. Even when there were no orders from Moscow and time was pressing, it was dangerous to act on one's own. In this event, even determined SMAG officials preferred to wait. In May 1947, the SED leaders had to respond to an invitation that the *land* minister presidents of the Soviet zone (who, with one exception, were party members) participate in an all-zonal conference to discuss national problems. There was extreme domestic pressure to accept, while no decision was forthcoming from the Kremlin. Tiul'panov at first recommended rejection but eventually allowed for tactical modification. The invitees were permitted to join the conference but instructed to present an ultimatum upon arrival. As was rightly anticipated, this resulted in obliging them to leave prior to any discussion.[27]

Their dependence on Soviet assent notwithstanding, East German cadres did exercise substantial influence. The occupation power often asked them for assessments and/or proposals. The USSR was also reliant on services by the KPD/SED, notably at the intra-German level: Being a foreign power, it was able to take action only through an indigenous stand-in. So the relationship had some elements of mutuality despite its gross asymmetry.[28] At the same time, however, the East Berlin leaders were careful to have a sense of Soviet expectations before offering assessments and suggestions. They prepared meetings with Stalin most thoroughly by sounding out what would be appropriate to submit to his judgment. Those SED leaders who enjoyed particular trust in Moscow had limited possibilities to voice deviating opinion internally. This was done when, in a conversation with Stalin on 31 January 1947, they were confronted with what they deemed a threat to their very existence: the prospect that, for the sake of their party's extension to West Germany, the SPD might be readmitted in the Soviet zone. They objected. But when Stalin refused to accept this, saying that the SED was not in a weak (power) position to cope with such a situation, further discussion was excluded.[29]

Decisions on Socio-Political Transformation

While, on instructions from Stalin, the KPD declared that Sovietization was not on the agenda, the occupation power began to lay the basis for systemic change. But in view of both Western attitudes and German "immaturity", its course was both cautious and gradual and allegedly served the interests of "bourgeois democracy". The real intent was indicated to cadres by the proviso that (full) introduction of the USSR's order was not appropriate given "current conditions of development in Germany".[30] The Kremlin started occupation policies by requisitioning major enterprises and all bank accounts and assets, introducing a centralized state banking system, and expropriating the owners of larger estates and farms. This was publicly justified by a need to punish supporters of nazism and to prevent them from bringing another Hitler to power. In fact, however, the purpose was – besides transfer of material value to the USSR – destruction of "bourgeois" social power and creation of people's financial dependence on jobs which were largely in the hands of administrative cadres.[31]

Contrary to what had been agreed with the Western occupation partners, the Soviet authorities invited the Germans to form central party organizations as early as on 10 June 1945. At that time, the USSR was in exclusive control of Berlin, the defeated country's center. Therefore, the SMAG was in a position to license the German parties and to pose corresponding conditions unilaterally. The applicants who created *Reichsleitungen*, i.e. national headquarters, were required to accept membership in the "antifascist-democratic bloc", location in the prospective Soviet sector, and hence exclusive SMAG control. As a result, the Kremlin's occupation authorities "constantly oversaw all processes under way in the licensed political parties and intervened actively. Their activities were based on a conception approved of by the CC of the All-Russian Communist Party (B) which also issued all necessary instructions."[32] While, in the interests of a democratic façade, the non-communists were spared the obligation to submit their statements and resolutions in advance, the Soviet control personnel was present at all their meetings of any relevance, both internal and public, thoroughly monitored their political output, and intervened ex post whenever they saw a significant deviation from Moscow's line. All kinds of manipulation, pressure, and outright repression were used to make recalcitrant people comply. Even during the comparatively tolerant initial period, countless persons were physically threatened, imprisoned and tortured by Soviet *organy*, sent to concentration camps with high rates of mortality and occasionally put to death directly. It was general practice to subject lower echelons, which enjoyed little publicity, to maximum pressure and to display more caution with regard to more prominent political actors whose fate was likely to be known in both the public at large and Western quarters. Particularly with regard to the central leaders in quadripartite Berlin, the SMAG sought to substitute obvious intervention by organizing intra-party pressure from below. This did not always work, however, as is demonstrated notably by the two CDU Chairmen's removal in December 1945.[33] When, as a result of inter-allied agreement, elections had become inevitable in the fall of 1946, the SMAG used all its possibilities to make the communists prevail – with but limited success.[34]

A crucial point in Moscow's 1944 program of German postwar development was that, as a first step, the KPD had to be gradually transformed into a CPSU-type "combat and cadre party" which, on the basis of "internal cohesion", would be capable of playing the "leading role" and of rallying a superior mass basis.[35] Only when this was achieved, could "restoration of the working class's unity" by unification with the SPD under communist conditions follow. Accordingly, the KPD was unwilling in the summer of 1945 to accept spontaneous social democratic suggestions that the two parties draw lessons from the Weimar Republic experience (which had resulted in Hitler's taking power) and overcome their organizational schism (which was seen to have been crucial in weakening the "forces of democracy"). Contrary to Moscow's estimate, it became increasingly clear in the fall of 1945 that the SPD rather than the KPD attracted the masses and, on this basis, felt justified to claim political leadership. The head of the relevant occupation authority, Colonel Tiulpanov, understood that future election results would remove the basis for assigning the "leading role" to the communists, if the social democratic party were to retain separate status. To prevent this, he reported to Moscow, the two "workers' parties" had to merge soon. His advice was taken by Stalin who issued the order to initiate formation of a "socialist unity party". During the following months, his department exerted unprecedented pressure on largely unwilling social democrats to accept the postulated union with the communists. On 20-21 April 1946, the KPD and the SPD merged to form the SED.[36]

Building a new German administration, the Soviet authorities pursued two objectives: putting reliable communist cadres into crucial positions and establishing fundamentally new structures. Since the appearance of a "bourgeois democracy" was to be created, it was general practice to fill seemingly leading posts that in fact wielded little power with non-communists while much less visible, but actually crucial functions were given to Soviet confidants. Administrative restructuring was sought by "breaking up the bourgeois state machine" as Lenin had posited. In practical terms, this implied notably concentration of all power in the "hands of the people", i.e. the leaders appointed by the occupation power who, according to official doctrine, defended the people's "objective" interest. Any division and/or separation of powers was seen to weaken "people's power". In principle, all executive, legislative, judicial, and economic functions had to rest with the same communist cadres who, on their part, acted essentially on Soviet instructions.[37] To be sure, this ideal was put into practice only insufficiently during the initial period given the fact that personnel was greatly lacking. This deficiency, however, was gradually overcome by massive KPD/SED cadre training on the one hand, and by intensified supervision and cleansing on the other.

During the early occupation period, the administrative patterns in the Soviet zone were shaped to be formally compatible with the principle of self-government agreed upon by the allied power. It soon turned out, however, that decentralized structures were inconsistent with Soviet occupation practice, which required ubiquitous fulfilment of the center's orders. Attempts to provide for homogeneous East German development through institutions of formal "self-government" resulted in a degree of heterogeneity that the Soviet side deemed unacceptable. The fact that the SMAG was internally factionalized as a result of Stalin's *divide et impera* further added to the problem. The very effectiveness of occupation control was seen to be in jeopardy. To redress the situation, the Kremlin centralized the German administration in its zone step by step from the fall of 1946 to the summer of 1947. As auxiliaries of the occupation authorities, two principal apparats emerged to guide regional and local administrative institutions: the German Administration of the Interior (GAI) and the German Economic Commission (GEC). They provided the nucleus of the future Soviet zone, and ultimately GDR, state apparat.[38]

The Kremlin took a specific approach when it came to maintenance of domestic security. In its view, it was natural that the security network of the occupation power was directly in charge of intra-German order. The Soviet *organy* used indigenous informers; the Red Army employed both watchmen and border guards on an individual basis. In the summer of 1945, the SMAG began to set up police commissariats under its direct control. Their personnel was recruited on the recommendation of trusted communist cadres. As a result, approximately 90 per cent of policemen were SED members in December 1946. Recurrent purges served to guarantee political reliability and proletarian composition.[39] Military units and secret services, while deemed indispensable for any communist regime, were taboo until mid-1947.[40] All security-related competence rested directly with the occupation power which, within the East German police, created special K 5 groups to perform auxiliary functions for the Soviet *organy*.[41]

Changes Resulting from Open Outbreak of East-West Confrontation

The announcement of the Marshall Plan on 9 June 1947 aroused open hostility in Moscow: The Kremlin understood that its previous hope for U.S. withdrawal from Europe, and hence for control of all Germany, was frustrated. It responded by greatly accelerating transformation of the SED into a "party of the new [i.e. Soviet] type".[42] The leeway that had been conceded to the "bourgeois parties", was also substantially narrowed.[43] As Tiulpanov saw it, the "reactionary circles" at the helm of either party had to be replaced by "progressive forces". In late fall, CDU refusal to participate in the Soviet-initiated SED-controlled "German People's Congress" provided a justification for long-decided intervention.[44] To a lesser extent, the LDP was deemed a political obstacle which had to be overcome.[45] Tiulpanov first sought to satellize the CDU: He had Chairman Jakob Kaiser deposed and replaced by a man of his choosing; he then initiated a fundamental change of policy top down and extensive purges in the party organization. But there was stubborn resistance, particularly at the grass roots. So it took much more than a year until he dared to have a party congress which, after all, was the only body legitimized to elect leaders. But even then, extreme effort was required to avoid a fiasco, and it was only much later that the CDU was fully subjugated.[46] To be sure, the LDP did not pose major problems to the occupation power's policy: In particular, it was willing to collaborate in the "German People's Congress". This, however, did not save it from the CDU's fate. The SMAG subdued the Liberals in the same fashion, if with somewhat less difficulty.[47]

Even though powerless and subservient at last, the CDU and LDP continued to appear potentially dangerous: Their support among the population was a thorn in Soviet eyes. On instructions from Moscow, Tiulpanov started to create pseudo-bourgeois parties to be directly controlled by communists in order to undercut both the Christian Democrats' and the Liberals' social basis. New cadres were sent from the USSR to lead the National-Democratic Party (NDPD) and the German Peasants Party (DBP) which were founded in the first half of 1949 to rally behind them nationally-minded people, former Nazis and previous Wehrmacht professionals, or, in the case of the DBP, the rural population. While the NDPD was rather successful in fulfilling its mission, the DBP failed to have much resonance.[48]

In Stalin's view, a communist party which had its organization all over the country was crucial for the achievement of German unity.[49] This requirement was missed when the Soviet side failed to extend the merger of KPD and SPD to the Western zones. Nor did its sustained effort produce result of making the British and U.S. occupation authorities license the SED besides a continuing social democratic party.[50] After the open breach with the West, there was no more hope that they might eventually do so. To build political influence in West Germany, Moscow instructed the SED to organize an allegedly non-party "German People's Congress" which tried to establish a network of regional and local committees all over the country.[51] When the attempt proved unpromising, Stalin told the SED leaders that, thus far, the struggle for Germany had been waged "too openly" and therefore needed to be "masked": The SED would have to cut its formal links with the KPD while simultaneously reinforcing its assistance.[52] Therefore, the West German communists were deprived of their regular presence in SED party bodies, except for participation in special sessions upon invitation.[53] But they continued to receive their instructions from the SED and the SMAG.[54] Stalin had also given the instruction that the East German party had to concentrate its work in the Western zones in one office and to nominate a special party secretary for the task.[55] On 2 February 1949, an SED West Commission was set up which, in the following months, received additional powers.[56]

Moscow, however, was not satisfied yet. To add efficiency to political work in West Germany, assertion of full control over the indigenous communist party appeared essential. The organization and performance of the KPD were seen to have many shortcomings; unconditional orientation on the USSR's model and policy had to be guaranteed as a pledge of future success. Only thorough guidance from East Berlin would eliminate current "ideological aberrations" and thus turn the political tide in West Germany.[57] In May 1949, Tiulpanov subjected two members of the KPD secretariat, Kurt Müller and Walter Fisch, to an embarrassing hearing. He accused them of manifold failure to pursue correct Marxist-Leninist policies, rejected their effort to excuse, or minimize, their mistakes, made them confess their alleged guilt, and lectured them on the decisions they would have to take in matters of policy, organization, and personnel. He concluded by ordering the KPD to accept unconditional control by the SMAG and the SED. The latter was obliged to render "powerful assistance" to the comrades in the West.[58] Similar conversations with other top KPD cadres including Chariman Max Reimann followed. The result was unlimited subjugation of the West German party: From then on, not only policy, but also the details of implementation and organization were determined by the SED which, in turn, depended on Soviet instructions.[59]

The Kremlin also reorganized the all-German effort by the non-communist parties and groups in the Soviet zone. As a general outline for this, an instruction was handed to the SED leaders in May 1949.[60] On this basis, the East German party apparat worked out a plan for a "National Front" which was to unite all "antifascist-democratic forces" in a common struggle for "national unity".[61] The resulting draft met with harsh criticism and underwent fundamental change by the Soviet side.[62] In the end, the East German parties and organizations built a political front designed to create regional and local branches in the Western zones.

Administrative Transformation and the Problem of Domestic Security
When, in the wake of the early Cold War, "intensified struggle" against internal and external "class enemies" was proclaimed, this entailed far-reaching consequences in the Soviet zone. Even before that, the USSR had seen a need to "promote restructuring of Germany" along its lines.[63] This became more outspoken from fall 1947 onward. Early in 1948, "people's justice" was proclaimed: Jurisdiction was obliged to obey political imperatives and executive authority. The SMAG ordered both courts and police to devote particular energy to fighting "political crime". Sentences in political cases were subjected to systematic monitoring; whenever they were deemed too mild, they had to be rendered more severe. Precise details were given on what form of punishment was obligatory for various categories of politically deviating behavior.[64] Another instrument to assert full political control over society, was a ban on private associations. In fall 1949, the

occupation power ordered their dissolution. From then on, all professional, sports, recreational, and similar non-political collective activity was permitted exclusively under the aegis of SED-controlled "societal organizations".[65]

In 1948, the SMAG issued strict rules of general administrative practice, with regard notably to organizational structure, confidentiality, personnel ranking, disciplinary measures, and statistics preparation. Continuous supervision was introduced to make sure that the orders were correctly followed. Soviet procedures and habits were made mandatory for administration.[66] The police continued under strict Soviet control but received better organization and equipment.[67] A Soviet directive of July 1948 introduced an equivalent to the early Red Army's commissars creating a network of political officers in all police and armed organizations.[68] Implementation was put into the hands of Erich Mielke who, under Ulbricht's guidance, maintained party liaison with the occupation power in all matters of security.[69]

The Soviet leaders also felt that the SED regime would need capabilities to cope on its own with upcoming challenges. As a first step toward creating a secret police (the *Stasi* as it was called later), the SMAG issued an order on 16 August 1947 which commissioned denazification and related tasks to the K 5 Department.[70] This organization, which, headed by Mielke, was directly subordinated to Soviet State Security, was to "fight against the enemies of the new democratic order and against their criminal activities", to put an end to anti-communist abuse, and to prevent any attempt at undermining Soviet measures. It was authorized to deal with problems of domestic security and to issue orders to the judiciary. In close co-ordination with the occupation authorities,[71] it had to "penetrate and investigate" public administration. Soviet advisors rendered "assistance" introducing *organy* practices such as covert observation and exhaustive interrogation. The staff was recruited from the "working class".[72] In 1948, the K 5 was authorized to arrest people on its own, if under Soviet supervision.[73] When, as another branch of the *organy,* "Committees for the Protection of National Property" (CPNP) were founded as a parallel organization, the problem of coordination was discussed with Stalin. As a result, the K 5 was merged with the CPNP in spring 1949 when a large number of security experts from Moscow began to train the personnel as the nucleus of a future East German state security apparat which, after having been formally constituted in January 1950, continued to be fully controlled by omnipresent Soviet *Chekists.*[74]

Facing an "intensifying struggle" for Germany, the Kremlin saw a need to equip the SED regime also with a military instrument. In early fall 1947, Ulbricht mentioned internally that the SMAG had begun to prepare creation of a "centralized powerful police unit".[75] Both he and two or three experts had been invited to participate in discussion of military detail.[76] In mid-1948, the occupation power formed border police units under its direct control and deployed them in barracks along the zonal demarcation line to support Soviet forces.[77] On 2 July 1948, Stalin issued an order that "barracked" units be put up and given both *Wehrmacht* weapons and "regular military training". Among German prisoners of war in the USSR, 5000 professionals, 100 officers and 10 generals were recruited as training personnel.[78] They were experts in tank, anti-tank, and artillery warfare, and also radio operators, sappers, sailors, and pilots.[79] The units were formed under the occupation forces' direct control. Soviet advisors were present everywhere and controlled both military activity and the soldiers' everyday life.[80] The occupation authorities frequently intervened by issuing instructions. Trouble was caused by an unexpected order which excluded a number of categories from service (notably all men who happened to have relatives in the Western zones).[81]

The following steps of the military buildup can equally be traced back to Soviet initiative, often to orders by Stalin himself: creation of "People's Police Schools" for cadet-like military training,[82] subsequent enlargement of their capacity as well as training of top cadres in the USSR,[83] restructuring of units and numerical increases,[84] foundation of a small navy,[85] preparation of air force cadres,[86] and a second reorganization of the ground troops.[87] All Soviet instructions thus far known show a keen interest in both regulating military service in every detail and strictly controlling implementation of orders and every-day troop activity. To ensure this, the ubiquitous Soviet advisors had to provide all-encompassing military guidance and to report everything they saw and heard. They were hierarchically organized to guarantee co-ordinated performance.[88] The Soviet army was in charge of all military matters including allocation of equipment, while the East German authorities provided administration, barracks, food, and finance.[89]

Creation of a Separate East German State

At the end of World War II, Stalin had hoped that Germany would emerge united under communist rule.[90] After the open breach with the Western powers, he had vainly tried to make them return to the *status quo ante* which had allowed for both unilateralist policy-making in the Eastern zone and vetoing undesirable economic policies outside Soviet-occupied territory. As early as in winter 1947-48, the Kremlin began to feel that, for the time being, its authority might only suffice to create an East German state.[91] When the Berlin Blockade of 1948-49 had failed to overcome this limit, Stalin decided to promote this project. He had a constitution and other founding documents worked out by a "German People's Council" (as a supposedly all-German non-partisan representative body) on the basis of detailed instructions to lay the foundations for a "German Democratic Republic" (GDR).[92] In the early fall of 1949, the SED leadership asked Stalin for permission to transform the "German People's Council" into a parliament which would then ratify the constitution, form a government, appoint leading personnel, approve of the government's declaration, vote postponement of elections, and introduce a five-year economic plan. Given the fact that a few West Germans had also been included in the Council, the state thus constituted was to claim all-German legitimacy.[93]

The Kremlin agreed but added modifications. On the basis of proposals worked out by both the SMAG and the SED party apparat and reviewed and corrected in Moscow, the final procedure was set. On the basis of Stalin's previous approval, the "German People's Council" declared itself the "Provisional People's Chamber", proclaimed the GDR and voted a number of laws and appointments. In this fashion, the Chairman of the Council of Ministers, the latter's members, and the State President were elected. Also, choice of leading personnel in the ministries required Soviet consent as did the government's rules of procedure which had to undergo fundamental revision before they were eventually accepted in Moscow.[94]

The SED leaders had cherished the hope that proclamation of the GDR would result in substantially easing the occupation regime. In September 1949, a draft had been submitted to Moscow which envisaged transfer of both administrative and decision-making powers to the emergent state's government and limitation of Soviet responsibilities to "general supervision". In an effort to demonstrate their trustworthiness, the East Berlin leaders expressly confessed German "guilt" and "responsibility" "for the aggressive policy of war" and promised "expiation". In practical terms, this amounted to an obligation to satisfy any of Moscow's reparation demands. The East Berlin regime also clearly committed itself to continuation of Sovietization policies and to full support of the USSR's all-German ambition by declaring willingness to pursue the "struggle against fascism and militarism" and determination to comply fully with the "Potsdam decisions".[95] SED Chairman

Pieck expressed confidence that the SMAG would "change its function in Germany fundamentally", "abandon administrative work" and limit its activities to supervising socio-political transformation. As a result, the emergent state would enjoy full freedom of action; "German sovereignty" would be guaranteed.[96]

The Kremlin, however, made its highest representative in Germany, General Chuikov, declare that the Soviet government took note of the fact that the leadership of the German state (i.e. the GDR) accepted the Potsdam decisions and was willing to fulfil the obligations resulting from the four power agreements. Therefore the administrative functions thus far exercised by the SMAG would be handed over.[97] The term "administration" (*upravlenie*) indicated transfer of executive functions under a higher authority's instructions; reference to powers of decision-making was conspicuously absent. This limited concession was made conditional on the GDR's compliance with a number of demands the fulfilment of which would be continuously monitored by special offices established in East Berlin and other major cities. They were accorded the right both to exact any information from the [East] German administration and to initiate all kinds of enquiries and checks. Regular reports on results would be sent to Moscow. Whenever the GDR would be found wanting in any respect, corrective intervention was envisioned. Additionally, the USSR reserved a number of responsibilities to itself: exclusive contact with the three Western powers, examination of international treaties, supervision of foreign trade, and decision-making on import and export of "strategically important raw materials". Unless exceptions were expressly authorized in the future, SMAG orders and directives would have to be maintained.[98]

Conclusions

Despite obvious disappointment, the East Berlin leaders articulated neither frustration nor discontent: They knew that all their power depended on their Soviet "friends". They saw no alternative to increasing their effort to seek the Kremlin's favor.[99] At the same time, their aspirations basically coincided with Moscow's purpose. For Stalin, the KPD/SED connection was equally beneficial. The East German communists provided his policies with an invaluable appearance of reflecting the occupied country's indigenous will. The services of their party, its organizational network (which, more often than not, claimed to represent suprapartisan opinion), and the "antifascist-democratic" allies (which presumably expressed non-communist interest) provided the Kremlin with exceptional options at the intra-German level. They were also used to justify both the occupation power's measures of socio-political transformation in the Soviet zone and the USSR's national appeals to the Germans outside its power sphere. To allow this effort to succeed, the scope of the Kremlin's impact on East German decision-making had to be kept from the public. Political steps which were actually initiated by the Moscow leadership were to be perceived as autonomous German action. The occupation authorities did not even want high-ranking KPD/SED cadres to learn the true origin of the policies that they had to advocate.[100]

Notes

[1] *Documents on Germany 1944-1985*, Department of State Publication 9446, Washington: Government Printing Office 1985, pp. 33-38.

[2] N. Lebedeva/M. Narinskii, "Rospusk Kominterna v 1943 godu," in: *Mezhdunarodnaia zhizn'*, 5/1994, pp. 80-88; M. Narinskii, "The Soviet Union and the Berlin Crisis, 1948-49," in: Francesca Gori/Silvio Pons (eds.), *The Soviet Union and Europe in the Cold War, 1943-53*, London: Macmillan 1996, p. 58.

[3] G. Keiderling (ed.), *"Gruppe Ulbricht" in Berlin April bis Juni 1945. Von den Vorbereitungen im Sommer 1944 bis zur Wiedergründung der KPD im Juni 1945. Dokumentation*, Berlin: Berlin Verlag 1993; P. Erler/H. Laude/M. Wilke (eds.), *"Nach Hitler kommen wir". Dokumente zur Programmatik der KPD-Führung 1944/45 für Nachkriegsdeutschland*, Berlin: Akademie Verlag 1994; R.C. Raack, "Stalin Plans his Post-War Germany," in: *Journal of Contemporary History*, 28 (1993), pp. 55-56, 64-65, 69-70.

[4] G. Keiderling, op. cit., pp. 256-259, 273-274, 277-280, 283-286, 296-297, 318-321, 323, 369, 383-389, 402-403, 416-417, 432-442, 475-476, 506-508; P. Erler, "'Moskau-Kader' der KPD in der SBZ," in: M. Wilke (ed.), *Die Anatomie der Parteizentrale*, Berlin: Akademie Verlag 1998, pp. 229-291; M. Kubina, "Der Aufbau des zentralen Parteiapparats der KPD 1945-1946," ibid., pp. 49-117.

[5] Cf. G. Wettig, "Der Konflikt der Ost-CDU mit der Besatzungsmacht 1945-1948 im Spiegel sowjetischer Akten," in: *Historisch-Politische Mitteilungen*, vol. 6 (1999), pp. 109-130.

[6] This is clearly reflected in the Politburo patterns: Iu. N. Zhukov, "Bor'ba za vlast' v rukovodstve SSSR v 1945-1952 godakh," in: *Voprosy istorii*, 1/1995, pp. 23-29. The same technique was used by Hitler: W.-U. Friedrich, "Formen des Totalitarismus," in: E. Jesse/S. Kailitz (ed.), *Prägekräfte des 20. Jahrhunderts*, Munich: Bayerische Landeszentrale 1997, p. 254.

[7] S. Bjornstad, "Soviet German policy and the Stalin note of 10 March 1952," Hovedopp-gave, University of Oslo, Department of History, Fall 1996, p. 8.

[8] J. Foitzik, "Die Sowjetische Militaeradministration in Deutschland [introduction]," in: Jan Foitzik (ed.), *Inventar der Befehle des Obersten Chefs der SMAD 1945-1949*, publ. by Institut fuer Zeitgeschichte, Munich: Oldenbourg 1995; S. Creuzberger, *Die sowjetische Besatzungsmacht und das politische System der SBZ*, Weimar: Boehlau 1996, pp. 29-43; A. Haritonow, *Sowjetische Hochschulpolitik in Sachsen 1945-1949*, Cologne: Boehlau 1995, pp. 20-24; M.I. Semiriaga, *Kak my upravliali Germaniei*, Moscow: Rosspen 1995, pp. 34-38; K. Arlt, "Das Wirken der Sowjetischen Militaeradministration in Deutsch-land," in: B. Thoss (ed.), *Volksarmee schaffen – ohne Geschrei! Studien zu den Anfängen einer "verdeckten Aufrüstung" in der SBZ/DDR 1947-1952*, Munich: Oldenbourg 1994, pp. 99-108.

[9] Cf. R.C. Raack, op. cit., p. 64.

[10] See for example G. Wagenlehner's statement in an expert discussion, quoted in: G. Wettig (ed.), *Die sowjetische Deutschland-Politik in der Ära Adenauer, 16. Rhöndorfer Gespräch*, Bonn 1997, p. 78.

[11] In similar vein S. Bjornstad, op.cit., p. 8.

[12] Cf. S. Creuzberger, op.cit., p. 60.

[13] See, *inter alia*, G. Koenen, *Utopie der Säuberung*, Berlin: Alexander Fest 1998.

[14] The KPD/SED was under constant Soviet surveillance including that of the secret services. Cf. P. Erler, "Zur Sicherheitspolitik der KPD/SED 1945-1949," in: S. Suckut/W. Suess, *Staatspartei und Staatssicherheit*, Berlin: Ch. Links 1997, p. 78; Pieck's notes, in: R. Badstübner/W. Loth (eds.), *Wilhelm Pieck – Aufzeichnungen zur Deutschlandpolitik 1945-1953*, Berlin: Akademie Verlag 1994, pp. 137-143, 147-151, 161-189.

[15] Cf. H. Weber, "Zum Transformationsprozess des Parteiensystems," in: H. Weber (ed.), *Parteiensystem zwischen Demokratie und Volksdemokratie. Dokumente und Materialien*, Cologne: Wissenschaft und Politik 1982, pp. 38-40.

[16] P. Erler, "Zur Sicherheitspolitik," op. cit., p. 80; M. Kubina, "In einer solchen Form, die nicht erkennen lässt, worum es sich handelt...", in: *Internationale Wissenschaftliche Korrespondenz*, 3/1996, p. 344.

[17] Pieck's notes on Stalin's conversation with KPD leaders on 4 June 1945, in: R. Badstübner/W. Loth, op.cit., p. 51; "Zur programmatischen Arbeit der Moskauer KPD-Führung 1941-1945," in: P. Erler/H. Laude/M. Wilke, op. cit., pp. 120-123.

[18] Pieck's notes on a meeting with Marshal Bokov on 23 Jan. 1946, in: R. Badstübner/W. Loth, op.cit., pp. 63-65; information by Serov, 7 Aug. 1946, ibid., pp. 77-79; information by Russkikh on CPSU procedures, 3 Nov. 1948, ibid., p. 242; information by Suslov, 28 Jan. 1949, ibid., p. 274.

[19] See e.g. preparation of the SED leaders' visit to Moscow on 16-18 Sept. 1949 and their internal statements there: R. Badstübner/W. Loth, op. cit., pp. 293-309/*Aus Politik und Zeitgeschichte. Beilage zur Wochenzeitung "Das Parlament"*, B 5/91, 25 Jan. 1991, pp. 12-14.

[20] Pieck's notes on preparations for the 2nd SED Party Congress in spring 1947, in: R. Badstübner/W. Loth, op.cit., pp. 131-134, 137-143, 147; Tiul'panov to Suslov (excerpt), 27 Sept. 1947, in: B. Bonvech/G. Bordiugov/N. Neimark, SVAG. Upravlenie propagandy (informatsii) i S.I. Tiul'panov. 1945-1949, Moscow: „Rossia molodaia", pp. 87-95.

[21] Cf. N. Naimark, "Die SMAD und die Frage des Stalinismus," in: *Zeitschrift für Geschichtswissenschaft*, 4/1995, p. 306.

[22] Report by Major Nazarov included in the protocol of the 19 Sept. 1946 session of the CPSU Central Committee commission set up to investigate SMAG Administration for Propaganda (excerpt), in: B. Bonvech/G. Bordiugov/N. Neimark, op.cit., p. 182.

[23] A. Malycha, "Die Illusion der Einheit – Kommunisten und Sozialdemokraten in den Landesvorständen der SED 1946-1951," in: M. Lemke (ed.), *Sowjetisierung und Eigenständigkeit in der SBZ/DDR (1945-1953)*, Cologne: Boehlau 1999, pp. 81-103; N. Naimark, *The Russians in Germany*, Cambridge: Harvard University Press 1995, pp. 69-140; K.-D. Müller, " 'Wir dachten, der Krieg ist vorbei...'," in: *Deutschland Archiv*, 3/1997, pp. 412-416; Alexei Filitov, "The Soviet Administrators and Their German 'Friends'," in: N. Naimark/L. Gibianski (eds.), *The Establishment of Communist Regimes in Eastern Europe, 1944-1949*, Boulder/CO: Westview 1997, p. 116.

[24] S. Creuzberger, op.cit., pp. 106-110.

[25] Ibid., pp. 113-116; P. Erler, "Zur Sicherheitspolitik," op.cit., p. 78.

[26] Even when the SED sought membership in late 1948 (R. Badstübner/W. Loth, op. cit., p. 253), Stalin rejected this as "premature" (S. Suckut, "Zur Vorgeschichte der DDR-Gründung," in: *Die Deutschlandfrage von Jalta und Potsdam bis zur staatlichen Teilung Deutschlands 1949*, Berlin: Duncker & Humblot 1993, p. 123).

[27] J. Laufer, "Auf dem Wege zur staatlichen Verselbständigung der SBZ," in: J. Kocka (ed.), *Historische DDR-Forschung*, Berlin: Akademie Verlag 1993, pp. 27-55.

[28] See in more detail M. Lemke, "Die deutschlandpolitischen Handlungsspielräume der SED 1949-1955," in: Gustav Schmidt (ed.), *Ost-West-Beziehungen. Konfrontation und Détente 1945-1989*, Bochum: Brockmeyer 1993, p. 308.

[29] "Zapis' besedy I.V. Stalina s rukovoditeliami SEPG," in: *Istoricheskii arkhiv*, 4/1994, pp. 38-39.

[30] P. Erler/H. Laude/M. Wilke, op. cit., p. 394.

[31] G. Kynin/J. Laufer, "Vvedenie," in: *SSSR i germanskii vopros, 1941-1949. Dokumenty iz Arkhiva vneshnei politiki Rossiiskoi Federatsii*, vol. 2 (1945/46), Moscow: "Mezhdunarodnye otnosheniia" 1999, pp. 35-43; J. Laufer, "Von den Demontagen zur Währungsreform," in: M. Lemke, *Sowjetisierung*, op. cit., pp. 174-176; J. Laufer, "Die UdSSR und die Einleitung der Bodenreform in der SBZ," in: A. Bauernkaemper (ed.), *"Junkerland in Bauernhand"?*, Stuttgart: F. Steiner 1996, pp. 22-30. – The anti-nazi argument was mere pretence. As was criticized by CDU politicians and other non-communists in the Soviet zone, even families whose members had taken part in the 20 July 1944 conspiracy against Hitler lost their landed property (S. Tiul'panov, "Trekhletnii opyt raboty Upravleniia informatsii SVAG (oktiabr' 1945 - oktiabr' 1949gg.)," document from the RTsKhDNI [former CPSU Party Archive for the period until 1952], pp. 65-66; V.S. Semenov/I.F. Filippov, "Spravka o bloke demokraticheskikh partii Germanii, 21 Dec. 1945," in: *SSSR i germanskii vopros*, op. cit., pp. 316-320.

[32] M.I. Semiriaga, *Kak*, op.cit., p. 53.

[33] Except for the SPD, the fate of which must be seen against the special background of its enforced unification with the KPD, Soviet repression has been best documented in the case of the CDU. Cf. B. Kaff (ed.), *"Gefährliche politische Gegner"*, Düsseldorf: Droste 1995; G. Buchstab (ed.), *Verfolgt und entrechtet*, Düsseldorf: Droste 1998; G. Wettig, *Der Konflikt*, op. cit., pp. 109-137.

[34] S. Creuzberger, op.cit., pp. 44-98, 111-176.

[35] See notably "Aktionsprogramm des Blocks der kämpferischen Demokratie" [final version], 21 Oct. 1944, in: P. Erler/H.Laude/M. Wilke, op.cit., p. 266; W. Pieck's explanations to course participants at the KPD party school in Moscow, 31 Oct. 1944, ibid., pp. 272-280.

[36] Tiul'panov's report included in the protocol of the session of the CC commission to inquire about the SMAG Propaganda Administration (excerpt), 16 Sept. 1946, in B. Bonvech/G. Bordiugov/N. Neimark, op.cit., p. 158; report by Tiul'panov (excerpt), 25 Feb. 1946, ibid., pp. 41-43; SMAG Propaganda Department to L. Baranov, 14 March 1946, ibid., pp. 43-46; Pieck's notes on a meeting with Marshal Bokov and S. Tiul'pnov, 22 Dec. 1945, in: R. Badstübner/W. Loth, op.cit., p. 62; Pieck's notes on a meeting with

Marshal Bokov, 21 Jan. 1946, ibid., pp. 63-64; Pieck's notes on a conversation with Stalin on 6 Feb. 1946, ibid., p. 68.

[37] W. Leonhard, *Die Revolution entlässt ihre Kinder*, Cologne-[West-]Berlin: Kiepenheuer & Witsch 1955, p. 356; G. Keiderling, op. cit., pp. 130, 262, 312-317, 327, 329-331, 343-344, 348-355, 357-358, 362, 417-419; P. Erler/H. Laude/M. Wilke, op. cit., pp. 266, 303; V.I. Lenin, *Polnoe sobranie sochinenii* (5th ed.), vol. 33, Moscow: Gos. izdat. pol. lit. 1962, pp. 1-120; Tiul'panov's report to the CC Commission set up to inquire about the SMAG Propaganda Department's activities (excerpt), 16 Sept. 1946, in: B. Bonvech/G. Bordiugov/N. Neimark, op.cit., p. 157; preparatory paper sent to Moscow by the SED leaders prior to their conversation with Stalin on 18 Dec. 1948, in: R. Badstübner/W. Loth, op.cit., p. 249; Pieck's notes, ibid.., pp. 63-65, 68, 82, 85-93, 148, 149-158, 248, 249-251, 260, 263-265, 265-274.

[38] Stalin's remarks in his conversation with the SED leaders on 31 Jan. 1947, in: Zapis', op. cit. , p. 36; GAI (DVdI) memorandum on SMAG Order no. 0212 of 30 July 1946 [with the Russian original enclosed], 9 Jan. 1948, BAAP [Central Government Archive of the former GDR], MdI 7/1, pp. 16-18; Third European Department of the Soviet Foreign Ministry to Smirnov/Semenov, 5 Jan. 1947, AVPRF [Russian Foreign Ministry Archive], 0457a, 5, 32, 25, .p. 4; Morenov to Gribanov, 10 Jan. 1947, AVPRF, ibid., pp. 25-28; Obzor Kynina, AVPRF, AOB, 11zh, 71, 20, p. 597; Serov, Vremennoe polozhenie o nemetskom upravlenii Vnutrennich del v Sovetskoi zone okkupatsii Germanii, 13 Jan. 1947, AVPRF, 0457a, 4, 19, 48, pp. 40-47; directive concerning the DVdI, confirmed by Ltn. Gen. Kurochkin, undated [May 1947], BAAP, MdI 7/1, pp. 19-28; Smirnov to Molotov, 19 June 1947, AVPRF, 06, 9, 43, 632, p. 15; directive concerning the DVdI [German and Russian version], undated [July 1947], BAAP, MdI 7/1, pp. 29-33; Ltn. Gen. Dratvin, Polozhenie. O nemetskom Upravlenii Vnutrennikh Del v Sovetskoi zone Germanii, undated [July 1947], AVPRF, 0457a, 4, 19, 48, pp. 48-56; J. Foitzik, "Einleitung," in: *Inventar*, op.cit., p. 46.

[39] Serov to Kruglov, 26 June 1946, GARF [Russian State Archive], 9401, 2, 138, pp. 49-58; T. Lindenberger, "Die Deutsche Volkspolizei (1945-1990)," in: T. Diedrich/H. Ehlert/R. Wenzke (eds.), *Im Dienste der Partei*, Berlin: Ch. Links 1998, pp. 97-98; P. Erler, "Zur Sicherheitspolitik," op.cit., pp. 82-83; Maj. Gen. Mal'kov to Gribanov, 19 Aug. 1947, AVPRF, 0457a, 4, 19, 48, pp. 24-35.

[40] Stalin's statement to the SED leaders on 31 Jan. 1947, in: Zapis', op. cit., p. 40.

[41] Maj. Gen. Mal'kov to Gribanov, 19 Aug. 1947, AVPRF, 0457a, 4, 19, 48, pp. 24-35; N. Naimark, *The Russians*, op. cit., pp. 360-361; S. Creuzberger, *Die sowjetische Besatzungsmacht*, op. cit., pp. 31-32; M. Kubina, "Die Schaffung von strukturellen Voraussetzungen," in: G. Wettig, *Die sowjetische Deutschland-Politik*, op. cit, p. 45.

[42] Pieck notes in: R. Badstübner/W. Loth, op. cit., pp. 1130, 131-134, 137-143, 147-149, 149-151, 161-172, 173-174; Tiul'panov to Semenov, 1 Aug. 1947, AVPRF, 0457a, 6, 32, 225, pp. 49-57; M.I. Semiriaga, *Kak*, op. cit., p. 59.

[43] Internal CDU paper by R. Tilmanns, 1 July 1947, in: S. Suckut, "Blockpolitik," op. cit., pp. 210-212; "Grundsatzerklärung der SED zur Blockpolitik," ibid., pp. 228-230; protocol of the 30th session of the party bloc, 31 Oct. 1947, ibid., p. 243.

[44] Baranov to Suslov, 25 Oct. 1947, RTsKhIDNI, 17, 128, 1097, p. 1; Tiul'panov's report to the CC of the All-Russian CP (M. Suslov), 15 Nov. 1947, RTsKhIDNI, 17, 128, 329, pp. 207-217; Tiul'panov to Shikin (excerpt), 9 Dec. 1947, in: B. Bonvech/G. Bordiugov/N. Neimark, op.cit., pp. 98-100.

[45] Documents ibid., pp. 51-53, 61-63, 85-87, 165-167.

[46] Ibid., p. 99; Smirnov to Semenov, 26 Jan. 1948, AVPRF, 0457a, 5, 28, 8, pp. 26-33; Tiul'panov to the Third European Department of the Foreign Ministry, 19 March 1948, AVPRF, ibid., p. 61; Polozhenie v ChDS, 19.3.1948, AVPRF, ibid., pp. 63-70; Tiul'panov's report on the situation of the CDU in the Soviet Zone and in Berlin, 3 May 1948, RTsKhIDNI, 17, 128, 568, pp. 74-93; Tiul'panov to Semenov, 28 Feb. 1949, AVPRF, 0457a, 7, 39, 11, pp. 11-42; Ltn. Gen. Guliaev to Semenov, 4 Dec. 1948, AVPRF, 0457a, 5, 28, 8, pp. 297-299; Col. Radionov to V. Semenov, 6 Jan. 1949, AVPRF, 0457a, 7, 39, 11, pp. 1-6.

[47] SMAG Information Administration to Baranov [excerpt], 16 April 1948, in: B. Bonvech/G. Bordiugov/N. Neimark, op.cit., p. 102; information paper of the SMAG Information Administration [excerpt], undated [16 April 1948], ibid., pp. 103-105; Sobolev/Poliakov/Fedoseev/Nemchinov/Konstantinovich to Zhdanov, undated [after April 1948], ibid., p. 212; M. Kaiser, "Sowjetischer Einfluss auf die ostdeutsche Politik und Verwaltung 1945-1970," in: K. Jarausch/H. Siegrist, op.cit., p. 116 [for the end of 1945]; Tiul'panov's report on the LDP to the CC of the All-Russian CP (Baranov), 19 April 1948, RTsKhIDNI, 17, 128, 569, pp. 3-9; M. Gribanov to A. Smirnov, 14 Feb. 1948, AVPRF, 0457a, 5, 28, 8, p. 36; Tiul'panov to Semenov, 2 Nov. 1948, AVPRF, ibid., pp. 214-231. According to a note by Pieck, Stalin told the SED leaders on 18 Dec. 1948 the LDP had to be "disrupted" (R. Badstübner/W. Loth, op.cit., p. 261).

[48] Tiul'panov to Baranov, 7 May 1948, RTsKhIDNI, 17, 128, 568, pp. 103-105; Tiul'panov to Semenov, 7 May 1948, AVPRF, 0457a, 5, 28, 8, pp. 99-102; Burzhuaznye partii sovetskoi zony okkupacii Germanii (po materialam PV GSOV v Germanii), 14 May 1948, RTsKhIDNI, 17, 128, 568, pp. 136-138; Tiul'panov to Semenov, 25 May 1948, AVPRF, 0457a, 5, 28, 8, p. 113; Tiul'panov to Baranov, 28 May 1948, RTsKhIDNI, 17, 128, 568, pp. 136-138; Tiul'panov to Baranov, undated [end of May 1948], ibid., pp. 140-145; Mamontov to Semenov, 6 Sept 1948, AVPRF, 0457a, 5, 28, 8, p. 183; Tiul'panov to

Semenov, Sept. 16, 1948, ibid., pp. 185-189; Tiul'panov to Semenov, 29 Sept. 1948, ibid., pp. 190-195; Tiul'panov to Semionov, 9 Feb. 1949, AVPRF, 0457a, 7, 38, 7, pp. 71-80; S. Tiul'panov to V. Semionov, 13 April 1949, AVPRF, 0457a, 7, 39, 13, pp. 53-61; documents in B. Bonvech/G. Bordjugov/N. Neimark, op.cit., pp. 107, 111, 229.

[49] Pieck's notes on Stalin's meeting with KPD leaders on June 4, 1945, in: R. Badstübner/W. Loth, op.cit., p. 50.

[50] Stalin during his conversation with the SED leaders on 31 Jan. 1947: Zapis´, op.cit., p. 38.

[51] Tiul'panov to Suslov, 9 Dec. 1947, RTsKhIDNI, 17, 128, 331, p. 95; Baranov to Suslov, 30 Jan. 1948, RTsKhIDNI, 17, 128, 1166, p. 68.

[52] Pieck's summary on the conversation with Stalin on 18 Dec. 1948, in: R. Badstübner/W. Loth, op.cit., p. 260; Pieck's report to the SED Central Secretariat, ibid., p. 267.

[53] "Innerparteiliche Massnahmen. Beschlüsse des PV der SED, 24.1.1949, und der I. Parteikonferenz der SED, 25.-28.1.1949," in: *Dokumente der Sozialistischen Einheitspartei*, vol. II, [East-]Berlin: Dietz 1950, p. 217; Patrick Major, "Big brother und little brother: Das Verhältnis SED-KPD 1948-1951," in: Elke Scherstjanoi (ed.), *"Provisorium für längstens ein Jahr"*, Berlin: Akademie Verlag 1993, pp. 156-158.

[54] Gribanov to Smirnov, 25 Jan. 1949, AVPRF, 082, 36, 187, 40, pp. 1-14.

[55] Pieck's notes on the results of Stalin's meeting with the SED leaders on 18 Dec. 1948, in: R. Badstübner/ W. Loth, op.cit., p. 260; W. Pieck's report to the SED Central Secretariat, ibid., p. 266.

[56] Rau to Ackermann (attention of Ulbricht), 6 Jan. 1949, SAPMO, DY 30/IV 2/1/73, p. 47; draft [worked out by the SED] for a resolution passed at the KPD party conference in Solingen on 5/6 March 1949, with two enclosures (letters by Dahlem to Ulbricht), 23 Feb. 1949, SAPMO, ibid., pp. 1-26; D. Staritz, "Die SED, Stalin und die Gruendung der DDR," in: *Aus Politik und Zeitgeschichte. Beilage zur Wochenzeitung "Das Parlament"*, B 5/1991, p. 4; P. Major, op.cit., p. 157.

[57] Ibid., p. 160; Tiul'panov to Semenov, 28 March 1948, AVPRF, 0457a, 2,28, 7, p. 43; Tiul'panov to Semenov, 12 May 1949, AVPRF, 0457a, 7, 39, 10, p. 1.

[58] Ibid., pp. 1-10.

[59] Tiul'panov to Semenov, 24 May 1949, AVPRF, ibid., pp. 28-46; Tiul'panov to Semenov, 29 July 1949, AVPRF, ibid., pp. 72-81; report by Maj. Mulin, 27 Oct. 1949, sent by

Col. Guliaev to Grigorian, 28 Oct. 1949, RTsKhIDNI, 17, 137, 93, pp. 38-42; Guliaev to Semenov (with enclosures), 17 Aug. 1949, AVPRF, 0457a, 7, 39, 10, pp. 85-110. Cf. KPD drafts submitted to the Soviet CC apparat: RTsKhIDNI, 17, 137, 93, pp. 43-92.

[60] Pieck's notes of Grotewohl's report at the SED Politburo on 23 May 1949, in: R. Badstübner/W. Loth, op.cit., p. 281; Tiul'panov to Smirnov, 26 July 1949, RTsKhIDNI, 17, 137, 92, pp. 3-10; Chuikov/Semenov to Malenkov/Vyshinskii (with 7 enclosures), 10 Aug. 1949, AVPRF, 082, 36,187, 40, pp. 53-81; Gribanov et al. to Vyshinskii, undated [Aug. 1949], AVPRF, 082, 36, 187, 40, p. 82; report by Ltn. Gen. Russkikh, 1 Nov. 1949, RTsKhIDNI, 17, 137, 92, pp. 40-42.

[61] Tiul'panov to Smirnov, 26 July 1949, RTsKhIDNI, 17, 137, 92, pp. 3-10; Russkikh's report at a session of the SED PV on 4 Oct. 1949, 1 Nov. 1949, RTsKhIDNI, ibid., p. 41.

[62] Chuikov/ Semenov to Malenkov/ Vyshinskii, 10 Aug. 1949, AVPRF, 082, 36, 187, 40, pp. 53-81; Gribanov et al. to Vyshinskii, undated [Aug. 1949], AVPRF, ibid., p. 82; Ltn. Gen. Russkikh's report, 1 Nov. 1949, RTsKhIDNI, 17, 137, 92, pp. 40-42.

[63] Vremennoe polozhenie o nemetskom upravlenii Vnutrennikh del v Sovetskoi zone okkupatsii Germanii, issued by Serov, 13 Jan. 1947, AVPRF, 0457a, 4, 19, 48, pp. 40-47.

[64] Vremennoe polozhenie o kriminal'noi politsii Sovetskoi zony okkupatsii Germanii, signed by Gorokhov, 17 May 1949, BAAP, MdI 7/1, p. 154; Gorokhov to K. Fischer, 24 June 1949, BAAP, 7/45, pp. 262-263; Gorokhov to K. Fischer, 14 July 1949, BAAP, ibid., pp. 240-241.

[65] Col. Dollada to K. Fischer (in Russian), 1 Oct. 1949, BAAP, MdI 7/47, pp. 84-98.

[66] K. Fischer to Lieutenant Colonel Dollada (in Russian), 12 Aug. 1948, BAAP, MdI 7/42, p. 34; K. Fischer to Gorokhov (in Russian), 29 Sept. 1948, BAAP, ibid., p. 61; Gorokhov to K. Fischer (transl. into German), 16 Dec. 1948, BAAP, ibid., pp. 88-90; Col. Dollada to K. Fischer, 11 Oct. 1949, ibid., pp. 100-104; Gorokhov to K. Fischer (transl. into German), 24 June 1949, BAAP, MdI 7/45, p. 262; Gorokhov to K. Fischer (with enclosure), 11 July 1949, BAAP, ibid., pp. 182-197; Gorokhov to K. Fischer (transl. into German), 12 Aug. 1949, BAAP, ibid., p. 271.

[67] Pieck's notes on a conversation with Tiul'panov/Nazarov on 14 May 1948, in: R. Badstübner/W. Loth, op.cit., p. 228; documents in: Günther Glaser (ed.), *"Reorganisation der Polizei" oder getarnte Bewaffnung der SBZ im Kalten Krieg? Dokumente und Materialien zur sicherheitspolitischen Weichenstellung in Ostdeutschland 1948/49*, Frankfurt/Main: [mimeographed on a private basis] 1995, pp. 276-279; Gorokhov to K. Fischer, 16 Dec. 1948 (date of transl. into German), BAAP, MdI 7/42, pp. 88-90; Gorokhov to K. Fischer (transl. from Russian), 11 July 1949, BAAP, MdI 7/45, pp. 182-197; Gorokhov to K. Fischer (translation from Russian), 24 June 1949, BAAP, ibid., p.

262; Gorokhov to K. Fischer (translation from Russian), 14 July 1949, BAAP, ibid., p. 240; Gorokhov to K. Fischer (transl. from Russian), 12 Aug. 1949, BAAP, ibid., p. 271; Col. Dollada to K. Fischer, 11 Oct. 1949, BAAP, MdI 7/42, pp. 100-104.

[68] Two versions of this directive were found in East German files: one passed by the SED Politburo on 19 July 1948 and another one differently phrased in bad German, which is obviously a translation of a Russian text (G. Glaser, Einführung, in: G. Glaser, *"Reorganisation"*, op.cit., p. 35.

[69] H. Schwan, *Erich Mielke. Der Mann, der die Stasi war*, Munich: Droemer Knaur 1997, pp. 82, 86.

[70] Order of SVAG chief no. 201: guidelines on the implementation of Control Council directives no. 24 and 38 on denazification (German transl.),16 Aug. 1947, BAAP, MdI 7/421, pp. 14-18.

[71] D. Gill/U. Schroeter, *Das Ministerium für Staatssicherheit*, Berlin: Rowohlt 1991, p. 76; Notes on a conversation with Mielke, undated [Nov. 1947], BAAP, MdI 7/421, p. 65; notes by Sächsisches Landeskriminalamt, Dezernat 5, on regulations issued by the provincial government with regard to order 201, 24 Nov. 1947, BAAP, MdI, 7/421, pp. 53-55.

[72] N. Naimark, *The Russians*, op.cit., p. 361; A. Haritonow, op.cit., p. 155; J. Laufer, "Die Ursprünge des Überwachungsstaates," op.cit., pp. 161-164. For regular detailed K 5 reports to the SVAG in 1947-1949 see BAAP, MdI 7/436.

[73] Report on a conversation with Mielke, undated [Nov. 1947], BAAP, MdI 7/421, Bl. 65; order by the Saxon K-5 on complementing and modifying the land goverment's decree for the impLementation of SMAG order no. 201, 25 Nov. 1947, BAAP, MdI 7/421, pp. 80-83. Cf. N. Naimark, *The Russians*, op. cit., pp. 361-362; D. Gill/U. Schroeter, op. cit., p. 76; Jochen von Lang (with Claus Sibyll), *Erich Mielke*, Berlin: Rowohlt 1991, pp. 69-70.

[74] SED answers to questions posed by Stalin in preparation of the 18 Dec. 1948 meeting, in: R. Badstübner/W. Loth, op. cit., p. 252; M. Tantzscher, " 'In der Ostzone wird ein neuer Apparat aufgebaut'," in: *Deutschland Archiv*, 1/1998, pp. 50-51; J. Gieseke, "Das Ministerium fuer Staatssicherheit (1950-1990)," in: T. Diedrich/H. Ehlert/R. Wenzke, op. cit., pp. 374-375; Walter Suess, " 'Schild und Schwert'," in: K.-D. Henke/R. Engelmann (eds.), *Aktenlage*, Berlin: Ch. Links 1995, p. 89.

[75] E. W. Gniffke, *Jahre mit Ulbricht*, Cologne: Wissenschaft und Politik 1966, p. 262.

[76] Heinz Hoffmann's reminiscences according to: *Ich schwöre. Eine Bilddokumentation über die Nationale Volksarmee*, [East-]Berlin: Militärverlag der DDR 1969, p. 251.

[77] Maj. Liul'ka to Gribanov, July 15, 1948, AVPRF, 0457a, 5, 33, 27, pp. 162-168; Piccek's notes on a conversation with Tiul'panov/Nazarov, 14 May 1948, in: R. Badstübner/W. Loth, op.cit., p. 228; Col. Dolladas's instruction to the DVdI President on reorganization of the"Ring um Berlin", Sept. 8, 1949, in: G. Glaser, *"Reorganisation"*, op.cit., p. 323.

[78] Ministerstvo inostrannykh del SSSR, Istorichesko-diplomaticheskoe upravlenie: Germanskii vopros vo vzaimootnosheniiakh SSSR, SShA, Anglii i Frantsii v period ot Berlinskoi konferentsii do obrazovaniia dvukh germanskikh gosudarstv (1945-1949 gg.). Obzor podgotovil G.S. Kynin. Redaktor: A.M. Aleksandrov. Chast' III (1963) [henceforth: Obzor Kynina], AVPRF, Arkhivno-operativnaia biblioteka [AOB], 11zh, 71, 20, p. 602. Cf. Piccek's notes on a conversation with Tiul'panov/Nazarov, 14 May 1948, in: R. Badstübner/W. Loth, op.cit., p. 228; R. Wenzke, "Auf dem Wege zur Kaderarmee," in: B. Thoss, op. cit., pp. 214-227.

[79] K. Fischer to Gorokhov, 11 March 1949, BAAP, MdI 7/48, p. 164. According to a high ranking NVA officer's assessment, this indicated long-term personnel planning which, at the very beginning, envisioned maritime and air forces (Maj. Gen. Kaekow's reminiscences on his military service in the Soviet Zone/GDR in 1948 - 1956. Manuskript der Arbeitsgruppe Befragungen/Erinnerungen, Militärgeschichtliches Institut der DDR, Potsdam, Juli 1990, Aufbewahrungsort MGFA Potsdam, p. 2).

[80] See G. Kaekow's testimony, ibid., p. 1.

[81] "Einführung," in: G. Glaser, *"Reorganisation"*, op.cit., p. 60; documentation, ibid., pp. 254-258.

[82] Order by the SMAG Supreme Commander no. 175, 26 April 1949, mentioned in: Order by the SMAG Supreme Commander no. 0036, 8 Aug. 1949, AVPRF, 0458, 264ss, 314, 0036, p. 11; Order by the SMAG Supreme Commander no. 175, 26 April 1949 (excerpt of German transl. and Russian orig.), in: G. Glaser, *"Reorganisation"*, op.cit., pp. 282-284.

[83] Decision by the Soviet Council of Ministers [chaired by Stalin] no. 2625-1044ss, 18 June 1949, AVPRF, 0458, 264ss, 314, 0036, pp. 1-5; conversation between Pieck/Dahlem and Kabanov/Gorokhov, 1 July 1949, in: G. Glaser, *"Reorganisation"*, op.cit., p. 56. Cf. W. Eisert, "Zu den Anfängen der Sicherheits- und Militärpolitik der SED-Führung 1948 bis 1952," in: B. Thoss, op.cit., p. 184.

[84] Order by the SMAG Supreme Commander-in-Chief no. 0035, 8 Aug. 1949, AVPRF, 0458, 264ss, 314, 0036, pp. 6-13; order by Army General Chuikov and Lieutenant General Lukianchenko [unnumbered], 9 Aug. 1949, AVPRF, ibid., pp. 17-19. Cf. R. Wenzke, op.cit., pp. 239-248.

[85] Decision by the USSR Council of Ministers signed by I. Stalin and countersigned by M. Pomaznev, no. 1708-665ss, 25 April 1950, AVPRF, 0458, 264ss, 314, 0036, pp. 24-38.

[86] Decision by the USSR Council of Ministers no. 4594-2025ss, 15 Nov. 1951, as mentioned in a letter by Army Gen. Maladin to Air Force Gen. Shigarev/ Col. Beloskokov made known to the SMAG Supreme Commander, 21 Nov. 1951, AVPRF, 0458, 264ss, 314, 0036, p. 40; Order by the USSR Council of Ministers no. 4594-2055ss to Air Force Gen. Shigarev, 15 Nov. 1951, Army Gen. Shtemenko's notes, 21 Nov. 1951, AVPRF, ibid., p. 42.

[87] R. Wenzke, "Auf dem Wege zur Kaderarmee," in: B. Thoss, op. cit., p. 253.

[88] Orders by the SMAG Supreme Commander nos. 0035 and 0036, 8 Aug. 1949, AVPRF, 0458, 264ss, 318, 0036, pp. 8, 13; regulation by the head of the SMAG Interior Administration on military advisors, 9 Aug. 1949, AVPRF, ibid., p. 22; Order of the SVAG Commander-in-chief, 11 Aug. 1949, ibid., p. 20.

[89] T. Diedrich, "Aufrüstungsvorbereitung und -finanzierung in der SBZ/DDR 1948-1953," in: B. Thoss, op. cit., pp. 278-305.

[90] Pieck's notes on a conversation with Stalin on 4 June 1945, in: R. Badstübner/W. Loth, op. cit., p. 50.

[91] M.M. Narinskii, "Berlinskii krizis 1948-1949gg.," in: *Novaia i noveishaia istoriia*, 3/1995, p. 18; Smirnov to Vyshinskii, 12 Jan. 1948, AVPRF, 06, 21, 16, 219, pp. 1-2; J. Laufer, "Die UdSSR und die Ursprünge der Berliner Blockade," in: *Deutschland Archiv*, 4/1998, pp. 572-573.

[92] Obzor Kynina, AOB, 11zh, 71, 20, pp. 608-610; Molotov to Stalin, 21 Oct. 1948, AVPRF, 06, 10, 36, 488, pp. 73-80; Gribanov to Smirnov, 25 Jan. 1949, AVPRF, 082, 36, 187, 40, pp. 1-12; Gribanov to Vyshinskii, undated [Aug. 1949], AVPRF, ibid., p. 82; G.N. Goroshkova, *Dvizhenie nemetskogo narodnogo kongressa za edinstvo i mirnyi dogovor*, Moscow: Politizdat 1959, pp. 73-80.

[93] Letter by the SED leaders to Stalin, 19 Sept. 1949, in: R. Bastübner/W. Loth, op. cit., pp. 294-297.

[94] Notes by Sergeev, 12 Nov. 1949, AVPRF, 082, 36, 183, 12, pp. 18-24; Il'ichev to Gribanov, 18 Nov. 1949, AVPRF, ibid., pp. 14-17; Gromyko to Stalin, 20 Oct. 1949, AVPRF, 07, 22a, 12, 138, pp. 10-12.

[95] Government declaration draft, 8 Sept. 1949, quoted by S. Suckut, "Zur Vorgeschichte," op. cit., pp. 183-186.

[96] Elaborations on W. Pieck's explanations on the 22nd (36th) meeting of the SED PV, 4 Oct. 1949, quoted by S. Suckut, "Die Entscheidung zur Gründung der DDR," in: *Vierteljahrshefte für Zeitgeschichte*, 1/1991, p. 157.

[97] Declaration by Army Gen. Chuikov, 10 Oct. 1949, in: *Dokumente zur Deutschlandpolitik der Sowjetunion*, vol. I, [East-]Berlin: Rütten & Loening 1957, pp. 236-238.

[98] Declaration by Army Gen. Chuikov, 11 Oct. 1949, in: "Dokumente zur Deutschlandpolitik," op. cit., p. 240; conversation between Chuikov, Il'ichev, Pieck, Grotewohl, and Ulbricht on 11 Nov. 1949, in: R. Badstübner/W. Loth, op. cit., p. 316; M. Lemke, "Die DDR und die deutsche Frage 1949-1955," in: W. Loth (ed.), *Die deutsche Frage in der Nachkriegszeit*, Berlin: Akademie Verlag 1994, p. 142.

[99] Cf. Grotewohl at the 23rd (37th) enlarged meeting of the SED PV, 9 Oct. 1949, quoted ibid., p. 139; Pieck's address, 11 Oct. 1949, in: *Dokumente zur Aussenpolitik der Regierung der DDR*, vol. I, [East-] Berlin: Rütten & Loening 1954, p. 14.

[100] For occasional hints before his party's CC, Pieck was severely criticized by the Soviet side: P. Erler, "Zur Sicherheitspolitik," op. cit., p. 80; A. Haritonow, "Unter Aufsicht. SMAD und SED in Berlin 1946," in: *Deutschland Archiv*, 6/1996, p. 902.

Gary Bruce

The Revolutionary Potential of GDR Society in 1950-1955

This chapter examines the revolutionary potential of GDR society in the 1950s through an analysis of two elements that are crucial to a revolution: leadership and the popular motive behind participation in a revolution. These two elements are investigated at several critical junctures in the 1950s in East Germany, namely the elections of 1950, the Saalfeld disturbances, the "building of socialism" in 1952 and its consequences, including the uprising of 1953, and finally the response of East Germans to the Geneva Conference of 1955. The chapter argues that there existed in the East German population a popular ideology that infused participation in a revolution, but that this ideology was not fully exploited due in part to the lack of leadership. Potential sources of such leadership had either left the GDR or had been driven underground and dispersed.

An essay which discusses revolutionary potential is, like revolution itself, fraught with danger, particularly if it deals with a period when, arguably, a revolution did not take place. The historian who undertakes such investigations must be diligent to avoid slipping into counter-factual history. This essay does not seek to impose a social model of revolutions onto the German Democratic Republic (GDR) of the 1950s and subsequently to determine whether or not GDR society of the time "met" the criteria possibly to undertake a revolution, for two reasons. First, space constraints dictate that the topic must be more narrowly defined. Second, the "model" approach does not adequately capture the complex nature of revolutions, nor their place and time specificity.[1] Rather, this essay seeks to deal with the human element of GDR society in the 1950s and two aspects in particular of this element that are crucial to a revolution. The first of these elements is one that Vladimir Lenin identified in 1915 – leadership. Lenin defines this component of revolution as "the ability of the revolutionary class to take revolutionary mass action, strong enough to break (or dislocate) the old government which never – not even in a period of crisis – 'falls' if it is not toppled over."[2] In other words, no matter the extent of popular unrest or rioting, there must be a seizure of the state in order for a revolution to be successful.[3] The second element is the popular motive behind participation in a revolution, a factor that George Rudé has championed. As Rudé has written: "The immediate – or even long term – causes of popular participation in revolution is one thing; popular ideology that infuses that participation, and without which there can be no popular revolutionary activity at all, is something else."[4]

I

The historian faces a daunting task in attempting to determine general developments in the GDR's population in the early 1950s, let alone identifying a specific feature such as revolutionary potential, for the simple reason that the source base is thin. Modern polling techniques did not exist, and secret police surveillance of the general population was in its infancy. It is indeed important to stress the humble beginnings of East Germany's Ministry for State Security (*Ministerium für Staatssicherheit* – MfS). Initially, the MfS was a small arm of the Soviet security apparatus in Germany, comprising a mere 4,000 workers in 1952.[5] During a 1955 speech by Ernst Wollweber, head of state security from 1953 to 1957, to a closed session of the MfS leadership, Wollweber stated that the original organization was so small that "everybody knew everybody."[6] Moreover, the department charged with monitoring the broader population, Department VIa, was not a major department in the organization.[7] Following the uprising of June 1953, the MfS greatly expanded its internal monitoring duties by creating "information groups" within the MfS.[8]

Neither the *Politbüro* nor the Central Committee had means for comprehensive assessment of the situation in the GDR prior to 1952. Departments within the Central Committee sent members to collect information on specific developments in the GDR, but these were not systematic assignments to evaluate the overall situation. The Central Committee's agricultural department, for example, might send its members to a certain region to assess the harvest, or the department of industry might send a delegation to determine the extent to which the latest economic plan was being met in a specific factory. Based on these isolated reports, one cannot draw overall conclusions on the situation in the population. With the founding of the Central Committee department *Leitende Organe der Parteien und Massenorganisationen* in 1952, the SED ·leadership became equipped with a tool for systematic assessment of the situation in the population. The reports and analyses that this branch generated are a valuable source of information, but begin only in 1952.

Reports of the non-Marxist parties in the GDR are only partially helpful for tracing developments in the GDR population prior to 1953. No information reports exist from local Christian Democratic Union (CDU) groups prior to 1953.[9] The situation with documentation from the Liberal Democratic Party of Germany (LDPD) is better, but reporting on the population was sporadic. The records of the Free German Trade Union

(FDGB) may prove a useful source for future researchers in assessing the mood of the population. These records are, however, limited, as they provide information solely on the situation in factories. Police reports offer important insights into popular developments, although the *Volkspolizei* in general did not systematically collect information on the population. During certain important events, however, such as the October 1950 election, the *Volkspolizei* collected information on the population. Nevertheless, the restrictive source situation is a fact which must be kept in mind in discussing the revolutionary potential of GDR society prior to 1953.

II

The first event of the 1950s that historians encounter in assessing the revolutionary potential of GDR society is the elections of 1950. These elections were the first in the GDR to be conducted under the "unity lists" typical of post-1945 East European People's Democracies, whereby voters either supported or rejected a list of candidates in its entirety. Voters did not have the option of indicating their choice of candidate. From the *Volkspolizei* reports summarizing the situation at election-related events throughout the GDR between 17 September and 2 October, it is possible to conclude in general terms that the GDR population showed little interest in the election rallies and election meetings. The police in Bautzen noted that the population stayed away from election meetings.[10] In *Gemeinde* Struholmersdorf and in Schmellbach, both in Thuringia, virtually no-one attended election meetings.[11] Leading SED functionary Fred Oelssner's campaign speech at the VEB Zeiss plant in Jena was greeted with derisive laughter, and an exodus ensued at the end of the work day, although Oelssner had not finished his talk.[12] The press regularly doubled in its reports the numbers of those in attendance to mask the poor turnout. Of the six summary police reports on election gatherings taken between 17 September and 2 October 1950, four reported a lack of interest in election-related events, with Saxony and Thuringia reporting the least interest in these events.[13]

Opposition to the elections also manifested itself in the removal or defacing of election posters. The police reported numerous incidents of anti-SED graffiti or destruction of election posters in the days leading up to the election, and established special detachments to guard elections posters.[14]

In certain instances, opposition to the 1950 election took a more serious form. One group of young Social Democratic Party members from Zwickau drove to Berlin in May to contact the Eastern Office (*Ostbüro*) of the West

German SPD.[15] The group, led by a certain Müller, returned to Berlin in September to obtain more information against the upcoming elections. In September 1950, the group produced and distributed pamphlets urging voters to vote against all candidates in the upcoming election. On 22 September, the group met at Müller's home and, in rudimentary fashion, wrote anti-SED slogans on pieces of paper for distribution. The police arrested all members of the group the same night, two on their way to distribute the flyers, and the rest at Müller's home. The members of the group received sentences between 3 months and four years in prison for "smearing [*Boykotthetze*] against democratic institutions."[16]

In Werdau, Saxony, members of the SPD *Ostbüro* distributed a large number of pamphlets during the night of 5 September 1950. Additionally, they sent 300 anti-Communist letters to members of the Socialist Unity Party (*Sozialistische Einheitspartei Deutschlands* – SED) – the ruling Communist Party.[17] The group also placed stickers in private mailboxes or house entrances. The *Ostbüro* found that unknown opponents of the regime would often spread these stickers.[18]

In response to the increased underground activity, the *Volkspolizei* undertook greater security measures. In the four days before the election, the SPD was unable to conduct resistance activities because of increased security. *Volkspolizei* officers and their dogs patrolled the streets nightly.[19] In response to the increased number of oppositional pamphlets entering the GDR, the *Volkspolizei* launched operations "Gustav," "Heinrich," and "Fritz."[20]

The 1950 elections reveal that there was, at best, broad antipathy to the 1950 elections in the GDR and, at worst, broad hostility to them. Source constraints may well prevent a more detailed analysis of the popular view of these elections. Perhaps of more importance, however, is the fact that an active underground SPD movement existed in the early 1950s. This movement represented an ideologically polar counterpart to the SED, and a potential braintrust of a revolution. Indeed, as the uprising of 17 June 1953 will demonstrate, SPD elements actively led the demonstrations in several GDR towns.

III

A little-known demonstration which took place in August 1951 in the small Thuringian town of Saalfeld provides valuable insights into popular developments in the GDR vis-a-vis governing structures.[21] At 6:40 pm on 16

August 1951, *Volkspolizei* officers arrested two workers from the Wismut mining operation on Saalfeld's market square because of drunken and disorderly conduct. Within a few hours, between 30 and 40 of their friends appeared in front of the police station to express their anger at the arrest of their colleagues. Two of the demonstrators were arrested because of the insults they hurled at the police.[22]

The second set of arrests sparked the angry demonstrators to proceed through town to gather more support. Although Wismut workers made up the majority of these new demonstrators, other social groups such as independent business owners also participated.[23] Upon their return to the police station, the crowd entered the police station and attempted to negotiate the release of the prisoners. After making little progress, 4 or 5 women suggested that the demonstrators should stop trying to negotiate, and free the prisoners themselves. In the meantime, 36 police officers arrived from the nearby Maxhütte station as backup. The demonstrators jostled and insulted the reinforcements.[24]

By evening, word of the disturbances had reached SED General Secretary Walter Ulbricht. Ulbricht gave both the MfS and the *Volkspolizei* clear orders not to use force to quell the disturbances. At roughly 10 pm, the *Volkspolizei* inspector Zahmel, on orders from inspector Odpadlik at the provincial police headquarters for Thuringia, released the prisoners. The crowd welcomed the prisoners joyously, but the crowd's demands had increased in the meantime. They suspected that there were others inside and demanded the release of all prisoners, as well as the handing over of the *Volkspolizei* officers Hoeg and Enders.[25]

Because the police were not willing to meet these demands, and due to increased numbers of demonstrators caused by the addition of Wismut workers who were driving past the police station because of the shift change, the crowd became violent.[26] About 50 demonstrators broke into the building with axes and picks, yelling: "Where are the criminals and scoundrels"; "Strike them dead;" "Throw them out the windows." At 11:15, more reinforcements entered Saalfeld, along with the head of the MfS in Thuringia, *Volkspolizei* chief inspector Menzel.[27] The arrival of reinforcements incited the crowd to further attacks on the police station. They destroyed desks, telephones, typewriters and windows, and stole documents which they later burned on the market square. They were not able to locate police officers, however, as the police had either already left the building or taken refuge on the roof.[28] The demonstrators left on their own accord at about 2 am, having caused roughly DM 25,000 in damages.[29]

The disturbances in Saalfeld prompted the Minister of the Interior for Thuringia, Gebhardt, to travel to Saalfeld and talk to the population on the following day.[30] Gebhardt's speech on the market square in Saalfeld was interrupted by "workers and Saalfeld business people" shouting insults such as: "Shut up you lying pig."[31] Gebhardt was not able to quell the unrest. On the evening of the 17th, approximately 150 workers gathered in front of the court prison demanding the release of 14 Wismut workers. A delegation from the crowd was permitted to enter the building, so that they could see that the workers were not imprisoned there. Satisfied that there were no other workers in custody, the crowd dispersed and by the night of the 17th, the disturbances had come to an end.

For the purposes of this essay, two aspects of the demonstrations in Saalfeld are worth stressing. First, the social makeup of the demonstrators is noteworthy. The documents do not allow for a definitive conclusion on the social makeup of the demonstrators on 16 August 1951 in Saalfeld, but there are, nevertheless, indications that suggest fairly broad social participation. Certainly, Wismut workers comprised the greatest number of demonstrators, but the fact that Wismut workers easily garnered support shortly before their first storming of the police station merits attention. Furthermore, the fact that "Saalfeld business people" interrupted Gebhardt's speech indicates that members of this social group took part in the demonstrations. According to the police reports on the events, a "vegetable dealer" shouted insults at Gebhardt and a clock maker also interrupted the speech. Following 17 August, the search for Saalfeld business people who had taken part in the demonstrations was a leading issue for the Saalfeld police.[32] This evidence suggests that, on 16 August in Saalfeld, there was a willingness to engage in civil disobedience that was prevalent in a variety of social groups. The importance of establishing the breadth of participation lies in an aspect of revolutions identified by John Dunn: "Where the desperate act of rebellion does not appear justifiable to the great majority there will not be a revolution."[33]

A second aspect to the demonstrations that deserves consideration is their political character, or, precisely, their apolitical character. The demonstrations in Saalfeld in 1951 lacked political slogans. The fact that the demonstrators did not deface political posters or propaganda surprised even the police: "It is extremely noteworthy that the bandits did not touch one political slogan, picture or poster during the plundering of the police department, not even in the slightest. For example, *Der Ruf*, the competition organ of the [Free German Youth] remained intact in the middle of a window, while the panes on either side of it were smashed."[34] There is no indication in the police reports on the events in Saalfeld that the demonstrators shouted political demands. In terms of revolutionary potential, there is little evidence of Rudé's popular ideology during the Saalfeld disturbances. There is, however, evidence of a fairly broad willingness to engage in revolutionary-like activities.

IV

Historians face a more advantageous situation for discerning popular developments in the GDR from 1952 on, both due to the greater source base, and the dramatic events of the summer of 1953. It thus becomes possible to trace a key ingredient in revolutionary potential – a popular, and sufficiently wide-spread, revolutionary ideology By the end of 1952, there were already signs of revolutionary sentiment as a result of the "building of socialism", the accelerated Communization of East Germany which the SED launched in the summer of 1952. It is important to stress that although these protests were linked to the economic situation, they revealed a much deeper motivation of fundamental political resistance. The economic situation was admittedly abysmal, however. Workers had to contend with material shortages in factories, poor supplies of energy, ineffective machines, a shortage of tools, and few spare parts.[35] In December 1952, the distribution of Christmas bonuses that favoured party functionaries sparked work stoppages in factories in Weissenfels, Glauchau, Schkopau, Plauen, Cottbus, Berlin, and Magdeburg – where 2,000 workers went on strike.[36] The work stoppage at the Magdeburger Werft in December 1952 reveals that workers addressed both economic and political issues, as they compared the GDR to the Nazi dictatorship and criticized East Germany's view of democracy.[37] Workers also voiced political demands during confrontations in December 1952 at the Ernst Thälmann and Karl Marx plants in Magdeburg.[38] In Rathenow the SED members in a factory reported the following criticisms by workers: "We do not have democracy. If somebody says something, he ends up in Siberia. These government measures would not be possible in any capitalist country. There would be strikes and rebellion." And: "In the press, everything is presented to the people so wonderfully, but in reality everything is a disgrace."[39]

Space constraints do not permit for a detailed discussion of the outbreak and course of the East German uprising of 17 June 1953.[40] It is important, however, for the purposes of this study to determine the political character of the uprising, its "popular revolutionary ideology." The most recent literature on the June 1953 uprising demonstrates clearly that the uprising was an act of political will.[41] Indeed, political slogans and demands were in evidence as early as 16 June in Berlin, and from the very early morning hours in Berlin and other sites in the GDR on June 17, not, as some authors have suggested, only starting in the afternoon of 17 June.[42] According to a report from the head of the political department of the *Volkspolizei* Presidium in Berlin, demonstrators were demanding the end of the SED on the evening of 16 June: "From the House of the Ministries, the crowd moved toward Chaussee street, and from this point on their slogans became antidemocratic. They demanded, among other things, a general strike on 17 June at 7 am and the overthrow of the government."[43] On Chaussee street, demonstrators were, in fact, able to steal a Free German Youth truck with a megaphone on top, and used it to shout slogans such as: "Down with the SED," and "Overthrow of the government."[44] From the outbreak of demonstrations on 17 June, demonstrators shouted political demands. At 7:15 am, workers from the Kabelwerk Oberspree shouted: "Down with the police, the people's army, and the government."[45] A report from the police Presidium in Berlin reported the political nature of the demonstration in typical SED jargon: "The placards and the slogans shouted by the demonstrators *in the early morning hours* indicate the strong presence of provocative elements in the demonstrations already at that time."[46] Political slogans were also prevalent elsewhere in the GDR. On the 18th of June, the deputy head of the *Volkspolizei*, Grünstein, reported the following as the main slogans of the demonstrators throughout the GDR: a) Against the raising of the work norms, b) Reduction in prices in the HO stores, c) Removal of the delivery quotas (in agricultural regions) c) Release of prisoners, e) Free elections, f) Resignation of the government, g) Against the SED, h) Removal of the zonal boundaries.[47]

The story of the June uprising reveals a lack of leadership. The demonstrators targetted symbols of the power apparatus – MfS buildings, Party buildings, courthouses and police stations – but did not engage in a systematic seizure of power, whereby a group would assume, or at least attempt to assume, the reigns of state. The closest that the demonstrators came to such an occurrence were those instances where members of another political party assumed leadership, such as in the town of Görlitz, where the

SPD was publicly refounded on Lenin square in the centre of town.[48] At other sites in Görlitz, such as the fine optics plant and the hospital, "initiative committees" of the SPD were formed.[49] In VEB Lowa, speakers at a rally demanded the unity of Germany, free elections, and the revival of the SPD.[50] The countryside surrounding Görlitz also experienced SPD activity. At least one SPD group was formed, and several SED members demanded to have their SPD membership books back.[51] SPD activity was not limited to Görlitz. SPD influence overall in the uprising was of considerable concern to the SED. Horst Sindermann, leader of the Central Committee Agitation and Propaganda department said in October 1953: "We should examine how it is that agents of the SPD *Ostbüro* have a relatively large influence with the working masses compared to other agents."[52]

Although the non-Marxist parties in the GDR, the Christian Democratic Union (CDU) and the Liberal Democratic Party of Germany (LDPD) had been largely co-opted by 1953, there were isolated instances of lower level members of the parties taking leadership during the uprising. In *Bezirk* Erfurt, *Kreis* Heiligenstadt, the CDU deputy chair of the *Kreis* council stated that the SED should resign and that the CDU should take over the leading role.[53] A CDU factory chair in Heiligenstadt agreed, saying: "If the government makes mistakes, then it must be dissolved."[54] In Ershausen, Steinbach, and Arenshausen, the CDU had already prepared a list for new elections to the *Gemeinde* assemblies.[55] In Strassfurt, *Bezirk* Magdeburg, the VEB Werk-maschinen und Apparatebau elected a four-person delegation, three of whom were CDU members, to negotiate with the chair of the VEB council. The delegation was arrested before talks took place, however.[56] In *Bezirk* Gera, a CDU member stated: "Now our time has come. After the fall of the government, we will bring our people into the government."[57] Soviet sources also reveal that there were elements in the CDU that felt the CDU should form the government in light of the failures of the SED.[58]

The LDPD also participated to a certain degree in the uprising. Dr. Hans Loch, chair of the LDPD in the GDR, acknowledged LDPD involvement in the uprising: "There were also certain members of our party [the LDPD] who had an idea of taking over leadership on [17 June]."[59] In Magdeburg, one of the leaders of the uprising was an LDPD member. In *Bezirk* Dresden, Ebersbach, *Kreis* Görlitz, the CDU and LDP replaced the SED mayor. In Halle, 22 LDPD *Kreis* secretaries voted to hold open, free, and secret elections. In many cases, LDPD members demanded the resignation of the party leadership at the same time. In Döring, *Kreis* Rosslau, *Bezirk* Halle, an LDPD member was involved in the leadership of the uprising.[60]

Overall, however, CDU/LDPD participation in the demonstrations was limited. In *Bezirk* Leipzig, out of 59 "ring-leaders," three were SED members, one LDPD, one former CDU and sixteen Free German Youth.[61] After extensive study of the documents of the non-Marxist parties, Leo Haupts has concluded that the non-Marxist parties did not firmly support the SED on 17 June, but they did not actively resist the regime either.[62] Haupts' conclusion is supported by police records. Of 2,916 people arrested between 17 June and 30 June for their part in the uprising, only 4.6% were members of the CDU or LDPD.[63] Thus, revolutionary leadership, which, by definition, would have had to come from an ideologically diametrical source, was lacking on 17 June 1953. The main potential leadership candidates – the non-coopted members of the CDU and LDPD, and underground members of the SPD – did not actively participate in a leadership role during the uprisings.

Leadership was also not forthcoming from the intellectual community of East Germany. There were only limited open protests by East German intellectuals, both in the months prior to the uprising and during the uprising itself.[64] The reasons for the lack of participation of the intelligentsia during the uprising are varied. First, their material situation had improved to the point that they did not have the same material grievances of the working classes. Secondly, many intellectuals had achieved their positions because of the political system in place, and were reluctant to oppose it. Perhaps most importantly, however, intellectuals comprised a significant percentage of the emigration population prior to 1953.[65] Thus, the potential for revolutionary leadership originating from the intellectual community in the GDR was slim. To return to the two "human" factors outlined at the beginning of this essay, the disturbances of the summer of 1953 demonstrated the existence of a popular revolutionary ideology, but a lacking leadership.

In defence of this latter statement, it is worth stressing the broad participation in the uprising. Although workers initiated the disturbances on 17 June, the latent resistance to the regime was visible in the speed with which these demonstrators gained support from other sections of society. According to a police report on demonstrations in Cottbus: "The demonstrators quickly gained adherents during the march through town."[66] A theme common to the police reports on Halle was the willingness of other people in the city to join the demonstrations. In Stadtroda, people eagerly joined the 200 protesting workers on the streets. Police also complained of the trucks transporting demonstrators between Gera and Greiz: "Over 50% of the people in the trucks were in my opinion not Wismut workers, but provocateurs from the population and youths."[67] In *Bezirk* Frankfurt/Oder, construction workers demonstrating at the border crossing of Dahlwitz/Hoppegarten were joined by other people in town. According to one police report: "When the construction workers, and other sections of the population who had gathered there, tried to break through, the comrades of the border police put an energetic stop to their efforts."[68] In Wittenberge, a demonstration of 400 people "from various societal groups" took place.[69] Police reports following the uprising indicate that in the majority of *Bezirke*[70] where disturbances took place, there were more demonstrators than strikers.[71]

V

The only known organized resistance group in East Germany between 1953 and 1955 is the Eisenberg Circle, a group which began in September/October 1953 as a loose collection of five or six high-school students from Eisenberg who were reacting against the expulsion of other students for being members of the *Junge Gemeinde* and against the general "Stalinization" of the school curriculum.[72] One of the founders recalled that SED repression in general, not solely against the *Junge Gemeinde*, contributed to deep fear in the population.[73] One of the founders attributed the group's longevity to the basic support in the population for its endeavours.[74]

Within a few months of its founding, the Eisenberg Circle had begun its first modest actions against the regime. They consisted of tearing down SED propaganda and symbols and distributing anti-Communist material. The Eisenberg Circle contacted West Berlin anti-Communist organizations like the *Ostbüro* of the SPD to procure material. At the end of 1955, the group undertook its first major action. Members of the group broke into the local museum to procure arms, but the raid was unsuccessful as the museum had only old guns, for which ammunition was not available.[75] Shortly after that action, the group took up contact with a group of oppositional students from Eisenberg studying at the University of Jena. To reduce risk of arrest, the two groups maintained their independence, so that members of one group were not necessarily known by the other group. The groups had loose organizational structures; they did not hold elections or membership meetings. On 21 January 1956 the Eisenberg Circle undertook a major action by burning down a shooting range of the East German army near Eisenberg.[76] The Eisenberg Circle continued its resistance work until February 1958 when the MfS began arrests of the group's members. The story of the Eisenberg Circle is significant because it reveals that the only known, organized resistance group in East Germany between 1953 and 1958 did not contemplate revolutionary action, nor revolutionary leadership. Revolutionary potential was missing a key ingredient.

VI

East German state reporting on the Geneva Conference of 1955 provides another glimpse into popular developments in East Germany, and in particular into potential in terms of revolutionary ideology. In July 1955, the leaders of the Soviet Union, Britain, France, and the United States met in Geneva to discuss the German question. SfS reports[77] on the population reveal widespread interest in East Germany in the Geneva conference: "On the overall opinion on the Geneva conference, it can be said that [...] rarely has a political event found such popular interest."[78] The SfS remarked on the numerous discussions in factories prior to and during the conference, noting that because of the overwhelming interest in the Geneva conference, all other concerns of the population had faded into the background.[79] Another report summarized the situation as the following: "The strong interest in the Geneva conference is largely due to the hope for a rapid solution to the German problem. This is true for all sections of society. The difference is that progressive elements are interested in a democratic Germany, while reactionary and enemy elements desire unity along the western model."[80] CDU *Bezirk* analyses also concluded that there existed broad support for free elections.[81]

The SfS information department was alarmed by the great "lack of clarity" in the East German population on the form of a united Germany, and suggested that the East German population was confused as to the nature of free elections as practiced in the West.[82] The SfS' own reports demonstrated that these views were widespread, although they were couched in terms blaming specific class enemies.[83] The SfS information department report summarizing the popular attitude towards the Geneva conference stated: "There is a great lack of clarity in all sections of the population about the manner of achieving German unity, and the form of a united Germany. Propaganda must be increased to deal specifically with these questions, but also why the carrying out of free elections is presently impossible."[84]

Ernst Wollweber, the head of East German state security from 1953 to 1957, complained of popular support for free elections: "We [state security workers] should have no illusions regarding the content of our fight for reunification. There were these illusions. There were these illusions in general. We see this in our daily information reports [...] We should have no illusions – we can't say this outside – that the situation is this simple: We hold free elections and then see what happens based on the result of the vote. We are Democrats, but not idiots. We support free elections, if at these elections the working class and its leading Party play the decisive role. We support free elections, where those who do not deserve freedom do not have freedom."[85] Wollweber's admission of popu;ar support for free elections demonstrates that the roots of a popular revolutionary ideology in the GDR existed both prior to, during and after the uprising of 1953.

Although a revolutionary ideology may well have been present, there was no concerted effort at rebellion, let alone revolution, during 1956, when other countries in the Eastern Bloc, namely Hungary and Poland, demonstrated revolutionary tendencies (although there were isolated strikes in Magdeburg in the fall of 1956[86]), nor in response to the highly provocative action of erecting the Berlin Wall in 1961.[87] Explanation for this phenomenon must inevitably return to the events of June 1953. The uprising had demonstrated in bloody fashion that it would not be possible to change the political system in East Germany without the acquiescence of the Soviet Union, or, perhaps equally unrealistically in the late 1950s, without Western assistance. Ultimately, further research is needed to determine precisely the nature of popular opinion in the months prior to the building of the Berlin Wall,[88] and why there was no concerted resistance. In attempting to answer the latter question, researchers in this area would do well to keep in mind the sentiment captured by an observer in Ralf Dahrendorf's *Reflections on the Revolution in Europe* who, when asked why the revolution of 1989 took place, replied that the revolution occurred because of the existence of a generation which did not know that it could not be done.[89]

To return to the areas of investigation outlined in the introduction, it is evident that a key ingredient for revolution as identified by Rudé – a popular ideology that infuses participation in revolution – had roots in the East German population in the first half of the 1950s. Indeed, the participants of June 1953 made evident their desire for a complete overthrow of the political system in East Germany and its replacement with a system based on free elections and respect for basic rights. This revolutionary ideology was not fully exploited due in part to the lack of leadership. Potential sources of such leadership had either, as in the case of the intellectual community, left the

GDR , or had been driven underground and dispersed, as was the case with the non-Marxist parties. The use of force on June 17 in particular assured that a revolutionary leadership could not materialize from the relatively spontaneous demonstrations, and increased surveillance in the aftermath of the uprisings further reduced the chances of an effective revolutionary leadership taking form.

Notes

[1] See John Dunn, *Modern Revolutions*, Cambridge: Cambridge University Press, 1989, 2nd. ed., p. 232.

[2] V.I. Lenin *Collected Works* , Moscow: Foreign Languages Publishing House, 1960-70, Vol. 21, pp. 213-214.

[3] Charles Tilly and James Rule have focused on the seizure of power in "Political Process in Revolutionary France 1830-32" in: John Merriman, ed., *1830 in France*, New York: New Viewpoints, 1975, pp. 41-85.

[4] Harvey Kaye, ed., *The Face of the Crowd: Studies in Revolutionary, Ideology and Popular Protest. Selected Essays of George Rudé,* Toronto: Harvester Wheatsheaf, 1988, p. 77. For a detailed account of Rudé's analysis of popular revolutionary ideology, see his "Revolution and Popular Ideology" in: G.R., *France and North America: The Revolutionary Experience,* Lafayette, Louisiana: USL Press, 1974.

[5] This contrasts sharply with the 96,000 employees who were on the Stasi payrolls by 1989. Cf. Clemens Vollnhalls, "Das Ministerium für Staatssicherheit," in: Hartmut Kaelble, Jürgen Kocka, Hartmut Zwahr, eds., *Sozialgeschichte der DDR*, Stuttgart: Klett-Cotta, 1994, p. 502; Jens Gieseke, "Die Hauptamtlichen 1962," *DA* 27 (1994), p. 940.

[6] *Bundesbeauftragter für die Unterlagen des Staatssicherheitsdienstes der ehemaligen DDR* (Federal Office for the Records of the State Security Service of the former GDR) (hereafter BStU), *Zentralarchiv* (Central Archive) (hereafter ZA), *Sekretariat des Ministers* (Secretariat of the Minister) (hereafter SdM) 1921, p. 74. "Referat des Genossen Staatssekretär auf der Dienstbesprechung am 5.8.1955."

[7] The BStU's internal researcher on this topic, Herr Wiedmann, defines Department VIa as an "extremely small apparatus"; Interview with Herr Wiedmann, 28 April 1997, Berlin. The reports of this branch have yet to be located within the labyrinth of the former MfS-archives. This information was provided verbally to the author by his caseworker in the BStU, Frau Karin Göpel, Berlin, 10 July 1996.

[8] For details on the establishment of an extensive surveillance system, see the author's forthcoming book *Resistance with the People: Resistance in Eastern Germany 1945-55*, Boulder, Colorado: Westview Press, 2001

[9] Stephan Zeidler, "Zur Rolle der CDU (Ost) in der inneren Entwicklung der DDR 1952-53," M.A. thesis, University of Bonn, 1994, p. 18.

[10] *Bundesarchiv - Potsdam Abteilungen* (Federal Archives – Potsdam Branches) (hereafter BA-P), DO 1 11/1121, p.24. 22 September 1950 report entitled: "Stimmungen in Wahlversammlungen und Kundgebungen."

[11] BA-P, DO 1/11/1121. 26 September 1950 report entitled: "Stimmungen in Wahlversammlungen und Kundgebungen."

[12] BA-P, DO 11/1150, p. 13. 16 September 1950 report by HVDVP taskforce.

[13] See the reports in BA-P, DO 1 11/1121.

[14] BA-P, DO 1 11/1121, p. 139. 18 October 1950 report: "Vorkommnisse während der Vorbereitungen und Durchführung der Volkswahl in der Deutschen Demokratischen Republik v. 15.9.-15.10.50."

[15] The SPD had been banned in East Germany except East Berlin from 1946. The West German Social Democratic Party (SPD) established the *Ostbüro* in 1946 as a contact post for SPD refugees coming from East Germany, and a contact post for SPD members that elected to stay in East Germany. The best account of the SPD *Ostbüro* is Wolfgang Buschfort, *Das Ostbüro der SPD* (Munich: R. Oldenbourg Verlag, 1991).

[16] *Archiv des Deutschen Liberalismus* (hereafter ADL), #2924. 11 November 1950 extracts from the trial of Müller and others.

[17] *Archiv der sozialen Demokratie* (hereafter AdsD), SPD-PV-Ostbüro 0368 a-c. 17 October 1950 report from "Source 13 688/8" entitled: "Final report of the Saxony resistance movement against the so-called elections of 15 October 1950."

[18] Ibid.

[19] Ibid.

[20] BA-P, DO 1 11/752, p. 14. 20 September 1950 task force order from deputy head of the *Volkspolizei* for Saxony-Anhalt, Dombrowsky, to the Criminal Police department of the *Volkspolizei* in Saxony-Anhalt.

[21] The demonstrations in Saalfeld have received treatment in Andrew Port's "When workers rumbled: the Wismut upheaval of August 1951 in East Germany", *Social History*

22 (1997), pp. 145-173. Port's account relies primarily on MfS and local Party documentation. The account here relies on police records.

[22] BA-P, DO 1 11/08, p. 27. 17 August 1951 report entitled: "Überfall auf das VPKA Saalfeld," by Mayer, deputy head of the GDR *Volkspolizei.*

[23] Ibid.

[24] Ibid., p. 28.

[25] Ibid.

[26] Ibid. The market square in Saalfeld where the police station was located was the gathering point for workers awaiting transport to the Wismut mining operation.

[27] Ibid., p. 62. 19 August 1951 report entitled: "Vorläufiger Schlussbericht über die Ereignisse in Saalfeld bis zum 19.8.1951 -12:00 Uhr," by the head of the *Volkspolizei* in Thuringia, König.

[28] Ibid., p. 64.

[29] Ibid., p. 42. Undated report: "Bericht über die im Auftrag des Chefs durchgeführte Untersuchung über die Ursachen der Vorkommnisse im VPKA Saalfeld in der Nacht vom 16. zum 17.8.1951," by Flechtner, deputy head of the *Volkspolizei* in Thuringia.

[30] BA-P, DO 1 11/08, pp. 27-30. 17 August 1951 report entitled: "Überfall auf das VPKA Saalfeld," by Mayer, deputy head of the GDR *Volkspolizei.*

[31] Ibid., pp. 42-43. Undated report: "Bericht über die im Auftrag des Chefs durchgeführte Untersuchung über die Ursachen der Vorkommnisse im VPKA Saalfeld in der Nacht vom 16. zum 17.8.1951," by Flechtner, deputy head of the *Volkspolizei* in Thuringia.

[32] BA-P, DO 1 11/08, "Bericht über die im Auftrag," p. 43.

[33] John Dunn, *Modern Revolutions*, p. 246.

[34] BA-P, DO 1 11/08, "Bericht über die im Auftrag," p. 69.

[35] Ilko-Sascha Kowalczuk, Armin Mitter, "'Die Arbeiter sind zwar geschlagen worden, aber sie sind nicht besiegt!' Die Arbeiterschaft während der Krise 1952/53," in: Kowalczuk/Mitter/Wolle, eds*., Der Tag X: Die 'innere Staatsgründung' der DDR als Erlebnis der Krise 1952-54*, Berlin: Ch. Links, 1995, pp.39-40.

[36] Ibid., p. 44.

[37] Ibid., p. 45.

[38] Ibid.

[39] Quoted in ibid., p. 46.

[40] For a detailed account in English of the outbreak in Berlin, see the author's forthcoming book *Resistance with the People: Resistance in Eastern Germany 1945-55*, Boulder, Colorado: Westview Press, 2001. See also Christian Ostermann, "New Documents on the East German Uprising", *Bulletin of the Cold War International History Project*, Spring, 1998. The most reliable account in German of the uprising overall is Armin Mitter, Stefan Wolle, *Untergang auf Raten*, Munich: Bertelsmann, 1993. Details of the uprising continue to emerge, however.

[41] See Armin Mitter, Stefan Wolle, *Untergang auf Raten*.

[42] Torsten Diedrich, *Der 17. Juni 1953*, Berlin: Dietz, 1991, p. 83; Arnulf Baring, *Uprising in East Germany*, Ithaca: Cornell University Press, 1972, p. 74. Political slogans were evident in the demonstrations of December 1952. See Mitter/Kowalczuk, "'Die Arbeiter sind zwar geschlagen worden, aber sie sind nicht besiegt!'," in: Kowalczuk/Mitter/Wolle, S. 44-45.

[43] BA-P, DO 1 11/304, p. 259. "Der Beginn der Streikbewegung in der Stalinallee," 13.7. 1953 from the Polit-Abteilung of the PdVP Berlin.

[44] Ibid.

[45] SAPMO, ZPA, J IV 2/202/14, "Über die Lage am 17.6.1953 in Gross-Berlin und der DDR." 17.6.1953.

[46] BA-P, DO 1 11/304, p. 258 "Der Beginn der Streikbewegung in der Stalinallee." 13.7.1953 by the Polit-Abteilung of the PdVP Berlin. Emphasis added by GB.

[47] BA-P, DO 1 11/45, p. 12. "Rapport Nr. 166, Gesamtbericht über die Ereignisse am 17.6.1953" 18.6.1953 by the deputy head of the *Volkspolizei*, Grünstein.

[48] SAPMO-BA, ZPA, DY 30 IV 2/5/546, p. 239 Report on 17 June 1953 based on reports from the *Bezirke*.

[49] SAPMO-BA, ZPA, DY 30 IV 2/5/535, p. 7. 17 June 1953 report from the *Bezirk* leadership in Dresden.

[50] AdsD, SPD-PV-Ostbüro 0434b. 22 June 1953 report on Görlitz strikers, reconfirmed in reports by sources 20984, and 20924.

[51] SAPMO-BA, ZPA, DY 30 IV 2/5/596, p. 42. 20 July 1953 report on the events of 17 June 1953.

[52] Bärwald, *Das Ostbüro der SPD*, Krefeld: Sinus, 1991, p. 78.

[53] Thüringisches Hauptstaatsarchiv, Weimar (hereafter THSA), B IV 2/4-49, p. 9. 3 September 1953 report on the events during and after 17 June 1953 in *Bezirk* Erfurt.

[54] THSA, B IB 2/4-48. July 1953 letter from KPKK Heiligenstadt to BPKK Erfurt.

[55] THSA, B IV 2/4-48, Bezirksparteiarchiv der SED Erfurt.

[56] *Archiv für Christlich-Demokratische Politik* (hereafter ACDP), VII-011-1268. 23 June 1953 report of CDU *Bezirk* association for Magdeburg to the CDU leadership.

[57] SAPMO-BA, ZPA, IV 2/5/534, p. 185. 20 June 1953 report entitled: "Über die Entwicklung des faschistischen Abenteuers im Bezirk Gera."

[58] 27 June 1953 report from Lieutenant General Fedenko, Operations Division, Main Operations Division, General Staff of the Soviet Army, to Lieutenant General Pavlovsky, reproduced in Christian Ostermann, *The Post-Stalin Succession Struggle and the 17 June 1953 Uprising in East Germany,* Washington: National Security Archive, 1996 (Document #25).

[59] ADL, #2367. FDP Ostbüro report from August 1953.

[60] Mecklenburgisches Landeshauptarchiv (herafter MLHA), IV 2/5/531, p. 71. Situation report of 18 June 1953 on the factories of the *Bezirk* Schwerin; ibid., IV 2/5/533, p. 164. Report on *Bezirk* Halle of 20 June 1953.

[61] Heidi Roth, "Der 17. Juni im damaligen Bezirk Leipzig," *DA* 24 (1991).

[62] Leo Haupts, "Die Blockparteien in der DDR und der 17. Juni 1953," *Vierteljahreshefte für Zeitgeschichte*, 40/3, 1992, p. 42.

[63] BA-P, DO 1 11/758, p. 4. 2 July 1953 report by Weidlich, head of the investigation department of the *Volkspolizei*, on those arrested in connection with the "fascist putsch."

[64] For an analysis of the role of intellectuals in the GDR in 1952-1953, see Ilko-Sascha Kowalczuk, "Volkserhebung ohne 'Geistesarbeiter'?" in: Kowalczuk/Mitter/Wolle, eds., pp.129-167.

[65] John Torpey, *Intellectuals, Socialism and Dissent: The East German Opposition and its Legacy,* Minneapolis: University of Minnesota Press, 1995, p. 28.

[66] BA-P, DO 1 11/305, p. 102. 27 June 1953 report from the Cottbus *Bezirk* police to the head of the *Volkspolizei.*

[67] BA-P, DO 1 11/45, p. 243. Extracts from the *Bezirk* police situation reports for the period 0:00 to 17:00 on 17 June 1953 signed by Weidhase, head of operations staff.

[68] BA-P, DO 1 11/45, p. 9. Extracts from the *Bezirk* police situation reports for the period 17:00 to 24:00 on 17 June 1953, signed by head of operations staff Weidhase.

[69] MLHA, IV 2/4/587. "Analyse über die Lage in *Bezirk* Schwerin am 17. Juni 1953" by the *Bezirk* leadership of the SED.

[70] There were 14 administrative districts (*Bezirke*) in East Germany.

[71] BA-P, DO 1 11/45, p. 11. June 18, 1953 report of HUDVP operations staff: "Rapport Nr. 166". Soviet sources offer different numbers, but suggest a similar trend. Soviet military officials reported 132,169 strikers in the GDR on 17 June, but 269,460 demonstrators. 27 June 1953 report from Lieutenant General Fedenko, Operations Division, Main Operations Administration, General Staff of the Soviet Army, to Lieutenant General Pavlovsky, reproduced in Ostermann, *The Post-Stalin Succession Struggle*, Document #25.

[72] The founding members of the Eisenberg Circle were Thomas Ammer, Johann Frömel, Günter Schwarz, Reinhard Spalke, and Ludwig and Wilhelm Ziehr. Patrik von zur Mühlen, "Widerstand in einer thüringischen Kleinstadt 1953 bis 1958. Der 'Eisenberger Kreis'," in: Poppe/Eckert/Kowalczuk, eds., *Zwischen Selbstbehauptung und Anpassung*, Berlin: Ch. Links, 1995, p. 165.

[73] Ibid., p. 166.

[74] Ibid., pp. 168-169.

[75] Ibid.

[76] Ibid.

[77] At the 15th Plenum of the SED, held in July 1953, the SED announced that the Ministry for State Security would henceforth be a State Secretariat for State Security (*Staats-sekretariat für Staatssicherheit*).

[78] BStU, ZA, AS 43/58 Vol. 4/1, p. 200. 4 August 1955 *Informationsdienst* report.

[79] BStU, ZA, AS 43/58 Vol. 4/2, p. 71. 22 July 1955 *Informationsdienst* report.

[80] BStU, ZA, AS 43/58 Vol. 4/1, p. 205. 4 August 1955 *Informationsdienst* report.

[81] ACDP, VII-013-1262. Undated report of CDU *Bezirk* association Erfurt to the CDU leadership; 19 July 1955 report from the CDU *Bezirk* association Magdeburg to the CDU leadership; 18 July 1955 report from CDU *Kreis* association Burg to the CDU leadership; 25 July 1955 report from CDU *Bezirk* association Karl-Marx-Stadt to the CDU leadership; political information report 19/55 of 14 November 1955; 30 November 1955 report from the CDU *Bezirk* Dresden association to the CDU leadership.

[82] BStU, ZA, AS 43/58 Vol. 7, p. 4. 21 September 1955 *Informationsdienst* report.

[83] BStU, ZA, AS 43/58 Vol. 7, p. 7. 21 September *Informationsdienst* report.

[84] BStU, ZA, AS 43/58 Vol. 7, p. 9. 21 September 1955 *Informationsdienst* report.

[85] BStU, ZA, *Sekretariat des Ministers* 1921, p.73. Transcript: "Rede des Genossen Staatssekretär auf der Dienstbesprechung am 5.8.55."

[86] Mary Fulbrook, *Anatomy of a Dictatorship*, Oxford: Oxford University Press, 1995, p. 188.

[87] Ibid., p. 90.

[88] For an introduction, see the chapter "Die DDR zu Beginn der sechziger Jahre: Der Weg ins sozialistische Ghetto," in: Mitter/Wolle, *Untergang auf Raten*.

[89] Ralf Dahrendorf, *Reflections on the Revolution in Europe*, New York: Times Books, 1990, p. 15.

Jeffrey Kopstein

Does Everyday Resistance Matter? Lessons from the Two German Dictatorships

Using the example of workers under Nazi and Communist rule in twentieth-century Germany, this chapter assesses the conditions under which everyday resistance can exercise significant influence on dictatorships. Because dictators cannot determine whether or not low-level resistance is a prelude to a large-scale rebellion, "the weapons of the weak" yield to the powerless a veto power in all sorts of policy realms. Ruling elites in both cases were hemmed in by tacit agreements made with their workers in matters of prices, wages and social policy. In the case of the Nazis, these social and economic tensions were alleviated through external war. In the case of communist East Germany, under the pressure of a bipolar and nuclear world order, the same kinds of resistance could not be displaced through external aggression and led instead to long-term economic decay. The East German dictatorship could therefore fall from within, while the Nazi dictatorship could only do so from "without".

In the historiography on Nazi Germany and the rapidly developing historiography on the GDR, one finds frequent use of what might be called the "everyday resistance hypothesis." This hypothesis maintains that the everyday, mostly non-political, acts and attitudes of ordinary people exercised an important influence on policies ranging from wages, prices, investment, and even such foreign policy matters as peace and war. This hypothesis is highly controversial and only a minority of scholars subscribe to it; nevertheless, its plausibility is worth investigating for two reasons. First, at a general level it is important to explore the comparative historical "record" for its power to adjudicate disputes about the importance of everyday resistance and the conditions under which it might matter for politics. Second, and at a more concrete level, such a comparison might be useful for allowing the contradictory evidence from the two German cases to speak to each other. In the case of Nazi Germany, for example, the everyday resistance hypothesis is highly contested: new scholarship stressing the centrality of race (as opposed to class) has led many scholars to reject the hypothesis outright. What can the trajectory of scholarship on the Nazi case tell us about possible pitfalls in our study of similar kinds of behavior in East Germany? And how might the East German experience influence our thinking about the National Socialist past?

The main argument of this chapter can be summarized as follows: although everyday resistance does not matter in "direct" ways that earlier structuralist accounts maintain, it does matter, especially in modern dictatorships that possess formidable surveillance apparatuses and care about popular opinion. In many ways the effects of everyday resistance in the two German dictatorships were remarkably similar: leaders in both regimes feared that amorphous discontent might lead to a "general strike." The differences, however, in the effects of everyday resistance on economic, social, and ultimately military policies had as much to do with the international position and intentions of the two dictatorships as they did with differences in behavior at the grass roots level. Both were militarized societies that were constrained by popular opinion as mediated through everyday resistance. In the case of the Nazi dictatorship, political rule was stabilized and everyday resistance negated, or at least muted, through racism, war, and plunder. Nazism could therefore only fall from "without." The East German regime did not have the "luxury" of war, extreme nationalism, or conquest to act as internal stabilizing factors and was thus paralyzed by everyday resistance, ultimately becoming susceptible to revolution from "within."

In such a short paper, these arguments can only be made in an introductory form. I tender them not in order to test them in a "rigorous" fashion but rather for the purpose of generating novel and provocative hypotheses. Beyond hypothesis generation, however, the comparison is also useful for highlighting the similarities and differences in the two German dictatorships; it is through analogical thinking that social reality is put into perspective. Even here, however, any complete catalogue of similarities and differences between the two twentieth-century German dictatorships must remain beyond the scope of this paper.

The Hypothesis and its Critics

In a fascinating series of books and articles, James Scott has maintained that everyday resistance (defined as everything, from shirking, grumbling, work to rule, jokes, machine breaking, but short of collective action) often constrains elites in unexpected ways.[1] Malay paddy farmers, for example, in a region where Scott has done intensive field work have long resented paying the official Islamic tithe. It is collected unfairly and unequally, the proceeds are sent to the provincial capital, and not a single poor person in the village has even received any charity back from the religious authorities. Quietly and massively, the Malay peasantry has managed to nearly dismantle the tithe system so that only 15 percent of what is formally due is actually paid. There have been no tithe riots, demonstrations, protests, only a patient and effective nibbling in a multitude of ways: fraudulent declarations of the amount of land farmed, simple failures to declare land, underpayment, and delivery of paddy spoiled by moisture or contaminated with rocks and mud to increase its weight.

It is easy to see why social historians of modern dictatorships might be attracted by the study of everyday resistance. First, aesthetically it is pleasing to put people other than tyrants at the center of our analysis. It would be nice if the true *dramatis personae* of history were somehow the powerless and not the powerful. Second, the thesis is pleasantly ironical and counterintuitive. Everyday resistance is akin to the "anthozoan polyps" that form the "reef" on which ships of state founder. Social historians cast their eye on the polyps (cause) while political historians, so the argument might run, concentrate – wrongly or superficially – on the shipwreck (effect). Third, and perhaps most important, by connecting what goes on at the bottom of society to politics, such an approach responds to some of the criticisms frequently made of social historians by political historians and political scientists: social historians often fail to connect their social narratives to narratives of political domination. *That* would be an interesting story – a narrative of socialism's rise, existence, and ultimate demise that found its focus somewhere other than in a study of party elites, dissident intellectuals, and those who mobilized politically in the final months of 1989.

There is another aspect to Scott's argument that also merits attention. His discussion of the "hidden transcript" – what people say and feel in the absence of their superiors – suggests that subalterns are not as fooled by the words and philosophies of their superiors as might usually appear to be the case.[2] For students of totalizing dictatorships, the idea of a hidden transcript that acts to break down the hegemony of rulers over a long period of time is especially appealing, because rebellions against authority in such situations frequently appear to come out of nowhere. The search for the hidden transcript in the East German case, for example, may provide insights into the big bang of 1989 in a way that studying mobilization of the last months can not.

But it is precisely at this point that social scientists have criticized Scott. In a recent joint effort by three "heavy hitters" of social movement theory,[3] Scott is subjected to a withering attack. While acknowledging the value of his earlier work[4] that sought to explain the factors underlying collective action, they argue that the newer work on resistance has "provided little purchase on the question of when these low level resentments would lead to mobilization and collective action and when they would remain at the level of individual *ressentiment*."[5] In other words, they question whether everyday resistance matters. To be fair to Scott, his argument is not that everyday resistance needs to move to mobilization for it to matter. Quite the contrary: his notion of "nibbling" suggests that the real events leading to state failures and crises frequently come well before the mobilization even starts. Even so, the question of the conditions under which everyday resistance matters remains an empirical one, and one that should interest students of state socialism's existence and demise.

The German Dictatorships

A parallel, if not identical, pattern of theorization has taken place in the historiography on Nazi Germany and the place of working class "resistance" within it. The study of resistance under the Nazis has become a subindustry of sorts within German history. Few historians or social scientists, however, seek to identify the ways in which this resistance influenced policies. The reason for most resistance studies is more to show which groups of Germans acted ethically under the most extreme circumstances than to show how it affected policy. As interesting as this literature is, from the standpoint of social science it misses the opportunity to say just how resistance actually mattered.

There are exceptions. The most consistent and bold statements on the role of everyday resistance among the working class in the Nazi period were penned by Tim Mason.[6] Mason's arguments are intricate and often subtle. For the purposes of this essay, however, they can be boiled down to a few simple propositions. First, the ideology of Nazi social policy, conceived at the broadest level as a *Volksgemeinschaft* (a racial, national community) in which notions of class would no longer inform either working-class consciousness or state policy, were received highly skeptically by the working class. Second, during the 1930s, policies designed to speed up work, weaken working-class institutions of representation, and increase national rates of accumulation and investment at the expense of wages, met with "resistance" in the form of shirking, high rates of absenteeism, the occasional and isolated strike, and consistent grumbling – all of which was assiduously reported and sent upwards by the political police. Third, Mason argued that this resistance reached a crescendo in 1938-39, as the Nazi leaders were pumping unprecedented sums of money into armaments. Such high rates of investment created labor shortages, pushed up wages, and yielded to the working class a form of power – to withhold their services on an individual basis – that threatened the rearmament program. The Nazi leadership, according to Mason, feared turning the terms of exchange against the working class more strongly than it already had because workers had demonstrated in 1918 their capacity to bring down an authoritarian government. The leadership was therefore cornered. Fourth, and this is his most controversial point, Mason maintains that the constraints imposed on the leadership by workers' resistance forced Hitler to go to war earlier, three or four years earlier, than he would have preferred because he believed that Germany could not increase its military output further without risking industrial unrest and in that case could not wait any longer because that would mean allowing Germany's opponents time to increase their own military output. These social constraints ultimately determined not only the timing of the war but also shaped the kind of war that Hitler fought. "Blitzkrieg" was not merely a type of tactic, but also a strategy that corresponded to the Nazis' precarious domestic situation. The Nazis needed a war but they did not want a long one and especially not one that would demand sacrifice from the population.

In a nutshell, this summarizes Mason's *ouevre*. It is an original, unified, and, in many ways, powerful argument. And nobody buys it anymore. His arguments have been attacked from multiple sides. First, the new emphasis on race and biological thinking among scholars of Nazi Germany, and especially their work documenting the significant public support for the various aspects of the *Volksgemeinschaft* ideology, has tended to render Mason's picture of working class resistance as a kind of quaint, romantic Marxism. Even if it can be categorized as resistance, however, such resistance may simply have functioned as an outlet for frustrations, and in many ways may have stabilized the system by precluding more organized forms of action. Second, to the extent that workers remained immune to Nazi ideology and developed their own sense of identity and personal space outside of the *Volksgemeinschaft*, it remains far from clear that such attitudes and behavior can be understood in any meaningful sense as "resistance." It can just as easily be thought of as "acquiescence" if not support. Third, Mason's argument that the system faced an economic crisis in the late 1930s has confronted devastating criticism from both social and economic historians as "objectively" wrong. Fourth, the notion that the crisis led to war and specifically "Blitzkrieg" is a conclusion that even people who otherwise buy much of what he has to say almost unanimously dismiss as not grounded in facts (other factors, especially foreign policy appear to explain the timing of the war much more parsimoniously) and at best speculative.

It is important to note that Mason's interpretation changed in subtle ways over time. Whereas his early work was a straightforward structuralist explanation for the origins of the war – workers constrained leaders and forced their hand – his later work contained an important cognitive component (though this too was not completely absent in the earlier writings) that did not deny the power of the Nazis to crush working-class resistance. His work did, however, continue to maintain that working class attitudes, as they filtered their way up to the leadership, influenced just how far Hitler and his cronies were willing to go in forcing savings, suppressing consumption, and the like.

What East Germany has to say to the Nazi Case

The volume of social history on the Nazi period, and more specifically on workers, is so large that it is far from clear who is right. Often the same documents and statements (especially Hitler's) are read in different ways. If one were to judge the matter from the sheer weight of scholarly opinion, there would be very little left of Mason's enterprise. What I want to do here is outline why elements of the East German case might lend a renewed credibility or plausibility to Mason's story, or at least provide a form of "replication" for part of it.

Obviously there are crucial differences between Nazi Germany and Communist East Germany, especially regarding ideology and behavior, and it is not my intention to play them down. Yet there are also some striking similarities. I have been continually impressed by how the internal interpretations of working class attitudes, everyday resistance, and a general fear of unrest that are to be found at every level of the archives, from factory reports to the monthly reports of the *Bezirksleitungen,* to Central Committee Department reports, to Politburo Meetings, reflect important continuities in political judgement in the two German dictatorships. Like the Nazi leadership in Mason's story, the East German leadership from very early on found itself hemmed in by shop floor resistance of the most elementary sort and, especially after June 1953, feared a mass uprising. It was always prepared to make concessions to rather than confront the working class.[7]

It is important to note here that Mason's Marxism and his putative romanticism in regards to the role of the working class need not be adopted in order to accept much of his structuralism. It is true that implicit in much of

Mason's work is the hope that the working class could indeed become the true driving force of history; he had very high hopes for workers, especially German workers. Ultimately, of course, these hopes were dashed not only in Germany but also in Great Britain and the rest of the world. Yet the essentially non-normative components of his essays may remain intact and the East German case may help us salvage (if only in modified form) the kinds of things that Mason was getting at.

I have elsewhere argued that resistance to the reintroduction of piece work, labor competitions, and the activist movement during the late 1940s prevented the SED from gaining complete control of the shop floor. The archival evidence on this point is quite overwhelming.[8] A cat-and-mouse game between the workers' state and the working class ensued that was never resolved successfully in one direction or the other. In the one instance where the state did seriously attempt to suppress wages through norm and price increases, in mid-1953, the working class rebelled *en masse*, and the regime quickly retreated after the protests were put down with Soviet assistance. Never again did the regime try to "tame" the working class through central policies. The few attempts to increase output or lower the overall wage bill through central policies were always subverted at the enterprise level with the tacit acquiescence of the leadership. The one genuine venture into reforming the socialist economy, the New Economic System of the 1960s, was in no small measure prevented from full implementation because of Ulbricht's fears that price increases and "socialist" unemployment might lead to a repeat of June 1953. Such constraints ultimately left Honecker with little alternative when he came to power but to pursue a sort of socialist consumer populism that led to under-investment, rapidly rising foreign debt, infrastructural decay, and ultimately political revolution.

One could argue, however, that such a structural – even *ouveriste* – approach is flawed in the East German case too. Again, the potential criticisms are reminicient of the critiques of Mason's work launched by labor historians of Nazi Germany: Nazi workers were encouraged, often successfully, to take pride in their work for the regime. The same, it appears, was true in East Germany. Rebellious impulses could easily be deflected by segmenting the labor force into groups of more and less loyal, enthusiastic, and productive workers. Between 1953 and 1989, not one instance of collective protest occurred of a magnitude large enough threaten the regime. Indeed, without too much difficulty one could find groups of workers and ordinary East Germans who benefited from the regime's policies and who most likely supported it for material and "ideal" reasons. Furthermore, the ubiquity of concern with mass public support emanating from the lower levels, as both scholars of Nazi Germany and East Germany have found in the archives in two different eras, could simply reflect bureaucratic strategies for increasing resource allocation from the center. ("Give us more or we run the risk of unrest" might have been the logic presented by factory directors and Bezirk party secretaries to their superiors in Berlin). In a similar vein, it is worth recalling that some of Mason's critics argued that his evidence was drawn disproportiately from Nazi sources, especially political police sources which, for the obvious reasons, had the tendency to cast all attitudes and behaviors in a political light (either pro or anti regime), even when they did not reflect tendencies that could easily have been translated into collective action. In short, so the argument runs, objectively the Nazis and the Communists need not have worried very much about the working class and neither should we.

But any analysis of the ebb and flow of wage policy, piece rate policy, price policy, housing policy, and consumer goods policy suggests very strongly that both the Nazis and the SED did worry. And it is the discrepancy between the *objective* political capacities of the state and the society, and the *perceived* potential for conflict that is most interesting. It is true that the "hidden transcripts" of everyday resistance may not amount to very much when elites are not aware of them, when they remain hidden. But the one thing we know about totalitarian regimes is that very little does remain hidden. The leadership in these societies had unprecedented access to the hidden transcript of subaltern groups, including workers. Perhaps the most we can say for everyday resistance in both Nazi Germany and Communist East Germany is that it fostered a culture of disrespect for authority in the work place and in the society at large. But while such a culture of disrespect may never, on its own, have overthrown the regime, it did lay the ground work for a potential overthrow, and the leadership of both societies were acutely aware of this. This, I think, is what Mason is really getting at and I see no reason to discard his approach.

Everyday resistance matters in a totalitarian dictatorship in a way that it does not in a democracy, or even in a traditional dictatorship. In a democracy, everyday resistance is marginal because the culture that it nurtures can be expressed quite openly in participatory behavior. In a traditional dictatorship, where rulers are satisfied simply to demobilize the population and foster political passivity, everyday resistance is expected and even accepted.

Modern totalitarians, however, because they wish to mobilize their populations, to politicize them for instrumental purposes, constantly keep an ear to the ground for signs that their projects might be rejected en masse.

It is wrong and ahistorical to argue that once the June 1953 strikes occur, the rest of the GDR's history is essentially one of a coercive state over a cowed society. But it is true that the events of the years running up to and culminating in mass unrest in June 1953, and the skirmishes of the class war in the work place that occur continuously after that, nourished the sentiment in the leadership that the whole operation was far more precarious than it probably was. Like Hitler, Ulbricht and Honecker lived with a "myth of the general strike" that threatened to bring the whole enterprise crashing down. In the communist case, since a general strike really did occur, the fear of working class unrest was probably more well-founded, though it is difficult to say whether it was more feared. Here, too, I think, Mason's model provides us with some very important insights. As in the Nazi case, the communist leadership found this dilemma paralyzing in the realm of economic policy.

What the Nazi Case Says to the East German Experience

The differences between the two cases, as noted above, are crucial. Perhaps the most important difference: one made war and committed genocide and the other did not. Indeed while the East German regime, after some flirtation with Khrushchevian utopianism in the 1960s, settled into a conservative, if rather drab, consumer socialism in the 1970s and 1980s, it is difficult to conceive of something similiar happening in the Nazi case. War and planning for war was the glue of the Third Reich. Consider, for example, the counterfactual put forth by Robert Harris in his novel (and later-to-be TV movie) *Fatherland*.[9] The year is 1964. Germany has won World War II. Churchill and his "warmongers" have long ago fled to Canada. Europe is now under Nazi control and all that remains of the fighting is a few guerilla skirmishes in the hinterlands of Siberia. The scene in the novel is set for the US President Joseph Kennedy to visit Germany to make detente with Hitler. Germany itself has become stable, a bit shabby, and very conservative. Its officials have become cynical and more than slightly corrupt. Its youth long for jazz, travel, and an end to militarization.

The reason that Harris's Brezhnevite/Honecker-like post war Nazi Germany does not ring true is that it is terribly difficult to imagine a peaceful Nazi Germany, a country satiated and contented to end the "struggle." It is this constant need for struggle, for outward expansion – for war – that historians have placed at the center of their analyses.

Mason's most bold claim, that Hitler started the war in 1939 because he needed to, may be moving beyond what his evidence might warrant. But even if the causal logic here is flawed, the functional logic remains powerful. War helped the Nazis. It increased national integration, gained new adherents for the party among the working class, provided new sources of wealth in the form of plunder, and brought "inferior" foreigners to Germany as workers who could preform functions that Germans would have had to and allowed German workers to occupy a place on the social ladder relatively higher than where they had previously been.[10] To some extent, racism and anti-semitism were equally integrative.

The depressing part of the comparative story is that Mason is only partially right and on crucial issues he missed something terribly important. For while Hitler may have "needed" the war, once he started it there was no reason why war would not increase his popularity. One need only read the *Sopade Berichte* for a taste of the pessimism that pervaded Social Democratic thinking on the willingness of Germans to resist Nazi war plans. Indeed, once the war had started the German working class appears to have supported the Nazi state, at least no less strongly than other segments of the society. Their everyday resistance was diminished or at least muted by the glories of war and the decadent pleasures of conquest and racism. That war has an integrative capacity should surprise neither the historian nor the social scientist. We have known this since Thucydides. It is disappointing, however, that the one class from whom history had hoped for the most – the German working class – supported the very people who were determined to destroy them as a class.

Why this was the case, why the working class supported a regime that was committed to destroying them as a "class," is intriguing, especially when we consider the other irony of the comparison. Everyday resistance among workers intensified in the eastern half of Germany once it was clear that the SED, a nominally working-class party, had taken over. Involved in a cat-and-mouse game with the working class from 1947 until 1953 and thereafter paralyzed by the specter of rebellion, a fear reinforced in the millions of words that flowed upward on the disrespect shown by ordinary people for "socialism," "peace," and the SED, the East German leadership ultimately had very little power. Unwilling or unable to engage in real combat, the party had to settle for an endless series of phoney, ritualized "combat tasks"[11] or what I have called elsewhere the "campaign economy"[12] (with such unconvincing, even laughable militarized slogans as "mein Arbeitsplatz ist mein Kampfplatz fur den Frieden") in which the disciplining virtues of real war were substituted with the metaphorical language of an organizational struggle for something as abstract as socialism. Ultimately the people knew the difference.

Conclusion

What does this comparison tell us about the role of everyday resistance and the dispute between Scott and McAdam, Tarrow, and Tilly? Does everyday resistance actually matter? Does it have any political impact or is it something that we study out of phenomenological curiosity (how did people understand their situation?), ethical reconstruction (who resists tyrannies?), or plain empiricism (history as it "actually happened")? Why should we care?

The history of the two German dictatorships yields some tantalizing clues about everyday resistance: precisely where we might expect everyday resistance to matter the least, it may matter the most. The greater the *Machtanspruch* of the ruling group, the stronger the capacity to infiltrate and monitor the hidden transcript of the oppressed, the more ambitious the transformative plans of the leadership – the more leaders may actually care about and react to what ordinary people are thinking as expressed in their everyday acts. Hard as they may try (and the East Germans certainly tried) tyrants can never really know what people are thinking, how far they can be pushed, and what might lead to rebellion. In the language of rational choice, dictators always suffer from the problem of preference falsification. Here democratic leaders have a genuine advantage. Since Plato we have known that the tyrant has no true friends. For this reason, everyday resistance may matter most in a totalitarian dictatorship – a counterintuitive finding in light of how we normally think about the idea of totalitarianism.

On the other hand, it is important to note that everyday resistance probably does not matter in the way more optimistic students of resistance hoped that it might. The lessons of the Nazi period are sobering ones. Whereas people cannot be easily mobilized to build abstractions such as socialism, they can be seduced by the possibilities for plunder or glory inherent in war. Seen in this way, the nuclear deterrent of the cold war years begins to loom much larger in our thinking; with the communist world unable to transform its militarized impulses into real war, it had to substitute an ersatz productivist war that it was destined to lose. Everyday resistance may have played no small part in this defeat.

Notes

[1] James Scott, *Weapons of the Weak*, New Haven, Conn.: Yale University Press, 1985; James Scott, *Domination and the Arts of Resistance*, New Haven, Conn.: Yale University Press, 1990.

[2] Scott, 1990

[3] Doug McAdam, Sidney Tarrow, and Charles Tilly, "Toward an Integrated Perspective on Social Movements and Revolution," in: Mark Irving Lichbach and Alan S. Zuckerman, *Comparative Politics: Rationality, Culture, and Structure*, New York: Cambridge University Press, 1996, pp.102-139

[4] See James Scott, *The Moral Economy of the Peasant*, New Haven, Conn.: Yale University Press, 1976.

[5] Lichbach and Zuckerman, p.120

[6] Tim Mason, *Sozialpolitik im Dritten Reich: Arbeiterklasse und Volksgemeinschaft*, Opladen: Westdeutscher Verlag, 1977.

[7] Jeffrey Kopstein, "Chipping Away at the State: Workers' Resistance and the Demise of East Germany," *World Politics*, vol.46, no.4 (1996), pp.397-430.

[8] For detailed archival references, see Jeffrey Kopstein, *The Politics of Economic Decline in East Germany 1945-1989*, Chapel Hill: University of North Carolina Press, 1997.

[9] Robert Harris, *Fatherland*, New York: Random House, 1992

[10] Ulrich Herbert, *Hitler's Foreign Workers*, Cambridge: Cambridge University Press, 1997.

[11] Ken Jowitt, "Soviet Neotraditionalism," *Soviet Studies*, vol. 35, no.3 (1983), pp.202-230.

[12] Kopstein, 1997.

Randall L. Bytwerk

The Pleasures of Unanimity in the GDR

The GDR was characterized by implausible unanimity in nearly every aspect of public life. Whether in elections in which 98.85% of the voters voted yes, in the comprehensive suppression of public dissent, or in the Politbüro itself, the GDR presented an image both to citizens and the larger world of a society unified in its outlook. This chapter considers the evidence for that unanimity and the reasons for building a Potemkin Village of public opinion, and concludes by discussing its ultimate failure.

> When someone is honestly 55% right, that's very good and there's no use wrangling; And if someone is 60% right, it's wonderful, it's great luck, and let him thank God. But what's to be said about 75% right? Wise people say this is suspicious. Well, and what about 100% right? Whoever says he's 100% right is a fanatic, a thug, and the worst kind of rascal.
>
> *An old Jew from Galicia*[1]

98.85% of those who voted in the 7 May 1989 GDR communal elections gave their "yes" to the candidates of the National Front. The voter turn-out was 98.77%.[2] Outside observers smiled at the results, yet year after year, election after election, the figures were the same. And not only there. In the party, the media, the schools, indeed all areas of public life, an implausible uniformity characterized public life in the GDR. American President Bill Clinton was ready to claim a landslide had he gotten over 50% of the vote in the 1996 election, but even 75% would have been a catastrophe in the GDR.

This chapter first considers the evidence of unanimity in the GDR, then discusses why the GDR needed such an implausible Potemkin Village of public opinion and ends by discussing its ultimate failure.

Kinds of Unanimity

Since learning from the Soviet Union was to learn victory, the GDR followed the Soviet model in which secrecy pervaded every aspect of life. One example of what might be provided is indicative. It describes Chernenko's report to his colleagues in 1980, and their responses.

> He stressed the fact that "Central Committee plenums last year [1979] were conducted in a spirit of complete unanimity," prompting Andropov to remark, "That is an entirely proper conclusion. The plenums really did proceed in complete unanimity," and Pelshe to add, "And their decisions were also adopted unanimously." And when Chernenko mentioned that fifty-one sessions of the Central Committee

Secretariat had taken place and that they had passed 1,327 regulations, Suslov and Andropov together piped up, "Like the Politburo, the Secretariat also conducted its business in complete unanimity."[3]

The GDR learned from the masters.
The Socialist Unity Party (SED) operated under rules that allowed for little public discussion. It was governed by the Leninist principle of Democratic Centralism. The last edition of the *Kleines politisches Wörterbuch* defined it clearly:

> Leadership of the party by an elected central, periodic election of all leading party organs by lower bodies, collective leadership, periodic reports of the party organs to those who elected them; firm party discipline and the subordination of the minority to the majority; absolute execution by lower organs and members of the decisions of higher organs [...] active participation by party members in their organizations to implement these decisions.[4]

Since the lower bodies had little real say in electing the higher ones and since the higher bodies saw no need to report accurately to lower ones, the result was a system far more central than democratic.

The situation was made even more clear in the SED's party statute, the preamble to the 1975 version of which stated: "Any sign of factionalism or group-building contradicts the nature of a Marxist-Leninist party and is incompatible with party membership."[5] Even at the upper levels of the SED, discussion was rare. Günter Schabowski reports two lively discussions in the Politbüro during his membership, one regarding the firing of Konrad Naumann, the Berlin SED first secretary, the second in September 1989 as things were already crumbling.[6] Lower level party officials knew that disagreeing with their superiors was not a wise career move. As those who questioned the wisdom of the SED's decisions were told, "Do you think you are smarter than the collective wisdom of the party?"[7]

The media were under tight supervision. The processes are covered well in Gunter Holzweißig's book *Zensur ohne Zensor*.[8] In brief, journalists were carefully chosen and knew that any mistake, whether intentional or not, could result in immediate assignment to factory work. As Klaus Raddatz told journalists in 1984: "We journalists are front-line fighters of a party we joined of our own free will. No one is forced to become a journalist."[9] His point was sufficiently clear. Given the choice of factory work or journalism, the great majority chose journalism.

One aspect of the media, however, is worth closer examination: humor. The GDR was not a funny state. I am not interested here in the jokes people told each other, of which several collections have been published,[10] rather in what was officially permitted.

Humor was not a standard feature in the GDR's newspapers. There were occasional editorial cartoons, though their number seems to have diminished as time went on. The single periodical that carried satire and humor was *Eulenspiegel*. The other major opportunity was the cabaret, both the nine professional cabarets in the cities and the many lay cabarets. Both were challenging endeavors for their participants. *Eulenspiegel* occasionally surprised, but rarely startled the reader. The cabaret could be more open. Still, it was carefully watched. Both provided a limited opportunity to comment critically on prevailing conditions.

Eulenspiegel was one of the most popular periodicals in the GDR, with a weekly circulation of about 500,000 in the 1980s; the staff estimated that 650,000 could have been sold if the paper allocation had been increased.[11] A major reason for its popularity was that it regularly dealt with the annoyances of everyday life in the GDR: rude shop clerks, shoddy goods, poor labor discipline, unresponsive bureaucracies.

The GDR bureaucracy may have felt nervous about permitting *Eulenspiegel* as much free reign as it did, but since the USSR had a satiric periodical named *Krokodil,* the GDR and the other socialist nations had theirs.

Although *Eulenspiegel* certainly contained more criticism of existing conditions than any other mass-circulated periodical, its boundaries were clear. It was allowed to criticize the problems of daily life, but never to suggest that anything might be amiss in the system that ultimately caused those problems. And the balance had to be right. That is, there had to be more satire aimed at the class enemy to the West than satire directed at domestic targets. As Peter Nelken, editor for many years, wrote in 1962, "The primary task of satire in our era is to direct its fire against imperialism, the main enemy of humanity."[12] The result was that a great deal of space went to unoriginal attacks on the Federal Republic of Germany or the United States.

People read *Eulenspiegel* for the domestic satire. Here the rules were clear, and enforced. As one early staff member put it, they had to operate by "street and house number."[13] That is, they could point out specific problems at the lower level. The few times they crossed the line, the results were swift. In 1953, *Eulenspiegel's* predecessor *Frischer Wind* published an attack on Manfred Ewald, who ran GDR sports. Four staffers were demoted to lower positions, two found themselves working in factories. As Joachim Jäger notes, it was the last time anything that risky was tried.[14] The result was that

Eulenspiegel printed little that shocked or surprised its readers, but simply gave expression to the common complaints of daily life.

Cabaret was more lively – but with a much more limited audience. I recall attending a performance of the Leipzig Pfeffermühle in 1988 that surprised me with satire more biting than that which I had seen in *Eulenspiegel*. The program covers alone were surprising (see page 113). The refrain to a song claimed that the SED leadership was having nightmares about "lauter kleine Gorbatschows." Cabaret satire still could not directly criticize the system, but its degree of pointedness was substantially stronger.

The reason was that the audience was small. The 220 annual performances of the Pfeffermühle in the early 1980s, for example, sold out nearly every performance, but the total annual audience was about 30,000.[15] The professional cabarets all had small venues. Furthermore, attendees had to remember what they had heard. The printed texts were not available. Cabaret was only rarely given space on television, and when so only for carefully approved segments. Requests from West German correspondents to film cabaret segments were invariably rejected according to West German correspondent Peter Merseberger, who cites Hermann Kant on the theme:

> We do not want to give the West something to exploit when we criticize or poke fun at something. We fear we will make ourselves laughable. If we do permit criticism, we are afraid the West German media will play it up. That is a regrettable lack of sovereignty.[16]

Kant's point is entirely accurate. The GDR lived in constant fear that any criticism would provide ammunition for the class enemy to the west, and satire was the worst kind of criticism, as it would render ludicrous those who took themselves seriously indeed.

Public life was another area of unanimity. In private, naturally, people spoke differently than in public, but my concern is with public behavior. The range of measures taken to encourage unanimity in public expression is simply astonishing. From the earliest years of schooling to the workplace, from the stamp collectors' club to the church, from humor to tragedy, the goal was to have agreement.

Children from the earliest age learned what it was appropriate to say in public. Teachers were carefully selected and textbooks rigidly guided. Membership in the youth organizations, the Young Pioneers, the Thälmann Pioneers and the Free German Youth (FDJ), was for practical purposes compulsory. A 1959 message to parents made this clear:

Front and Back Covers from a 1988 Pfeffermühle program

The beginning of your child's education begins an important stage of life: the systematic preparation for a life in service to our socialist community. An important helper in socialist education is the Pioneer Organization Ernst Thälmann, the socialist

mass organization for children. [...] It will be most beneficial for the development of
your child if you agree to his membership in the Pioneer Organization.[17]

Not surprisingly, the vast majority of children joined, and even parents who
opposed membership found it hard to see their children standing outside the
group. Membership in the groups grew steadily. The beginnings were rough,
and even into the 1950s FDJ membership was stagnating at around 35% of
the age cohort. But by the 1960s the percentages had reached entirely
satisfactory levels of near-unanimity.

The various mass organizations had enormous memberships. The
Society for German-Soviet Friendship (DSF), for example, was 6,400,000
strong in 1988.[18] This enormous number was motivated less by passionate
interest in the USSR than by the accurate conclusion that it was a cheap and
easy way to demonstrate loyalty. Moreover, unanimous membership in the
DSF was frequently a requirement for groups to win awards or benefits.
Sylvia Mangoldt, a school psychologist, for example, testified to the Enquete
Kommission about the arguments she encountered for not being a DSF
member:

> There were arguments that membership showed one's attitude toward the state,
> toward socialism and the Soviet Union, that membership in the DSF was an essential
> characteristic of a socialist teacher, and that otherwise the teacher collective could not
> earn the title "Socialist Teacher's Collective."[19]

The last argument is the one I am interested in here. The system was such that
not only the individual suffered disadvantages from failing to joint the proper
groups, but also his or her work mates. Given the importance of the *Kollektiv*
in the GDR, it took a person of fortitude to do something that not only
brought himself difficulties, but also his friends.

The Church was an area to itself. It did not fade away as rapidly as the
SED had hoped. I do not wish to discuss the tangled relations between
Church and state here. Rather, I am interested in the efforts the state took to
make the activities of the Church as invisible as possible.

I remember visiting the Statt-Kirchentag in Leipzig in July 1989, an
alternative gathering with a heavy ecological emphasis held during the
Evangelical Kirchentag. Much there was far more open than one expected to
find in the GDR. Of course, things were already beginning to move, but the
experience confirmed what Pfarrer Wolfgang Gröger of Leipzig, the
Church's youth pastor in the early 1980s told me of his visits to city hall to
secure permission for various Church activities. "You can do anything you
want as long as it is inside the walls of a church," he was sometimes told.
That was not strictly true, of course, since the state's organs kept careful

watch on what happened inside as well as outside the walls, but there clearly was more flexibility if things happened where they could not be seen. Gröger reports, for example, trying to secure a permit for a church-organized bike-ride to promote environmentalism. About 100 participants were expected. The authorities were unwilling to permit such a visible demonstration of church popularity, so Gröger finally compromised: groups of ten would leave at five-minute intervals. However, the leaders moved rather slowly, and soon the groups had merged.

Still, the group was not carrying signs or banners, something that would have brought rapid action. Consider a police report of a 1988 march after the prayer for peace at the Leipzig Nicolaikirche: "Attempts to form chains or circles were blocked by official forces. The participants in the procession carried no banners, symbols or other signs; there was no other public display. There was no harm to public safety, and they had very little public visibility."[20] The point was that the procession was essentially invisible. There was no public display of dissent.

The Church remained a problem throughout the GDR's history. In part, the SED simply did not understand it. As Mary Fulbrook observes:

> The main miscalculation on the part of the SED here, however, was to assume that the Church operated according to the same hierarchy of command – in other words, that it was essentially characterized by the same democratic centralist structures – as the SED itself. To the SED's dismay, it discovered too late that it could not rely on the leadership of the Church to contain unruly spirits below; that "turbulent priests" had greater leeway in the Church than did their secular counterparts under the iron hand of communist party discipline.[21]

Still, Church membership steadily dropped. Once the SED adopted the policy of making Church membership increasingly uncomfortable (but not impossible), those wishing a quiet life decided it was not worth the trouble.

The GDR began with 82% Protestant membership. By 1964, the Evangelische Kirche had under 50%, and by the mid-1980's 30-40%. In 1987 in East Berlin, only 7% claimed any church affiliation. In the new satellite towns, it may have been as low as 3%. The expectations were that national membership would drop to 20-25% by 2000.[22]

Dissent as Heresy and Disease

We have surveyed a variety of ways in which the GDR sought unanimity in every area of life. Why did it do so? Why would a society allegedly striving for a world described by Marx as one where people could express their full interests insist that everyone, at least in public, behave in monotonous and predictable ways? I suggest two reasons. The first has to do with the fundamental nature of the Marxist-Leninist system, which is similar to a state church that can tolerate no dissent, the second to the pragmatic conclusion on the part of the SED that dissent once allowed would spread as a plague, a fear that the events of 1989 proved wholly justified.

The comparison to religion, frequently made in passing, is worth developing in more detail. Modern totalitarianism is best compared to a particular form of religion: an established church with compulsory adherence. Such a form of religion has not been seen in the West since the Peace of Westphalia in 1648 (which generally ended European attempts to require the adherence of all citizens to the religion of the state).

This variant of religion compels public adherence to an established creed, an adherence which within the individual takes varied forms. Some accept the established religion with genuine faith, believing in its tenets and seeking to realize them in their lives. Others accept the creed for pragmatic reasons: their careers or personal security depend on outward adherence. Another, and large, group does not quite disbelieve. That is, the forces of the church, and of the society that seem universally to accept the church, produce acceptance without passion. Citizens go through the motions of adherence, but their faith is lukewarm at best. A large cadre of priests promotes and enforces public adherence, and church and state are deeply intertwined. Finally, there are heretics and infidels. Heretics share the basic theology, but interpret it in ways other than those of the established church. They are worse than infidels who hold to another (and false) religion, but have the courtesy to practice it elsewhere.

The GDR was a professedly atheistic state whose intellectual father viewed religion as an opiate of the masses, a historical relic that assuredly would fade with time. Still, the SED realized that the needs religion fulfilled could not be wished away. Over forty years it erected a secular religion. As one writer who experienced the system puts it:

> East Germany resembled the huge temple of a pseudo-religious cult. It had all the trappings: godlike veneration of the leader, pictures of "saints" and quotations from their teachings, processions, mass rituals, vows, and strict moral demands and commandments administered by propagandists and Party secretaries who held priestly "rank".[23]

This is perhaps extreme. Still, the SED used the language of religion to speak of its "unshakable" faith in Marxism-Leninism. The university departments of Marxism-Leninism, which offered courses required of all students, were called departments of "religious studies."[24] The SED was "the

Institute of Eternal Truth." These are the kinds of jokes that are only partially in jest. Walter Ulbricht proclaimed "Ten Commandments" for his citizens.[25] Jürgen Kuczynski, the perennial "faithful dissident" of the GDR, even wished for a secular equivalent of Christian prayer.[26]

Like state religions, socialism had to respond to varying levels of commitment. Some people were passionate Communists. They believed in the system. Propaganda needed to inspire them to live out the precepts of their faith. Others were believers from expediency. Without public assent to the political faith, their jobs, their well-being, the future of their children were uncertain. They needed to be persuaded to behave in the right way and to say the right things (in public, at least).

The major threat to state theologies is heresy. One expects infidels to have false views, whether theological or economic. They are the object of missionary endeavors; they need to be converted. Heretics, however, are domestic enemies. Given the blessing of the "truth," they choose falsehood. The history of Marxism is similar to that of Christianity in that there has been a seemingly endless series of sects. When the sect is a breakaway from a church it threatens only the church, but when the church and state are one, heresy threatens the entire structure.

Thus, as we saw earlier, SED members were obligated to follow the decisions of the party. Unlike Roman Catholics for whom the pope is infallible only when speaking *ex cathedra* on matters of faith and morals (which he rarely does), the SED's decisions were all seen as infallible. "Die Partei, die Partei, die Partei hat immer Recht," the song said. The result was that members did not publicly question party views often, even when they had great personal reservations. Wolfgang Leonhard writes:

> I have often seen it myself, that in conversation with people from the West an official who is wrestling with the severest internal doubts will stubbornly, and apparently with complete conviction, defend the official Party line. His Western interlocutor then leaves him with the firm conviction of having been talking to a 150% Stalinist.[27]

The hearings of the Enquete Kommission are filled with accounts of people who said the right things in public, knowing that doing otherwise would have unpleasant consequences.

The intellectuals were worst of all. Robert Van Hallberg has an interesting explanation of their near universal willingness to "go along to get along":

> The reason they did not do so [i.e. object] was rarely the threat of imprisonment or torture but, rather, fear of professional obstacles. My claim is not simply that certain professional structures, such as the Writer's Union or the Central Institute for

Literary History, enforced particular kinds of conformity. The more interesting
phenomenon is that the elaborateness of GDR professional organizations seemed to
have rendered intellectual life devastatingly predictable: one knew that one would
indeed be read carefully, if only by censorious authorities; one thought one knew
what would happen if something in particular were said. Even when the organization
itself produced no pressure to write or repress something in particular, colleagues
with whom one collaborated closely were assiduous in warning of repercussions and
asking for revisions in anticipation of what – often wrongly – they thought would be
the authorities' response. [...] In addition, the sense of consequence given
intellectuals, partly by their organization, was something no one was willing to
sacrifice or even place in jeopardy.[28]

In short, a wide range of pressures nicely joined to keep citizens generally in
line. It was unpleasant to risk speaking openly in most situations.

But what about the government? Why did it insist on implausible
unanimity? As one pastor testified to the Enquete Kommission, the GDR had
a government that feared nothing more than publicity.[29] Part of it, naturally,
was fear. The leadership knew well that considerably less than 99% of the
population favored its policies. Günter Schabowski made an interesting
statement during the Enquete Kommission hearings:

The SED was a party that – although there may have been some who thought
otherwise – never had majority support. We could proceed only by ignoring whether
or not we had a majority. If I have to wait for a majority, I have to choose the path of
social democracy, and that we despised. We lived continually by suppressing the
reality that a large part of the population, perhaps the majority, was against us.[30]

Another reason was probably a kind of common-sense understanding
that public dissent spreads, sometimes with astonishing rapidity. This was
clear in the events of 1989 across Eastern Europe. An interesting approach
taken by police departments recently helps to explain the intolerance of
dissent. Police departments have discovered that suppressing minor crimes
also reduces larger crimes. Going after visible offenders like subway cheaters
and graffiti artists persuades the public that the police are doing their duty,
and increases the perceived risk of criminal behavior.[31]

Another way of looking at it is Noelle-Neumann's Spiral of Silence
approach to public opinion. She argues that we have a fine sense for
distinguishing the opinions that can be safely expressed from those than
cannot.[32] Those opinions that are "dangerous" fade from public discussion.
Even bringing them up risks at the least unfriendly looks from one's fellow
citizens. We know what will lead to unpleasantness, and seek to avoid it.
Citizens of the GDR knew well what could be said in public and what was
better avoided. Once views lose their place in the public square, they fade

quickly. They may not vanish – many may indeed still hold them – but the absence of hearing them discussed in public leads those who hold them to wonder just how alone they are. Dirk Philipsen quotes a Leipzig dissident speaking of the situation in the mid-1980s:

> The really terrible thing about all of this is that nobody knew that these things were going on in other places. Just knowing about it would have made a big difference. Then you wouldn't have felt so alone. It would have encouraged us a great deal. Only a small number of people knew about anything going on outside of their own hometown, mostly about things that happened in Berlin.[33]

That was Leipzig. What must the feelings have been in smaller towns and villages?

The Failure of Unanimity

The GDR enforced public unanimity both for reasons of insecurity and because of a justified fear that public criticism, once on the move, would be difficult to stop. Even at the end of the GDR, the SED, the Stasi and all the weighty apparatus of party and state were joined in ensuring unanimity. Honecker and Hager made widely publicized statements to the effect that the GDR had no intention of making changes, despite the Soviet example. Consider as another example a 1988 FDJ report: "It is interesting how strong the 'Opposition Movement' in the GDR is and what its aims are. Some have the naive view that one should give such people the opportunity to express their opinion in public and discuss it."[34] Even near the end, the clear sense was that contrary views should not be given time in the public forum.

The major reason the GDR's attempt at unanimity failed is that is attempted too much. As Jacques Ellul observes, all modern propaganda systems, democratic ones included, strive for unanimity.[35] The difference is that democratic systems settle for general agreement on the central issues. Few think that the foundations of the United States are crumbling because the number of jokes about the President is rising. *Eulenspiegel,* on the other hand, got in trouble in 1963 for a gentle mention of Walter Ulbricht's goatee.[36]

As a result, people were forced to say and do things they knew conflicted with their actual attitudes. Just as people under a state church may say their ritual prayers and attend divine services without feeling deep faith in the reigning theology, so many citizens of the GDR went through the motions. Many, probably most, did not believe any longer by 1989, but neither did they quite disbelieve. To admit that one was serving a dubious cause with artificial passion is psychologically uncomfortable. It is equally uncomfortable to admit that one's behavior is the result of cowardice. The more congenial solution is to go through the motions, not quite disbelieving what one is called upon to believe.

The tension in Leipzig in September 1989 demonstrated the truth of Goebbels' statement that a sharp sword stands behind effective propaganda.[37] As long as public expression was risky, most were silent. Once a few had the will to speak, the rest followed quickly.

When I visited Leipzig for three weeks in July 1988, I was surprised by the energy with which people criticized the system to me in private conversation. Surely, I thought, I was encountering those with enough courage to invite an American to dinner. They could not be typical of the population. I was hardly alone in my defective analysis.

In short, the contagion of dissent was contained. The problem was that the disease was virulently contagious, requiring constant efforts to contain it, including the harshest measures when necessary. As the SED leadership aged, and grew comfortable in the organized adulation and managed unanimity, they became in some sense captives of their own propaganda, They lost the will, and with the advent of Gorbachev also the ability, to take the vigorous measures necessary to contain the disease. Once the epidemic began, there was no stopping it.

The SED's propaganda had produced widespread, but shallow acceptance.[38] To use a biblical metaphor, it was a house built upon the sand that could not resist the storm.

Notes

[1] Cited by Czeslaw Milosz, *The Captive Mind*, trans. Jane Zielonko, New York: Octagon Books, 1981, p. v.

[2] "98.85 Prozent stimmten für die Kandidaten der Nationalen Front," *Neues Deutschland*, 8. Mai 1989, p. 1.

[3] Dmitri Volkogonov, *Autopsy for an Empire: The Seven Leaders who built the Soviet Regime*, trans. Harold Shukman, New York: Free Press, 1998, p. 280.

[4] *Kleines Politisches Wörterbuch*, 7th ed., Berlin: Dietz, 1988, pp. 179f.

[5] *Statut der Sozialistischen Einheitspartei Deutschlands*, Berlin: Dietz, 1975, p. 16.

[6] Günter Schabowski, *Das Politbüro: Ende eines Mythos. Eine Befragung*, Reinbeck: Rowohlt, 1990, p. 20.

[7] Enquete Kommission, *Rolle und Bedeutung der Ideologie, integrativer Faktoren und disziplinierender Praktiken in Staat und Gesellschaft der DDR*, 9 vols., vol. III, *Enquete-Kommission ìAufarbeitung von Geschichte und Folgen der SED-Diktatur in Deutschland,î* Frankfurt a.M.: Suhrkamp, 1995, p. 332.

[8] Gunter Holzweißig, *Zensur ohne Zensor. Die SED-Informationsdiktatur*, Bonn: Bouvier Verlag, 1997.

[9] Argu of 9 February 1984, SAPMO, DY 30/IV 2/2.040/16.

[10] See, for example, Clement de Wroblewsky, *Wo wir sind ist vorn. Der politische Witz in der DDR oder Die verschiedenen Feinheiten bzw. Grobheiten einer echten Volkskunst*, Hamburg: Rasch und Röhring Verlag, 1986.

[11] Heinz-Werner Tzschichhold, "Personal Communication," 1987.

[12] Cited by Joachim W. Jäger, *Humor und Satire in der DDR. Eine Versuch zur Theorie*, Frankfurt a.M.: R. G. Fischer, 1984, p. 43.

[13] Karl Kultzscher, *Links und rechts der Dumme. Lebensdatenverarbeitung eines DDR-Satirikers*, Köln: Tiberius Verlag, 1993, p. 28.

[14] Jäger, pp. 113-114. Peter Merseburger, *Grenzgänger. Innenansichten der anderen deutschen Republik*, München: C. Bertelsmann, 1988, pp. 194-195.

[15] Jäger, p. 88.

[16] Peter Merseburger, *Grenzgänger. Innenansichten der anderen deutschen Republik*, München: C. Bertelsmann, 1988, pp. 194-195.

[17] Cited by Heinz Elmar Tenorth, Sonja Kudella, and Andreas Paetz, *Politisierung im Schulalltag der DDR. Durchsetzung und Scheitern einer Erziehungsambition*, vol. 2, Bibliothek für Bildungsforschung, Weinheim: Deutscher Studien Verlag, 1996, p. 155.

[18] *Statistisches Taschenbuch der Deutschen Demokratischen Republik 1989*, Berlin: Staatsverlag der DDR, 1989, p. 22.

[19] Enquete Kommission, vol. II, p. 166.

[20] Christian Dietrich and Uwe Schwabe, *Freunde und Feinde. Friedensgebete in Leipzig zwischen 1981 und dem 9. Oktober 1989. Dokumentation*, Leipzig: Evangelische Verlagsanstalt, 1994, p. 198.

[21] Mary Fulbrook, *Anatomy of a Dictatorship: Inside the GDR 1949-1989,* Oxford: Oxford University Press, 1995, p. 116.

[22] John P. Burgess, *The East German Church and the End of Communism: Essays on Religion, Democratization and Christian,* New York: Oxford University Press, 1997, p. 48.

[23] Hans-Joachim Maaz, *Behind the Wall: The Inner Life of Communist Germany,* trans. Margot Bettauer Dembo, New York: W. W. Norton & Company, 1995, pp. 2f.

[24] Robert Von Hallberg, *Literary Intellectuals and the Dissolution of the State: Professionalism and Conformity in the GDR,* trans. Kenneth J. Northcott, Chicago: University of Chicago Press, 1996, p. 39.

[25] Dieter Vorsteher, ed., *Parteiauftrag: Ein Neues Deutschland. Bilder, Rituale und Symbole der früheren DDR,* München: Koehler & Amelang, 1997, p. 37.

[26] Schriftsteller-Verband der DDR, X. *Schriftstellerkongreß der Deutschen Demokratischen Republik. Arbeitsgruppen,* Köln: Pahl-Rugenstein, 1988, p. 24.

[27] Wolfgang Leonhard, *Child of the Revolution*, trans. C. M. Woodhouse, London: Collins, 1957. p. 373.

[28] Von Hallberg, p. 317.

[29] . Enquete Kommission, vol. VI, p. 373.

[30] Enquete Kommission, vol II, p. 502.

[31] Malcolm Gladwell, "The Tipping Point," *New Yorker,* June 3, 1996, 32-38.

[32] Elisabeth Noelle-Neumann, *Die Schweigespirale. Öffentliche Meinung – unsere soziale Haut,* Frankfurt a.M.: Ullstein Sachbuch, 1982.

[33] Dirk Philipsen, *We Were the People: Voices from East Germany's Revolutionary Autumn of 1989,* Durham, NC: Duke University Press, p. 49.

[34] "Information zur politisch-ideologischen Arbeit beim bisherigen Verlauf des 'FDJ-Angebots DDR 40'," SAPMO DY 30/IV 2/2.039/336, 1988, p. 8.

[35] Jacques Ellul, *Propaganda: The Formation of Men's Attitudes,* trans. Konrad Kellen and Jean Lerner, New York: Alfred A. Knopf, 1968, p. 11.

[36] "Nelken an Norden am 27. Juni 63," SAPMO DY 30/IV A2/2.028/64.

[37] Joseph Goebbels, *The Goebbels Diaries: 1942-1943*, trans. Louis P. Lochner, Garden City: Doubleday, 1948, p. 430.

[38] For a more detailed analysis of the failure of GDR propaganda, see Randall L. Bytwerk, "The Failure of the Propaganda of the German Democratic Republic," *Quarterly Journal of Speech*, 85 (1999), 400-416.

David P. Harding

The Demoralization of the East German Officer Corps and the Prussian Military Tradition

Most historical accounts of the *Nationale Volksarmee* (NVA) portray it as an unshakeable pillar of state security. In a political system that left few avenues for dissent, reform-minded party members and military personnel adopted creative means to press for change. Reformist military officers noted the decline of East German society and expressed their views on the urgent need for state reform. In the 1980s, some used military history, especially the example of the Prussian military reformers of 1807-1813 who advocated social reform during the Napoleonic Wars, as their medium to criticize the regime and call for reform of the GDR.

Introduction

The investigation of the reasons behind the demise of the GDR is far from ended. Much of the research has focused on cultural and social change, politics, and the influence of the international system, especially the Soviet Union, on the events of 1989. Missing from much of the discourse is the role of the Party's security organs, which in the end stood by and watched as the Wall came down and a new generation of politicians scrambled to save the GDR.

By security organs, I do not mean the just the Stasi, although it played perhaps the most prominent role in controlling society and maintaining the SED's power. I would like to take a look at the National People's Army (*Nationale Volksarmee*, NVA). When it is mentioned at all, it is generally referred to as a "tool of the Party," "instrument of state power," or some other such general description. One gets the impression that the NVA was comprised of relatively like-minded individuals whose vested interest in the system's survival made them unquestioningly throw their support behind the Party. But I am not inclined to think that this was necessarily the case, that the NVA was monolithic, that it was so simple or easy. Rather, based on my research, admittedly still ongoing and in its formative stages, I am inclined to believe that there were fissures within the NVA as elsewhere in the GDR, and that these reflect a social institution under pressure to adapt to changing domestic and international situations.[1]

As a social institution, the NVA was subject to many of the same pressures that afflicted GDR society. It developed its own means to cope with these pressures, although the Party's official position on social and political reform in the 1980s was to reject it outright. Within the Party and the NVA, however, there were members, usually from the post-war generation, who were sympathetic to Gorbachev's calls for renewal under perestroika and glasnost. As the crises of the 1980s intensified a growing number of East German officials, including military officers, began to question the Party's ability or willingness to act in the best interests of the East German *Volk*. For the military, technological change and events in the GDR's last decade further shook its self-confidence and made it clear to many that the Army's role would no longer be to defend socialism from the West, but to defend the regime from the people it swore to protect. Many of those same officials recognized that the GDR could only survive if it reformed its socialist system.

In a political system that left few avenues for dissent, reform-minded party members and military personnel adopted creative means to express the need for change. As is common in many organizations, in the NVA there were groups of what one could generally categorize as the "old guard" of conservatives who rejected the call to reform from the east; the vast majority of officers who were content to "go along to get along" so as not to jeopardize their careers or families, and those to whom I will refer as the "intellectual vanguard." This last group is the focus of my inquiry: they are the military intellectuals who taught in the military academies, published in the professional journals, and who were responsible for developing and maintaining the NVA's traditions and culture. By the 1980s, however, things had changed and some military historians took the example of the Prussian military reformers of the Wars of Liberation and used them to criticize the regime and present a model for reform in the GDR. Thus, by looking at the military history published in the period 1972-1989, we can see how the Prussian example evolved to suit a reformist agenda. The example of the Prussians, and the East German military historians' writings about them, is significant because it reflects the beginnings of a change in culture in one of the Party's most powerful and reliable organs of regime security.

Evidence: the Prussians
Anticipating social instability resulting from increased exposure to the West during détente, the SED stepped up its use of history as a tool for propaganda and legitimization. This effort became known in the West as the "Second Prussian Renaissance."[2] An especially useful example for both civilian and military historians, but especially for the military, was the Prussian military

reformers of 1807-1813. They had called for social reform to revivify the Prussian state, and military reform to defeat Napoleon after the army's defeats at Jena and Auerstädt. The Prussians provided the Party with the means to emphasize:

1. the progressive and revolutionary nature of socialism,
2. the close ties between the army and the people,
3. the necessity of "throwing off the yoke of foreign domination,"
4. and the virtues of close ties to the "brotherly" Soviets.

This last tradition resulted from the alliance between Prussia and the Russian Tsar after the Treaty of Tauroggen in 1812.[3] The wide range of applications to the Party's and the army's concerns accounted for this example's prominence in the canon of East German traditions.

Prior to 1971, East German military historians had used the Prussians to justify socialism as a progressive and revolutionary tradition.[4] At that time, socialism's prospects for the future appeared bright relative to the West, and the NVA historians could easily link the two situations. The Prussian reformer General Gerhard von Scharnhorst led the way to early nineteenth century reform, and commentators observed that he, as well as the army, had been at the vanguard of social as well as military change in Prussia. Erich Honecker's declaration at an NVA Party Conference illustrates how this idea had become part of the party line: "The words of the great reformers of the Wars of Liberation still hold true. The army always must stand at the forefront of social progress."[5] By subsuming their class interests to the interests of the State, the Prussian reformers had swept away "feudalism" and cleared the way for a bourgeois society, which Party ideology considered the necessary precursor to socialism. The NVA considered itself the inheritor of this tradition, because, as the defender of socialism, it perpetuated the tradition of the revolutionary fighters *(Kämpfer)* and defended the German People against counterrevolutionary Western imperialism.[6] Here, under the rubric of the class struggle, historians conjoined the themes of progressive socialism and *Feindbild* (threat portrayal).

According to tradition common to both the East and West, the social progress that the Prussian reformers introduced resulted in an army that, in conjunction with the militia or *Landwehr,* avenged the humiliations of Jena and Auerstädt[7] and drove Napoleon's *Grande Armée* from the Fatherland. But for historians in the GDR, the modern-day equivalent of the Napoleonic yoke from which the Prussians were to free themselves was the U.S. occupation of the Federal Republic. Finally, Carl von Clausewitz provided an archetype to East Germans who commemorated his activities at Tauroggen, where he arranged the defection of Yorck's Prussian Corps from Napoleonic service to the Tsar. Yorck later fought with great distinction against Napoleon. Thus we see the beginnings of the German-Soviet cooperation that figured prominently in SED propaganda.[8]

The SED managed to get through the early 1970s with minor difficulties. Party officials expected a mass exodus when they eased travel restrictions as a result of increased contact with the West, but this did not materialize right away.[9] East German officials did not have to contend with a major dissident problem until the mid- to late seventies. The NVA officer corps remained firm in its belief in socialism as a progressive political program at this time: it had little reason to doubt the Party's claims because the SED could still deliver on its promises. In other words, at this point, the NVA elite's collective faith in socialism remained unshaken and its sense of "self-legitimacy"[10] was still intact. However, the combination of developments such as the Czech invasion in 1968, the stationing of nuclear missiles in central and eastern Europe after 1978, the Polish Crisis in 1980-81, economic decline beginning in the early eighties related to rising fuel prices, the SED's rejection of perestroika, and an increasingly restive East German society boded ill for the future. In time, it occurred to many officers that suppression of popular unrest would become the NVA's main mission.

The Call to Reform

Contrary to many contemporaneous Western accounts of the NVA, the declining East German social cohesion and economy affected the military.[11] By the mid 1980s, as perestroika began to sweep from the Soviet Union through eastern Europe, the situation became critical for the GDR and the NVA. Perestroika put pressure on the East German state to implement domestic reforms, which Honecker and the SED gerontocracy refused to pursue. A rift developed between the post-World War II generation of Party officials and the senior leadership.[12] The survivors of Nazi persecution and the horrors of World War II had a different perspective than those born after the war. To those who survived the war's hardship and mass destruction, post-war East Germany represented an improvement over the last years of the *Hitlerzeit*. For many in the post-war generation, however, the limited information from the West and the reports of those allowed to travel outside the communist bloc convinced them that, in terms of quality of life, the GDR had actually *lost* ground relative to the West. Over time, the regime found it harder to hide the growing discrepancy between East and West, and people's discontent grew. In the 1980s, emphasis on human rights and ecological concerns heralded a new generation's entrance onto the political scene similar to the Green Party's appearance in the Federal Republic.[13]

A similar process occurred in the army. The realization that everyone would lose in a nuclear war convinced many military intellectuals that there could be no war in central Europe. The image of "nuclear winter" brought on a *Sinnkrise* as some debated the prospects for winning a European war in the nuclear age.[14] In spite of absolute material decline for the civilian economy, insufficient manpower, and shortages of funds for field training, the army continued to modernize and field expensive new equipment. The contradictions in the socialist system relating to the failed economy and the SED's promises that "more sacrifice will set things right," the claims for democracy implicit in the name German Democratic Republic, and the basic failure to act in the people's interests were too great to ignore. Some in the army felt that the Party betrayed them by expecting them to suppress popular dissent so the Party could maintain its monopoly on power.[15] The growing awareness that the army would likely be called upon to suppress dissent intensified the sense that the NVA was living a Kafkaesque existence. As a result, the meaning of the Prussian reformers changed for some in the intellectual vanguard of the NVA between the "Prussian Renaissance" of the early 1970s and the end of the GDR in 1989. This change in meaning reflected changes in East German society, and the Army's role within the state. Yet in a neo-Stalinist regime, the consequences for dissent are too great for most people to do anything more than share their thoughts with carefully selected friends or family members.

As in the Soviet Union during this time, some GDR officials were able guardedly to use the system to spread a message of concern about the state of the State and the need to reform. Thus, they were able to take the officially sanctioned version of the Prussian reforms and through them propose "reform in the name of the Volk." It is apparent from looking at publications from the mid-80s on that a rift of sorts, or perhaps a diverging *Weltanschauung,* developed not only between reformist army officers and Party hardliners, but between senior and mid-level leaders within the army itself.

Conditions in eastern Europe in the 1970s and 1980s in many ways recall pre-revolutionary France. Robert Darnton has reconstructed the underground publishing industry that helped spread the Enlightenment's criticism and ideas throughout the realm in defiance of royal censors.[16] Similarly, a lively trade in *samizdat* literature throve during the Brezhnev years and helped spread dissident messages across the Soviet imperium. To continue the analogy, much like Montesquieu's use of metaphor in the *Persian Letters,* NVA historians used the image of the Prussian reformers as a device to criticize the regime without attacking it directly. Whereas Montesquieu invoked the image of his protagonist's family in Persia to illustrate the despotism of the Old Regime, the East German historians used the example of the Prussian reformers' resistance to oppression to criticize indirectly their neo-Stalinist government.[17] In both cases, to have attacked the regime directly would have elicited the wrath of the censors, or worse. Here is where we begin to see the divergence between the "establishment" version of Prussian military reform and the version the reformist minded historians promulgated.

The evidence shows a clear qualitative difference between those who supported the SED resistance to perestroika and reform in the 1980s, and those who did not. Reinhard Brühl, the chief of the Military History Institute and senior author of the official NVA history published in 1985, wrote after unification that the book suffered from a "fundamentally flawed basis" and that it served primarily as a "legitimizing historical representation."[18] In that book the reformers are treated cursorily as heroes because they gave priority to "throwing off the yoke of foreign domination" over "maintaining long-standing social conditions."[19] The part of the narrative referring to the necessary change to bourgeois society remained unchanged from the official 1970s version appearing elsewhere. Meanwhile, the authors devote twenty pages to informing the reader of how close a relationship between Volk and Armee had developed since 1956.[20] General Brühl later claimed that the authorities carefully controlled the content of this book, and so it forms a nice counter-example to what others, who managed to get around the party line, wrote at this time.

In the spring of 1987, the new Minister of Defense, General Heinz Keßler, published an article in Brühl's journal *Militärgeschichte* (Military History) extolling the "untiring" work of Comrade Erich Honecker "for the well-being of the people and a secure peace."[21] To justify the Party's actions, Keßler reached back into the past: Without a Party *hard as iron* and steeled in struggle, without a Party that enjoys the support of all those whom it actually represents, without a Party that understands what it is to pursue and influence the desires of the masses, it is impossible to successfully lead such a struggle.[22]

Keßler defines the "welfare of the people" as "defending the peace" and measures taken to ensure that nuclear war will not visit central Europe. One finds striking, in the midst of perestroika, the recurrence of references to "class conflict" and Western "imperialism, especially that of the United States and its NATO allies."[23] Nowhere does one find reference to the types of issues affecting East German society that the reformist officers address. Readers gain the impression of a society under siege, and of the Party's steely resolve to protect its citizens from Western imperialism and nuclear extinction. Reading between the lines, one also gets the feeling that the NVA's senior leadership sensed trouble brewing. This article illustrates an official effort to project the GDR's problems onto the "other" rather than accept responsibility for its shortcomings. Keßler further proclaims how much the SED, especially Comrade Honecker, has done to protect the "achievements under revolutionary and progressive socialism of the working class" for those whose faith may have begun to waver.

Some writers revised their work and slipped criticism of the regime into carefully worded passages in later editions. Edgar Doehler's book on tradition in the NVA appeared in two versions, one in 1979, and another in 1989. Both books treat the Prussian reformers and bring up familiar elements: the need for social reform, the necessity to rid Prussia of feudalism and foreign domination, the establishment of military ties to Russia as the foundation for the current alliance with the Soviet Union. In the 1979 version, the author also describes the close ties between the military and the Volk. Doehler laces his narrative with quotes from Franz Mehring[24] to illustrate how the Prussian reformers contributed to overthrowing the "exploitative classes" and eliminating the "Junker Army" in the interests of the people. Above all, Mehring's writings reflected the "positive relationship of the revolutionary workers' movement to the progressive traditions"[25] of the reformers.

Doehler's 1989 edition of *Military Traditions* includes some notable changes. Although it includes quotes from Friedrich Engels, it excludes Mehring completely. Whereas the lessons from the 1979 edition centered on arming the masses to defend the gains of socialism, in 1989 he emphasizes different themes. Doehler notes that the Prussian king and his reactionary Junker clique were "more afraid of the people than the foreign oppressor."[26] In a lengthy quote borrowed from Engels, Doehler argues that the "Volk had armed themselves without waiting for the most gracious permission of the nobility so that they might restore the national honor. Yes, the dictators compelled us quickly to the front; we quickly became the source of state power and appeared as sovereign people. That was the greatest gain of those years." In 1989, Doehler concludes that the military "must remain closely tied to the people, and that it acts as the military champion of the people's interests [...] and stands for social progress. [...] That is above all what the NVA has taken from the *Landwehr* (citizens' militia in the reformers' time) and included in its traditions."[27]

Doehler's later interpretation illustrates a shift in emphasis from justifying the Party's control of state power to indicating subtly where the power really resides. The reference to a monarch more afraid of his people than foreign domination points implicitly to the GDR's rulers. Doehler's use of Engels' words to cover his tracks recalls the Rosa Luxemburg counter-demonstration in 1987, where anti-government protesters disrupted the official celebration under the banner "Freedom is always the freedom of those who think otherwise." In the years of arms control, perestroika, and Gorbachev's "Common European Home," the image of the U.S. danger lost its saliency. The threat from the foreign oppressor, i.e. the U.S., is exchanged for the dangers inherent in the rule of domestic "dictators," whether the Junker-clique or the ruling SED. Doehler succeeded in altering his message over time to express a viewpoint calculated to resonate with those who had already felt doubts about the SED's willingness to act in the interests of the people.

The example of Count Yorck von Wartenburg illuminates another major concern of GDR military men during perestroika: the relationship with the Soviets. Already we have seen how some recognized the need to redefine who the enemy was. Karl-Heinz Riemann, a professor at the "Karl Liebknecht" Military Training College in Potsdam, published a 1987 article in *Militärgeschichte* that took the theme of "the domestic enemy" one step further. His article describes how Yorck, in defiance of his king, played a key role in effecting the transfer of Prussian troops to the anti-Napoleon coalition. Riemann warns against "blind loyalty to one's king." Later he pointedly quotes Yorck's reaction to the Prussian King's dismissal of the liberal reformers Karl von Grolman, Wilhelm von Humboldt, and Hermann von Boyen: "Unfortunately, in our Fatherland great shocks must first occur before we wake up to reality." Riemann concludes by praising "that rebellious Prussian General, who in 1812, against the will of his king, took an important step toward molding the comradely relationship between the German and the

Russian peoples." When set against the background of perestroika and the SED resistance to Gorbachev's call for reform, the message seems patent.[28]

A final point for illustration concerns the need for internal reform of the military and democratization. Perestroika demanded social restructuring and greater democratization. Although the SED resisted such reform, there were those in the NVA who believed that the period of the Prussian reformers required above all further research into the role of the armed forces and into the relationship between the masses of the people and the armed forces. The efforts in a succession of German states toward a democratic form of bourgeois military affairs deserve closer attention.[29]

By 1988, military historians began to spend more time investigating the relationships between army and Volk, even going so far as to study the Bundeswehr example of *innere Führung,* or civil-military relations in a democratic state.[30] Clausewitz's study of French society to discern how the Napoleonic armies achieved successes over the rest of Europe provided them with another paradigm for studying civil-military relations. The historians discerned that Scharnhorst had originally identified the source of Prussian misfortunes as "woven deep within the internal relationships of the coalition armies who met in the French Revolutionary Wars and those of the French Nation."[31] Clausewitz built on Scharnhorst's foundation and identified reform of Prussian society as the antidote. But curiously, one East German author pointed directly to Clausewitz's understanding of socio-economic conditions as key to his success in determining why the French were superior to everyone else. Clausewitz had considered it most important, in the course of the reforms, to give the peasantry more property. Once the way to free property ownership was opened, which was in the true economic interests of the Prussian state, the defense readiness of the peasantry rose.[32] The NVA historians used this as more evidence that liberalization would strengthen the state.

In Clausewitz's eyes, it remained essential to harness the power of the Volk, for ultimately they provided the necessary leverage to defeat Napoleon. In the end they, that is, the Volk, brought the Prussian state back from the dead. The lessons from French Revolutionary experience suggested the enduring importance of popular support for state survival. The transition to the liberal bourgeois society proved important for the Prussians, but it remained up to the King to keep his contract with the Volk, and to retain their support. Whereas for Clausewitz the "holy trinity" had comprised "king – army – people," the SED had revised his concept with "Party – army –

people."[33] The underlying principles remained relatively unchanged over a century and a half.

Conclusions

The NVA suffered from many of the same problems that plagued East German society. Since Unification, former East German military historians have reported that, as the GDR's crises intensified, many military intellectuals experienced a crisis of purpose. That *Sinnkrise* reflected a growing sense of confusion over the NVA's mission as a conventional armed force in the nuclear age as well as the deterioration of East German society. As East German society grew more restive, especially after 1985, it became increasingly apparent that the NVA's primary mission would be to maintain civil order. With that in mind, it appears as though some in the intellectual vanguard of the NVA grew concerned about the future relevance of the NVA as an institution and sought an outlet to express their concerns.

These men addressed their concerns through their writings. Just as the self-identification of the NVA as a Soviet invention had to be replaced with a German identity, the example of the Prussian reformers provided a metaphor for Soviet-led perestroika. The close ties with fraternal Russia evolved into a call to support the type of reform that the contemporary SED resisted. As superpower tensions eased in the 1980s, the SED replaced the West as the enemy of the people. Finally, employing the words of Clausewitz and Yorck, the historians could press their call to reform without interference from the authorities.

This is not to say that the Nationale Volksarmee was a democratic movement like *Neues Forum* or *Demokratische Aufbruch*. Far from it. What I am suggesting is that even in a "tool of the Party" like the NVA, there were those who began to have their doubts and who tried to do something positive to try and improve things. Wolfgang Scheler attributes the army's restraint in 1989 to the *Sinnkrise* dating back to the missile deployments of the late seventies. At this point in my research, I am not so sure that I would go that far; however, it appears as though we should take his claim that there were "little groups" of disillusionment seriously. What is important is that by the mid-eighties the NVA appeared to be experiencing the first stages of a cultural shift, one that the vast majority of East Germans had begun to experience long before 1989. How far it developed among the officer corps requires further research. However, it is encouraging to note that even among those granted privilege in a society like the GDR, there are a few who can see beyond their immediate self-interest and recognize the need to improve their society. Although typically few in number, they are often the harbingers of a larger movement to come.

When the test came in 1989, the hope for the future resided with the Volk who were pushing for social reform,[34] and not with the Party, which clung tenaciously to its corrupt, oppressive, and inefficient neo-Stalinist system. The precedent lay with the Prussian military reformers of 1807-1813. Only by standing aside during the popular demonstrations in 1989 and letting the will of the people play itself out did the NVA represent the interests of the Volk. In November 1989, the NVA took a major step toward legitimizing its claim as a *Volksarmee*. Ironically, in doing so it laid the groundwork for its dissolution.

Notes

[1]The literature on the GDR in general is not yet mature, but for a start see the following: John Torpey, *Intellectuals, Socialism, and Dissent: The East German Opposition and Its Legacy*, Minneapolis: University of Minnesota Press, 1995); Mary Fulbrook, *Anatomy of a Dictatorship: Inside the GDR, 1949-1989*, Oxford: Oxford University Press, 1995), 45; Timothy Garton-Ash, *In Europe's Name: Germany and the Divided Continent*, Oxford: Oxford University Press, 1994; Charles S. Maier, *Dissolution: The Crisis of Communism and the Collapse of East Germany*, Princeton: Princeton University Press, 1997.

[2]Paul A. Koszuszek, *Militärische Traditionspflege in der Nationalen Volksarmee der DDR: Eine Studie zur historischen Legitimation und politisch-ideologischen Erziehung und Bildung der Streitkräfte der DDR*, Frankfurt a.M.: Haag & Herchen, 1991, p. 150.

[3]Reinhard Brühl, "Carl von Clausewitz – Patriot und Militärtheoretiker," *Einheit* 35, no. 3 (1980), 317.

[4]See Gerhard Bogisch, "Zu einigen Aspekten der Traditionspflege in der NVA." *Zeitschrift für Militärgeschichte* 8, no. 4 (1969) 413-14.

[5]Hansjürgen Usczeck, "Die Nationale Volksarmee und Scharnhorst," *Militärgeschichte* 11, no. 6 (1989), 711; Erich Honecker, "Der Freundschaftvertrag mit der UdSSR ist von großer militärpolitischer Bedeutung für die Sicherung des Friedens in Europa und in der Welt," *Parteiarbeiter*, 1964, special edition 4, quoted in Ibid. (Translations into English are my own.)

[6]Bogisch, "Aspekte," 414.

[7]These are the two defeats that drove the Prussian Army from the war against Napoleon in 1806.

[8]Hansjürgen Uszcek, "Die Nationale Volksarmee und Scharnhorst," *Militärgeschichte* 11, no. 6 (1989), 713. The tradition of cooperation between the NVA and other socialist armies, especially the Soviet Red Army, remained a prominent and enduring theme until the end of 1989. It purported to legitimize the NVA and serve as the example upon which the NVA modeled itself. During perestroika, however, this relationship posed problems for East German officials. They reacted by sealing off the GDR and the NVA from reformist tendencies emanating from the Soviet Union.

[9]Michael J. Sodaro, *Moscow, Germany, and the West From Krushchev to Gorbachev*, Ithaca: Cornell University Press, 1990, p. 254.

[10]Vladislav M. Zubok identified three components of political legitimacy in the Soviet Union that also apply to the GDR: popular legitimacy, external legitimacy, and self-legitimacy. For our purposes I will focus on the self-legitimacy of the NVA officer corps, which entails a "set of beliefs that justify to rulers themselves their power and actions." As we shall see, its "self-legitimacy" eroded over time, and accounts in part for the GDR leadership's willingness to stand by and let the revolution in 1989 peacefully run its course. See Vladislav M. Zubok, "The Collapse of the Soviet Union: Leadership, Elites, and Legitimacy," in: Geir Lundestad, ed., *The Fall of Great Powers: Peace, Stability, and Legitimacy*, New York: Oxford University Press, 1994, p. 158.

[11]See Douglas A. MacGregor, *The Soviet-East German Military Alliance*, Cambridge: Cambridge University Press, 1989; A. Ross Johnson, Robert W. Dean, and Alexander Alexiev, *East European Military Establishments: The Warsaw Pact Northern Tier*, New York: Crane Russak & Co., 1982; Thomas Forster, *Die NVA: Kernstück der Landesverteidigung der DDR.*, Cologne: Markus Verlag, 1980. Additionally, most unclassified U.S. Department of Defense and official government assessments paint the NVA in a positive light. For example, see the Defense Intelligence Agency's *Soviet Military Power* series, published between 1982 and 1990.

[12]Vladislav Zubok described a similar process in the Soviet Union and ascribed it to increased contact with Western ideas and consumer society as a result of television, printed media, and official travel. The speed with which Egon Krenz and some of the younger generation SED leadership replaced Honecker and his associates during the fall 1989 crisis provides evidence that this occurred in the GDR. Evidence also exists that East German military intellectuals had similar access to the West. Looking in bibliographies of historical literature from the 1980s, one is struck by the inclusion of Western sources, including military historians from the Bundeswehr. Prominent military historians began to participate in conferences sponsored by Western military organizations. The director of the Military History Institute in Potsdam, Major General Reinhard Brühl, published a 1987 article in the West based on a conference paper. See Reinhard Brühl, "Historische Leitlinien für Erziehung und Ausbildung in der Nationalen Volksarmee und ihre Bedeutung für die

Zukunft," in: Detlef Bald, Paul Klein, eds., *Historische Leitlinien für das Militär der neunziger Jahre,* Baden-Baden: Nomos Verlag, 1988.

[13]Fulbrook, *Anatomy,* 39-40; Torpey, *Intellectuals,* 90-1.

[14]Professor Wolfgang Scheler, a philosopher and the Chair for Marxism-Leninism at the Friedrich Engels Military Academy in Dresden during the 1980s, began publishing on this topic in party organs in the early 1980s and continues to this day. See especially Wofgang Scheler, "Die Sinnkrise des Militärs. Eine geistige Vorbereitung für das Verhalten der NVA in der demokratischen Revolution" in: Andreas Prüfert, ed., *Die Nationale Volks-armee im Kalten Krieg: Militärisches Denken und Handeln an Schnittpunkten des Kalten Krieges. Zur Rolle der NVA in internationalen Krisen- und Konfliktsituationen,* Bonn: Karl-Theodor-Molinari-Stiftung, 1995, pp. 133-145, and *Von der marxistisch-leninistischen Lehre vom Krieg und von den Streitkräften: zum neuen Denken über Frieden, Krieg, und Streitkräfte,* Dresden: Dresdner Studiengemeinschaft Sicherheitspolitik (DSS) e.V., 1996.

[15]Reinhard Brühl, "Die Nationale Volksarmee der DDR. Anmerkungen zu ihrem Platz in der Geschichte," in: Detlef Bald, Reinhard Brühl, Andreas Prüfert, eds., *Nationale Volksarmee – Armee für den Frieden. Beiträge zu Selbstverständnis und Geschichte des deutschen Militärs 1945-1990,* Baden-Baden: Nomos Verlag, 1995, p. 27.

[16]Robert Darnton, *The Literary Underground of the Old Regime,* Cambridge: Harvard University Press, 1982, pp. 144-5.

[17]Charles de Secondat Montesquieu, *Persian Letters,* translated by John Ozell, introduction by William Graves, New York: Garland Publishers, 1972; Mark Hulliung, *Montesquieu and the Old Regime,* Berkeley: University of California Press, 1976, pp. 117-39, passim.

[18]Reinhard Brühl, "Klio und die Nationale Volksarmee. Gedanken zur Militärgeschichts-schreibung der DDR," in: Manfred Backerra, ed., *NVA: Ein Rückblick für die Zukunft. Zeitzeugen berichten über ein Stück deutscher Militärgeschichte,* Cologne: Markus Verlag, 1992, p. 251.

[19]Reinhard Brühl, *Armee für Frieden und Sozialismus. Geschichte der Nationalen Volksarmee der DDR,* East Berlin: Militärverlag der Deutschen Demokratischen Republik, 1985, p. 23.

[20]Ibid., 499-518; in a further example of the "cosy" relationship between the army and the people, the "unreconstructed" military historian Paul Heider argued consistently in 1975 and in 1985 that "for the first time in German military history, the century-long conflict between the army and the people could be swept away as a result of the creation of the socialist armed forces under the leadership of the working class and its Marxist-Leninist Party." Paul Heider, "Erbe und Tradition der DDR aus militärhistorischer Sicht,"

Militärgeschichte, 24, no. 1 (1985), 73; Paul Heider, "Militärgeschichte und lebendige Bewahrung der revolutionären Traditionen in der Klassenauseinandersetzung unserer Zeit," *Militärgeschichte* 14, no. 4 (1975), 391.

[21]Heinz Keßler, "Unermüdlich für das Wohl des Volkes und einen gesicherten Frieden. Zum militärpolitischen Wirken des Genossen Erich Honecker," *Militärgeschichte* 26, no. 3, (1987), 291. Whether Keßler realized it or not, it is interesting to note that one of Hitler's favorite phrases was "hard as Krupp steel" [hart wie Kruppstahl]. NVA leaders always went to great lengths to divorce themselves from the fascist past; from the outset, the Communist Party's anti-fascist tradition formed one of the central pillars of the SED's mythology.

[22]Erich Honecker, *Protokoll des VIII. Parteitags der Sozialistischen Einheitspartei Deutschlands,* vol. 1, East Berlin: Dietz Verlag, 1971, p. 34, quoted in ibid., 291.

[23]Keßler, "Unermüdlich," 300-2.

[24]According to Mehring's (1846-1919) biographical note in *Militärgeschichte,* he was "one of the most important historians and journalists after Marx and Engels. [...] Since 1914 he was in the first row of the German Left's struggle. [...] He made a considerable contribution to the creation of the group 'Internationale' as well as the formation of the Spartakus group [...] and therefore contributed to the preconditions that led to the creation of the German Communist Party." Mehring wrote extensively on eighteenth- and nineteenth-century German and Prussian history. The SED considered him a true socialist hero; the NVA honored his memory by naming a unit after him. See Heinz Karl Hoffmann, "Traditionsnamen in der Nationalen Volksarmee und in den Grenztruppen der DDR," part 3, *Militärgeschichte* 26, no. 1 (1987), 66.

[25]Edgar Doehler and Rudolf Falkenberg, *Militärhistorische Traditionen der DDR und der NVA,* East Berlin: Militärverlag der Deutschen Demokratischen Republik, 1979, p. 42.

[26]Edgar Doehler and Horst Haufe, *Militärhistorische Traditionen der DDR und der NVA,* East Berlin: Militärverlag der Deutschen Demokratischen Republik, 1989, p. 30.

[27]Doehler and Haufe, *Militärhistorische Traditionen,* 33.

[28]Karl-Heinz Riemann, "Graf Yorck von Wartenburg – preußischer General feudalem Konservatismus und Patriotismus," *Militärgeschichte* 26, no. 6 (1987): 586, 589, 589-91; Jeffrey Gedmin, *The Hidden Hand: Gorbachev and the Collapse of East Germany,* Washington: American Enterprise Institute Press, 1992, p. 47.

[29]Brühl, "Aktuellen Aufgaben," 525.

III. Modes of Memory

Karen Ruoff Kramer

Imag(in)ing the GDR: Gender in Projected Memory

"Projection" is here understood in the double sense of calculating the future and of casting film images onto a screen. Presuming that DEFA images will, with time, supplant the lived and recollected experience of 'real socialism' and hence become decisive for what the GDR will have become in the collective memory of a (possibly, eventually) united Germany, this chapter attempts to anticipate how gender relations in the GDR will "look" to future generations on the basis of five films of the middle decades (1960s and 1970s).

I. The Future of the Past

> "Blicke ich zurück in die ferne Kindheit, ist mir
> als sähe ich Bilder aus einem alten Film."
>
> Konrad Wolf [1]

The plethora of conflicting "memories" of the GDR in public representation and in recollected experience have the cumulative effect of canceling out the GDR altogether as a point of reference. Mutually exclusive positions, each emphatically true from one perspective or another, negate one another; each truth in this negation game is, by correlation, also a lie. *Bleibt was?*

The multifarious and contradictory things the GDR is remembered as having been to its contemporaries in East and West will be irretrievably forgotten when the locus of recollection shifts from human memory to the archive. Future historians will conjure and concoct a GDR from the meager residue of documents, texts, and preserved images and will proliferate their interpretations to the educated classes through the institutions of education, scholarship and the museum. But what the GDR will have come to be in *popular consciousness* will not be a product of the research of such historians. The cinematic image, broadcast via TV, will determine for the mass of people what, if anything, they associate with the term "GDR". The image is today already stronger than the word; our notions of the Weimar and Nazi periods are not only *illustrated* by, they are significantly *shaped* by the films from or about those eras – *The Blue Angel* and *Cabaret, Triumph of the Will* and Steven Spielberg's sundry variations.

The future "GDR" will "look" a lot like its movie images – if for no other reason than that they will be the only thing left for people to *see*. What people will see in them will depend in part, of course, on the exigencies of their respective social arrangements. Histories are constructed for present purposes, and present purposes change. In providing reassurances for, or challenges to, a present which wants explication, histories acquire a retroactively teleological structure. The arbitrariness of this process was nicely exemplified in the (dual) 750th anniversary celebration of the cities Berlin in 1987. For 750 years Berlin had been headed – so much was clear – toward the present. Fine... but *which* present? One Berlin had lumbered with historical–materialist resolve toward the first workers' and farmers' state on German soil; the other had marched inexorably towards its (sur)really–existing Capitalist city–state. The fact that these teleologies were mutually exclusive did not temper competing claims from either side of the Wall, it made them all the more adamant. The present finds the precursors it needs, just as children create the parents they need.

The images "canned" on celluloid with which we will here be concerned are instable, and not only in the sense that film stock disintegrates in the course of time. The shifting utilities of viewing contexts temper, distort, sometimes even invert, films' original contextual meanings. An experience from a seminar I taught on Weimar film demonstrates this effect of receptive inversion. Asked to interpret the introductory shot sequence of the 1932 Brecht/Dudow film *Kuhle Wampe,* in which a fleet of unemployed workers on bicycles race fruitlessly from one potential employer to the next in an industrial landscape of plant chimneys and "no help wanted" signs, a student replied that the sequence is clearly an *ecological* statement. The bicycles, he contended, present an alternative to the automobile, the chimneys symbolize industrial pollution. With due respect to the valid insights of reception theory, this student simply got it wrong; the cinematic composition of these images of 1932 had nothing to do with ecology. Brecht used the chimney more than once to symbolize the peaks and troughs of the business cycle; the smoking chimney was *good*, it signified employment. To hold forth about trees, on the other hand, was in Brecht's view an almost criminal undertaking in troubled times.[2]

DEFA films are particularly vulnerable to interpretive inversions of this sort, especially by viewers who had little first–hand experience of the GDR. Superficial encounters with the GDR often left the impression that it was a simple place with many secrets but no mysteries. Upon closer view it proved to be complex and puzzling. The better DEFA films provide a closer view, but they present the neophyte with sometimes inscrutable narratives. My students, having had no first–hand encounters with "real socialism," often have difficulty understanding central features of these films: Why did the

Party care if comrades got divorced? What's all the dancing about?[3] Or: Hey, what's so interesting about work?

Such questions signal the deep experiential divide which so sorely inhibits relations between east and west in contemporary Germany. Seldom has a people conducted such a massive and protracted lab experiment as the Germans did, under duress, in the postwar period: Put a fourth of the population in a box and change the rules; forty years later, open up the box and watch what happens. One can learn much about human behavior – e.g., about the differential effects of post–modern capitalism – by studying the experiment and its behavioral legacies. DEFA films are not simple mirrors of that Germany–in–the–box, but they do provide routes of access to a disputed history which continues to shape public and individual experience in the united Germany. Their images will play an increasing role in defining popular conceptions of what the GDR will have been. DEFA will have, if not the last word, the last image.

II. (Disad)Vantage Point

We shall in the following do blind screenings of several DEFA films – "blind" because film's constitutive component, the moving image, is not reproducible on the printed page. The reader's part in this paradoxical activity is blind viewing, for which we shall in the following provide various sight aids: short characterizations of the corpus from which films were selected in their sociopolitical contexts; synopses of the main characters, plots, and dilemmas depicted in the films; and a brief analysis of their gender representations. We shall be focussing on gender in partnerships as articulated, explicitly or by implication, in five films from the middle decades of the GDR (1960s and 1970s) whose artistic quality and thematic focus have already now set them apart from the mass of the some 750 feature films produced by the DEFA.

Two of the films under review *(Lots Weib, and Das Kaninchen bin ich)*, produced in 1965, were conceived and approved for production in the brief cultural–political hiatus which ensued after the erection of the Berlin Wall; the majority of films produced that year, including *Das Kaninchen bin ich*, came under sharp criticism at the Eleventh Plenum of the Socialist Unity Party (SED) and were confiscated before their release. This corpus bears aesthetic resemblance to Socialist Realism (condensation of conflicts, didacticism, relatively clear character types/masks, hero/foil structures), but aggressively exposes abuses and inconsistencies of real–Socialism while continuing to endorse its ideals and to acknowledge its historical legitimacy.[4] Prevalent themes of the corpus include anti–fascism; problems in the socialist workplace and in the organization of work;[5] conflicts between old communists, new bureaucrats, and youth; the West as «other»; corruption and hypocrisy (individual and institutional); the role of individuals in Socialism; gender problematics.

The three other films to be discussed here *(Bis, daß der Tod Euch scheidet, Der Dritte,* und *Die Legende von Paul und Paula)* are *Gegenwarts– filme* from the corpus of 1970s subjectivist films (some of which were also forbidden for a time). Whereas these films touch on some of the themes prevalent in the 1965 films, they are more centrally concerned with the problems of private life in socialism: isolation and longing, the search for meaningful relationships, disintegration of the family, redefinition of gender roles, sexuality. Although the characters tend to be less type–determined than those in the films of 1965, the recurrence of the relatively self–sufficient heroine who yearns for a man capable of a sensitive and enduring partnership in effect forges a new character–type – one so frequently played by actress Jutta Hoffmann that one could name it after her. These films share with the (west) German literary genre New Subjectivity of the same era an increased authenticity and a focus on the private sphere as a locus of the political.[6]

III. Movements and Change

"Gender" was once a term used primarily in the contexts of grammar and biology. What moved the term onto the terrain of contemporary social discourse in western democracies was the feminist formulation of women's concerns in contexts of alterity. A real–socialist discourse on women's economic emancipation, invoked from the top down, was a salient component of GDR political culture from the outset, but development of an autonomous feminist movement was curtailed until the soft revolution of 1989/90. The lack of such a movement and its discursive paradigms led many western feminists to conclude that women in the GDR had made no notable progress toward emancipation.[7] Female figures in DEFA films were mockingly referred to as "socially romanticized *Stehaufmännchen*" (punching dolls that always manage to bounce back).[8] But the absence of a movement does not mean things aren't on the move; under conditions that impede the emergence of autonomous movements in the public sphere, change must be gauged by other indicators.[9]

A case in point: The fact that almost all GDR women of working age worked was, in the West, generally tossed aside as merely a function of an unproductive socialist economy. To be sure, over half of the real–socialist work force was female in the period covered by this study (a GDR propaganda flyer on women in socialism sites 50.8% in 1975, 51.2% in 1979);[10] approximately nine out of ten women of working age worked or were in professional training. The economy would have foundered without them. *And:* the fact *that* almost all women worked outside the home clearly changed not only their objective role and mode of participation in society but also the way they viewed themselves, what they hoped to achieve, and what constituted fulfillment. There is substantial evidence, massively underscored in these films and born out by the subjective experience of GDR women after unification, that the conditions of life in real–Socialism had profound effects on women's relative self–sufficiency, professional options, and structures of desire.

The official "emancipation of women", formally endorsed by the Party from early on, was strongly motivated by the need to maximize women's contribution in the productive sphere. The manifesto of the "Antifascist Women's Committees", established in May and June 1945 in the Soviet Sector of Berlin, called for the "active participation of women in public life and education, in the professions and the economy," and for massive re–training programs to qualify women in areas previously reserved largely for men; it called for equal pay for equal work, independent of gender and age.[11] It would, of course, be wrong to assume that all women, in those years, *wanted* to be "emancipated" in all of those ways. Indeed, as late as 1962 Walter Ulbricht felt called upon to address a convention of the Women's Committees with the following words:

> I realize that there are old attitudes around that contend women should, first and foremost, do so–called light work. But, dear Comrades, we can't build socialism with hairdressers alone. I, too, like a good coiffeur, but the most important and most interesting jobs are those in technology.[12]

The point is not that emancipation can be achieved by Party decree, nor that women's massive integration into the productive sphere and into "male" professions was primarily a result of an emancipatory project, nor indeed that GDR women could properly be called "emancipated." The dual burden of women in socialism was clearly immense, and their representation in positions of highest authority was virtually nil; vestiges of patriarchy were ever present, not *only* in but *also* in the nuclear family, that institution in which demands and expectations which found no satisfaction in the public sphere were often played out. But significant formal components or preconditions of emancipation were implemented in the GDR, and, despite the tenacity of sexist traditions in the family, in relationships, and in professional life, the behavior and attitudes of women did change markedly.[13] The frequent articulation of the problems of women in DEFA films attests to a foregrounding of gender issues in the experience and consciousness of the anticipated viewer.

IV. Family Matters

Or does it? It is not surprising that realist films produced in the country with one of the world's highest divorce rates should tend to represent the nuclear family as breaking or broken.[14] Two thirds of divorces granted in the GDR were initiated by women.[15] The disintegration of a two–parent family forms the central action of two of the five films we shall blind–screen here; in each of these films, it is the wife who indicts the marriage.

Lots Weib (1965)

Egon Günther's first film, Lots Weib (Lot's Wife), is a relatively early depiction of gender impasses in the family. Filmed in black–and–white with sometimes ironic camera techniques, this witty and urbane film succeeds in maintaining the subtle tension of tragi–comedy. An upbeat jazz theme marks the major points of transition, mirroring protagonist Katrin's creative energy and assertiveness while commenting bitterly on the sober realities with which she contends. Katrin is a sports teacher, her husband Richard a Captain in the People's Navy. Since Richard is more often at sea than not, Katrin raises her sons, with whom she interacts with playful fantasy and humorous warmth, as a usually–single parent. Richard enters the film on a short visit home. Their initial interaction is pleasant and intelligent; they have a well–appointed apartment, engaging children, and their interaction displays the easy wherewithal of social privilege without the coolness which sometimes attends it. A model family? Not so. After a few moments, Katrin asks Richard for a divorce; she reminds him that they don't love one another and never did, that she dreads his homecomings, knowing that when night falls she will have to sleep with him again. She tells him they both know it was a mistake ever to have married, and that it's time to draw the consequences. Richard, driven both by complacency and a desire to avoid scandal (i.e. the prodding inquiries of the Party and of his fellow officers), refuses; for him, such a relationship is an acceptable, functional arrangement. In conceding that theirs is not a great beaming love "like in a TV film", he dismisses Katrin's notion of love as naive and unrealistic. Richard asks how long she's wanted a divorce; she responds that it's been since she found out about his other women. He is taken aback for an instant, but immediately gains his composure – these things happen. He accuses her of jealousy. It's worse than that, she counters: in fact, she hardly cares. He appeals to her sense of responsibility to the children and to the society. "What about living a lie?" she retorts.

In order to leverage herself out of a marriage she has too little social clout to terminate (she knows that, given her husband's social position, a court would not likely grant her a divorce against his will), she intentionally commits a crime (shop–lifting), knowing that her husband is likely to find the scandal of staying married to a known criminal to be even more humiliating than divorce. She refuses to discuss her reasons for having committed the crime at her criminal trial, in the disciplinary hearing at her school, or in her divorce trial; the female judge in the divorce court senses, however, that something doesn't add up and probes until the true motive is revealed. The judge exposes Richard as having doubly failed: in having refused a divorce even though the marriage was devoid of love, then for divorcing his wife when she was in a tight spot. "Ich bin immer für die Frauen," says the female judge with a wink. Katrin is granted the divorce, but the price is high: she is suspended from teaching and sent "into production" for three years for the shoplifting offense. And what appears to be a budding relationship with a teacher who had the guts to support her during the disciplinary process crumbles as he, at the end of the film, walks off with a younger woman.

This 1965 film documents women's position of disadvantage in real–socialist society of the sixties. It exposes the double standard in divorce litigation, takes on hypocrisy and empty convention, and depicts the Party's "concern" for individuals in the work collective to be as manipulative as it is inept. Perhaps most importantly, it endorses Katrin's desire for a partnership that is more than just an expedient arrangement and thereby asserts that the degree of personal happiness is a valid measure of the relative success of real–socialist society.

While putting forward this progressive agenda, the film draws on traditional sexist conventions and Kino clichés. Katrin is a beautiful woman who styles her hair and dresses for effect. Her body is repeatedly filmed in a leotard as she masterfully executes gymnastics routines. Whereas these elements by no means replicate the sexist display of the female body recurrent in classical Hollywood cinema of the time, and whereas the gymnastics scenes could perhaps be read, instead, as validation of her mastery and physical strength, this heroine's body does seem to be displayed also for the male gaze. And if the spell of that gaze is partially grounded in castration fear, as psychology–based feminist film theory has contended, then Katrin's body drives it home – it scores *all* the goals in a handball game with her male students, who leave the field drained and exasperated. But if this film invites the male gaze, it also repeatedly undercuts it with ironic distancing techniques. The introductory sequence features dancing couples filmed at a 90 degree tilt; the camera thus captures the motion of seduction in jiggling horizontals—a projection of projection, if you will. Moments of weary intimacy between Katrin and Richard are shot in unconventional angles. These more and less subtle distancing devices and the flip musical theme establish a sovereign and anti–sentimental narrative tone, thereby under–cutting any inclination on the part of the viewer to view the dissolution of this marriage as lamentable.

Bis, daß der Tod Euch scheidet (1979)
The above–described incompatibilities are dwarfed by the conflicts presented in Heiner Carow's 1979 film, *Bis, daß der Tod Euch scheidet ('Til Death do you Part)*. The title of the film lends the opening sequence an air of foreboding: the credits are inscribed in red against a long–shot of foliage while the off–screen voice of a female justice–of–the–peace gently recites the socialist marriage vows:

> With the development of our society, new kinds of familial relations have emerged. Equal rights for man and woman and the educational possibilities in all fields are good prerequisites for structuring your marriage in an enduring and happy manner. You wish for a happy and harmonious marriage, based in mutual love, respect and fidelity [...]. These, your wishes, are also the concern of our society, at whose center the human stands. [...] I wish for you that in old age you are still united in love as you are today united in your hopes and wishes. 'Til death do you part.

The marriage thus commenced begins to deteriorate in the very first scene, at the wedding celebration. The husband, Jens, a seemingly gentle and sensitive construction worker, is visibly jealous and insecure. His wife, Sonja, a cashier in a supermarket, is modest, hard–working, caring; she defers in nearly all things to her husband, to whom she is devoted. But despite her acceptance of the support–role "wife", Sonja also wants a life of her own in the most mundane of senses: After giving birth to their son, she wants to go back to her job at the supermarket. Jens is outraged at this wish and smashes the dinner she has carefully prepared; he belittles her job and says she just wants to flirt with the customers. After he calms down, Jens pardons himself by describing how he had hated his mother's working when he was a child, and how he had yearned for nothing so much as one day having his own family with wife–mom at home. Sonja acquiesces, but she secretly enrolls in a continuing–education course, which she finishes in six months' time with excellent marks. When she proudly discloses this clandestine success to her husband (who has come home to find her a bit tipsy, dancing around in her wedding dress as she celebrates her success with a female colleague) he hits her and accuses her of dishonesty. She apologizes. Their marital conflicts become increasingly martial. Jens drinks often and heavily, beats Sonja on several occasions, and rapes her in a fit of possessive rage. When Sonja becomes pregnant with their second child, she secretly has an abortion. Sonja's mother and girlfriend urge her to leave Jens, but she keeps coping, constrained by a sense of duty (if *she* doesn't help him, she asks, who *will?*). The title of the film lurks for the duration as an ominous premonition in the viewer's mind; Jens tells Sonja more than once that if she ever left him he would kill her; she swears she never will. But it is, in the end, the caring, accommodating Sonja who nearly commits murder: When she sees her drunken husband mistakenly grab a mineral water bottle in which she stores household acid, she does not stop him from drinking it; he nearly dies. The close–call with death stabilizes Jens's behavior to a degree, but the relationship is beyond repair. The film ends with Sonja's public confession – at a friend's wedding party – to Jens and to all present that she knew there was acid in the bottle when he drank it. Tormented by guilt (and presumably also afraid to deliver herself into her husband's hands after revealing the truth), Sonja turns herself in to the police.

Bis, daß der Tod... breaks with western Kino cliché in depicting the violent husband not as a macho from whom one might expect such behavior, but rather as a boyish young man who suffers from self–doubt of nearly psychotic magnitude. Nor is he depicted as being an "asocial element", a rowdy, or a saboteur on the model of earlier DEFA typecasting of the violent male.[16] The figure is thus less easy to vilify than the above exercise in blind viewing might suggest. Likewise, Sonja's contributions to her own victimization undercut the viewer's ability to endorse her fully. Although Sonja has grasped the opportunities of the empowered socialist woman as asserted in the marriage vows (professional life, further education), these "prerequisites for [...] structuring [...] marriage in an enduring and happy manner" threaten hers to the core. They collide not only with her husband's traditionalist behavior and attitudes but also with her own. Although Sonja is undoubtedly the stronger and better person in this marriage, central aspects of her character are indicted – her avoidance of confrontation, her servile "caring", and her inability to act (even the "act" of would–be murder is passive).

A flat reading of this film could hold that Sonja's cardinal error is to stay with a man who impedes her contribution to the socialist project. But the complexity of the characters counter–indicates that reductionist reading; although the social parameters of gender equality posited in the marriage vows explicitly form the contrastive backdrop for this catastrophic partnership, the tragedy which ensues is more personal than social. The elusive dream is, simply, happiness. There is a social component, to be sure – the anguish is grounded in *Ungleichzeitigkeit* (non–contemporaneity), in a fateful mix of new expectations and left–over constraints – but the focus is on *individual* suffering. The film's strength lies in its candor, not in an idealized role model of the new woman. Sonja's tragic flaws (traits in and of themselves worthy of emulation: compassion, adaptability, a desire to give of herself) buttress a patriarchal model which persists in times which require (and are purported to enable) a radical redefinition of relations. The fact that she facilitates her own victimization does not, as some have contended, reduce her husband's culpability.[17]

V. «Emancipated, but without a man...»

A strikingly large number of DEFA *Gegenwartsfilme* of the sixties and seventies feature a single woman as protagonist.[18] The female protagonists of two of the films selected for review here are single mothers in search of the sort of male partner the wives in the above described films wish they had but don't, and one film is about a single woman having an affair with a married man who appears to be the kind of man all the protagonists long for but turns out not to be. In all five films, the heroines find their previous or current male partners unacceptable; but instead of giving up on men altogether, they continue to yearn or search for a man who fits the bill.[19]

Das Kaninchen bin ich (1965)

Kurt Maetzig's *Das Kaninchen bin ich (I'm the Rabbit)* recounts the story of the orphan Maria, a beautiful young woman of proletarian origin who works as a waitress at a bar, having been denied entrance to the university because her brother was sentenced to prison for political reasons never specified in the film. Maria falls in love with her brother's judge, Daster, a married man who secretly sets her up in his *Datscha* while she convalesces from a malnutrition–induced back ailment. Maria has myriad negative experiences with men. She recollects having been seduced by Uli, her sports teacher (of whom her off–screen voice says he belongs on the police department's black–list of criminals who get off scott free). She constantly has to fend off the advances of male customers in the bar where she works, commenting: "In the half year that I've been running around this place [I've had] about a thousand offers, but I stay firm – though it would sometimes be easier just to go ahead and sleep with them, in order to get them off my case." Her brother brutally beats her, angry that she has taken up with his judge. Daster seems to be different, a sensitive and charming man of balanced temperament. In the course of the film, however, he is revealed to be an unprincipled opportunist whose sentencing is inspired not by the spirit of justice but by opportunism: He's a hard–liner when the line is hard, then attempts to use Maria (through a mock suicide attempt) to enable a professional about–face when the political climate thaws. The film ends with a final jab at the sexism of GDR men: Having been admitted to the university after all, Maria is pulling a cart of her belongings through Berlin traffic toward a room of her own; while her off–screen voice triumphantly fills in the entries on the questionnaire for university enrollment, the on–screen image shows her warding off yet another advance by a random male. Her final words answer the question on citizenship with an emphatic "German Democratic Republic!" This last line reads rather like a political concession to the censors, but it is rendered forcefully in a way which, instead of equivocating on the film's critical stance, asserts Maria's intention of creating a socialist society worthy of the name.

In *Das Kaninchen bin ich* (as in Frank Beyer's film of the same year, *Spur der Steine)* sexism and gender discrimination, while articulated with a candor striking for the times, were embedded in a broader criticism of the incongruities of the socialist project (opportunism, corruption, a persistence of class privilege, political abuse of the justice system), with the consequence that these films, unlike *Lots Weib,* were withheld from the public. Maria's problems are rooted not only in traditional gender inequities but also in systemic ills whose transformation seemed to many artists and intellectuals – in that brief cultural thaw which ensued between building of the Berlin Wall and the deposing of reformer Nikita Khrushchev – imminent.[20] That optimism, which resonates in the final sequence of the film, proved illusory.

Der Dritte (1971)

Egon Günther's film *Der Dritte (The Third Man)* depicts a female protagonist's relationships with three men (two ex– and one potential). It is at the same time a film about women in the absence of men: women in a Lutheran convent, women whose men have left them, daughters in early puberty. The film begins with what appears to be a black–and–white documentary about a computer center in which a male technician describes a compiler; at the end of the sequence, the camera focuses on the back of a woman standing at the computer, pans down her legs and stops at her high–heeled shoes. A women exits the computer center into the space of urban Berlin, filmed in color; it is the protagonist, Margrit. We see what she sees: streets, bikes, busses, traffic lights. She is one person in a nameless mass. The moment she enters her apartment she blankly switches on the TV, then asks/scolds herself aloud: "Du hast doch keine Angst –?" ("Come on – you're not afraid now, are you?"). Margrit's herstory is recounted in a series of flashback sections with headings: the death of her mother (in which female relatives abscond with the corpse's clothing); her youth (as an orphan in a Lutheran convent, which includes suggestion of lesbian temptation); her first partner (a chemistry teacher who seduces her in her blue FDJ shirt and is then too cowardly to admit having fathered her first child); her second partner (a sensitive blind pianist who flees to West Berlin when he is not admitted to the conservatory; he asks her to follow with their – her second – child; she does not). Two sections are devoted to her friend from the factory, Lucie. Lucie and her boyfriend have broken up; she visits Margrit and explains that she, too, is now alone. During the visit they comfort one another and kiss in an almost lesbian embrace that suggests one option for addressing loneliness, but they break off with a sigh: "We have all rights – emancipated, but without a man."

   The now–time narrative punctuated by the flashbacks has introduced us to a man who works at Margrit's factory and who has caught her attention. We sense, correctly, that he will become the third man in her life. She is intensely interested in him, but does not show her interest; she stalks him and even looks up his mother to find out more about him. She twice follows him onto the train he customarily takes to the countryside to go hiking, but when she ends up in his compartment she pretends the encounter is accidental.

When she accepts his second invitation to go hiking, they fall passionately in love within the hour. He comes home with her; her two daughters walk into the room. "Oh – there are three of you..." he says; the viewer detects ambivalence. Margrit embarks on an emphatic, rapidly–spoken monologue while he sips coffee off–screen, having given up trying to get a word in edgewise:

> I've been working in prognostics for two years. My tool is the CPU, computer... I'm a mathematician. I work, think and feel in harmony with the technical–scientific niveau of the socialist scientific–technical revolution. But when a man appeals to me – when I need him in my life, when I want him – I most likely still make a fool of myself if I say so. No, if I am in love I have to keep my love a secret, have to hide my desire very deep, for it might bother him. Only *he, he* can take that liberty. Just like in grandmother's times, I have to sit there well–behaved and wait for benevolent fate [her daughters, bewildered, turn to leave at this point, but she stops them:] – Stay here, stay here, you should listen to this – wait for benevolent fate that I will be noticed, that he will find me desirable. I can only distinguish myself in his eyes by silent restraint, by strictly waiting–it–out in matters of love. Even if he embraces me it is still advisable to mince, to lower my eyes and to say "no" for the time being. [Frank display of interest on the part of the woman] is something he doesn't want, it puts him off. He's had experience in these things. And was raised that way. And his father and mother, too.
>
> Do you understand that I don't *want* that, that I can't *do* that? That I feel untruthful if I board the same train, just by accident, and make up a story about a sick girl–friend so that you won't notice that I'm following you? I want you to see me, I want you to recognize me. I didn't want to play that game but I did, I did... I played that game.

The "game she played" is the ritualized double standard; she recognizes its absurdity and tips her hand immediately, once she's won. Number three is more intrigued than put off by this speech, which is less a confession than a test. He passes it. They marry. It's a joyous, lively celebration. As he dozes, his head in Margrit's lap, during the wedding party, having enjoyed too many spirits, Lucie looks him over and comments that he looks a little like *both* of Margrit's daughters. That's fitting, Margrit quips, "after all, he *is* their first father."

For a film which makes such sobering observations on the state of male–female partnerships, *Der Dritte* is disconcertingly upbeat. The single–mother Margrit is lonely but whimsical. She is convincingly self–sufficient; she wants a man and goes after him, and once she's got him she promptly makes it quite clear just who she is: not a passive mate but a self–assertive and outspoken woman with a clear agenda. She is not one to trade her identity for a wedding ring. We never learn the third man's given name, and his unusual family name is mumbled so quickly that the viewer can't understand it: a generic male to be numbered, not named. Number three is manly but reserved, a sensitive man who takes walks alone in the woods. We get only one closer glimpse of this man, independent of his union with Margrit: at a Party conflict hearing, where he takes the side of the accused (a corpulent father of eight who's in trouble for continually falling asleep on the job and nods off even during the hearing), arguing that the man's significant contribution to the socialist project is to produce children and implying that if that occupation prevents his getting sufficient sleep at home, then he should get it at work. This scene suggests that the third man is a thoughtful, unconventional and generous fellow who might prove to be a genuine counterpart for Margrit. This film ends optimistically but with an open, rather than a decisively happy, end (which would tend to obviate the gender critique articulated through Margrit's previous experiences). Will this relationship prove to be as rewarding as it portends? "Well," says Margrit with a wry smile in the final words of the film, "we'll just have to see – Right, Lucie?" No trepidation, no desperate hope. The heroine has shown that she can manage perfectly well alone; she will do so again, if needs be.

Die Legende von Paul und Paula, 1974

The final film we will consider here is Heiner Carow's *Die Legende von Paul und Paula (The Legend of Paul and Paula)*, one of the best–known DEFA films of the 1970s. The first and final shots of the film show the demolition of old housing blocks, being blown away to a soundtrack by the popular rock–band "Die Pudhys." Paula, a single mother with a son and a daughter from different fathers, has a monotonous job at a supermarket. She has been multiply disappointed by men. All we know about the father of her first child is that he is no longer around; early in the film, she finds the father of her second child making love to another woman when she returns from the hospital with their newborn baby. Paula is a lonely and unhappy woman; she broods alone at home, gloomy over the emptiness of her life: "Go to bed at nine. Sleep, work; then sleep and work again." She yearns for a man and instills this value in her small daughter; their bedtime dialogue:

"You must sleep now."
"Why must I sleep?"
"So that you will grow up to be big and beautiful!"
"Why do I need to be big and beautiful?"
"So that you can get a man – later."
"And why do I need to get a man?"
"Why, why, why? Why is a banana bent?"[21]

Paul is a shy, educated, sexually inexperienced man who is ensnared by Ines, a sexy, callous woman he meets at a traveling fair. Paul loves her, but she is interested only in his social status. They marry and have a child. Ines is contemptuous of Paul and takes lovers. Even after he catches her in bed with one of them, Paul stays, but he grows bitter and ever more lonely. Paul and Paula eventually get together; theirs is an intense and desperate love, but Paul is unwilling to divorce his wife out of solicitude for his son and because he fears it will damage his career (he is a *persönlicher Referent* in what appears to be the Foreign Ministry). They can still be friends, he offers. Paula is devastated; in the depression which follows the break–up, she sends her children off to an afternoon movie instead of taking them to the zoo as she had promised, and her son is killed crossing the street. Paul soon realizes that his life is empty without Paula and desperately tries to win her back; she won't have him, holding him partly responsible for the death of her son. She entertains an offer of marriage from a kindly, elderly suitor, whom she finds physically repulsive; she is appalled at the thought of marrying him but does not want to live alone. Paul intervenes; he camps out on Paula's stairwell in drunken despair, begging to be let in. He finally breaks the door down with an ax borrowed from a nosy neighbor (who has been observing this relationship with that furtive curiosity fostered by Berlin stairwells). Love triumphs – to the cheers of all the neighbors, who come to witness the reunion: Lovers finally united in what promises to be a beautiful, lasting relationship. A happy end? Not so. Within a jump–cut or two, Paula becomes pregnant, refuses an abortion despite her doctor's warning that she will not survive another birth, and dies bearing the child.

Having taken the risk in full awareness of its probable consequences, Paula's all–or–nothing wish to bear the child amounts to a death wish. Paul and Paula's love was bigger than life, and life proved too small to accommodate it. A happy ending would have trivialized the problems to which the film gave voice and would have tipped the balance in the direction of kitsch. But the sad end is not entirely tragic; the film ends with a pan shot of Paul in bed with his arms around three children (his son, Paula's daughter, and their common child): The father positioned at the center of domestic responsibility.

This aesthetically complex and uneven film integrates hyper–realism, surrealism and symbolism. The depiction of Paula's living conditions are soberly realistic: a poor woman who lives behind a cinema, she lugs coal, bucket by bucket, walking with an ever grimier face past posters of glamorous movie stars (a touch of self–referential irony, to be sure, but also an underscoring of the humble world being depicted in *this* film). Her contribution to socialism – her "professional life" – consists in paying out deposits on empty bottles to thirsty construction workers who subject her to sexist remarks. The hyper–reality of this milieu is undercut, however, by Paula's spontaneity and child–like fantasy, often rendered in surrealistic or absurdly comic scenes that burst the sober boundaries of her lower class life. After she meets Paul, for example, her mundane world is instantly transformed. Still in the thrall of their first night together, she starts her shift with only her slip on, to the whooping delight of the bottle–bearing construction crew. After donning her uniform, she breaks out in song at the cash register and all the customers in the supermarket join in (one of the wittiest commentaries on mug–shot socialism in DEFA film). Her fantasies of marrying Paul play in a mythic setting, as does one of their encounters. The symbolic register is apparent in the building detonations (suggestion that one cannot create without destroying), and in the names of the dual hero/ine – Paul and Paula. The name–pairing suggests a symmetry of kindred souls; indeed, there is something almost sibling–like about their interaction. More interesting for present purposes, however, is the fact that the names echo what is, among the films here described, a new quality: a mutual, instead of a one–sided, recasting of gender relations.

Whereas the ambitious aesthetics of *Paul und Paula* are not uniformly successful, the film is striking in its positing of a symmetry of desire. Paul and Paula's "legend" validates thereby the relationship–ideal which the heroines in the other films miss: a buoyant partnership in which the partners' needs match. This is possible because Paul learns from Paula. He follows her lead, or, in the words of the theme–song's refrain, he lays himself "in her shadow" – and is thereby infected by her courage. When Paul entreats Paula to let him into her apartment after their breakup, he first pleads, "this is about *you*, Paula"; then he pauses, reconsiders, and concedes softly: "No, Paula – it's about me." This is a concession: He recognizes and acknowledges his need for Paula. The only other film in which the male lead comes even close to such interactive responsiveness is *Der Dritte;* but unlike Paul, the "third man" is a marginal character until the very end of the film and remains a largely unknown quantity; the viewer can only surmise whether Margrit's hopes are warranted, since the film ends at the beginning of their relationship. *Paul and Paula* enacts the transformation of a partnership initially constrained by convention (as opposed to merely positing an abstract alternative to the real), but does not subject it to the test of time.

VI. Patterns and Puzzles

The DEFA films described above depict a private sphere characterized by conflicts (particularly in the eroding nuclear families) and loneliness (especially in the single–mother families), tension between traditional gender roles and new economic realities, and a search for meaning and happiness. The films are political by omission and displacement; they refuse to rehearse the stock consciousness–building themes of an overly politicized society, and they assert that subjective happiness is a measure of the success of the socialist project.

The particular happiness here under scrutiny is that of women, at once a heavily gendered issue and a litmus test of the socialist project *per se*. In the words of scriptwriter Wolfgang Kohlhaase (referring to the film–heroine he created in *Solo Sunny),* "Men adapt much more readily to conventions that originate from times when men exclusively had the say. Women, in their demand for change, signal much more clearly a general need for change in society."[22]

The new woman was real–socialism's product and its touchstone: Maria was not only the *Kaninchen* (rabbit), she was a *Versuchskaninchen* (guinea pig). Because GDR women shouldered the lion's share of subjective adaptation under real–Socialism, they reflected the specific impact of systemic change on individual experience more fully than did men. Full involvement in production was new to women; they entered that world without being able to abandon the very traditional world of reproduction. It was more than a dual burden, it was a double bind. In giving voice to women's frustrations and desires, the films variously indict and validate real–Socialism's ability to enable the new sort of interpersonal relations endorsed by the utopian ideal. This metonymic use of heroines to reflect on the relative success of the real–socialist project in individual lives critiques by implication the utopia deficit not only in male consciousness but also of the society as a whole.

Gender policy in the GDR was internally contradictory, caught between anachronism and progress. Formal prerequisites for emancipation (near equality in professional qualification and professional life, for example) effected relative economic self–sufficiency and unleashed forces beyond the direct control (and to some extent beyond the perception) of the Party, the

State, the men, and the women. Demographers and planners had a tiger by the tail: It was essential that women work, and it was also essential, given the declining birthrate, that they bear more children. Measures adopted to address one problem often aggravated another. Incentives were put into place to encourage couples to produce children (loans, child money, priority access to housing). But policies with predictably opposite effects were adopted as well: legal abortion with no questions asked and at state expense, easy divorce.

Family policy continued to be based on the assumption that women bore primary responsibility for the reproductive sphere.[23] To be sure, extensive institutional support structures were put in place to facilitate their combining productive and reproductive work (child–care facilities, centralized laundry service, additional vacation days and sick–leave for mothers, etc.). But these services and policies, well–intentioned though they appear to have been, may have reinforced the traditional division of labor in the family rather than destabilizing it, easing "women's" burden sufficiently that male partners could continue to opt out.[24] The necessity of change in the familial division of labor was not officially acknowledged[25] (a telling omission in a society which was not known for mincing its words when it came to consciousness–building exercises) and the lack of an independent women's movement hindered the formulation of such demands from below.

The situation in the West was just the reverse. On the one hand, lower levels of professionalization and economic self–sufficiency, a more limited support infrastructure; on the other, a public discourse initiated by women's groups which overtly challenged traditional gender roles and exploitative practices in public and private domains. K. Weller has asserted that

> [i]n contrast to the West, where the practice of reform often lagged behind rhetoric, in the GDR practice ran ahead of theory. [...] We can therefore talk of "forced emancipation" in the GDR, where a lack of democratization prevented the subjective realization of liberation – although in the West the opposite situation prevailed, resulting in pseudo–emancipation.[26]

Western critics who judge DEFA films on the basis of critical paradigms of feminist–engendered discourse may be disappointed, perhaps even annoyed. DEFA films aren't P.C. But precisely the seeming incompatibilities with Western discourses and approaches make DEFA films useful vehicles for comprehending the differential experience and attitudes of women in the GDR/new Länder. Furthermore, their study prompts a rethinking of some assumptions of Western feminism and provides challenging case studies for feminist film theory.

These films present more puzzles and challenges to the Western viewer than can be addressed in this brief study.[27] Let us address, in closing, one enigmatic characteristic of the films surveyed, namely the fixation of the strong, self–sufficient heroine on the elusive male partner. The ideal of the rewarding, lasting partnership figures in these films as a perpetual point of reference. That the heroines should prefer a rewarding partnership to a bad one or to living alone is not surprising, in and of itself; but the status of longing in these films is sometimes so pervasive that the elusive male seems to be quasi–constitutive of the self–identity of the woman.

How can we account for the incongruity between the self–sufficient heroine and her hankering for a man? Does it confirm the western German commonplace that the GDR was an open air museum of traditional German values despite the socialist rhetoric? Does it reflect the biases of male directors and scriptwriters who, experiencing the problems of women only vicariously, got it wrong? Does it indicate an objective shortage of acceptable partners in the GDR, a function of women's having moved more quickly and further beyond traditional gender roles and thereby developing standards and expectations few males could meet? Does the elusive Herr X perhaps figure as a functional abstraction from the *misère* of really–existing relationships, rather than as an actual object of yearning? Does he instantiate the disparity between real–Socialism and its founding myths? Each of these posited explanations has some degree of plausibility, but none of them alone offers a compelling explanation.

The "yearning–for–a–man" in these films must be positioned in an aesthetic negotiation of proxied reference, but without thereby being reduced to a mere *Stellvertreterdiskurs* (stand–in) for the shortcomings of real–Socialism. Women's (full) emancipation was a salient component of the holistic utopian projections which legitimated the real–Socialist project from the outset (the transformation of productive relations being only the material basis for the transformation of human life). The rendering of its shortfall in cinema is a metonymic device, the part which indicates (also) the social order as a whole: "Heldinnen stehen stellvertretend für die Entwicklungs-möglichkeiten des Menschen im Sozialismus überhaupt."[28] Granted – so long as one bears in mind that they are thereby also "standing in" for themselves! The incessant longing for (and pervasive absence of) the compatible male encoded in these films, far from rehearsing a backwardness in women's attitudes, indicts the asymmetry of gendered identities and practices in real–Socialism: "idealized expectations of men on the part of women, traditionalist images of woman on the part of men, a clear divergence of the images of one's own and the other gender, led to mutually false expectations."[29] These DEFA heroines do not long for just *any* man, they yearn for fitting counterparts. The men they meet or marry are unacceptable because these males' conceptions of a satisfactory partnership are posited on a woman who no longer exists.

Notes

[1] Introductory caption of *Die Russen kommen* (Heiner Carow, 1968/1987).

[2] "Wirklich, ich lebe in finsteren Zeiten! /...Was sind das für Zeiten, wo / Ein Gespräch über Bäume fast ein Verbrechen ist / Weil es ein Schweigen über so viele Untaten einschließt!" Bertolt Brecht, "An die Nachgeborenen," *Gesammelte Werke,* Vol. 9, Frankfurt a.M.: Suhrkamp, 1967, pp. 722–23.

[3] A question to which their professor has no compelling answer, but striking it is. Dance scenes (set in work collectives, bars, schools, weddings, private homes) are so frequent in DEFA films of the 60s and 70s that, when screening a film for the first time, one wonders when, not whether, the dancing will start. Films include *Lots Weib, Das Kaninchen bin ich, Karla, Spur der Steine, Paul und Paula, der Dritte, Berlin um die Ecke, Bis daß der Tod uns scheidet, Das Versteck, Die Russen kommen, Jahrgang 45.*

[4] The notable exception is renowned documentarist Wolfgang Boettcher's *Jahrgang 45,* which, though a dramatic film, is filmed in documentary style.

[5] See Karen Ruoff Kramer, "Representations of work in the Forbidden DEFA Films of 1965," in: Sean Allan and John Sandford, ed., *DEFA – East German Cinema 1946–1992,* Oxford: Berghahn Books, 1999, pp. 131–145.

[6] The term "New Subjectivity" was coined by western literary critics to celebrate literature's presumed withdrawal from political to private concerns; the "new subjectivist" authors, among them the first writers to emerge in the context of the feminist movement, rejected this reading of their texts, insisting that the private sphere was the real locus of the political. A similar (though differently motivated) shift is perceptible in DEFA films of the seventies. The frontal political indictments of the 1965 films had been terminated by direct state intervention, the locus of critical discourse displaced. "Diese Art Filme [...] gab's [danach] nicht mehr. Die neuen Leute kamen mit kleinen Geschichten. Sie wußten, was night geht [...]" (Frank Beyer, "Menschen in ihrer Zeit," *Film und Fernsehen,* 8/90, p. 10). For an excellent analysis of the complex interaction of public and private spheres in the GDR see Prue Chamberlayne, "Transitions in the Private Sphere in Eastern Germany," in: W.R. Lee and Eve Rosenhaft, *State, Social Policy and Social Change in Germany 1880–1994,* Oxford/New York: Berg, pp. 286–313.

[7] "After 28 years of existence it is clear to the GDR politicians and scholars that no new person has yet emerged as a result of the socialization of the means of production.[...] Women in the GDR have never fought openly for their rights. They were awarded rights as if they were favors" (Christel Sudau, "Women in the GDR," *New German Critique,* Nr. 13, Winter 1978, pp. 79–80). This informative study of the contradictory situation of women in real–Socialism is inhibited by its tendency to judge the relative emancipation of women only in terms of indicators developed in a western feminist paradigm, which impedes a nuanced understanding of the complex socio–psychological phenomenon under investigation.

[8] From the transcript of a post–unification film seminar on DEFA Frauenfilme, quoted by Andrea Rinke, "Models or Misfits? The role of Screen Heroines in GDR Cinema," *Triangulated Visions: Women in Recent German Cinema*, Albany: State University of NY Press, 1998, p. 217. Rinke's article provides an excellent contextualized treatment of female DEFA protagonists, including an extended analysis of two films from the decade following the corpus of the present study, *Unser kurzes Leben* (Lothar Warneke, 1981) and *Das Fahrrad* (Evelyn Schmidt, 1982).

[9] In the years since unification, at least some western feminists have begun to revise their negative estimation of the relative emancipaton of GDR women; in a 1988 interview, Alice Schwarzer had stated: "Natürlich gibt es in den sozialistischen Ländern zumindest auf dem Papier den Anspruch, daß die Frau auch ein Mensch ist, ein Anspruch, der nur sehr halbherzig eingelöst worden ist... Zwar haben die Frauen das Recht, die Hälfte der Berufsarbeit zu tun, aber die Männer haben nicht die Pflicht, sich die Hälfte des Privatbereichs an die behaarte Brust zu nehmen." In a 1998 *Emma* article, however, responding to the question of "warum Frauen in der deutschen Politik so groß rauskommen," Schwarzer praises the impact of East German women on politics in the united FRG: "Hinzu kommen die Frauen aus dem Osten. Die waren den Westmännern zunächst hochwillkommen, schienen sie doch keine Ahnung zu haben von dem so lästigen Feminismus. Doch siehe da, die Lebensrealität ist auch ein Stück Feminismus. Die in der DDR geprägten Frauen finden es mithin selbstverständlich, ein Recht auf Beruf und Kinderhilfe zu haben." Both interviews are excerpted in *Konkret*, Dec. 1998, p. 11.

[10] The photos printed in this flyer are telling: a half–size shot of a woman studying, a half–size shot of a woman working in technical production, and a full–sized shot of a couple playing with their toddler. (No publ. date, no title – these were presumably printed on a portion of the flyer that was torn off).

[11] Jutta Menschik and Evelyn Leopold, *Gretchens rote Schwestern: Frauen in der DDR*, Fischer Verlag: Frankfurt a.M., 1974, p. 13.

[12] "Ich weiß, daß es alte Auffassungen gibt, wonach die Frauen vor allem sogenannte leichte Berufe ausüben müßten. Aber liebe Genossinnen, wir können den Sozialismus nicht

nur mit Friseusen aufbauen. Ich bin auch für schöne Frisuren, aber das wichtigste und interessanteste sind gerade die technischen Berufe." Menschick/Leopold, p. 32.

[13] For a concise and differentiated review of the literature on the tension between emancipation and perpetuated patriarchy in the GDR see Chamberlayne, pp. 286–296.

[14] The GDR ranked fifth globally in divorce rates (Jutta Gysi, Dagmar Meyer, "Leitbild: berufstätige Mutter – DDR–Frauen in Familie, Partnerschaft und Ehe", in: Gisela Helwig/Hildegard Maria Nickel, eds., *Frauen in Deutschland 1945–1992*, Bonn: Bundeszentrale für politische Bildung, 1993). This volume is a very informative, statistically based and nuanced analysis of motherhood and family relations in East and West Germany.

[15] Sudau, p. 71.

[16] Such characters are recurrent but tend to be cast in supporting or minor roles; see especially*Berlin um die Ecke* (Gerhard Klein, 1965), *Denk bloß nicht, ich heule* (Frank Vogel, 1965), and *Spur der Steine* (Frank Beyer, 1965).

[17] Although the casting and texting reveal in each character a tense inner mix of contradictory traits, complicating the "battered wife and pugilant husband" scenario and impeding a stock response on the part of the viewer, Gisela Bahr's criticism that Carow shows a clear "bias toward the male hero [...]" is in my view unwarranted. She writes that "the injured Jens gets all the sympathy, while Sonja is seen as the perpetrator of a shocking, incomprehensible act, rather than as the battered wife who could bear it no longer." This reading suspends most of what has taken place on the screen for the duration of the film (see Gisela Bahr, "Film and Consciousness: The Depiction of Women in East German Movies", in: Sandra Frieden, Richard McCormick, Vibeke Petersen, Laurie Vogelang, eds., *Gender and German Cinema: Feminist Interventions, Volume I: Gender and Represen-tation in New German Cinema*, Providence/Oxford: Berg Publishers, 1993, pp. 125–139).

[18] In addition to the films discussed here, the reader's attention is drawn particularly to *Karla, Spur der Steine, Das Versteck, Unser kurzes Leben, Die Beunruhigung, Das Fahrrad, Die Schlüssel, Solo Sunny, Sabine Wulff, Der geteilte Himmel, Paulines zweites Leben*.

[19] Maria *(Das Kaninchen bin ich)*, is the sole exception; the youngest of the protagonists, she has broken off her relationship with Daster and is, at the end of the film, focussed entirely on building a new life; a partner is not, at this point, part of that project.

[20] Director Kurt Maetzig had met briefly with Khrushchev during his last visit to Berlin; Khrushchev reportedly urged him to embrace films with greater courage, "to abandon worn–out paths" despite the fact that he should reckon with critique in so doing. Christiane Mückenberger, ed., *Prädikat: Besonders schädlich*, Berlin: Henschel Verlag, 1990, p. 319.

[21] The original German is a well–known, rhymed slogan which loses much in translation –
"Warum ist die Banane krumm?" The phallic connotation is presumably intended.

[22] Wolfgang Kohlhaase, "Was heißt denn 'happy end'," *Film und Fernsehen* 1980/81, p.
15, cit. Rinke, p. 210. In a similar vein, Helke Misselwitz, explained that the primary
motivation for making her highly acclaimed documentary film, *Winter Adé,* was "that I
believe women's fate is the best indication of the quality of life in a society" (Karen
Rosenberg, "Goodbye to Winter: Women in the GDR – An Interview with Helke
Misselwitz," *International Documentary: The Newsletter of the International Documentary
Association,* Winter 1990, p. 6).

[23] "Die Familienpolitik der DDR war Frauen – oder, besser gesagt, Mutterpolitik." Jutta
Gysi, Dagmar Meyer, "Leitbild: Berufstätige Mutter – DDR–Frauen in Familie,
Partnersschaft und Ehe," in: Helwig/Nickel, *Frauen in Deutschland,* p. 139; the article is a
very informative analysis of the tense interface and tension between *Frauenpolitik* and
Familienpolitik in the GDR.

[24] E.g., Anita Grandke, specialist in family law at the Humboldt–Universität, while
endorsing the reforms of 1972 (which sought to facilitate the combination of motherhood
and professional life in the GDR with institutional incentives), criticized these reforms for
tending to prop up the traditional division of labor in the family (quoted by Gisela Helwig,
"Einleitung", Helwig/Nickel, *Frauen in Deutschland,* p. 17). Sudau detects this tendency as
well: "Certainly, such awards help women, but at the same time, women's dependence on
that kind of help is perpetuated; these subsidies do not even attempt to make child–care the
responsibility of both parents" (p. 75). Whereas there is concensus in the literature that the
primary burden of private sphere logistics and parenting continued to rest on women's
shoulders in real–Socialism, it is difficult to get a precise and definitive reading on
whether, or to what extent, the division of labor in household and parenting might have
been in flux. Gysi/Meyer endorse the consensus position while presenting interesting
sociological data which give one pause to wonder whether some shift in the division of
labor did occur (Gysi/Meyer, pp. 157–162).

[25] See Irene Dölling, "Gespaltenes Bewußtsein – Frauen– und Männerbilder in der DDR,"
in: Helwig/Nickel, *Frauen in Deutschland, 1945–1992,* p. 27.

[26] K. Weller, "Die Zwangsemanzipation, das Los des Feminismus, der Mythos von der
Doppelbelastung", in *Frauen im Umbruch? Feminismus im Aufbruch: Einspruch,*
Leipziger Heft 4, 1992, pp. 10–17, quoted by Chamberlayne, p. 294.

[27] To name just a few: How accurately do these films by male directors reflect GDR
women's attitudes and experience? E.g., does the scarcity of scenes depicting household
and parenting chores reflect the myopia of male directors; or does it suggest a higher
tolerance by East Germans of the old division of labor, or a more substantial involvement

of males in household work than the sociological literature reflects; or does it simply reflect a sense that such themes make for boring movies? To what extent were the films shaped – through inclusion or omission – by the need to pre–empt the censors? What smuggled messages does the western viewer not see that a GDR audience, sensitive to the specific filters of censorship, might have spotted "between the frames"? In what ways do the biases of the outsider impede our viewing? For example: even as we note the "lack" of feminist critical paradigms in the films, should we not be wary of reduplicating Freud's ill–conceived "penis envy", reducing difference to lack? To what extent do or do not these films rehearse the patriarchal strategies identified by feminist film theory? What would the answers to that question tell us about the society in which they were produced, and what would be the implications for theory?

[28] Hans–Rainer Mihan, "Sabine, Sunny, Nina und der Zuschauer," *Film und Fernsehen* 8 (1982), 12, quoted in Rinke, p. 209.

[29] "Idealiserte Erwartungen der Frauen an die Männer und traditionelle Vorstellungen der Männer von den Frauen, ein deutliches Auseinanderklaffen der Selbst– und Fremdbilder der Geschlechter, führte zu wechselseitigen Fehlerwartungen. [...]": Gysi/Meyer, p. 151.

Bernd Lindner

Medien der Zeitgeschichte: Die Aufarbeitung der DDR-Geschichte am Beispiel des Herbstes '89

Using the example of the treatment of the events of the autumn of 1989, this chapter shows that GDR history has been taken up in several distinct phases and through different media since 1990. The first phase, concurrent with the events themselves, was a process of self-understanding through the collection and preservation of artefacts from the peaceful revolution; its medium was the exhibition. The following, more market-oriented phase of political evaluation of the past lasted until 1995 and was based on the media of books and, later, of film and television. The third period of historicisation is still underway and occurs in two very different ways: repression of memory and musealisation.

Die Geschichte gescheiterter gesellschaftlicher Systeme läßt sich von zwei Enden her betrachten, von ihrem Beginn wie von ihrem finalen Schluß. Das Ende als Beginn der Analyse zu setzen, liegt um so näher, je überraschender der Zusammenbruch eines eben noch übermächtigen Herrschaftsapparates für alle – Beteiligte wie Außenstehende – kam. Doch soll es hier im folgenden nicht nur darum gehen, von welchem Ende her die Geschichte der DDR am 'besten' zu erzählen ist, sondern auch darum, mit welchen Medien dies bevorzugt getan wurde und noch getan wird. Dann wird schnell sichtbar, dass es seit 1990 nicht nur verschiedene Stufen der Aufarbeitung der DDR-Geschichte gab, sondern ihnen partiell auch jeweils eigene Medien immanent waren. Exemplarisch soll das hier am Beispiel des Herbstes 1989 dargestellt werden.

Wir erinnern uns: Berlin, 4. November 1989, Alexanderplatz. Zirka eine halbe Millionen Menschen haben sich versammelt, um von der SED-Führung friedlich ihr Recht auf Meinungs- und Versammlungsfreiheit einzuklagen und um für eine Erneuerung der sozialistischen Gesellschaft in der DDR zu demonstrieren. Davon handeln die Reden bekannter Schriftsteller und Schauspieler, aber auch der Vertreter der neu gegründeten Bürger-bewegungen. Davon handeln aber auch die ebenso witzigen wie kämpferischen Sprüche auf den Transparenten der Demonstranten.[1] Und nur langsam dämmert es allen Beteiligten: Hier, in diesem Augenblick, wird Geschichte geschrieben. Nicht (mehr) von den Mächtigen, sondern von vielen namenlosen Akteuren. Alle Beteiligten waren sich spontan einig: Dies gilt es festzuhalten, diese Spuren sind zu sichern! Am Ende der Kundgebung der Aufruf: Alle Losungen und Transparente an der Tribüne abzulegen, um daraus später "eine Art neuer Kunstausstellung"[2] zu gestalten. Die meisten Demonstranten folgten dem Aufruf.

Noch nie ist eine Revolution so schnell musealisiert worden, wie die friedliche des Herbstes 1989 in der DDR. Und dies nicht nur, weil sich schon wenige Tage nach der benannten Groß-Demonstration, mit der Öffnung der Mauer, die Frage nach ihren Zielen völlig neu stellte.

In Berlin – wie in vielen anderen Orten der DDR – machten sich Einzelne wie Gruppen (meist aus dem Umfeld der Bürgerbewegungen) daran, die Spuren ihres eigenen Protestes zu sichern und zu archivieren. Und dies z.T. bereits lange vor dem 4. November 1989. Noch hatten in vielen Orten die Demonstrationen ihren Höhepunkt nicht überschritten, da wurden ihre Zeugnisse bereits der Gegenstand von Ausstellungen. Vielleicht ist 'Ausstellung' der falsche Begriff für dieses spontane Vorzeigen von Dokumenten jener Ereignisse, welche die meisten Bürger nur Wochen vorher noch für unmöglich gehalten hätten. Eher waren diese Präsentationen ein Medium der Selbstverständigung, mitten im laufenden, individuell so schwer zu erfassenden Prozeß, in dem jeder Tag wie ein halbes Leben war!

Die ersten Präsentationen dieser Art waren noch stark wortdominiert. Sie fanden in Kirchen oder in den Versammlungsräumen der Künstlerverbände statt. Ihr Inhalt: Erlebnisprotokolle von 'zugeführten Demonstranten'. Sie berichteten darin, was ihnen von den Sicherheitskräften auf Geheiß der SED-Führung im September und Anfang Oktober 1989 (insbesondere aber am 7. Oktober, dem 40. Jahrestag der DDR) an Schikanen und Demütigungen angetan worden war.[3]

Neben diesen schockierenden Berichten hingen auch erste Fotodokumente. Im Verlauf des Oktobers 1989 mehrten sich dann die Ausstellungen von Fotografien, die den Prozess der zurückliegenden Wochen, insbesondere die machtvollen Demonstrationen der Bürger in Leipzig, Dresden, Plauen und anderen Städten, bildlich dokumentierten. Schaufensterflächen in den Stadtzentren, Foyers von Theatern und Kinos, kleine Galerien des Kulturbundes wie der autonomen Szene wurden dafür genutzt. Der Zulauf war gewaltig. So stauten sich vor dem Schaufenster der "Internationalen Buchhandlung" in Leipzig wochenlang die Passanten, Fotografien betrachtend, auf denen sie selbst zum Motiv geworden waren. Und staunten über ihren eigenen Mut. Selten wohl in ihrer Geschichte hat das Medium Fotografie so unmittelbar soziale Funktionen erfüllt wie in diesen Wochen.[4]

Später kamen die ersten Transparente und Losungen dazu. Direkt von der Straße wurden sie in Ausstellungen überführt. So in Dresden und Berlin, wo Mitglieder des Verbandes Bildender Künstler sie in bereits langfristig geplante Kunstausstellungen[5] integrierten. Dort reagierten sie mit Wandzeitungen, Podien, spontanen Diskussionsrunden unter Beteiligung gerade 'heimgekehrter' Remigranten aus der Künstlerszene,[6] aber auch neuen, originären Kunstwerken auf die Ereignisse vor den Ausstellungstoren. Zugleich wurde dem Neuen Forum und anderen Bürgerbewegungen dort ein Platz für Präsentation ihrer Ziele gegeben, den ihnen die meisten DDR-Medien zu dieser Zeit noch vorenthielten. Für wenige Wochen entstanden hier – wie bei anderen, ähnlichen Ausstellungsprojekten in Potsdam, Leipzig und anderswo – Orte einer direkten, lebendigen, Demokratie.[7]

Ein halbes Jahr später, am 12. April 1990, wurde dann in Ostberlin die Ausstellung *TschüSSED* eröffnet. Sie präsentierte jene Plakate und Transparente, die am 4.11.1989 nach der Demonstration auf dem Alexanderplatz spontan zusammengetragen worden waren, erstmals in einem musealen Kontext. Auch sie wurden in das Interieur einer vorhandenen Exposition – der zum 40. Jahrestag der DDR eröffneten Jubelausstellung des Museums für Deutsche Geschichte – montiert. Erstmals trat gemeinsam mit der Initiativgruppe 4.11.89, dem Organisator jener großen Demonstration, eine staatliche Einrichtung der Bundesrepublik als Mitveranstalter solch einer Ausstellung auf: Das Haus der Geschichte der Bundesrepublik Deutschland, welches die Ausstellung leicht verändert, später auch in Bonn präsentierte. Eine 'deutsche Revolution' war endgültig zur Besichtigung freigegeben.

Die *erste Phase* der Aufarbeitung des Herbstes '89 – noch mitten im Prozeß selbst[8] – war von seiner Funktion her ein *Prozeß der Selbstverständigung*. Ihr Tenor war *Sammeln, Bewahren und Motivieren* in einem. Ihr *Hauptmedium* war das der *Ausstellung*. Hieran schloß sich ab dem Sommer 1990 die *Phase der politischen Aufarbeitung* des Herbstes '89 an, die zugleich eine *Phase seiner politischen Verwertung* war. Ihr *Hauptmedium waren Bücher, das gedruckte Wort*. (Was nicht ausschloß, daß weiterhin auch Ausstellungen zum Thema stattfanden, wie auch die zeitliche Begrenzung der einzelnen Phasen der Aufarbeitung partiell Überlappungen aufweist). Diese *zweite Phase* reichte in etwa bis 1995. Auch sie war an ihrem Beginn in sehr starkem Maße vom Bestreben des Sammelns und Dokumentierens geprägt. Doch wurden hier weniger die dinglichen Zeugnisse der Ereignisse gesammelt, sondern es ging verstärkt um eine Dokumentation des Verlaufes des Herbstes 1989. Zugleich trug diese Phase von Beginn an auch den Stempel der Vermarktung. Großen politischen Ereignissen folgt heutzutage deren kommerzielle Vermarktung auf allen 'Kanälen' stets auf dem Fuße.

Dieses eherne Gesetz des Medienzeitalters griff spätestens nach dem Fall der Mauer auch in der DDR.

Die Wende war noch im vollen Gang, ihr Ausgang nur bedingt gewiß, da erschienen bereits die ersten Bücher über die geschichtsträchtigen Tage jenes Herbstes. Nicht von ungefähr trugen die meisten von ihnen Chronik-Charakter und/oder sammelten Aussagen der Beteiligten zum Geschehen und zu seiner Vorgeschichte. In dieser veränderungsreichen Zeit, in der sich die Ereignisse überstürzten, war das Bedürfnis, sie chronologisch festzuhalten und sich damit des eigenen Erlebens zu versichern, besonders ausgeprägt.

Die Nachfrage nach den Büchern war vor allem in der 'Noch-DDR' groß. Ganze Buchauflagen konnten an einem Nachmittag von der Ladefläche eines Lastwagens herab verkauft werden (so Ende November 1989 in Leipzig mit dem Buch *Jetzt oder nie – Demokratie. Leipziger Herbst '89*[9] geschehen). Das zog auch viele gestandene staatliche Verlage der DDR an. Beteiligt an der Edition von Wende-Chroniken haben sich u.a. der Mitteldeutsche Verlag Halle, der damals noch gewerkschaftseigene Verlag Tribüne, der Kiepenheuer Verlag Leipzig, der Henschel Verlag Berlin.[10] Die Gründe für ihr Engagement schwankten dabei zwischen schnellen Absetzbewegungen aus dem Schatten der ehemals Mächtigen und echtem Beteiligtsein. Gleichfalls bauten viele, im Umfeld der Bürgerbewegungen oder aus ihnen heraus gegründete Verlage ihre ·(oftmals kurze) Publikationsgeschichte auf Anfangserfolgen mit solchen, zumeist stark regional geprägten Chroniken des Herbstes '89 auf (Die Sammlung dieser Wendechroniken im Bestand des Zeitgeschichtlichen Forums Leipzig umfaßt derzeit zirka 50 Einzelpublikationen).[11] Viele der Chroniken, insbesondere der überregionalen, waren allerdings echte 'Schnellschüsse'. Oft ausschließlich auf der Grundlage der bereits lückenhaften bzw. politisch einseitig motivierten Berichte der noch existierendcn SED-Bezirksleitungen und ihrer Medien zusammengestellt, sind sie mehr Meta-Chroniken als eigenständige Quellenwerke.

Das gilt partiell auch für die 1. Auflage des Buches *Wir sind das Volk!* von Hannes Bahrmann und Christoph Links, das innerhalb der Wende-Editionen eine besondere Stellung einnimmt. Es erschien erstmals im Januar 1990; damals noch gleichzeitig in der Bundesrepublik und in der DDR.[12] Christoph Links nutzte den kommerziellen Erfolg des Buches, um damit einen eigenen Sachbuchverlag zu gründen, der heute zu den erfolgreichsten Verlagen im Osten Deutschlands zählt. 1994 erschien, nun im eigenen Verlag, eine stark überarbeitete Neuauflage der erfolgreichen Chronik. "Der

Abstand von fünf Jahren ermöglichte" es – wie die beiden Autoren im Vorwort ihrer neuen *Chronik der Wende* betonen – "auf vielfältige Momente des Umgestaltungsprozesses einzugehen, die damals nicht im unmittelbaren Wahrnehmungshorizont lagen."[13] Doch blieb es nun nicht bei dem Buch allein. Der Ostdeutsche Rundfunk Brandenburg (ORB) produzierte auf der Grundlage des Buches eine 73teilige Fernsehserie gleichen Namens, die allabendlich zwischen dem 7. Oktober und dem 18. Dezember 1994 im 1. Programm der ARD, des ORB und um einen Tag zeitversetzt im Nachmittagsprogramm des Mitteldeutschen Rundfunks (MDR) lief. Bei der Serie handelt es sich jedoch nicht um eine einfache Illustration des Buches mit bewegten Bildern. Im Gegenteil: Die Spezifik des Mediums voll ausschöpfend, hatte das Fernsehen für die Rekonstruktion der Ereignisse eines Tages im Herbst 1989 – die im Buch auf knapp zwei Seiten abgehandelt werden mußten – jeweils eine Viertelstunde Zeit. Mittels Originalsequenzen der Medienberichterstattung aus Ost und West und historischen Dokumentaraufnahmen aus dem Herbst 1989 sowie später gedrehten Zeitzeugen-Interviews wurde ein filmisches Porträt jener stürmischen Tage erstellt. Und dies mit großem Erfolg: Nach einem 45minütigen Auftaktfilm, Anfang Oktober 1995 noch im Nachmittagsprogramm gesendet, verbannten die Programmplaner die tägliche Chronik anfangs auf Sendeplätze um 0.00 Uhr. Erst der Protest vieler Zuschauer, vor allem aber die ungewöhnlich hohen Einschaltquoten brachten die filmische *Chronik der Wende* im Sendetermin um ein, zwei Stunden nach vorn. Am Ende gab es für sie sogar einen Grimme-Preis, die höchste deutsche Fernsehauszeichnung. Von dieser medialen Öffentlichkeit profitierte auch das Buch. Wochenlang befand es sich auf den ostdeutschen Bestseller-Listen ganz vorn. Ausgewählte Beiträge der Serie kamen später zusätzlich auf zwei Kaufkassetten in den Handel. (Inzwischen liegt längst auch ein 2. Teil der Wendechronik vor, der die Ereignisse bis zum 3. Oktober 1990 fortschreibt.[14])

Nicht von ungefähr wurde erst die zweite Auflage der "Wendechronik" im Jahr 1994 von einer filmischen Variante begleitet. In der ersten und in weiten Teilen auch der zweiten Phase der Aufarbeitung der Geschichte des Herbstes 1989 dominierten nicht ohne Grund die traditionellen Medien: Buch, Fotografie und Ausstellung. Fernsehen und Film konnten da nur bedingt mithalten, obwohl sie heute doch eigentlich die "schnelleren" Medien sind. Das hatte Ursachen: Der Herbst '89 war in seinem Verlauf (zumindest bis zum Fall der Mauer) filmisch weitgehend undokumentiert geblieben. Und das galt nicht nur für einen der zentralen Orte des Geschehens, die Stadt

Leipzig. Dort konnten am 4. September 1989 letztmalig für mehr als acht
Wochen Kamerateams aus dem westlichen Ausland die Ereignisse nach den
wöchentlichen Friedensgebeten filmen.

In dieser Woche fand in Leipzig traditionell die Internationale
Herbstmesse statt. Fernsehgesellschaften aus aller Welt hatten ihre Reporter
entsandt. Doch standen deren Kameras nicht in den Messehallen um die
vermeintlichen Wirtschaftserfolge der DDR zu filmen, sondern auf dem
Nikolaikirchplatz. Die Kirchgemeinde von Sankt Nikolai veranstaltete, trotz
massiver Versuche der Einflußnahme von seiten des Staates, an diesem 4.
September ihr erstes Friedensgebet nach der Sommerpause. Einem Sommer,
in dem der DDR ihre Bürger zu Zehntausenden über die ungarisch-
österreichische Grenze davon gelaufen waren. Leipziger Bürgerrechtler
nutzten an diesem Tag gezielt die Anwesenheit der westlichen Medien, um
mit Transparenten ihre ungebrochene Bereitschaft, für eine demokratische
Veränderung der DDR-Gesellschaft einzutreten, deutlich zu machen. Sie
forderten Reise- und Versammlungsfreiheit. Auf einem Transparent stand
"Für ein offenes Land mit freien Menschen!", auf einem anderen
"Reisefreiheit statt Massenflucht!"[15]

Allerdings waren die Transparente nur kurz zu sehen, bevor sie von
Stasi-Mitarbeitern in Zivil heruntergerissen wurden. Lang genug aber, damit
sie die Kameras der internationalen Medien aufnehmen und um die Welt
senden konnten. Das brachte ihnen ein Leipzig-Verbot bis zum 9. November
1989 ein. Aber nicht nur in Leipzig waren westliche Kameras unerwünscht.
Auch bei der Belagerung des Dresdner Hauptbahnhofes am 4. und 5.
Oktober, als die Botschaftszüge aus Prag auf ihren Weg in den Westen die
Stadt passierten, fehlten sie, wie auch bei den Demonstrationen in Arnstadt,
Plauen, Karl-Marx-Stadt, Erfurt und anderswo. Daß die Medien der DDR
über diese Ereignisse nicht berichteten, verstand sich in den Augen ihrer
(An)Leiter von selbst.

Filmische Quellen für die unmittelbaren Ereignisse des Herbstes '89 sind
dennoch vorhanden. Es handelt sich dabei vor allem um:
- vereinzelte illegale Aufnahmen, die von Privatleuten oder Mitgliedern der
  Bürgerbewegung mit (aus dem Westen eingeschleusten) Videokameras
  gemacht und dann z.T. über diplomatische Vertretungen dorthin zurück
  geschmuggelt wurden (so geschehen am 9. Oktober bei der wohl
  wichtigsten Demonstration des Herbstes '89 in Leipzig;[16])
- Aufnahmen der Staatssicherheit, die sie entweder von ihren (mehr oder
  minder versteckten) Beobachtungskameras auf den Dächern entlang der

Demonstrationsstrecken oder von durch sie engagierte Kamerateams des DEFA-Dokumentarfilmstudios aufnehmen ließen;[17]

- 4 Filme von Studenten der Hochschule für Film und Fernsehen Potsdam-Babelsberg, die sie mit einer Sondergenehmigung ihres damaligen Rektors[18] in Berlin, Leipzig und Dresden[19] anfertigten;
- Filmmaterial des Dokumentarfilmregisseurs Andreas Voigt, der von seinem Studioleiter die Herausgabe von Technik und Material ertrotzte und auf eigene Gefahr in Leipzig zu drehen begann; Ausgangspunkt seiner mittlerweile sehr bekannten Filmtetralogie zu dieser Stadt in und nach der Wende.[20]

Dieses Filmmaterial zu finden und für die (Medien-)Öffentlichkeit zu erschließen war selbstverständlich schrittweise möglich. Das gilt insbe-sondere für das Bildmaterial der Staatssicherheit oder die privaten Amateur-aufnahmen, deren Existenz erst nach und nach bekannt wurde. Dies alles berücksichtigend, ist die langanhaltende Dominanz der traditionellen Medien in den ersten beiden Phasen der Aufarbeitung des Herbstes '89 plausibel.

Hinzu kommt, daß schon bald nach dem unmittelbaren Umbruch in Ostdeutschland die publizistischen und sozialwissenschaftlichen Analysen dieses Prozesses einsetzten. Beteiligt daran waren Autoren aus Ost und West; wobei letztere – nach einem verzögerten Start – nicht nur zahlenmäßig schnell die Oberhand gewannen. Nicht zuletzt weil die meisten Stimmen der östlichen Seite nach und nach verstummten.

Zentraler Punkt aller Analysen war bereits früh die Frage, ob es sich bei dem soeben erlebten Prozeß um eine Revolution gehandelt habe oder nicht. Die Spannbreite der Interpretationen reichten dabei von der "Revolution" über einen "Umbruch" oder die "Wende" bis hin zur "Implosion" oder einem "Zusammenbruch". Aber selbst jene Analytiker, die sich entschlossen von einer Revolution zu sprechen, taten dies lange Zeit (z.T. bis heute noch) nur in Anführungszeichen. Auch stellten sie – je nach Intention, aber auch politischer Einstellung zu dem Vorgang – dem Wort Revolution unter-schiedliche Adjektive voran. Da war von einer "friedlichen", "freiheitlichen", "protestantischen", "volkseigenen" oder gar "(gesamt-)deutschen" Revolution die Rede.[21] Bei alledem gerieten die eigentlichen Akteure des Herbstes '89, die Bürgerrechtler und die Demonstranten, z.T. auch die DDR-Flüchtlinge, bald an den Rand des Geschehens. Nach der Lektüre nicht weniger westlicher Interpretationen, vor allem von Seiten tragender politischer Kräfte (und dabei hebe ich nicht nur auf die damals regierende

Koalition von CDU, CSU und FDP ab), bekam man jedoch zunehmend den Eindruck: "Der Westen war's !"

Versuche, dieses verrutschte Bild wieder gerade zu rücken, gab es von Seiten des Ostens bzw. der ehemals Aktiven immer seltener. Zu sehr war man mit der täglichen Bewältigung der neuen gesellschaftlichen Zusammenhänge der sozialen Marktwirtschaft beschäftigt als das für die Mehrzahl der ehemaligen "Herbstrevolutionäre" noch von unmittelbar praktischer Relevanz gewesen wäre, ob es sich bei dem eigenen Tun um eine Revolution gehandelt hat oder nicht.

Und selbst dort, wo dies Thema – partiell mit großem Aufwand wie bei der Berichterstattung der Enquete-Kommission des Deutschen Bundestages zur Aufarbeitung von Geschichte und Folgen der SED-Diktatur – noch einmal behandelt wurde, versuchten nun ihrerseits die an deren Aufarbeitungstätigkeit beteiligten Ostdeutschen (vor allem Bürgerrechtler) ihren Part in dem gesamten Prozeß besonders hervorzuheben. So finden sich in dem Doppelband VII dieser Edition, der sich mit den Möglichkeiten und Formen abweichenden und widerständigen Verhaltens und oppositionellen Handels in der DDR wie auch mit der friedlichen Revolution im Herbst 1989 auseinandersetzt, viele gelungene Analysen zur Rolle der Bürgerbewegung (oder einzelner ihrer Gruppierungen samt ihrer historischen Genese) in diesem Prozeß.[22] Auch wird die Entwicklung des Fluchtverhaltens im Sommer und Herbst 1989 breit analysiert.[23] Ja, selbst (fast) jede ehemalige Blockpartei der DDR hat ihr eigenes "Coming-Out" bekommen.[24] Doch ist in den insgesamt 18 Bänden kaum von der Rolle der Demonstranten auf den Straßen und Plätzen der DDR und von der Bedeutung ihres Massenprotestes die Rede.[25]

Damit sind wir bereits *in der dritten Phase der Aufarbeitung des Herbstes 1989* angekommen: *seiner Historisierung.* Sie ist gegenwärtig im vollen Gange und geschieht auf zweierlei Weise:
1. Historisierung durch Verdrängung und Vergessen
2. Historisierung durch Musealisierung.
Verdrängung und Vergessen ist auf nahezu allen gesellschaftlichen Ebenen, in Ost wie in West, wenn auch aus z.T. sehr unterschiedlichen Gründen, zu verzeichnen: Den einen hilft die Erinnerung an den Herbst 1989 in ihrem täglichen Orientierungs-, partiell auch Überlebenskampf, kaum noch weiter. Nur einmal im Jahr, immer wenn es Herbst wird, glimmen die "Feuer der Erinnerung" im Osten wieder auf, organisiert wie privat. Den anderen war –

genauer betrachtet – der 9. November 1989 schon immer näher als der 9. Oktober des gleichen Jahres.

Die Ignorierung der Verdienstes des Herbstes '89 fing schon früh – 1990 – mit der Wahl des Tages der Deutschen Einheit an, der per politischer Willensbildung auf den 'geschichtsträchtigen' 3. Oktober gelegt wurde, dem in der Chronologie des Herbstes 1989 keine wichtige Bedeutung zukommt. An diesem Tag setzte die DDR-Regierung den visafreien Reiseverkehr mit der CSSR aus. Die Belagerung des Dresdner Hauptbahnhofes begann erst einen Tag später...

Aber bei dieser Kür war den politischen Entscheidungsträgern – West wie Ost(!) – jeder Tag recht, Hauptsache er lag vor dem 7. Oktober 1990; sonst wäre die DDR gar noch 41 geworden. Auf die Idee aber, den 4. September zu wählen, von dessen Bedeutung im Herbst 1989 hier bereits die Rede war, oder den 25. September, den Tag der ersten großen Demonstration in Leipzig, ist eigenartiger Weise scheinbar niemand gekommen. Selbst der 11. September, der Tag, an dem sich 1989 für die DDR-Bürger in Ungarn endgültig die Grenzschranken gen Westen öffneten oder der 30. September, an dem Außenminister Genscher den Besetzern der Prager Botschaft ihre Ausreise in die Bundesrepublik verkündete, wären dafür zehnmal besser geeignet gewesen als der nichtssagende 3. Oktober.

Aber auch um die bürgerbewegten Akteure des Herbstes '89 ist es still geworden. Politisch sind sie, so überhaupt noch aktiv, heute in allen demokratischen Parteien der Bundesrepublik zu Hause. Eine tragende Rolle spielen sie – will man von der Berufung Wolfgang Thierses zum überparteilichen Amt des Präsidenten des Deutschen Bundestages einmal absehen – aber in keiner der Parteien. Da macht selbst Bündnis 90/Die Grünen keine Ausnahme, die wenigstens noch in ihrem Parteinamen einen leichten Anklang an die Geschichte der DDR-Bürgerbewegung tragen, ansonsten aber – wie der bekannte Bürgerrechtler Wolfgang Templin in einem großen deutschen Nachrichtenmagazin bekannte – längst wieder zu einer "reinen Westpartei"[26] geworden sind.

Bleibt also nur die Musealisierung? Vorab: Ich bin beruflich an diesem Vorgang aktiv mit beteiligt.[27] Ich gebrauche den Begriff also durchaus nicht im negativen Sinne! Was kann dem Herbst '89, was kann der DDR besseres geschehen als im Museum zu landen! So ist er/sie ständig präsent als ein Gegenstand der Auseinandersetzung: zumindestens für die Besucher. Historisierung durch Musealisierung schafft zwar auch Abstand, zugleich aber – vorausgesetzt, sie ist gut gemacht – auch Reibeflächen für den

Betrachter. Entscheidend für mich ist, daß alle beteiligten Seiten ihren realen Platz in solch einer musealen Einrichtung finden. Dafür stehen heute alle Medien, tradierte wie neue, zur Verfügung.

Nachtrag – am Beginn des 21. Jahrhunderts

Inzwischen ist mehr als ein Jahr vergangen, seit der hier abgedruckte Vortrag von mir auf dem Montrealer Symposium gehalten worden ist. Eine Zeitspanne, in deren Verlauf die in dem Aufsatz beschriebene Aufarbeitung von DDR-Geschichte, in sich wandelnden Formen und Medien, weiter vorangeschritten ist. Im Mittelpunkt des öffentlichen Interesses stand dabei eindeutig die demokratische Revolution des Herbstes 1989. Geschuldet war das vor allem dem zehnjährigen Jubiläum der geschichtsträchtigen Ereignisse zwischen Massenflucht, Straßenprotest und Mauerfall. All diesen Jubiläen wurde 1999 in Feierstunden, unzähligen Medienbeiträgen, großen und kleinen Ausstellungen sowie Enthüllungen von Gedenktafeln und Denkmälern gedacht. Zugleich wurde damit *die dritte,* von mir *als Historisierung benannte Phase* der Aufarbeitung dieser Revolution entschieden vorangetrieben.

Noch einmal glimmten überall im Osten Deutschlands die "Feuer der Erinnerung" auf. Doch gab es bereits auch nachhaltige Anzeichen dafür, daß die Strahlkraft ihrer Glut im Nachlassen begriffen ist. Oder waren es nur Vorzeichen einer sich langsam einstellenden Übersättigung? Wie auch immer: Zu spüren bekamen sie gerade jene, die vor fünf Jahren mit ihren Aufarbeitungsprodukten zur Geschichte des Herbstes '89 noch landesweit große Publikumserfolge feiern konnten.

So auch die (bereits erwähnte) *Chronik der Wende*, deren Herausgeber – Hannes Bahrmann und Christoph Links – bei diesem Jubiläum gern an ihre früheren Erfolge angeknüpft hätten. Die bisher in zwei getrennten Büchern vorliegende Chronik wurde von ihnen erneut überarbeitet und zu einem einzigen Band von über 300 Seiten zusammengefügt. Dieser stellt nun die Ereignisse vom 7. Oktober 1989 bis zum 18. März 1990 in einem geschlossenen Überblick dar.[28] Gleichzeitig veröffentlichte der Ch. Links Verlag eine, stärker auf die visuelle Seite der Ereignisse abhebende *Bilderchronik der Wende*.[29] Neben Fotos von den Ereignissen des Herbstes '89 aus der gesamten DDR sind darin auch Auszüge aus vielen Interviews mit Zeitzeugen enthalten, die 1994 für die Fernsehadaption der Wendechronik geführt worden sind.

Aber auch diese TV-Variante der Wendechronik erlebte einen erweiterten "Neustart". Doch anders noch als vor fünf Jahren, hielt sich die Zuschauerresonanz diesmal in Grenzen. Die ARD sah sich nicht erneut durch hohe Einschaltquoten veranlaßt, den für die späten Nachtstunden gewählten, landesweiten Sendetermin[30] auf zuschauerfreundlichere Zeiten zu verlegen. Lediglich der für die Senderreihe verantwortliche ORB hielt eisern an seinem täglichen Ausstrahlungstermin um 22 Uhr fest. Andere regionale Sender in den Neuen Bundesländern, wie der MDR (Sendeanstalt der Bundesländer Sachsen, Sachsen-Anhalt und Thüringen) oder der Berliner Sender B1, verlegten die Ausstrahlung der "Chronik" gleich in die zuschauerschwachen Morgenstunden.[31] Erinnerungen an eine Revolution, die kaum einer mehr sehen will? Auf jeden Fall deutlich weniger Menschen als noch fünf Jahre zuvor!

Wo die Historisierung durch Vergessen im vollen Gange ist, folgt ihr die durch Verdrängung stets auf dem Fuße. Dies wurde spätestens beim Streit um die Rednerliste für den offiziellen Festakt des Deutschen Bundestages zum 10. Jahrestag des Mauerfalls am 9.11.1999 deutlich: Bei der ersten, durch den Bundestag getroffenen Auswahl der Redner fehlte ein Bürgerrechtler aus der DDR (wenn man einmal von Wolfgang Thierse absehen will, der jedoch wegen seiner Funktion als Bundestagspräsident und nicht wegen seiner Rolle im "Neuen Forum" im Herbst 1989 auf der Rednerliste stand). Entgegen allen späteren Beteuerungen bundesdeutscher Politiker, mag man hier kaum an einen Zufall glauben.

Das Protokoll sah – neben dem damaligen Generalsekretär der kommunistischen Partei der Sowjetunion und Inspirator der Perestroika, Michail Gorbatschow – nur westliche Politiker als Festredner vor: den ehemaligen Präsidenten der USA, Georg Bush, den Altbundeskanzler Helmut Kohl und den gegenwärtigen Bundeskanzler Gerhard Schröder. Alles Staatsmänner, deren Verdienste um die Überwindung der deutschen Teilung hoch einzuschätzen sind. Dennoch fand mit dieser einseitigen Nominierung jene Umdeutungspolitik des Herbstes '89 ihre Fortsetzung, die mit der Wahl des 3. Oktobers zum Tag der Deutschen Einheit 1990 bereits begonnen hatte. Es bedurfte erst des massiven Protestes ehemaliger DDR-Bürgerrechtler, bis mit Joachim Gauck einer von ihnen für die Rednerliste nachnominiert wurde. Hätten die Bürgerrechtler nicht protestiert, wäre das peinliche Defizit kaum jemand im westdeutsch dominierten Politikgefüge der neuen "Berliner Republik" aufgefallen.

Solche Erfahrungen sind geeignet, latent schwellende Vorbehalte gegenüber dem Westen in der ostdeutschen Bevölkerung weiter zu nähren. Dies
hatten zuvor bereits eine Reihe von Ausstellungen zu spüren bekommen, die
sich mit der deutschen Nachkriegsgeschichte bzw. Teilen der DDR-
Hinterlassenschaft auseinandersetzten, also Historisierung durch Musealisierung betrieben. In diesem Zusammenhang wurde auch der Herbst '89
häufiger thematisiert. Dort, wo der Prozeß der Musealisierung vor allem
durch das Bemühen geprägt war, den Akteuren von damals, die selbst-
gemachte Geschichte wieder ins Bewußtsein zu rufen – wie es in vielen
lokalen Ausstellungen zwischen Merseburg, Plauen, Weißenfels und Werdau
der Fall war – überwog (nach wie vor) der Stolz auf das Geleistete. Auch
wenn dies, bedingt durch den zeitlichen Abstand der Ereignisse und den
vorherrschenden "östlichen Blickwinkel" ihrer Macher, mitunter etwas
verklärt geriet. Dennoch war in diesen Ausstellungen deutlich zu spüren, daß
hier der zeitgeschichtlichen Ereignisse gedacht werden sollte, ohne bereits
eine endgültige Wertung über sie festschreiben zu wollen. Der Wirkungsgrad
dieser Präsentationen blieb allerdings meist auf ihr unmittelbares territoriales
Umfeld begrenzt; was von den großen Überblicksausstellungen in Berlin
oder Leipzig kaum zu behaupten ist.

Am 23. Mai 1999 wurde im Berliner Gropiusbau die offizielle "Geburts-
tagsschau" der Bundesrepublik Deutschland zum 50. Jahrestag ihrer
Gründung eröffnet: *Einigkeit und Recht und Freiheit. Wege der Deutschen
1949-1999*. Konzipiert wurde sie von einem gemeinsamen Arbeitsteam des
Deutschen Historischen Museums Berlin, des Bonner Hauses der Geschichte
und der ebenfalls in Bonn ansässigen Bundeskunsthalle. Ursprünglich einmal
als Ausstellung allein zur Geschichte der alten Bundesrepublik gedacht,
wurde sie im Zuge ihrer Realisierung um einige ausgewählte Aspekte der
DDR-Geschichte erweitert. Dies schien von allen Seiten akzeptiert zu sein,
bis Ende Juli – nach mehr als sechs Wochen Laufzeit der Ausstellung – in der
Berliner Zeitung ein Artikel erschien, der sich damit auseinandersetzte, "wie
die Jubiläumsausstellung [...] mit der DDR fertig wird". Er trug den
provokanten Titel "Hinten links in der Ecke"[32] und bemängelte eine politisch
einseitige Sicht der Präsentation auf den, in der friedlichen Revolution im
Herbst '89 untergegangenen Staat: "Wer die DDR auf Massenaufmärsche und
[...] auf die Überwachungskameras reduziert, kann dem Land keine
historische Dimension geben. Er kann weder die Existenz noch den
Zusammenbruch erklären. Letztlich ging dieser Staat nicht an Gängelei und
Repressionen zugrunde, sondern weil seine Funktionäre ihre Versprechungen

von einem besseren Leben als in dem benachbarten deutschen Staat nicht einlösten." Kritisiert wurde neben einem Primat der Politik, vor allem daß "die DDR [...] an eine BRD-Ausstellung einfach drangepappt wurde."[33]

Der Artikel zeigte Wirkung: Nicht nur daß die Berichterstattung der Medien zur Ausstellung schärfer wurde, auch im Besucherbuch häuften sich jetzt Aussagen wie: "Zu einseitig aus der BRD-Sicht aufgebaut"; "der DDR-Anteil ist zu kurz gekommen" oder "typische Wessi-Ausstellung." Daran konnte auch nichts ändern, daß die Ausstellungsmacher Journalisten zu einer Extraführung einluden, um zu belegen, daß in ihrer Exposition die DDR hinreichend thematisiert worden wäre. Die Kritik an der Art der Darstellung blieb jedoch ungebrochen: "Sie bedienen in ihrer Ästhetik vielfach westliche Klischees."[34] Noch Anfang September legte *Die Zeit* scharf nach. Unter der Überschrift "Gewinner und Verlierer" konstatierte sie: "Die Schlagworte sind klar: Diktatur, Staat der Funktionäre, Bevormundung, totale Überwachung, Repression, Planwirtschaft, militaristische Erziehung [...] der westdeutsche Besucher [...] wird [...] froh sein, dass keines der Bilder in seinem Kopf infrage gestellt wird. Diese Ausstellung hat auch gar nicht vor, mit den uralten Klischees vom unglücklichen Leben in einem verriegelten Land zu brechen. Sie inszeniert lieber die 10.000 Wiederholung von dem, was alle schon wissen."[35]

Noch heftiger umstritten als diese zeitgeschichtliche Ausstellung waren im fünzigsten Jahr der Bundesrepublik Deutschland verschiedene Expositionen mit Werken der bildenden Kunst aus der DDR[36]; vor allem die Ausstellung *Offiziell/Inoffiziell. Die Kunst der DDR*, welche im Rahmen des europäischen Kulturstadtjahres 1999 in Weimar stattfand. Am 9. Mai 1999 mit großem Pomp eröffnet, wurde sie – nach erfolgreicher gerichtlicher Klage betroffener Künstler gegen die Ausstellungsleitung (ein Novum in der deutschen Kunstgeschichte) und trotz partieller Neugestaltung der Exposition – bereits am 26. September 1999 vorzeitig wieder geschlossen. Vor allem die Besucher aus den Neuen Bundesländern erhoben massiv Einspruch gegen das Konzept des westdeutschen Ausstellungsmachers: Unter kunstunwürdigen Bedingungen hingen die Bilder, dicht an dicht auf grauen faltigen Kunststoffplanen, im halbdunklen Rund einer ehemaligen Lagerhalle; nur eine Etage getrennt von Kunstwerken aus der Zeit des Nationalsozialismus.[37] Auch wenn hier nicht der Platz ist, um die Besucherreaktionen darauf ausführlicher darzustellen,[38] so ist für unseren Zusammenhang daran doch bemerkenswert, daß das Museumspublikum in den Neuen Bundesländern offensichtlich nicht mehr gewillt ist, alles hinzunehmen. Oder, um mit den

Worten eines ostdeutschen Besuchers der Weimarer Ausstellung zu sprechen: "Die von Herrn Preiß[39] [...] gezeigte Ignoranz und Überheblichkeit ist selbst-entlarvend. Leider leistet der Ausstellungsverantwortliche dem Eindruck Vorschub, wieder einmal habe ein Westdeutscher das letzte Wort zum Geschehen in einem Land, von dem er offenkundig keine Ahnung hat, das er nicht ERLEBT hat. Frei nach dem Motto, wir wissen von nichts, aber wir reden geschwollen darüber und leisten uns ein finales Urteil."

Unter all diesen Bedingungen war der Eröffnung des Zeit-geschichtlichen Forums in Leipzig mit großer Spannung entgegenzusehen. Die, am 9. Oktober 1999 – zehn Jahr nach der entscheidenden Demonstration des Herbstes '89 in dieser Stadt – von Bundeskanzler Gerhard Schröder eröffnete Einrichtung stellt sich unter der Leitung des Bonner Hauses der Geschichte die Aufgabe, die Geschichte von Opposition und Widerspruch in der DDR in den Mittelpunkt einer ca. 2000 m2 umfassenden Dauer-ausstellung zu stellen. Dieses spezielle Segment der DDR-Geschichte wird auf dem Hintergrund des SED-Staates, seines Repressionsapparates sowie der deutschen Teilung erzählt. Natürlich stand – angesichts der beschriebenen Erfahrungen mit anderen Ausstellungsprojekten – die Frage im Raum, wie das Publikum in den Neuen Bundesländern auf diese thematische Ausrichtung der Leipziger Exposition reagieren und ob es die damit verbundene Sicht auf die DDR akzeptieren würde? Über 100.000 Besucher in einem halben Jahr sprechen erst einmal für ein anhaltendes Interesse am Gegenstand! Und wenn auch viele Besucher den DDR-Alltag in der Ausstellung zu gering vertreten sehen, so überwiegt allen bisher vorliegenden Besucherreaktionen zufolge doch die Zustimmung dazu: "In der Ausstellung spüre ich manchmal einen Klos im Halse, aber manchmal überkommt mich auch ein (befreiendes) Lachen!" Und ein anderer Besucher schrieb ins Besucherbuch: "Unsere Vergangenheit berührt uns mehr als wir gedacht haben."[40]

An der Gestaltung dieser Ausstellung als Wissenschaftler selbst mit beteiligt, ist es unangemessen, hier eine Wertung über sie abzugeben. Dies müssen und sollen andere tun. Für den Kontext des vorliegenden Beitrages bleibt jedoch festzuhalten, daß die Musealisierung von DDR-Geschichte, inklusive der Geschichte des Herbstes 1989, mit dem Zeitgeschichtlichen Forum erstmals eine feste räumliche Hülle erhalten hat, die über die bisherigen Möglichkeiten temporärer Auseinandersetzungen in Aus-stellungen deutlich hinausgeht. Zugleich bleibt zu hoffen, daß es ein Haus sein wird, das einer Historisierung der DDR durch Verdrängung und

Vergessen keinen weiteren Vorschub leistet und damit zum Prozeß des weiteren Zusammenwachsens der Deutschen beitragen kann

Anmerkungen

[1] Die Texte aller Reden und eine umfangreiche Auswahl der Transparentaufschriften sind enthalten in: *4. November 89.* Hrsg. von Annegret Hahn u.a.. Berlin: Henschel Verlag, 1990.

[2] Hennig Schaller, Mitorganisator der Demonstration, in: a.a.O. (Anm. 1), S. 204.

[3] Eine Auswahl daraus findet sich in: *Oktober 1989 – Texte. Temperamente. Blätter für junge Literatur*, 1/1990, S. 45f. (Thematisches Heft) und taz (Hrsg.): *DDR-Journal zur Novemberrevolution. August bis Dezember 1989: Vom Ausreisen bis zum Einreissen der Mauer*, taz: Berlin,1989, S. 39f.

[4] Vgl. Bernd Lindner: "Leipziger Zeit-Bilder: Ein Prozeß," *Fotografie*, 8/1990. S. 308-314.

[5] Die 11. Kunstausstellung des Bezirkes Dresden (6.10. - 26.11.1989) in den Ausstellungshallen am Fucik-Platz, auf dem immer die Dresdner Demonstrationen endeten, und die Leistungsschau der Berliner Designer und Kunsthandwerker (7.12.1989 - 13.1.1990) am Fernsehturm (vgl. dazu Wolfgang Kil: "Ein Stück Hyde Park am Fernsehturm," in: Hans-Werner Schmidt, Hrsg., *Bilder vom Neuen Deutschland. Eine deutsch-deutsche Ausstellungscollage*, Düsseldorf: Stefan Bollmann Verlag, 1990, S. 20/21).

[6] So lasen, diskutierten und sangen der Maler A. R. Penck, die Dichter Sascha Anderson, Katja Lange-Müller, die Liedermacherin Bettina Wegner, der Kunsthistoriker Diether Schmidt u.a. in den Räumen unterm Fernsehturm.

[7] Dazu ausführlicher Bernd Lindner: *Wie lange gehört uns unsere Geschichte? – Der Herbst 89 im Spiegel der Ausstellungen von "oben" und "unten" Vergleich.* Hrsg. vom Museum der Arbeit. Hamburg, 1993, S. 61-67.

[8] Zum Verlauf des Herbstes 1989 bis zur ersten freien Volkskammerwahl am 18. März 1990 vgl. Bernd Lindner: *Die demokratische Revolution in der DDR 1989/90*, Bonn: Bundeszentrale für politische Bildung, 1998, S. 48f.

[9] *"Jetzt oder nie – Demokratie. Leipziger Herbst 89".* Hrsg. vom Neuen Forum Leipzig. Leipzig: Forum Verlag, 1989.

[10]Hannes Bahrmann/Christoph Links, *"Wir sind das Volk!"*, Berlin: Aufbau Verlag, 1989/90; Zeno und Sabine Zimmerling, *Neue Chronik DDR* (in acht Folgen). Berlin:

Tribüne Verlag, 1990; Wolfgang Schneider, Hrsg., *Leipziger Demontagebuch*, Leipzig: Kiepenheuer Verlag, 1990; Annegret Hahn u.a., *4. November 89*, Berlin: Henschel Verlag, 1990.

[11] Chroniken liegen u.a. zu den Ereignissen in Auerbach, Coswig (Sachsen), Dessau, Dresden, Eisenach, Erfurt, Freiberg, Gotha, Greifswald, Güstrow, Halberstadt, Halle, Karl-Marx-Stadt, Magdeburg, Malchin, Meißen, Merseburg, Mühlhausen, Neubrandenburg, Neuruppin, Nordhausen, Plauen, Potsdam, Rostock, Rudolstadt, Schwerin, Stralsund, Suhl, Teterow, Waren (Müritz), Weimar, Weißenfels, Werdau, Wittenberg, Wismar u.a. vor.

[12] a.a.O., Anm. 10.

[13] Hannes Bahrmann/Christoph Links, *Chronik der Wende. Die DDR zwischen 7. Oktober und 18. Dezember 1989*, Berlin: Ch. Links Verlag, 1994, S. 5.

[14] Hannes Bahrmann/Christoph Links, *Chronik der Wende. Die DDR zwischen dem 19. Dezember1989 und dem 3. Oktober1990*, Berlin: Ch. Links Verlag, 1995.

[15] Vgl. dazu Uwe Schwabe, "Geschichte einer Losung," in: Bernd Lindner, Hrsg., *Zum Herbst 89. Demokratische Bewegung in der DDR. Begleitbuch zur gleichnamigen Ausstellung in Leipzig, Berlin und Bremen*, Leipzig: Forum Verlag, 1994, S. 9/10.

[16] Als der Ostberliner Bürgerrechtler, Fotograf und Amateurfilmer Siegbert Schefke (der Ende der achtziger Jahre mit Freunden aus Ost und West ein Informationsnetz geknüpft hatte, "daß jedes in der DDR zum Tabu erhobene Thema publik machte – via westliche Medien") die Ereignisse vom 9. Oktober 1989 in Leipzig vor Ort filmte. Er machte seine spektakulären Aufnahmen – u.a. vom Turm der Reformierten Kirche, die direkt an der Strecke der Montagsdemonstration lag – mit Hilfe ortsansässiger Bürgerrechtler und Kirchenleute. Mit den Aufnahmen raste er gegen 19 Uhr zurück nach Berlin, wo er sie einem westlichen Journalisten übergab. Noch am selben Abend um 22.30 Uhr wurden die Bilder in der Sendung "Tagesthemen" des 1. Fernsehprogrammes der Bundesrepublik gesendet. Vgl. dazu Renate Olschies, "Wir wollten Kirchenmauern durchbrechen," *Berliner Zeitung – Magazin "Wendespuren – Die Wege der Bürgerbewegung"*, 30. November 1996.

[17] Da die eigenen Aufnahmen sehr unscharf waren und maximal dazu genutzt werden konnten, die Stärke der Demonstrantenströme festzustellen; während die Profis vom Dokumentarfilmstudio ihnen gestochen scharfe "Porträts" einzelner Demonstranten lieferten, die dann erkennungsdienstlich behandelt werden konnten.

[18] Das war übrigens Lothar Bisky, heute Vorsitzender der PDS.

[19] *10 Tage im Oktober* (Film über die Ereignisse in Berlin um den 7. Oktober 1989;

Regie: Thomas Frick); *Es lebe die R...*(Film über die Ereignisse in Leipzig, Mitte Oktober 1989; Regie: Jörn Zielke); *Aufbruch 89 Dresden* und *Aufbruch 89 (Epilog)* (Film über die Ereignisse in Dresden um die Belagerung des Hauptbahnhofes am 4./5. Oktober 1989; Regie: Studentenkollektiv der HFF). Mit Ausnahme des Dresdner Epilogs beschäftigen sich alle diese Dokumentarfilme mit der Frühphase des Herbstes 89.

[20] "Leipzig im Herbst" (1989), "Letztes Jahr Titanic" (1991), "Glaube Liebe Hoffnung" (1994) und "Grosse weite Welt" (1997); in gewisser Weise gehört auch bereits Andreas Voigts Diplomfilm "Alfred" (1987) in diese Reihe, nicht nur weil er in Leipzig spielt.

[21] Vgl. dazu Ilko-Sascha Kowalczuk, "Artikulationsformen und Zielsetzungen von widerständigem Verhalten in verschiedenen Bereichen der Gesellschaft," in: *Materialien der Enquete-Kommission des Deutschen Bundestages zur Aufarbeitung von Geschichte und Folgen der SED-Diktatur*, Bd. VII,2 . Baden-Baden: Nomos Verlag, 1995, S. 1270f.; Bernd Lindner, *Die demokratische Revolution in der DDR 1989/90* (a.a.O., Anm. 8), S. 148f.; Michael Richter: "Die Revolution in Deutschland 1989/90. Anmerkungen zum Charakter der 'Wende'," *Berichte und Studien des Hannah-Arendt-Instituts*, Nr. 2/95. Dresden 1995.

[22] Autoren von Expertisen oder kommentierende Zeitzeugen waren in der Enquete-Kommission u.a. bekannte Bürgerrechtler wie Bärbel Bohley, Michael Beleites, Stephan Bickhardt, Rainer Eppelmann (zugleich Vorsitzender der Enquete Kommission), Hans-Jürgen Fischbeck, Carlo Jordan, Irena Kukutz, Ludwig Mehlhorn, Ulrike und Gerd Poppe, Wolfgang Templin.

[23] Vgl. Richard Hilmer, "Motive und Hintergründe von Flucht und Ausreise aus der DDR," in: *Materialien der Enquete-Kommission*, Bd. VII, 1/1995 (a.a.O., Anm. 21), S. 322-329; derselbe, "Übersiedler aus der DDR (Tabellen)," in: *Materialien der Enquete-Kommission*, Bd. VII, 1, S. 430-449.

[24] Günter Buchstab, "Widerspruch und widerständiges Verhalten der CDU der SBZ/DDR," in: *Materialien der Enquete-Kommission*, Bd. VII, 1/1995 (a.a.O., Anm. 21), S. 504-539; Siegfried Suckut, "Widerspruch und abweichendes Verhalten in der LDP(D)," in: ebenda, Bd.VII, 2, S. 1492-1655.

[25] Lediglich am Ende des Beitrages von Christian Dietrich, "Fallstudie Leipzig 1987-1989. Die politisch-alternativen Gruppen in Leipzig vor der Revolution," wird auf vier Seiten auf die Entwicklung der Montagsdemonstrationen in Leipzig Bezug genommen. In: *Materialien der Enquete-Kommission*, Bd. VII, 1/1995, S. 650f..

[26] In *Focus*, 46/1998.

[27] Der Autor ist als wissenschaftlicher Mitarbeiter am Zeitgeschichtlichen Forum Leipzig beim Haus der Geschichte der Bundesrepublik Deutschland tätig, das im Herbst 1999 in

der Leipziger Innenstadt eröffnet wurde (siehe unten).

[28] Hannes Bahrmann/Christoph Links, *Chronik der Wende. Die Ereignisse in der DDR zwischen 7. Oktober 1989 und 18. März 1990*, Berlin: Ch. Links Verlag, 1999.

[29] Hannes Bahrmann/Christoph Links, Hrsg., *Bilderchronik der Wende. Eindrücke aus der Zeit des Umbruchs 1989/90*, Berlin: Ch. Links Verlag, 1999.

[30] Der Sendebeginn schwankte zwischen 0.30 und 1.30 in der Nacht.

[31] Die Ausstrahlungszeit schwankte in den einzelnen Sendern zwischen 7.45 (B1) und 11.30 (MDR).

[32] In: *Berliner Zeitung* vom 22. Juli 1999. Autor: Frank Herold.

[33] Ebenda.

[34] "DDR-Bilder zwischen Funktionärsstaat und Alltag," *Leipziger Volkszeitung*, 31. Juli 1999.

[35] Jeanne Otto,"Gewinner und Verlierer," *Die Zeit*, 37/1999 (9. September 1999)

[36] Ausstellungen dazu waren 1998/99: *Rahmen-Wechsel. Fragen an die Kunst-sammlungen der Parteien und Massenorganisationen der DDR* auf Burg Beeskow bei Berlin; die Präsentation der Sammlung des westdeutschen Unternehmers Siegfried Seiz: *Kunst der achtziger Jahre aus der DDR* in Potsdam /Altes Rathaus; *Enge und Vielfalt. Auftragskunst und Kunstförderung in der DDR*, eine Ausstellung des Kunstfonds des Freistaates auf der Festung Königstein; *Dialoge. Werke aus der Sammlung der Grund-kredit Bank* im Kunstforum der Bank in Berlin; *Jahresringe. Kunstraum DDR. Eine Sammlung 1945-1989* im Kunsthaus Apolda.

[37] Die unter dem Titel *Die Kunst dem Volke – erworben: Adolf Hitler* erstmals nach 1945 wieder in diesem Umfang in Deutschland zu sehen waren.

[38] Vgl. dazu: Bernd Lindner, "Subversives Salz im klassischen Kompott? Die Weimarer Ausstellung 'Offiziell/ Inoffiziell – Die Kunst der DDR' im Spiegel ihrer Besucher-bücher", in: Kunstsammlungen zu Weimar, Hrsg., *Der Weimarer Bilderstreit*, Weimar: VDG-Verlag, 2000, S. 329 - 338; derselbe, "So war es nicht!" – "Genau so war es!" Deutsch-deutsche Dialoge in Ausstellungen mit Kunst aus der DDR," in: Heiner Timmermann, Hrsg., *Jahrbuch der DDR-Forschung*, Berlin: Duncker & Humblot 2001 (im Erscheinen).

[39] Achim Preiß, Kunsthistoriker aus Wuppertal, der jetzt in Weimar an der Bauhaus Universität lehrt, war Kurator der Ausstellung.

[40] Eine erste Übersicht über die Besucherreaktionen auf die Dauerausstellung des Zeitgeschichtlichen Forums gibt Rainer Eckert, im "magazin" des Hauses der Geschichte 3/2000, S. 30/31.

Roswitha Skare

"Real life within the false one"[1]
Manifestations of East German Identity in Post-Reunification Texts

Beginning with a short review of the question of East German identity, this chapter analyses texts by Daniela Dahn, Thomas Rosenlöcher and Hans-J. Misselwitz to show how history is recounted through stories. Despite the authors' different biographical backgrounds and their varying styles, the three chosen texts have two things in common: the central positioning of an 'East-We' and the use of small literary forms – be it in the form of anecdote, joke, almanac story or by example – guarantee not only the preservation of individual and collective experiences but their reproduction as well.

I

Following the historical events of the autumn of 1989 and the reunification of the two German states in October 1990, nothing seemed to be as misguided as the SED's claim that two different states had created two nations and two identities, and a 'Socialist GDR identity' in particular. Although the question of a separate GDR identity had been pursued occasionally before 1989, even in the West,[2] the mutualities between East and Western Germans seemed to predominate. The continuation of the German *Kulturnation*,[3] which many claimed to be still in existence, seemed to redeem the justified hopes for a quick knit of the two states, in part because the people on the other side were 'brothers and sisters', after all.[4] The East-West condemnations and misunderstandings of the past few years have shown that in many respects the Germans in the East and the West have developed different worlds and accordingly different identities.

In light of the fact that 60 percent of the new federal citizens were born after the founding of the GDR, grew up there and were socialized distinctly by the GDR, it is not really surprising that there was and is something like an East German identity. Even those GDR citizens who opposed the system still grew up with different role models and ideals, as well as other conceptions of an enemy and other kinds of resistance, than West Germans of the same age. Binding and fundamental to a common identity are common experiences, such as the collective East Germans experience of dichotomies, such as who 'ruled' and who 'was ruled' or 'private' and 'public' within the political context of the GDR, especially since the 1980s. Many citizens of the GDR found a way out of the relentless schizophrenia of juggling the official, conformist political consciousness with private attitudes with counter-identity orientations.[5] With the help of such counter-identities, one could dissociate oneself from the 'outside' and 'above' and clearly distinguish between 'us' and 'them', a boundary that was expressed not least in the autumn of 1989 with the slogan "Wir sind das Volk".

Nonetheless, it comes as a surprise in this regard that differences in approach to life, attitudes and values between East and West Germans are not decreasing with time. Instead, they are becoming more and more pronounced, or at least more apparent. Consequently, it was established in early 1991 that East and West Germans agreed on most points,[6] while representative polls of recent years note the differences between East and West more clearly than ever.[7] According to polls, East Germans now consider themselves primarily to be East German and secondarily German,[8] only 36% of East Germans continue to associate negative feelings with what they had experienced as Socialism, 40% agree with the Marxist hypothesis that the capitalist private ownership of production is the source of exploitation, and even 76% (in contrast to 50% in the West) feel that they can do without the kind of freedom in which millions are unemployed.[9]

The probable causes for the poll results reviewed here cannot be treated within the context of this essay, as they lie beyond the realm of my line of questioning. It should simply be emphasized that many have made the observation that the East German population has developed a more differentiated and critical view of their new lives in the Federal Republic. The fact that a new German identity,[10] as well as the existence of an East German identity and "Ostalgie",[11] is in consideration all over confirms the fact that at times of social upheaval questions of identity are accorded greater importance. This is the case particularly because such issues tend to go hand in hand with private crises in which individuals begin to question their personal histories. At times like these, the desire to be able to identify oneself with others increases, while at the same time the drive to differentiate oneself from the 'Other' is unmistakable. We need these images of ourselves and of the 'Other', we need stereotypes "zur Strukturierung der Welt, benötigen vereinfachte Darstellungen der Andersartigkeit, um unsere Ängste zu lokalisieren, um uns selbst zu beweisen, daß das, was wir fürchten, nicht in uns selbst liegt".[12] Although East and West Germans naturally have much in common, the emergence as well as the continued existence and development of an East German identity after the fall of the GDR can be explained by the human need for cohesiveness and mutuality, as well as by the need for delimitation. Since we all strive to live in concurrence with ourselves, our lives up until now and with our social environment, many experienced the events surrounding the *Wende* and the reunification as a break with their lives, their ideals and their goals up until that point, irrespective of whether one was for or against the regime. Past experiences and achievements were put into question, often by the West, and declared to be wrong or invalid. Self-doubt and inferiority complexes[13] in the new Western system increase the desire for confirmation and concurrence with other people. It is no wonder, then, that one tends to recall positive experiences in such situations, and to seek out others who share these experiences and can claim a similar frame of reference. In this sense, a voluntary East German identity that continues to exist in delimitation to the West German identity appears to have grown from the imposed collective GDR identity.

Some individuals feel moved to recount 'how things really were in the GDR', based on their own recollections. This is a result of the constant emphasis on the differences between East and West Germans in the media, as well as the judgement and condemnation of the GDR that is felt by many to be unfair and without nuance, as it simply allows for culprits and victims. Furthermore, the idea that authors have to exercise an educational function and should make themselves into the voice of the 'silent masses' seems not infrequently to play a role in academic circles in both East and West Germany. It should be assumed that many GDR writers continue to make an effort to be involved and, like Christa Wolf, see the writer's commission in an "Identitätsstiftung für das unglückliche, zerrissene Volk".[14]

Identity and the search for identity are in no way constant in content and intensity. On the contrary: identity changes constantly and thus is a reflection of an immediate social and private necessity. Based on the example of several 'memoirs', I would like to show in the following how the book trade transposes such a need, while seeking to satisfy it in its public.

II

I have chosen three texts for this analysis. They appeared in 1996 and 1997 and are by authors that can be included in the 'middle' generation.[15] Daniela Dahn, Hans-J. Misselwitz and Thomas Rosenlöcher were born either shortly before or shortly after the founding of the GDR and therefore spent the largest part of their politically conscious lives in that state. Many members of this generation identified themselves with the new and 'better' state. However, by the beginning of the 80s – if not earlier – they had to come increasingly to terms with the fact that their hopes and dreams could not be realized in the 'really existing Socialism' of the GDR. Accordingly, many had to ask themselves whether they should continue to participate in the system in spite of this realization or step out of these pre-ordained biographies and seek a 'third way'. The social changes that have taken place since reunification have in part triggered existential crises in this group, crises that concern not only reorientation in the new social circumstances, but of course also taking stock of one's own life. The members of this very generation of the GDR have fought back, in certain sense, and survived morally, but the professional as well as the political boats in united Germany have long since disembarked: at the time of the *Wende*, West Germans of the same age were already established and had created their own institutions.[16] Already as early as 1991, the East German psychotherapist Hans-Joachim Maaz diagnosed a "DDR-Verlust-Syndrom"[17] as a result of the historical events of 1989-90. Maaz speaks of his "verwirrten Identität" and of an "Identitätsbruch", his reason for why many East Germans are not able to allow themselves any real joy in the reunification. He feels that they are living in two worlds, but are at home in neither.

The titles of the three texts alone (*Westwärts und nicht vergessen. Vom Unbehagen in der Einheit,*[18] *Nicht länger mit dem Gesicht nach Westen. Das neue Selbstbewußtsein der Ostdeutschen,*[19] and *Ostgezeter*[20]) promise a critical, but in part also ironic, examination of German unity, its results and of the role of the East Germans in the process.

Along with the individual experiences of the three authors since the autumn of 1989, retrospectives of the GDR-period also play an important role, albeit to varying degrees. Looking back on their lives and the questioning of past decisions are not least an expression of the need the authors have to confirm their own lives, to justify to themselves the decisions they made and to consider them to be good decisions even in hindsight. Autobiographical reflections such as these are naturally quite selective, in content as well as in form. To conjure up the feeling of East German life, there has to be much generalization and a lot that is left out or repressed. Despite the authors' different biographical backgrounds and their varying literary styles, these three texts have two things in common, according to my theory: the central positioning of an 'East-We' and the use of small literary forms – history is recounted through stories. Telling stories, be it in the form of anecdote, joke, almanac story or by example, guarantees not only the preservation of individual and collective experiences, but their reproduction as well.

Furthermore, it is interesting to note which stories get told. Which symbols, images and myths[21] enter into these stories? Which stereotypes[22] of the 'East-We' and of the 'Other' become apparent?

III

The establishment of an 'East-We' while simultaneously delimiting the 'Other', the West German, plays an important role in all three texts:

1) giving the compass directions in the titles of the texts as an indication of East and West Germany already contributes to this aspect.

Rosenlöcher's title *Ostgezeter* simply offers information on the geographical source and on the kind of statements he makes. However, the use of the word *Gezeter* ('clamor') indicates an undertone that can be interpreted both as pejorative and as ironic. In contrast, Dahn's title establishes a sense of solidarity with her East German readers with the help of allusions. While the title tends to remind many West Germans of the advertising slogan "Go West!" at first, it awakens memories of the GDR for East Germans. Common prior knowledge and experiences are activated by the allusion to the solidarity song "Vorwärts und nicht vergessen".[23] It depends on the reader's socialization[24] as to whether the first part of the title is recognized as a play on the worker's movement song that the GDR appropriated for itself. Dahn's subtitle, however, points to Freud's work, *Vom Unbehagen in der Kultur*, leading one to anticipate cultural critique from Dahn's approach.[25]

The title of Misselwitz' essay, *Nicht länger mit dem Gesicht nach Westen*, makes a play on the fact that East Germans spent 40 years looking to the West. The state of the GDR only existed by nature of the division from the Federal Republic, citizens of the GDR measured their own life against the West, identified themselves with people on the other side. Western consumer goods became symbols of prosperity and freedom. After the West came into the East, however, the line of vision and the object of interest changed: East Germans' sights were turned to themselves. In this respect, it is decisive that identifying with oneself is always an option. We choose with whom and/or with what we want to identify ourselves. The years 1989 and 1990 create a historical demarcation in this process, one that determines whether the East Germans consider themselves to be primarily German or East German. Misselwitz asserts a new self-awareness of the East Germans that allows them to stop looking to the West and instead to make nearby conditions of the East the object of their reflections.

2) Statements by West German politicians and publicists are turned into the point of departure for one's own portrayal. Accordingly, one's own view of the events, which encompasses explanations and corrections, appears as counterpoint to the western side. Counter-examples from the history of the Federal Republic, as well as from that of the U.S. confirm one's own view and prove the necessity of correction and differentiation (DD 20f.; DD 163; DD 46ff.; DD 58; DD 65ff.; HJM 30; HJM 41). Usually summarizing such a correction, the opposition between "us" and "them/the others" is named explicitly. (DD 65: "Laß sie, sie reden über ein Land, in dem ich nicht gelebt habe."; DD 68: "Ihr werdet es *nie* verstehen!"; DD 8: "Wir stellen die Angeklagten, ihr die Richter."; DD 191: "Verschont uns mit euren Phrasen. Hört auf, uns und euch selbst weiszumachen, wir seien in einer schönen neuen Welt angekommen. *Unser Weg ist richtig*, das hatten wir schon mal.") Although personal experiences are used as the starting points, they are generalized with the assistance of the examples, such that East Germans as well as West Germans are referred to (TR 17: the "Hauptunterschied zwischen ihnen und uns"; TR 73: "euer Honecker" and "unser Bundeskanzler"). Nonetheless, this does not mean that this duality cannot also be differentiated. Thus, Rosenlöcher primarily refers to a geographical region, to the region of Saxony (TR 12: "Die Sachsen") and in so doing, does not claim to speak for all East Germans in any way. Rosenlöcher describes regional differences that are expressed through the delimitation to other regions by the disparity between the Saxons/"us" and the Berliners/"the others". Misselwitz for his part distinguishes between those who did participate in the demonstrations of the autumn of 1989 and those who didn't (HJM 46). In the recollections of her life in the GDR, Dahn also distinguishes between those who resisted and stood up for their own opinions and those who assimilated themselves and kept quiet (DD 82). Apart from this, continuities are pointed out in their portrayals that are supposed to make it clear that the contrast between 'upper' and 'lower' still exists, although the 'upper' has changed and is now to be found in the West (cf. above: "*Unser Weg ist richtig*, das hatten wir schon mal"; DD 11: "Reich der Besitzenden"; DD 8: "neue Herrlichkeit"[26]). With this fatalistic view of the historical developments, Dahn touches on the myth shared by many East Germans: that the holders of powers may indeed have changed, but otherwise everything has remained the same. To the benefit of the social home GDR with its potential for evolvement, the political home GDR is being faded out or reduced to a dichotomy between rulers and the ruled. Problematic in this

approach and the intended comparison between the GDR and the Federal Republic is not the fact that the comparisons are being made, but rather the result of the comparison, namely, that supposedly there is no real difference between 'really existing' Socialism and Western Democracy after all.

Rosenlöcher recalls a differentiation that there was in the GDR days, that between those "mit FDJ-Bluse" (TR 104) and those without, that is, a contrast between Party and State on the one hand and the populace, or rather a part of the populace, on the other.

Using the example of his visit to the Spree Forest, Rosenlöcher demonstrates that segmenting the population into different groupings is not unproblematic:

> Wo ich denn eigentlich herkäme?
>
> "Aus Stuttgart", sagte ich.
>
> "Das haben wir uns gleich gedacht", rief der Spreewaldhüne. Aber man habe hier keine Berührungsängste. (TR 70)

Rosenlöcher becomes the observer of his own group, and from an outsider's point of view he finds the irony in the assigning of groups by individuals. That a Saxon should pretend to be from Stuttgart and, further, that this is not doubted at all shows the irony and the tragedy of such stereotyping. It becomes clear in the answer of the Spree Forest local that prejudices and preconceptions of 'the other' exist, but that they deny having them. Admittedly, these prejudices have no particular social behavior as a result: the supposed West German is neither idolized nor is he excluded; instead he is treated as a peer.

The very fact that the one group knows little about the other and many statements are based on stereotype is one that Rosenlöcher makes a central theme under the caption "Die Frage des Dreikäsehoch" (TR 149). Rosenlöcher puts the question "Sind die Westdeutschen böse?" in the mouth of a child. For Rosenlöcher, the question triggers memories of childhood and youth, as well as reflections on his own development in recent years. The author's thoughts are constantly interrupted by the boy's repeated question whether the West Germans are evil and wander off in new directions again and again. It is hardly coincidental that Rosenlöcher quotes Theodor Storm, who commented in 1867 on the situation in Schleswig and Holstein, duchies annexed by the Prussians. This quotation also precedes Daniela Dahn's collection of essays,[27] which appeared in 1998, and in a certain sense exemplifies the intellectual proximity of the two authors. As does Günter Grass in his novel *Ein weites Feld,*[28] Rosenlöcher and Dahn draw a connection between the German unification in 1990 and the events that led to the foundation of the "Second German Reich".

Rosenlöcher formulates a fundamental problem of German unity, the lack of understanding for the 'Others', in a childlike and naïve fashion and completely without emotion. Ironically, the text ends with a question by a West German student who reverses the point of view and the question and ask whether the East Germans are evil (TR 155). Rosenlöcher concludes his thoughts with the ascertainment that one really only need the evil West German as a counterpart to oneself, as a counter-image to the *Ich*, which one wants to preserve even though it has not existed for quite a while.

3) Anecdotes, almanac stories, examples, sayings and images illustrate the discriminative practices of East and West Germans and consequently confirm one's opinion of one's own group and of the others. Arguments are based on incidents and events of common knowledge to the readers, ones which recall their own experiences and with which they can identify. With the help of such illustrations, abstract scenes can be translated into the reality of history, and the reader may become convinced of the correctness or incorrectness of a given theory. Furthermore, the same circumstances can be illuminated with several differing examples, making it absolutely possible to present a differentiated picture (e.g. Dahn's various experiences entering the USA). The use of example can be seen as part of an oral tradition that can be traced back to ancient rhetoric.[29] On the other hand, though, examples can hinder discussion and line of argument, for the very reason that they lay claim to authenticity. Admittedly, the prerequisite to using them 'successfully' is the self-recognition in the stories told on the part of the readers, that their own experiences and opinions are confirmed. Only by self-identification can a sense of belonging and eventually collective identity be produced or developed.

> Die Form der Anekdote scheint nun immer da benützbar, wo eine wirkliche Übereinstimmung zwischen dem Erzähler und dem Zuhörer und auch, wenn es mehrere sind, zwischen den Zuhörern besteht. Dann beleuchtet die Anekdote, wie es sehr schön heißt, blitzartig eine Situation (die dann eben allen bekannt vorkommt)[30]

Brecht's comments on the anecdote in connection with Naturalist drama point right to "das ethische Moment, das unwiderlegbare, weil auf authentische Quellen fußende Exemplarische, die konsensschaffende, blitzartige Erhellung einer Situation durch *ein* Beispiel".[31] It is probable that Dahn, Rosenlöcher and even Misselwitz, due to their socialization in Brecht's literary tradition, at least that of the Marxist Brecht, affiliate in the use of anecdote to Brechtian images as they are expressed in the *Geschichten vom Herrn Keuner*,[32] for example. At the same time, it has to be expected that the stories told meet with the desired identification of one part of the readership (supposedly the East German part) and that another part may become irritated and resentful.[33]

It is interesting that the stories told concentrate on a few themes that seem to take a central role in view of one's own situation. These themes surface in all three books, although they differ in forms of representation. While Dahn quotes from the respective laws, that is, from authentic sources, in order to demonstrate the differing laws used in the Federal Republic to process the Nazi past in comparison to the GDR past, Misselwitz relates the following anecdote:

> Ein ehemaliger General der NVA fragte schriftlich beim Bundesverteidigungs-
> minister nach, ob er sich – ohne Pensionsansprüche versteht sich – wenigstens
> "General a.D." nennen dürfe. Natürlich bekam er abschlägigen Bescheid. Daraufhin
> schrieb er dem Minister erneut und bekannte, daß er in der Wehrmacht bereits
> Leutnant gewesen sei. Selbstverständlich, meinte der Minister, dürfe er sich
> "Leutnant a.D." nennen. (HJM 61)

This anecdote is inserted into Misselwitz' reflections on the changing of the elite in the East without any commentary at all and illustrates his elaborations on the process of repression taking place, which in his opinion is taking the place of overcoming the past more and more often. No information regarding this former general of the NVA (on his character, for example) is entered into the anecdote, nor is there any reflection on the fact that there were obviously continuities in personnel from the *Wehrmacht* in the NVA. All that is important to the author is the fact that occupations in the GDR and in the "Third Reich" are valued so differently. Through this anecdote, the image of the unfairly treated East German takes shape for the reader. Its brevity and factuality and, furthermore, the fact that it is additionally supported by a reference point to typical attributes of the genre:

> erstens, was den Stoff angeht, *Faktizität*, zweitens, was ihren Gehalt angeht,
> *Repräsentanz*, das heißt Spiegelung eines Großen im Kleinen, drittens, was die Form
> angeht, *Kürze* und äußerste Sachlichkeit der Darbietung und viertens, was die
> Wirkung betrifft, die Haltung der *Nachdenklichkeit*.[34]

The plausibility and the notability of the example make not only for a convincing argument, but also make instrumental the shaping of political ideas.

Dahn illustrates similarly unfair repercussions of the new legal situation in an anecdote on the repercussions of the law regulating unresolved property issues for East Germans:

> Der Ostberliner Schriftsteller Walter Kaufmann stellte nach der Wende den Antrag,
> die Duisburger Villa seiner jüdischen Eltern, die von den Nazis ermordet worden

waren, rückübertragen zu bekommen. (Zu DDR-Zeiten war es den Bürgern untersagt, mit offiziellen Behörden der Bundesrepublik zu korrespondieren.) Anwalt Otto Schily übernahm den Fall und meinte: Das erledigen wir mit links. Doch er mußte sich von Rechts wegen belehren lassen. Das Bundesministerium der Finanzen teilte Herrn Kaufmann im Juni 1995 in einem Brief mit: "[…] Ansprüche nach dem Gesetz zur Regelung offener Vermögensfragen sind nicht gegeben, da dieses Gesetz nur für im Beitrittsgebiet belegenes Vermögen gilt." (DD 13)

Dahn herself says that several such cases had been brought to her attention, but that she only selected this single example. Thus, it is suggested that the other cases met with the same fate as that of the author Walter Kaufmann. By referring to actually existing individuals by name, as well as by the verbatim rendering of the letter, she proves what the results of the law have been for the East German populace.[35]

In both anecdotes, reference is made to discrepancies in the Federal German legislation. These events are related as stories of encroachments on East German citizens: the general and the author have both become victims of the new system. In this way, a myth of victimization is constructed and developed further in writing. Stemming from Party propaganda, this myth lives on in the memory of the East Germans, albeit unconsciously, namely that a lack of provisions in the GDR, for example, was blamed on 'imperialist manipulations' in the West. The stereotype of the disadvantaged East German and of the unfair West finds further elaboration in these stories. Simultaneously, the dichotomy of 'upper' and 'lower' is passed on also and supports the idea that there is no use in rebelling against the 'upper', since the power lies there and there's no fighting against it anyway.

Rosenlöcher illustrates the new conditions of ownership with an almanac story:

Bekanntlich kam vor vielen, vielen Jahren, als der Mensch noch ein Fußwesen war, ein Handwerksbursche von Tuttlingen nach Amsterdam. Staunend verharrte er vor einem Haus, wie er es auf seinem ganzen Weg nicht gesehen hatte. […] "Wem gehört dieses Haus?" fragte er. Die Antwort hieß "Kannitverstaan". "Donnerwetter", dachte der Johann-Peter-Hebelsche Bursche: "Das muß ein grundreicher Mann sein, der Herr Kannitverstaan." – "Kannitverstaan" ist holländisch und heißt auf sächsisch "Hä". "Der hiesige Herr Hä ist aber auch nicht der Ärmste", hätte der Handwerksbursche gedacht, wenn er anstatt nach Amsterdam nach Dresden gekommen wäre. […] Und wäre der Bursche neulich gekommen, hätte er erst recht Grund zum Staunen gehabt und fassungsloser denn je vor jenem Haus gestanden: "Wem gehört denn die Bruchbude hier?" […] Doch nun ist es an unsereinem, vor diesem und jenem Haus verwundert stehenzubleiben. So wie etwa ich schon nach ein paar Monaten Abwesenheit von Dresden allenthalben nachfragen mußte, was jetzt wohl wem gehöre. […] Und als ich in der Tieckstraße Silvester feierte, blieb dort in den Häusern schon manches Fenster dunkel, und ein Einwohner warf mit Raketen um sich, um auch im neuen Jahr für die richtige Stimmung zu sorgen. (TR 15f.)

Like all almanac stories, this one has a moral that de-emphasizes the importance of the historical context:

Das macht die Schwierigkeit allen Nachdenkens über die Gegenwart aus. Daß die neuen Möglichkeiten, noch eben erst kaum erträumt, mit neuem Zwang einhergehen. Daß selbst das schöne Geld, das uns so unabhängig macht, vom Geld abhängig macht. (TR 16f.)

However, this moral is not edifying in the traditional sense. Rather, it is much more a reflection of present conditions. In so doing, blame is neither laid nor sought in the 'others' – instead, problems are named and thereby recognized as such.

Another thematic constellation is the way the Federal Republic deals with dissidents. Dahn cites several examples illustrating how people with differing opinions, such as teenagers, are dealt with and comes once again to the conclusion that also in this context, there are few differences between "*Rechtsstaat BRD*" and the "*Unrechtsstaat DDR*".

Am Abend des 14. Juli dieses Jahres, ca. 20.30 Uhr, wurden über 50 Jugendliche, zumeist im Alter zwischen 13 und 17 Jahren, von der Polizei festgenommen. 160 Beamte stürmten überfallkommandoartig die Krämerbrücke, warfen einige von uns auf den Boden und drohten den anderen mit Gewalt, wenn sie sich nicht hinlägen. Unter Androhung von Schlägen wurden ihnen Gespräche sowie das Pinkeln verboten. [...] (DD 169)

Der Platz war durch Metallzäune in einen inneren Zirkel für besonders Auserwählte in Tribünennähe und in einen äußeren Bereich getrennt. Dort gelang es uns, ein großes Transparent zu entrollen und hochzuhalten: '*Danke Helmut für §218, Arbeitsamt + Armut.*' Sofort schoben sich Sicherheitsbeamte in Zivil dazwischen und versuchten, unsere Schrift durch ein eigenes Transparent mit dem sinnigen Spruch '*Jugend für Helmut Kohl*' zu verdecken. Unser Tuch war aber doch größer. Der Kanzler beschimpfte uns verärgert als "Fußkranke der sozialistischen Völkerwanderung", offenbar sein Urteil über jeden, der freiwillig in der DDR geblieben ist und trotz dieses Stigmas immer noch wagt aufzumucken." (DD 172)

The first example quoted refers to a message that was posted by teenagers in Erfurt on the Krämer Bridge. The report of the event is made in the form of a *Memorabile*. According to Jolles, the essential aspect of the *Memorabile* is the "Geistesbeschäftigung" and therefore the form "in der sich für uns allerseits das Konkrete ergibt",[36] which is achieved here by the exact documentation of the date, time of day, numbers present, etc. In contrast, the second example is an oral report by teenagers that the author quotes in her articles. The audience at this campaign demonstration allow themselves to be divided into Kohl's supporters and his opponents, but it appears to be more important to the author that the dissidents are not accepted and instead, like in the GDR days, are hindered by security forces. Here too, a story of victimization is told, although it is unimportant whether it has to do with East or West German youth (cf. the Hamburg story, DD 174ff.). Dahn is much more interested in showing that non-conformism is regulated and segregated.

What Dahn proves and illustrates in the form of concrete examples, Rosenlöcher abstracts with a joke, the punch line of which consists in the fact that all 'complainers' are sent back to the GDR:

> "Haben Sie das auch gelesen? Von dem Regierungsbeschluß? Daß jeder, der gar zu sehr schimpft, wieder in den Osten muß? Durch eine eigens eingerichtete Tür, dahinter schon ein Gummibaum steht. Und ein Bemützter mit Schäferhund: 'Ihren Personalausweis. DDR-Zollkontrolle!'"
> Bitte, ich sage kein Wort. (TR 166)

While Dahn's and Misselwitz' stories flow into the narrative structure of the essays and loosen up the text, the anecdotes, almanac stories and jokes that Rosenlöcher tells are a literary formation principle unto themselves. The anecdotes are inserted into the text in the form of dialogue, like in the short story or the travel section for example, such that they give structure to the text and return to the actual question over and over again. It becomes obvious, as in the following example on the subject of the past, that there are no clear answers, that culprit and victim are hard to distinguish from each other in many cases.

> "Haben Sie eine DDR-Identität?"
> "Ich war bei den Jungpionieren."
> "Wie bitte?"
> "Nichts", sagte ich.
> [...]
> "Was sagten Sie?"
> "Nichts", sagte ich.
> Und doch war ich bei den Jungpionieren.
> [...]
> "Ob Sie so etwas haben wie eine DDR-Identität?"
> "Können Sie mich nicht was anderes fragen?"
> "Was?"
> "Wie es mir geht, zum Beispiel."
> "Nun gut, wie geht es Ihnen?"
> "Blendend", sagte ich.
> Und doch war ich bei den Jungpionieren.
> [...]
> "Keine DDR-Identität?"
> Ich schüttelte den Kopf.

"Nie im Leben", sagte ich.

Und war doch bei den Jungpionieren. (TR 19, 23, 24, 26)

These dialogues lend structure to a longer text in which a possible GDR identity is reflected upon. For Rosenlöcher, identity has much to do with recognition, but also with barely explicable, hazy feelings of loss. Although this dialogue between an East German and a West German reproduces the communication problems in an ironic form, it clarifies nonetheless how East and West Germans talk past each other and – because of their differing points of reference – misunderstand each other.

IV

On the basis of personal experiences as well as with the help of facts and statistics from opinion polls, research studies and articles by other (East and West German) authors, Dahn and Misselwitz describe in their essays the present situation in unified Germany. The search for identity, the continuation of one's life to date and the new function of the authors all play an important role here. The statements are lent a universal validity through references to other authorities, often in the form of citation. With the help of little stories, illustration and argumentation are laid out, although any further discussion is hampered by the examples. For although counter-examples could certainly be found, these examples are held up as proof of the authors' point of view. By way of their claim to factuality, improbable events receive credibility. In contrast to the classically entertaining anecdotes, there is no comical element – instead, they tend to conclude rather with a shocking point that prompts reflection on the present situation in Germany.

Life in the GDR and the ramifications of reunification for East Germans are the primary considerations in these stories. In the process, the authors make it apparent that justice and equality are two important elements in the consciousness of many East Germans. It is left out, however, that the image of and the desire for an egalitarian and just world for all have to do with the founding myths of the GDR which could only carried through in fits and starts, but never completely. That which one forgave in the GDR or was ready to accept as a 'childhood disease' finds sharp criticism in the 'new' society.

Another story that is told in all three texts is the one about the autumn of 1989 as a people's revolution, one which defended such values as equality, justice and freedom.[37] Conjuring up the 'us' feeling of the peaceful revolution in the autumn of 1989 is essential for creating and maintaining an East German identity. The fall of the Berlin Wall is usually seen as a symbol for the downfall of communism[38] and as proof of the superiority of Western democracy. However, these three authors counter this with the memories of those who took part in the autumn of 1989 by describing traces that this event left in the collective memory[39] of the East Germans. With the help of anecdotes and examples, they make it clear that the events of the years 1989-1990 represent "politisch generierte Schwellen"[40] of historical experience for the East Germans. As with the two World Wars, June 17, 1953, the construction of the Berlin Wall, "Prague Spring" and the student protests of 1968, this event is conceived of either as a fortunate or unfortunate accident in one's biography and is remembered as an important event in the stories by those affected. The consciousness of broad segments of the East German population of having carried out a 'peaceful revolution' of their own accord and in this way contributed to toppling the regime left behind a sense of self-confidence and pride regarding what they achieved. For many East Germans, however, along with this confidence in being able to bring about change comes the feeling more and more often that they were not really the 'victors' of this revolution after all. Instead, the pressure of expectation of having to conform to West German standards is articulated, as well as the experience of not being recognized by West German as regards their own lifestyles, experiences and achievements.

In this way, all three texts call the memories of the autumn of 1989 to life. The recollection of these – for many East Germans, positive – experiences of individual strength and initiative give the reader a chance for identification and thereby establish a binding element between differing people and groups – a feeling of belonging arises:

> Die DDR ging unter, als sie gerade anfing, Spaß zu machen. [...] So viel Selbstbestimmung war nie. Und damit soviel neues Selbstbewußtsein. Das darf nicht vergessen werden, wenn man sich wundert, wie hartnäckig viele Neubundesbürger ihre Erfahrungen und Biographien verteidigen. (DD 11)

> Das Volk hatte sich als Souverän über die Verhältnisse erhoben. Es brauchte seine Macht einmal nicht zu delegieren. Ein Fest der Fre[i]heit als "Akt der Selbstverständlichkeit". In der Wirklichkeit jener wunderbaren Tage mußte sich vorübergehend kein Mensch ausweisen. Name, Herkunft, Beruf und Rang waren eine Zeit lang gleichgültig. Es ergab sich, daß jemand in den Straßen Westberlins seinen Vorgesetzten traf und ihn umarmte. Sogar Uniformierte der DDR-Organe mischten sich problemlos unters westwärts wandernde Volk. (HJM 10f.)

> Ich selbst stand eine kurze Zeit im Gedränge dicht neben zwei Grenzoffizieren, die sich vergeblich um einen Rest von Ordnung im Geschehen mühten und gegen die Menschenflut eine Absperrung verteidigten, um wenigstens den Schein eines regulären Grenzübergangs zu wahren. War es ihre Hilflosigkeit, die mich rührte, oder ein eigenes Bedürfnis nach Rückversicherung, daß ich einem von ihnen die Hand auf die Schulter legte und halb tröstend, halb beschwichtigend sagte: "Laßt mal. Es ist gut so. Wir kommen wieder."? (HJM 22)

In contrast to the varying attempts to explain the reasons for and precedents to the fall of the Berlin Wall,[41] the myth of the sovereign people is perpetuated here. For a brief moment, the difference between 'upper' and 'lower' appears to have been lifted, the goal of 'real' socialism to be within reach, equality, freedom and justice finally achieved. The "Reich der Freiheit" (DD 11) had been broached, utopias seemed to be true – all of which lasted only a short time, as the "Reich der Besitzenden" (ibid.) dawned with capitalist conditions. The new social conditions reincarnate the old dichotomy of 'upper' and 'lower'; continuities between the old system and the new are demonstrated. The tale of the 'third way' is told again by Dahn and Misselwitz and declared to be the only history of East Germans. How far present conditions have distanced themselves from the ideals of the peace and civil rights movement of the 70s and 80s in the GDR is apparent by the phrase Dahn uses: "Märkte schaffen ohne Waffen" (DD 12), an allusion to the GDR peace movement slogan: "Frieden schaffen ohne Waffen". An appeal is made here, albeit an ironic one, to the common memories and experiences and the associated values and ideals of a group of people with a common socialization.

Although the recollection of the autumn of 1989 does not play such a large role in Rosenlöcher's texts, he does connect the most-quoted sentence of the *Wende* to the region he calls home: "Ein einziges Mal in der sächsischen Kummergeschichte ist Sächsisch nicht die Sprache der Verlierer gewesen. Sie erinnern sich: 'Wir sind das Volk' war vor allem auf sächsisch gerufen worden." (TR 14) Given all the differences in the authors' biographical backgrounds and in the formation of their texts, there are an astonishing number of mutualities in the way history is related. History is told through stories, in which the authors make use of the literary elements of the factual texts in order to illustrate their own views of the events. These mutualities probably have their source in the authors' generation and, accordingly, their own socialization. The existence of an East German identity is, then, in no way simply an invention of the West.[42] The problem lies rather more in how the West reacts to its existence and how the East Germans experience these reactions.[43]

The following anecdote from Rosenlöcher will conclude my remarks. An analogy between the Spree Forest and the GDR and/or the East in general can be established: both continue to be written about, although neither exists any longer and although for this reason much is seen in a different light:

– Ob ich über den Spreewald schriebe? –
"Wie kommen Sie denn darauf?"
"Das sieht man Ihnen doch an."
"Was?"
"Daß Sie keine Ahnung haben."
"Wovon?"
"Vom Spreewald natürlich."
"Ist das weiter schlimm?"
"Im Gegenteil. Eine Voraussetzung. Den Spreewald gibt's nicht mehr, junger Mann."
(TR 67f.)

Translated by Heather Fleming

Notes

[1] This essay is the revised and expanded version of the paper I presented at the conference. The title is borrowed from Christoph *Dieckmann's Das wahre Leben im falschen. Geschichten von ostdeutscher Identität* (Berlin: Ch.Links, 1998), which itself is a play on Adorno's comment: "Es gibt kein richtiges Leben im falschen". Cf. Theodor W. Adorno, *Minima Moralia. Reflexionen aus dem beschädigten Leben*, Gesammelte Schriften, vol. 4, ed. Rolf Tiedemann, Frankfurt a.M.: Suhrkamp, 1980, 43.

[2] Cf. Werner Weidenfels, ed., *Die Identität der Deutschen*, München: Carl Hanser, 1983 or Harold James, *Deutsche Identität 1770-1990*, trans. Wolfdietrich Müller, Frankfurt a.M.: Campus, 1991.

[3] Günter Grass is certainly one of the best-known advocates of this thesis, which reaches back to Herder's conception of the "culture-nation", and according to Grass it has found a pragmatic application as the last point of reference of the conflicted German territorial consciousness since the 1970s. Looking back at German history, Grass notes that for centuries Germany has been represented only by its literature, or rather, by its literati. Cf. Günter Grass, *Kopfgeburten oder Die Deutschen sterben aus*, Neuwied: Luchterhand, 1980, 153f.

[4] At the beginning of the '70s, two thirds of the West German population were of the opinion that the inhabitants of the GDR were their compatriots. Although these numbers shrank during the years that followed, 50 percent still agreed with this statement in 1989.

Cf. Werner Weidenfeld and Karl-Rudolf Korte, eds. *Handbuch der deutschen Einheit*, Bonn: Bundeszentrale für politische Bildung, 1996, p. 248. Similarly, prior to 1989, the majority of the East German population considered itself to be primarily "German" and only secondarily "East German".

[5] Cf. Iris Häuser, *Gegenidentitäten. Zur Vorbereitung des politischen Umbruchs in der DDR. Lebensstile und politische Soziokultur in der DDR-Gesellschaft der achtziger Jahre*, Studien zur DDR-Gesellschaft 3, Münster: LIT, 1996. Joachim Gauck refers to "double and multiple identities". Cf. Joachim Gauck, "Vom schwierigen Umgang mit der Wahrnehmung," in: Stéphane Courois et al., *Das Schwarzbuch des Kommunismus. Unterdrückung, Verbrechen und Terror*, trans. Irmela Arnsperger et al., Munich and Zurich: Piper, 1998, 885-894, here 891. Using these different terms, Häuser und Gauck describe the fact that there was of course not one unifying identity of all East Germans in the GDR. East German identity was and is a diversely assembled patchwork in which opposing attitudes had to exist. Therefore, when I speak of an East German identity, I am ignoring that someone from the citizen's and peace movement of the GDR quite naturally had an identity that was assembled differently than a former SED functionary, for example.

[6] *Das Profil der Deutschen. Was sie vereint, was sie trennt,* Spiegel Spezial 1/1991: "Obwohl in der gesamtdeutschen Bundesrepublik die einen im Licht, die anderen noch im Schatten leben, stimmen die Deutschen in den meisten Meinungen überein. Das zeigte sich, unabhängig davon, ob die Interviewer allgemeine Themen nannten oder aktuelle Fragen stellten. Da wirkt kaum nach, daß die Deutschen vier Jahrzehnte lang in verschiedenen Systemen lebten und daß sie sich noch vor gut einem Jahr kaum kannten und nur über Bildschirme und Briefe sowie bei seltenen Beuschen voneinander erfuhren." (14)

[7] Cf. *Psychosozial,* 18.1 (1995), special topic: "Ossis und Wessis: Psychogramm deutscher Befindlichkeiten"; Wolfgang Hardtwig and Heinrich A. Winkler, eds., *Deutsche Entfremdungen: zum Befinden in Ost und West*, Munich: Beck, 1994; and Wolf Wagner, *Kulturschock Deutschland*, Hamburg: Rotbuch, 1996, 16ff.

[8] In 1990, only 28% still considered themselves to be citizens of the GDR, and 66% thought of themselves as Germans, but as early as 1992, as many as 51% saw themselves as GDR citizens again, and only 40% as Germans. Cf. Elisabeth Noelle-Neumann, "Aufarbeitung der Vergangenheit im Schatten der Stasi," *Frankfurter Allgemeine Zeitung,* 6 August 1992, p. 8. Cf. also Christoph Dieckmann, "In der Niemandszeit. Drei Kapitel über die ostwestdeutsche Ungleichzeitigkeit," *Die Zeit,* 17 September 1998, pp. 6f.

[9] These figures come from a study conducted by the Allensbach Institute for Public Opinion Research in 1992. Cf. Also Klaus Harpprecht, "Im Niemandsland. Die Crux der Ex-DDR ist ihre geistige Heimatlosigkeit," *Die Zeit,* 10 September 1998, p. 48.

[10] Cf. Margarethe Mitscherlich and Irene Runge, *Der Einheitsschock. Die Deutschen suchen eine neue Identität*, Hamburg: ECON, 1993; *German Studies Review. Special Issue: German Identity*, ed. Harold James, Winter 1992; *Die Deutschen auf der Suche nach ihrer neuen Identität?* eds. Eduard J. M. Kroker and Bruno Dechamps, Frankfurt a.M.: Königsteiner Forum, 1993; Rainer Härtwig, "Ost-West-Konflikt: Auf dem Weg der Annäherung zur neuen deutschen Identität und Integrität," *Report Psychologie*, March 1992, 9-19.

[11] Even in the *Handbuch zur deutschen Einheit*, there is a section on "Ostalgie oder DDR-Verklärung" under the rubric "Einstellung zur deutschen Einheit" (pp. 246-263). Cf. also Lothar Fritze, "Identifikation mit dem gelebten Leben. Gibt es DDR-Nostalgie in den neuen Bundesländern?" in: Ralf Altenhof and Eckard Jesse, eds., *Das wiedervereinigte Deutschland. Zwischenbilanz und Perspektiven*, Düsseldorf: Droste, 1995, pp. 275-292, and Thomas Ahbe, "Ostalgie als Selbstermächtigung. Zur produkitiven Stabilisierung ostdeutscher Identität," *Deutschland Archiv*, 30.4, 1997, 614-619.

[12] Sander L. Gilman, *Rasse, Sexualität und Seuche. Stereotype aus der Innenwelt der westlichen Kultur*, Reinbek: Rowohlt, 1992, p. 308.

[13] Polls verify over and over that many East Germans feel like "second-class citizens" in united Germany. Cf. Michael Lukas Moeller and Hans-Joachim Maaz, *Die Einheit beginnt zu zweit. Ein deutsch-deutsches Zwiegespräch*, Berlin: Rowohlt, 1991, as well as Margarethe Mitscherlich's discussion with Irene Runge (note 10) and with Brigitte Burmeister, *Wir haben ein Berührungstabu. Zwei deutsche Seelen − einander fremd geworden*, Munich: Piper, 1991.

[14] Quoted from Ursula E. Beitter, ed., *Schreiben im heutigen Deutschland. Die litera-rische Szene nach der Wende*, Loyola College in Maryland Berlin Seminar. Contemporary German Literature and Society 1, New York: Lang, 1997, p. xvii.

[15] In this regard, Misselwitz speaks of "generation bearing the brunt of thc political upheaval" in the GDR. Hans-J. Misselwitz, *Nicht länger mit dem Gesicht nach Westen. Das neue Selbstbewußtsein der Ostdeutschen*, Politik im Taschenbuch 15, Bonn: Dietz Nachfolger, 1996, p. 107. See also pp. 86f.

[16] The marginal role of the *Bündnis '90* in the East as well as amongst the West German Greens is an example of this lack of simultaneity in the East and West, also as concerns personal development.

[17] Hans-Joachim Maaz, *Das gestürzte Volk. Die verunglückte Einheit*, Berlin: Argon, 1991.

[18] Daniela Dahn, *Westwärts und nicht vergessen. Vom Unbehagen in der Einheit*, Berlin: Rowohlt, 1996. The following citations are from the Rowohlt 1997 edition and are identified in the body of this article by 'DD' and the page number.

[19] Cf. note 15. The following citations are identified in the body of this article by 'HJM' and the page number.

[20] Thomas Rosenlöcher, *Ostgezeter. Beiträge zur Schimpfkultur*, Frankfurt a.M.: Suhrkamp, 1997. The following citations are identified in the body of this article by 'TR' and the page number.

[21] *Der Duden. Deutsches Universalwörterbuch A-Z* (Mannheim: Duden, 1989) defines "myth" as: "1. Überlieferung, überlieferte Dichtung, Sage, Erzählung o.ä. aus der Vorzeit eines Volkes [...] 2. Person, Sache, Begebenheit, die (aus meist verschwommenen, irrationalen Vorstellungen heraus) glorifiziert wird, legendären Charakter hat." The adjectives used in the second part of the definition signal the negative connotation of the word in everyday speech; myths and 'objective' historiography appear to be mutually exclusive. Conversely, Lévi-Strauss demonstrated the similarities between European historiography and the myths of pre-literature peoples as early as 1962 (*La pensée sauvage*). Cf. also Thomas Hylland Eriksen, *Kampen om fortiden. Et essay om myter, identitet og politikk*, Oslo: Aschehoug, 1996.

[22] Cf. Sander L. Gilman (note 12) as well as Werner Koller, "Stereotypes und Stereotype. Sozialpsychologische und linguistische Aspekte", in: Hildegunn Brunland and Peter Langemeyer, eds., *Nationale oder kulturelle Identitäten? Zur Landeskunde der deutschsprachigen Länder*. Trekkfugl. Studien zur Didaktik Deutsch als Fremdsprache. Tagungsberichte und Arbeitsmaterialien zur Lehrerfortbildung in Norwegen 4, Tromsø: Nordoffset, 1997, pp. 71-92.

[23] The song of solidarity was written for the film "Kuhle Wampe" at the beginning of the '30s using Bertolt Brecht's lyrics and a melody by Hanns Eisler and was sung frequently in the GDR on official occasions.

[24] Naturally, Dahn's allusion was understandable to many West Germans, since the song of solidarity was also a component of social democratic and union culture in the West.

[25] Dahn refers to the work itself and quotes from it (cf. P. 200).

[26] Dahn awakens associations with Günter de Bruyn's novel *Neue Herrlichkeit* (1984), in which the corrupt, almost feudal-absolutist conditions in the GDR are satirically described.

[27] Daniela Dahn, *Vertreibung ins Paradies*, Reinbek: Rowohlt, 1998, n.pag.

[28] Göttingen: Steidl, 1995.

[29] Cf. Christoph Daxelmüller, "Narratio, Illustratio, Argumentatio. Exemplum und Bildungstechnik in der frühen Neuzeit," in: Walter Haug and Burghart Wachinger, eds., *Exempel und Exempelsammlungen*, Tübingen: Niemeyer, 1989, pp. 77-94.

[30] Bertolt Brecht, *Gesammelte Werke* 15, ed. in cooperation with Elisabeth Hauptmann, Frankfurt a.M.: Suhrkamp, 1967, p. 174. Quoted from Christian Klein "Die Anekdote als Moment des Politischen in der Dramaturgie von Georg Seidel," in: Horst Turk and Jean-Marie Valentin in association with Peter Langemeyer, eds., *Aspekte des politischen Theaters und Dramas von Calderón bis Georg Seidel. Deutsch-französische Perspektiven*, Jahrbuch für Internationale Germanistik. ser. A, vol. 40, Bern: Lang, 1996, pp. 421-435, here 424.

[31] Christian Klein, "Die Anekdote…," loc. cit., 424.

[32] Bertolt Brecht, *Geschichten vom Herrn Keuner*, Frankfurt a.M.: Suhrkamp, 1972. In this edition, the stories are published separately for the first time. On the history of the origins and reception of the Keuner stories, cf. Jan Knopf, *Brecht-Handbuch. Lyrik, Prosa, Schriften. Eine Ästhetik der Widersprüche*, Stuttgart: Metzler, 1984, pp. 311-322.

[33] In interviews, Daniela Dahn reports of the positive reactions of many West Germans during a book tour. Cf. for example Daniela Dahn, "Im Westen was Neues? Impressionen von einer Lesereise," *Neues Deutschland*, 15/16 Feb. 1997. The border between identification and irritation is not identical, then, with the 'border' between East and West.

[34] Hans Peter Neureuter, "Zur Theorie der Anekdote," *Jahrbuch des Freien Deutschen Hochstifts* (1973) 458-480.

[35] Cf. also Stefan Heym, *Auf Sand gebaut. Sieben Geschichten aus der unmittelbaren Vergangenheit*, Munich: Bertelsmann, 1990. In the title story, the results of the law regulating unresolved property issues are related through the example of fictitious individuals.

[36] André Jolles, *Einfache Formen. Legende, Sage, Mythe, Rätsel, Spruch, Kasus, Memorabile, Märchen, Witz*, Tübingen: Niemeyer, 1982, p. 211.

[37] Daniela Dahn portrays this brief period in the autumn of 1989 as a "Reich der Freiheit, in dem die bürgerlichen und die sozialen Menschenrechte garantiert waren" (DD 11).

[38] Cf. François Furet, *Das Ende der Illusion. Der Kommunismus im 20. Jahrhundert*, trans. Karola Bartsch, Eliane Hagedorn, Christine Krieger and Barbara Reitz, Munich: Piper, 1996. Furet describes the history of the illusion, as it also existed in the West, of the

inevitable triumph of communism as a now-concluded era "die mit der Oktoberrevolution begann und mit der Auflösung der Sowjetunion zu Ende ging" (11).

[39] On the concept of collective memory, cf. Jan Assmann, "Kollektives Gedächtnis und kulturelle Identität," in: Jan Assmann and Tonio Hölscher, eds., *Kultur und Gedächtnis*, Frankfurt a.M.: Suhrkamp, 1988, pp. 9-19.

[40] Cf. Lutz Niethammer, "Diesseits des 'Floating Gap'. Das kollektive Gedächtnis und die Konstruktion von Identität im wissenschaftlichen Diskurs," in: Kristin Platt and Mihran Dabag, eds., *Generation und Gedächtnis. Erinnerungen und kollektive Identitäten*, Opladen: Leske + Budrich, 1995, pp. 25-50, esp. 37f.

[41] Misselwitz himself refers to Henryk M. Broder's theory of the revolution as an "Opus magnum der Stasi" (HJM 13). Other attempts at explanation can also be found in literary form, such as Erich Loest's *Nikolaikirche* (Leipzig: Linden, 1995) or Thomas Brussig's *Helden wie wir* (Berlin: Volk und Welt, 1995).

[42] Stefan Berg, "Die neue deutschen Sippenhaft," *Der Spiegel*, 39/1996, 51-53.

[43] Cf. the letters to the editors in *Die Zeit* of October 1, 1998, p. 80 ("Solche Klischees schmerzen") oder Annette Simon: "Osten: 'Alles Kriecher und Spitzel?' Die Beschämung des Ost-Zwillings ist der Schamlosigkeit des West-Zwillings geschuldet," *enfant t./Zeitschrift für Kindheit*, 5.2 (1992), 81-88.

IV. Politics and Political Culture in the New *Länder*

Lothar Probst

Transition from Community to Society?

Western scholars tend to argue that community orientations in East Germany are typical features of a modernization backlog. Criticising this perspective, this chapter stresses the productive potential of community orientations in the shaping of East German identities and explores three dimensions of the communitarian heritage of the GDR: 1. The feeling of national togetherness promised an escape from the authoritarian state. 2. Small political communities and opposition groups were the forerunners for the citizens' movements which emerged in 1989. 3 Lacking the opportunities of a liberal and democratic public sphere, private networks and interpersonal relationships fostered communication and solidarity between the citizens.

The demand of a majority of the East Germans for national unity in 1989 and the ensuing process of unification triggered a new debate about nation and national identity in Germany. Ralf Dahrendorf put his finger on the problem when he said regarding the German case: "No matter how you look at it: the nation is back and with it the nation state, and in fact, it is back in the middle of Europe, in Germany."[1] Facing this problem many intellectuals expected a relapse into the disastrous traditions of German history, and believed that a strong feeling of national unity would dominate the new agenda in post-unification Germany.

In 2000, ten years after the unification, the problems look quite different. Contrary to expectations, it looks like as if "Germany is a nation which doesn't want to be a nation", as the historian Christian Meier put it in a book title.[2] Institutionally, Germany is united. With regard to the political culture, however, it is still a divided country. Culturally the East and West Germans are distinct from each other. In the West values and attitudes of East Germans are regarded as anti-modern, traditional and community-oriented, whereas many East Germans take the WestGermans for arrogant, aggressive, self-interested, and materialistic. Many surveys indicate a deep gap between the values of East and West Germans.[3] In general, East Germans place value much more than West Germans on social security and equality, close social relationships and a sense of community. West Germans, on the other hand, emphasize the preferences of a liberal society such as self-realization, individualism and political freedom. One of the surveys summarizes the differences as follows: "The East Germans live more in community, whereas the West Germans prefer to disassociate from each other."[4]

Many scholars interpret these differences from the perspective of modernization theory.[5] The basis of this theory is a particular understanding of modernity. Societies which are determined by certain "objective" features such as urbanization, the rationalization of thought structures, economic efficiency, and differentiated societal subsystems are, according to this theory, modern. Additionally, the process of secularization, the decline of traditional patterns of interpretation and the enlargement of individual options for action are regarded as typical modern charcteristics. Many social studies in recent years, however, also focus on a sphere of "subjective modernization",[6] particularly highlighting the differentiation of social milieus, the pluralization of lifestyles, the development of new social movements, a new gender relationship, the evolution of expressive claims for autonomy and self-realization and a turn to postnational and post-materialistic values.

Contrasting the GDR with these features of "modernization" many scholars assume a modernization deficit in East Germany.[7] On the one hand, they admit that the process of industrialization also produced partial forms of an "objective" modernization in the GDR, such as urbanization, mobility by the development of motorization, and an advanced education system focused on technical skills. On the other hand, they point to the deficiencies in the sphere of subjective modernization. Features of a "modernization gap" in East Germany are, following these scholars, privatism, the highlighting of family values and family life-styles, community orientation, materialism, and the longing for social security. These characteristics, according to the theory, can be traced back to the legacy of GDR state socialism, which combined traditional and antiliberal elements of German political culture with specific socialist elements such as comprehensive state subsidies. This legacy represents continuing effects of political socialization under communism and is accompanied by attitudes such as conformism, authoritarianism, and traditionalism. In the mainstream of modernization theory, particularly the longing for community indicates a lack of socio-structural and socio-cultural fragmentation of society. Against this background the therapy to overcome East Germany's modernization backlog seems to be clear: East Germany has to catch up to the Western standards of modernization.

Without ignoring that the socialist legacy and traditional elements of German culture still play an important role in the shaping of East German identities after unification, I think it is too easy to attribute the East German feeling of "uneasiness in unity" only to deficits of "subjective" modernization. Of course, the electorate and the milieu of the Party of Democratic Socialism (PDS), for example, represent many aspects of this legacy – particularly the resistance against the Westernization of the East. A *Spiegel* survey from 1996 (issue no. 45), however, indicates that a majority of members and voters of the Christian Democrats (CDU) and the Social Democrats (SPD) in East Germany share the feeling of uneasiness with those of the PDS, although they in principle support unification and the institutions of liberal democracy.

Against this background we have to develop a more differentiated view in order to understand East German dissatisfaction in the unification process. In almost all surveys, the reason for the discomfort with the outcome of unification doesn't result from economic deficiencies and social problems in the period of transition.[8] Many East Germans concede that their personal economic situation is much better than before unification.[9] Another argument, however, helps us to explain the East Germans' discomfort. A majority of respondents of the *Spiegel* surveys in 1993 and 1996 expressed a strong feeling of cultural exclusion and rejection by a majority of the West. The main point is that a pure Western perspective neglects that community orientations played in at least three respects an important role in East German society: 1. The feeling of national togetherness was much deeper than in the West, not least because national unity promised an escape from the authoritarian state; 2. Small political communities and opposition groups were the forerunners of the citizens' movements which emerged in 1989; 3. Lacking the opportunities of a liberal and democratic public, private net-works, communities and interpersonal relationships fostered communication and solidarity between the citizens. I will explore these three dimensions in the following section.

West German Postnationalism and the Ignorance of the East German Feeling of Togetherness
The first explanation goes back to 1989 and refers to the intellectual dis-course about German unification. When the demonstrators in the streets of Leipzig shouted "We are one people," West German intellectual skeptics such as Günter Grass and Walter Jens opposed unification, pointing out that a two-state concept would take into account the German responsibility for Nazi dictatorship. Their objections corresponded to the warnings of those East German intellectuals who, educated in the antifascist tradition, also opposed the East German citizens' demand for unification and pleaded for the con-

tinued independence of the GDR. Even after unification was already a fact, many intellectuals and part of the media continued to discuss the reestablishing of the German nation state in the old German tradition of dichotomizing between *Gemeinschaft* and *Gesellschaft*. Andreas Huyssen stressed in this context the continuation of a negative nationalism among left intellectuals when he said: "Nation and democracy, nation and modernity – these are the questions that are raised in the international debate about nation, a debate, which is unfortunately ignored in Germany."[10] On the contrary: in the postnational discourse of the '68 generation, national community was considered to be something premodern and retrogressive. Many intellectuals believed that "after Auschwitz, the Germans had gambled away the right of national unity".[11] Not only the change in the political and intellectual self- perception of the Federal Republic but also the cultural shift to the patterns of Western civilization and society contributed among many West Germans to a growing lack of interest in the GDR, which they regarded as a foreign country.

Against this background, the call of East German citizens for unification did not find an adequate resonance in the West and was misinterpreted as a kind of nationalistic enthusiasm. Many East Germans, however, just asked for a feeling of national solidarity, but then they experienced ignorance and refusal. Relevant parts of the West German intellectual public did not even respond to the desire of the East German citizens to be "one people" and, instead, defended the two-state concept. The experience of a rejection of their basic emotional demands contributed, as I would like to argue, to a revival of an East German identity centered around social and community-oriented values. In the beginning of the unification process more than 80% of the East Germans saw themselves as Germans; by 1993, however, the figures had already changed dramatically. Now 54 % expressed that they primarily felt East Germans (*Spiegel* 3/1993). Although most surveys did not indicate a general East-West antipathy, it is nevertheless true that, in the wake of unification, "das teilnationale Wir-Gefühl"[12] increased on both sides of the old East-West demarcation line.

Regarding German unification from this point of view it is quite obvious that a majority of the intellectual public and political class failed to integrate the East German demand for unity into a republican concept of national identity. A majority of the intellectual elite stuck to its postnational attitudes and did not respond to the desire of the East-German citizens to be "one people". The conservative-liberal Kohl government, on the other hand, treated the "Beitrittsgebiet" predominantly from an administrative and economic perspective, ignoring the fact that the simple transfer of Western institutions would provoke cultural counterreactions in the East. In both cases, the contribution of the East German citizens to freedom and unity was devalued. I think that Dieter Henrich was right when he emphasized that "national unity in 1989/1990 was generated by the East Germans' will for freedom. For the first time in our history," as Henrich continues, "we can found national unity on an historical event which is comparable with the founding events of Switzerland, the Netherlands or the United States, although Germany in general does not belong to the nations with a republican tradition."[13] Instead of emphasizing, however, that the East Germans' struggle for political freedom and unity constituted a break in the German tradition of separating freedom and unity, the mainstream of left intellectuals defined unification in terms of a continuity of the catastrophes of German history, ignoring the republican and democratic moment of the 1989 revolution. This republican moment contained in principle the potential for creating a common "political WE", which takes responsibility for the burden of the history and shapes the future.

Having German history in mind, it is, however, rather difficult to define a new national identity in postunification Germany beyond what Habermas called "Verfassungspatriotismus" with its postnational orientation. Originally the term "Verfassungspatriotismus" was coined by Dolf Sternberger. He used this notion in order to characterize "the will for a good, free order for the people to whom one belongs."[14] The more familiar Habermasian version, however, neglects that Sternberger connected the principle of universal rights with the feeling of togetherness. Lacking this feeling of togetherness and experiencing that they were not accepted as mutual members of a common German polity, many East Germans resigned and turned to the revitalization of an East German identity which includes elements of a stronger social coherence and feeling of community.

The Power of Antipolitics and the Democratizing Effects of Communitarian Networks in East-Central Europe

My second explanation represents a more general view of the transition of East-Central European societies from communism to liberal democracy. After the brutal suppression of the Czechoslovakian experiment for a humane socialism and the disillusionment of many intellectuals about communism in 1968, new types of opposition-building emerged in many East-Central European countries. Reacting to the atomizing tendencies of the one-party state which monopolized power and the public space, dissident groups started to reformulate the classical concept of civil society under the conditions of communist dictatorship. They generated channels of an autonomous public space with independent forms of publishing, teaching, and acting, in order to reestablish "truth," "truthfulness and "morality" in a society which was poisoned by lies and ideology. Antipolitics was created in order to overcome "the power of ideologies, systems, bureaucratic apparatus, artificial languages, and political slogans," as Vaclav Havel from Charta '77 put it in 1987.[15] The politics of antipolitics was, however, more than a mere proclamation of goals. It also was a practical attempt to organize forms of solidarity and assistance for persecuted citizens under the conditions of extreme political repression. The ethos of solidarity, community and participation dominated the discourse of the concept of antipolitics. We also have to remind ourselves in this context that the independent Polish opposition movement called itself "solidarnosc". In the wake of the seventies and eighties a broad network of independent groups and organizations, taking up the principles of antipolitics, emerged in nearly all East Central European countries and challenged the power of communist dictatorship.

The situation in the GDR was – in comparison with other East Central European countries – different. The political opposition was rather weak and, predominantly, oriented towards a reform of the socialist state instead of establishing a broad civil society. However, the socio-cultural sphere in the GDR was less homogeneous than the modernization approach would make us believe. Already in the seventies processes of a "subjective" modernization started to change GDR society in spite of the mechanisms of political control by the SED. GDR citizens could manage to develop more autonomy in personal relationships and networks, in niches, and in minor cultural and literary institutions. Particularly among the younger generation a growing number of people refused to follow the ideological guidelines and intentions of the official agents of socialisation and created their own spaces of self-expression concerning, for example, questions such as fashion, music, and lifestyle. These tendencies fostered not only the evolution of alternative subcultures but also a broader political opposition. In the beginning of the eighties peace and environmental groups emerged under the roof of the protestant church and started to establish an infrastructure for communication, political activities and an alternative public sphere. They organized meetings, conferences, exhibitions, lectures about peace, ecology and human rights issues, and published illegal leaflets and journals. In the

course of the eighties, broad networks such as "Kirche von unten", "Konkret
für den Frieden", and "Ökologisches Winterseminar" were built. Thousands
of people joined these networks, experiencing how to act in concert and to
oppose policies of the authoritarian regime. Community orientations and
solidarity played a very important role in these value-oriented groups. One of
the peace groups in Rostock called itself "Schalomgemeinschaft", pointing to
the common grounds of its members. Without overestimating the influence of
the opposition movement in the GDR among ordinary citizens, the literature
on this movement[16] reveals that these groups established the infrastructure
and the communication channels for the rise of the citizens' movement in
1989.

Political opposition groups were, however, only the spearhead of a
broader counter-culture which emerged in and outside of the Protestant
church in the course of the eighties. Joachim Gauck, in 1989 one of the
speakers of the citizens' movement *Neues Forum* in the city of Rostock,
highlights, for instance, the importance of non-oppositional networks inside
of the Protestant church when he argues: "Beside the peace and
environmental groups which opposed SED politics, there was a kind of
counter-culture in the daily work of the Protestant church. In the youth,
senior and women groups of the church, many citizens experienced
alternatives to the ideological goals of the SED state. People in these groups
acquired the ability to speak frankly with each other, to develop confidence
and trust."[17] And Dietlind Glüer, who worked for the Protestant church in
Mecklenburg, adds: "There was a whole ring of families in Mecklenburg,
families which stuck together all the time and supported each other for many
years."[18] Basic values such as mutual help, solidarity, and openness were the
glue which held these family networks together.

This sense of solidarity and community was, however, not limited to
connections inside of the Protestant church or the political opposition. Family
ties, neighborhoods, close friendships, private groups, and workplace
relationships were central elements of a communitarian network in the GDR
society in order to deal with the deficiencies of the economy and to
circumvent the repressive structures of the communist state. In the Western
discourse these networks are often devalued as partnerships of convenience
or needs-communities. This perspective not only ignores the differences
between value-oriented communities and needs-communities but also
neglects the positive effects of needs-communities on social cohesion even if
they were not explicitly political.

Regarding the value-oriented communities and opposition groups, many studies reveal that they developed a social and cultural obstinancy against the imperatives of communist dictatorship.[19] But also in their everyday life communities and networks, people experienced confidence, developed trust and channels of free communication, and learned how to deal with differences in a non-violent and non-friend-foe way of thinking. Moreover, we know from the empirical results of communication studies that interpersonal relationships in social networks foster political learning and stimulate political debate.[20]

Summarizing these experiences, it is obvious that the East-Central European societies including the GDR were much more determined by elements of a collective and communitarian culture than were Western societies. But this collective culture was a culture from the "bottom up" of the society and should not be confused with the artifical collective culture which was decreed from above. Against this background the public lament of many East Germans for the loss of "community" does not necessarily express an "Ostalgia" but a feeling for the loss of close interpersonal social relationships in a new individualistic environment. The rapid implementation of a new social, political and economic system requires new social capabilities and cultural attitudes, and many East Germans experience social and cultural differentation, individualization, and the imperatives of economic competition in the current process of modernization as a loss of solidarity and community-based relationships and friendships. Old protest networks, for instance, which stimulated courage and opposition-building under the conditions of dictatorship, collapsed after 1990 and lost support in the new democratic environment. One of the members of these networks summarized his experiences as follows:

> I was member in a group which encouraged political activities. [...] This group no longer exists. [...] The actions we were involved in and which were rather risky are no longer necessary. [...] We were only a few courageous people with a strong feeling of togetherness. But this feeling is gone, and I have no longer such a close circle of friends. The ties by which we were welded together are lost.[21]

The needs-communities lost their function in the new market and consumer society which provided everybody with sufficient goods. To maintain interpersonal relationships in order to obtain certain consumer goods did not make sense any longer. One GDR citizen describes the new situation with the words: "Before unification we were forced to stick together. Everybody helped each other to get this or that. We were in a certain sense a 'Solidargemeinschaft der Beschaffung'. And this is gone."[22]

Last but not least the people were confronted with the collapse of GDR-typical social institutions such as "Betriebskollektive", "Betriebssport-vereine", and other workplace arrangements. These institutions were places of interpersonal exchange and connectedness, though they were in many cases under the political control of the SED.

Summarizing these experiences, the East German "Modernisierungs-schmerz" does not necessarily represent a longing for the reestablishing of the old structures of the communist system. Instead of interpreting the East Germans' sense of community and solidarity only as an antimodern affect against the imperatives of modernization and individualization, we should keep the positive effects of the communitarian culture for social cohesion in mind. Furthermore, we should even take into account, and that is what I want to suggest, that liberal societies in the West could also benefit from the experiences which were represented in the communitarian culture of East Central European citizens and dissident groups. This brings me to my last point which concerns challenges of modern liberal societies.

Communitarianism and Democracy
The main discourse on the transition of East-Central European countries is centered on the question of how these societies can incorporate as quickly as possible the values of liberal society and market economy. Constitutional and political engineering, the implementation of institutions and the rule of law, party-building and parliamentary representation are regarded as the best preconditions for the stabilization of the new democracies. To make it clear: All these features are indispensable means to overcome the heritage of the communist dictatorship and to make democracy work. Moreover, social, political, and cultural differentiation and fragmentation are unavoidable in the ongoing process of modernization in the East-Central European societies, and every attempt to return to an artificial homogenization of society will fail.

But what happens when institutions do not work, when people experience the shortcomings of a market economy, and when parties turn out to be corrupt (a very topical issue in the light of the CDU party donations scandal)? Usually we rely on the capacities of the modern welfare state and its institutions which have to guarantee social security, social opportunity, individual rights, and political participation of the citizens. In fact, however, the political agenda is often determined by bureaucracy, political corruption, lobbyism, the dominance of economic interests, and a selfish culture of individualism. Also established liberal democracies are "suffering from a kind of legitimacy crisis, a growing and widespread concern that its institutions are no longer adequate, that they fail to live up to their own professed ideals, to support coherent public policy, a meaningful way of life, or a sense of popular empowerment."[23] There are many symptoms of this crisis: frustration with politicians, political parties and institutions, withdrawal from politics, resentment, apathy, distrust, or attitudes of authoritarianism. And there is a deep feeling in the electorate of many western societies that voters are only the objects of an elitist model of democracy. The rise of right-wing populist movements and parties is one of the results of this development.

Furthermore, the ongoing process of denationalization makes the world much more complex. Political decision-making depends more and more on the coordination of a complicated network of institutions and administrative agencies. This increasingly gives institutional politics the appeal of a "cold project," as Ralf Dahrendorf put it, not reaching the feelings and passions of the people. On the contrary, many people do not feel very comfortable with this development and react with a loss of confidence in political institutions.

In the light of these considerations, it is not surprising that also in the West the communitarian discourse has gained momentum over the last decade. The idea that the identity of modern societies can solely be centered around institutions turns out to be an insufficient answer to the loss of confidence in the benefits of liberal democracy. Common values, the feeling of togetherness and community orientations are still indispensable resources for the social and political cohesion of modern pluralistic societies. Local communities, interpersonal networks and voluntary associations – as the experience of East Central European societies shows – constitute the political and social space in which citizens develop civic attitudes, experience mutual solidarity, and learn how to act in concert. They support the cohesion of the people against the tendency towards atomization and disempowerment in the modern world. They are value-creating and democracy-(re-)generating, and they remind us that democracy is not only grounded in institutions but is also dependent on a working and active civil society. Politically and socially active citizens foster the development and strengthening of a moral infrastructure which is substantial for the support of political institutions in a liberal society.

In the light of the ongoing process of denationalization, the importance of local networks and communities is even growing. The philosopher Manuel Castells argues that one of the new conflicts in a globalized world is the conflict between the huge transnational economic and institutional nets on the one hand and the small personal nets on the other hand. The question of how to bridge the tension between these two nets will be one of the central challenges in the years to come. No matter what form of "global" democracy we expect to emerge, communitarian networks will remain important in order to create a feeling of togetherness and security in a fragmented and secularized society.

Notes

[1] Ralf Dahrendorf, "Die Sache mit der Nation", in Karl-Heinz Bohrer, ed., *Umbruch. Merkur Sonderheft* (Stuttgart, 1990), p. 823.

[2] Christian Meier, *Die Nation, die keine sein will,* Munich: Hanser Verlag, 1991. My own translation, as are all following translations from German unless otherwise indicated.

[3] See, for example, survey results published in *Der Spiegel* no. 3 (1993) or no. 45 (1996).

[4] Elmar Brähler and Horst Eberhard Richter, "Deutsche Befindlichkeiten im Ost-West-Vergleich", *Aus Politik und Zeitgeschichte,* B 40-41 (1995), p. 14.

[5] See, for example, Wolfgang Zapf, ed., *Die Modernisierung moderner Gesellschaften*, Frankfurt a.M.: Campus, 1991.

[6] Cf. Stefan Hradil, "Die 'objektive' und die 'subjektive' Modernisierung. Der Wandel der westdeutschen Sozialstruktur und die Wiedervereinigung", *Aus Politik und Zeitgeschichte,* B 29-30/92 (1992); Stefan Hradil, "Überholen statt Einzuholen? Chancen subjektiver Modernisierung in Ostdeutschland", in: Raj Kollmorgen et al. eds., *Sozialer Wandel und Akteure in Ostdeutschland*, Opladen: Leske und Budrich, 1996.

[7] Hradil, 1992.

[8] Cf. Karl-Dieter Opp, *Die enttäuschten Revolutionäre*, Opladen: Leske und Budrich, 1997.

[9] Thomas Gensicke, *Die neuen Bundesbürger. Eine Transformation ohne Integration*, Opladen/Wiesbaden: Westdeutscher Verlag, 1998.

[10] Andreas Huyssen, "Wider den negativen Nationalismus", in: F. Meyer-Gosau and Wolfgang Emmerich, eds., *Gewalt – Faszination und Furcht, Jahrbuch für Literatur und Politik in Deutschland*, vol. 1 (1994), p. 39

[11] Richard Schröder, *Vom Gebrauch der Freiheit*, Stuttgart: Deutsche-Verlags-Anstalt, 1996, p. 12.

[12] Bettina Westle, "Einstellungen zur Nation und zu den Mitbürgern", in: Oscar W. Gabriel, ed., *Politische Orientierungen und Verhaltensweisen im vereinigten Deutschland,* Opladen: Leske und Budrich, 1997, p. 80.

[13] Dieter Henrich, "Deutsche Identitäten nach der Teilung," *Politisches Denken. Jahrbuch 1991* (Stuttgart/Weimar: 1991), p. 31.

[14] Dolf Sternberger, "Verfassungspatriotismus", in: Dolf Sternberger, ed., *Schriften* ,vol. 10 (1990).

[15] Vaclav Havel, "The Power of the Powerless", in: Vaclav Havel, *Living in Truth,* London: Faber and Faber, 1987, p. 153.

[16] See among others: Jürgen Israel, *Zur Freiheit berufen: Die Kirche in der DDR als Schutzraum der Opposition,* Berlin: Aufbau Taschenbuch Verlag, 1991; Helmut Müller-Enbergs et al., *Von der Illegalität ins Parlament. Werdegang und Konzept der neuen Bürgerbewegungen,* Berlin: LinksDruck Verlag, 1991; Detlef Pollack, *Die Legitimität der Freiheit. Politisch alternative Gruppen in der DDR unter dem Dach der Kirche,* Frankfurt a.M.: Peter Lang, 1990; Lothar Probst, *Ostdeutsche Bürgerbewegungen und Perspektiven der Demokratie,* Köln: Bund Verlag, 1994.

[17] Lothar Probst, *'Der Norden wacht auf' – Zur Geschichte des politischen Umbruchs in Rostock im Herbst 1989,* Bremen: Edition Temmen, 1994, p. 103.

[18] The quote is from an unpublished interview by the author with Dietlind Glüer.

[19] Detlef Pollack, "Sozialstruktureller Wandel, Institutionentransfer und die Langsamkeit der Individuen", *Soziologische Rundschau,* no. 19 (1996), p.419.

[20] Lutz Erbring and Hossein Shala, "Politische Kommunikation im sozialen Umfeld. Über die Folgen und Funktionen aktiver interpersonaler Kommunikation in einer Phase turbulenter politischer und sozialer Veränderungen", in: Hans-Dieter Klingemann et al., eds., *Zwischen Wende und Wiedervereinigung. Analysen zur Politischen Kultur in West- und Ost-Berlin 1990,* Opladen: Westdeutscher Verlag, 1995.

[21] Opp, 1997, p. 113

[22] Ibid, p. 112.

[23] Jeffrey C. Isaac, "The Meaning of 1989", *Social Research,* vol 63, no. 2 (1996), p. 330.

Catherine Perron

Eastern German and Czech Democratization from the Perspective of Local Politics

This chapter focuses on the effects of "democratization by institutional transfer" on new democratic political elites at a local level. Its aim is to analyse to what extent the new eastern German local politicians benefited from the very rapid integration into the western German stable democratic system. Did it strengthen democratic practices and attitudes, and if so, how? What were the negative effects, if any, compared to the democratization process of other countries such as the Czech Republic, where the transformation process was much slower and the outcome more uncertain? Are the perspectives for the creation of a stable democracy better in the German case than in the Czech one? Which of these two systems provides the best foundations for political stability?

This chapter intends to be a contribution to the comparative study of post-communist transformation in Central Europe. It will focus on the democratisation process in local politics in Eastern Germany and in the Czech Republic.[1] These countries share similarities in their communist pasts which allow the comparison of their transformation processes. Both countries were industrialised, had developed societies, and were of comparable size and population. Both experienced rigid communist parties with almost no reform movements inside and a very weak opposition completely cut off from society. Both regimes broke down in a comparable way: under the pressure of massive demonstrations and with a rapid and complete overthrow of the Communist parties (no concerted process between communists and counter elites as in Poland or Hungary happened). Their situations in 1989 are therefore comparable, especially as far as elites are concerned.[2]

Of course, one could wonder what the Czech Republic and Eastern Germany have in common today, except their shared past as satellite states of the USSR. Eastern Germans are part of the richest and most powerful nation in Europe, whereas the Czechs, separated from the Slovaks, are still waiting to become members of the European Union. The common history of these two countries did not end with the 1989 revolutions, the defeat of communist power and the end of Soviet domination. In this paper, I argue that the post-communist transition in Eastern Germany, although in many ways unique, could nevertheless share similar features with the post-communist transitions in other Central European states. It is especially useful to compare with the other Eastern European cases the way in which the Eastern German transformation process by "institutional transfer" affected the construction of democracy, and to examine its success and failures. What occurred in Eastern Germany can be considered as a perfect example of a "transition to democracy" and is instructive to our understanding of this process in other post-communist societies. Moreover, since the foremost goal of these countries is to be integrated into the European Union, which in some ways is an integration into a more complex and developed system, the Eastern German experience might be useful to study. It provides insight into the feasibility of transformation processes in post-communist societies in general, and in a more general way, as A. Pickel and H. Wiesenthal argue,[3] Eastern European and especially Eastern German transformation processes challenge the "theory of political modesty" according to which no holistic social reform is feasible.

Here I will limit my study to an Eastern German/Czech comparison and focus the paper on the democratisation process at a local level from 1989 onwards.[4] The comparison between local politics will allow us to draw conclusions about elite renewal, about factors favouring the creation of new democratic culture; breaks and continuities with the past; and finally political stability and adherence to the values of the new regime.

1. The transformation of local politics

There are two aspects to the restructuring of politics at a local level. The first is linked to the transformation of the institutions: local administration and local government. The second is linked to the creation of a pluralistic political landscape. The latter requires the creation and transformation of political organisations (parties or movements) and the transformation of the patterns of mobilisation and participation.

The institutional aspect of the transformation of local administration and government will not be analysed in depth. Instead I will focus here on the "political" aspects and examine the emergence of a new political elite at a municipal level. The reorganisation of political life is of course closely connected with the emergence of new actors, meaning political parties as well as the individuals who act in these movements as leaders. Here we can call them "elites" (even though this term is controversial). These leaders are the ones who do the "management of meanings" in a context of institution-building and of very unfocused rules. They are important in a time of paradigmatic shift because "leadership is also about the interpretation of events [...] The functions of political leaders are more comprehensive than merely decision-making or the articulation of interests of the electorate."[5]

Political leaders are the ones who indicate the direction for changes. They shape the new system and are in turn shaped by the new position they hold and the obligations connected to them. Observation of leading politicians helps predict future orientations and the extent of democracy of the system which is being built.

The democratisation of the political landscape
The first step towards democracy after regime change is the removal of former power-holders and the accession to power of the opposition. As far as elites are concerned, they have to move from the totalitarian, monolithic type of elite structure to a pluralistic and consensually unified one in order to build a stable democratic system.[6]

Measuring the degree of political pluralism at a local level is a complex matter. There are several indicators for renewal. Some are obvious and easy to grasp, as for example election results. The loss of majority of the former ruling parties is one such indicator. Another is the creation of new political parties and movements and the accession to power of uncompromised people. Beyond these more obvious signs, one has to look more closely and examine the process of "elite circulation" in order to measure the renewal inside parties themselves, the proportion of newcomers versus traditional members in these political movements, as well as among representatives of the locally elected bodies. The measure of the turnover in personnel will tell us to what extent "elite circulation" (Szelenyi) occurred or if to the contrary a process of "elite reproduction" (Hankiss) happened. Nevertheless, in order to measure democratisation one has to go further. It is necessary to highlight the changes in political culture and practices of new and old political elites. The results obtained here can be contradictory to the ones obtained in measuring renewal from a party-political and personnel point of view. The capacity of old and new elites to reach an agreement over new rules, to settle their disputes and to stabilise the system has to be added to all these indicators of democratisation.

A comparison of the changes that occurred at a local level in Czech and Eastern German city-councils enables us to assess the possible impact on local democratisation of national transformations, to measure to what extent external factors exert an influence on the building of democracy (by accelerating, stabilising or facilitating the process), and to isolate these variables and their possible positive or negative effects.

One could assume that unification, with all the support provided to Eastern Germans, has greatly facilitated the transformation process and accelerated the construction of democracy, even at the local level of politics and administration. As Wollmann argues,[7] no "tabula rasa" has happened at this level, unlike other political levels, which were either cancelled like the *Bezirke* or created like the *Länder*. Transformations at a municipal level had to occur within the existing system, which implies that it was done by restructuring the existing administration and with local recruitment of people. From a political, partisan point of view, this process is very similar to the Czech one. "The existence and survival of bureaucratic structures and its at least partial organisations and personnel continuity on the local level provides a degree of similarity with other formerly socialist countries in East-Central Europe that would suggest and invite comparison between these countries, as the local level development in East Germany would not have to be considered as 'uniquely' different on this score, but as a variation within the cross country variability of local level institutions."[8]

Elections as a factor of renewal: the introduction of pluralism
As stated above, the first steps towards democracy are a renewal of the political landscape and the renewal of its actors. We will therefore consider election results.[9]

A review of the general election results for municipal elections, should focus first on the score of the Communist party or its successor. In 1990 the Communist party won 17.2% in the Czech Lands, which is comparable to the New *Bundesländer:* 14.5%, though results varied from one *Land* to another (19% in Mecklenburg-Vorpommern, 16.6% in Brandenburg, 11.6% in Saxony, 12.7% in Sachsen-Anhalt, 10.5% in Thüringen). These initial local elections can be considered as a clear victory in both countries of the new democratic forces. If one looks at the concrete examples of the six city councils I have studied more closely (three in the Czech Lands : Plzen, Kladno, Olomouc; three in the new *Bundesländer*: Dresden, Potsdam, Hoyerswerda), in none of these were former communists the strongest fraction. They lost to "independent" political parties or movements, the Civic Forum (OF)[10] in the Czech Lands (with 35.8% of the votes) and to the CDU (34% of the votes) or the SPD (21.2% of the votes) in the former GDR[11]. Not only did the Communist parties lose their position as leading parties, but, in addition to the big parties or movements like OF or CDU, SPD, several small, independent, democratic political movements entered the city councils (the ecological movements, for example).

These local election results confirm the ones of the first free parliamentary elections which led at a national level to a very broad political renewal, and brought to power the former opposition. These changes stand for a far-reaching transformation that went as deep as the local level. From an electoral point of view the Communists had lost their monopoly position. They were voted out of power even at the lower levels of government. Pluralism was installed.

This renewal that took place in city councils was confirmed by the second elections in 1994. In the Czech Lands, the successor parties to the OF: the Civic Democratic Party (ODS) and the Civic Democratic Alliance (ODA) (28.8% of the votes for the ODS, and 6.5% for the ODA) and new political parties like the Social democrats (CSSD, 8.1% of the votes) were elected almost everywhere, whereas with a few exceptions the SPD or CDU maintained their positions in the New *Bundesländer* (the only notable exception is Hoyerswerda – the largest city in Eastern Germany in which a PDS[12] mayor managed a political come-back).

In 1990, ruling coalitions were formed without the Communist parties, which everywhere became opposition parties. These coalitions were "grand coalitions" in the first years. They were a continuation of the "common front strategies" that had prevailed during the revolutions. In Eastern Germany they brought together parties from the right (CDU) to the left (SPD) with the support of the former dissidents (Bündnis 90) and other smaller parties and movements. In the Czech lands it was usually under the banner of the OF that the smaller parties like the Civic Democratic Alliance (ODA), Christian Democrats (KDU-CSL), Social Democrats (CSSD) or the Greens (SZ) were united.

The review of election results and analysis of their meaning for the renewal of the political landscape shows a similar process in both countries. Change has been far-reaching. There is no major difference between the Czech case and the Eastern German one, and the processes were very similar except for the fact that in Eastern Germany parties appeared earlier (we will come back to this point later).

Renewal from a personnel point of view: measuring "elite circulation"
Assessing the degree of elite circulation inside city-councils gives another measure of renewal, this time from the perspective of personnel. We will try to investigate how many of the newly elected representatives are political newcomers and how many were already members of a party in the former

system. Here we do not consider only the Communists as part of the former system, but we consider also that membership in one of the puppet parties[13] was a sign of at least acknowledgement, if not active political support of the Communist system. We argue, too, that a former member of one of these puppet parties cannot be considered a complete political newcomer.

Seen from this point of view, a clear difference appears between Czech city councils and Eastern German ones. Even though it was not possible to obtain exact numbers for the first legislature in Eastern German city councils, one can guess that there were almost half of the representatives who were members of a former GDR party : SED, CDU, LDPD, NDPD or Bauernpartei[14]. In the Czech Republic these numbers are significantly lower. In the three city councils that were studied, about 21% of the representatives in Plzen, about 28% in Olomouc and about 40% in Kladno were already members of a party (KSCM, CSL, CSS[15]) under the communist regime, which is almost half less than in Eastern Germany. This tendency gets even stronger if one looks at the second city councils elected in 1994. There they are only 27% in Kladno, 17% in Olomouc, and 14% in Plzen, whereas in the GDR, they are still up to 50% in Hoyerswerda, 40% in Potsdam and 42% in Dresden. Thus, from a personnel perspective, "elite circulation" has been greater in the Czech Republic than in Eastern Germany.

The explanation is to be found in the structuring of the new party systems. Here the external factors had a strong influence in the GDR. In the Czech Lands the party system was established at a national level in 1991, when the OF split between Vaclav Klaus's ODS and the OH.[16] At a local level, this had an impact from 1992 on, when parties had to get organised for the parliamentary elections.[17] Only then did a truly differentiated party system emerge. At a local level a whole set of grass-root organisations arose, which mostly originated in the division of the OF. Inside the city councils, the OF clubs[18] tended to split too, and to give way to new political streams like the ODS, ODA, OH.

This was of course not the case in Eastern Germany, where a real party-system was established almost two years earlier, before the first free elections (the *Volkskammerwahlen* in March 1990) with strong influences from the West. The political landscape was structured according to the western German model despite the fact that people were still acting in a sovereign GDR. Dissident movements like *Neues Forum, Demokratie Jetzt*, or *Demokratischer Aufbruch* virtually disappeared. Only party-like organisations remained, which took over western names and programmes. From the first communal elections which were held in June 1990, the political landscape was already articulated in a very classical way between right and left (Christian Democrats and Social Democrats).

However, despite this apparently rigid structuring along well established party-lines, there has been a noticeable instability among elected city councillors in Eastern Germany, who made up fractions inside the city council. They often changed fraction and party in the midst of a legislature. This was the sign of a political system in which political identities lacked time to establish themselves firmly, and in which cleavages had had no time to appear. All this resembled the Czech process of emergence of a new political landscape. In the New *Bundesländer*, many former dissidents entered structured parties. This process, in which the model of political parties prevailed rather than looser organisations like *Neues Forum* or the OF – despite the legacies of forty years of Communist party rule, happened in a very similar way in both countries. In the Czech Lands, many new politicians entered a party after the dissolution of the OF and most of those who did not disappeared from the political scene after the 1994 elections.[19] From these second elections on, a tendency towards a right/left structuration of the political scene appeared. The only big innovation in the Czech case which merits further attention was the creation of the ODS and ODA representing a liberal stream, which had no past record in Czech political tradition. For the rest of the parties, the First Republic was used as a model (People's Party, and the Social Democrats) and the resulting political landscape was very close to the German one.

Impact of transition by "system transplantation" on the political landscape
The difference between the Czech and the German transformation lies in the fact that unification and the speed at which it took place left Eastern Germans with no other solution than to inherit old party structures. They had no time to renovate them or to establish new ones as the Czechs did. The general atmosphere of political competition was too keen. Removing old party members was therefore a more difficult task in Eastern Germany than in the Czech Lands. That the *Block* parties had their counterparts in the West and were already endowed with large networks of grass-root organisations would serve as a major advantage in the intense German political contest. The cost of establishing a new independent political movement was too high, and the chance to settle in the new landscape very small. The existence of the western party models, which had little in common with eastern parties but shared the

same name or origin (the CDU, for example), was a powerful incentive to maintain those structures. During the first elections in Eastern Germany (at a national as well as at a local level) people voted less for the Eastern German political parties than for the Western ones. The unexpectedly good results of the CDU[20] were less linked to the performance of the Eastern German CDU during the electoral campaign, than a plebiscite for the western CDU and unification.

The direct consequence of the fact that all the attention was focused on the West was that the renewal was less far-reaching. Former structures were kept alive. Even though *Block* parties were transformed, many of their members stayed on and retained influence. In the Czech Republic a much more radical break with the former political system occurred; especially from a personal and organisational point of view. Except for the Communist party, the People's Party (CSL) which represents between 6 and 10% of the electorate is the only party that has survived, united with the Christian democratic union: KDU (a newcomer). All other parties, such as the very powerful ODS, were creations or, like the CSSD, recreations[21].

The opposite is true for Eastern Germany. There, most of the political forces originated in the former regime. Only the Social Democrats (SPD) and the Greens together with Bündnis 90 have no links with the communist regime. The percentage of the electorate they represent is small[22] compared to that of the CDU, FDP and PDS. The effects of unification clearly led more to the maintenance of old structures than to their renewal.

While unification maintained existing structures in order to allow parties to compete inside the new Germany, another factor made renewal in Eastern Germany less deep than in the Czech Republic: the persistence and increasing power of the PDS. The former Eastern German Communist Party, even though it has been renewed, has established itself as a central political force of the Eastern political landscape. There is no doubt that this is a consequence of the pattern of unification, which left Eastern Germans without a voice to represent them inside the new united Germany.[23] Because Western German politics and orientations prevailed after 1990, a broad spectrum of Eastern Germans was left with no other solution than voting for the PDS in order to be heard at a national level. Eastern German interests, when they were represented through representatives of SPD, FDP or CDU, were obscured by big western German fractions in which Eastern German politicians did not have sufficient weight to impose their views.

This was not the case in the Czech Republic, where KSC (later KSCM)[24] retained a position[25] albeit with diminished support. It is too early to predict the disappearance of the Communist Party in the Czech Lands. It seems that its position is stable and will remain around 10%.[26] In the City councils its results have tended to worsen.

One could argue that it is the Czech Republic that is unique, with its absence of threat of a communist comeback, whereas the strong results of the PDS in Eastern Germany could be compared to what happened in all Eastern European states: Lithuania, Poland, Hungary etc. during the second elections.[27] But this fails to recognise that Poland and Hungary lacked a social-democratic type, left-wing party to attract those who suffered under the transformation process. In Eastern Germany, such a democratic left-wing party existed in the SPD, which could potentially have benefited from popular discontent with reform policies. Nothing like that happened, however, and the SPD stayed weak. Thus the PDS vote must be interpreted rather as a protest vote against the West and the way unification took place.
The effects of unification were double: first, the very slow economic recovery of the New *Bundesländer* and the high unemployment rate,[28] combined with the dominant presence of Western Germany, made Eastern Germans willing to re-examine their past as a socialist country and long for certain of its aspects, which now were viewed in a more positive light. Even though this might be an ex-post artificially created protest identity, embodied in the PDS, unification by "system transfer" had the effect of creating dissatisfaction. Second, this high degree of dissatisfaction, which has nothing to do with the real material well-being of Eastern Germans, was expressed as a continuing protest vote in favour of the former Communist party.

All this was possible because in Eastern Germany the transformation process (into a market economy and a liberal democracy) is perceived as irreversible. Through unification with the powerful, well functioning and established democracy of the FRG, the Eastern Germans knew they would be anchored in stable system which is deeply rooted and would need more than their dissatisfaction to be overturned. They immediately benefited from this institutional stability and no longer had to fear the return of an authoritarian system.

Eastern German feelings of powerlessness vs. Czech fears of destabilisation
Eastern Germans are the only case in which one could speak of "transition to democracy," for the destination was precisely known: the western German

model. Only time and speed were unknown, and widely underestimated. Therefore one could argue that Eastern Germans, certain by some means to attain a liberal western type of democracy, were able to experiment, to innovate, perhaps even to take the risk of voting massively for the ex-Communist party, because the implications of such an act were not as far-reaching as they could be for the Czechs. They did not risk the loss of the major achievements of the revolution: freedom of speech, rule of law, political pluralism etc., for these were ensured by the federal system and institutions, which were deeply anchored in the West.

In the Czech Republic the situation differs. After the experience of 1968, to experiment is out of the question. The failure of the Prague Spring and "socialism with a human face" spelled the end of any kind of experiment in reforming communism. Since the normalisation that followed the crushing of the Prague Spring, it was clear to Czechs that the only way out of communism was the establishment of a clearly western type of democracy and market economy and rejection of a "third way". In addition, after 1989 the achievements of the revolution are much more fragile, much easier to reverse than in the new *Bundesländer*. Experimenting is a far too dangerous game. The West and the European Union are watching. The main objective of the Czechs is still, almost ten years after the 'velvet revolution', to consolidate their young democracy, to stabilise their political system. They need to ensure the success of reforms, and to keep their orientation towards a reform policy to enter the EU. This situation is much more constraining than the Eastern German one. Czechs cannot allow themselves any mistakes. The Slovak example with Meciar provided them with a good example of what can happen to a government that tries to go its own way.[29] It can turn out to have a very high price. Czechs are aware of this.

Therefore a massive vote for the KSCM is unlikely to happen as a protest vote. People worry more for the government's stability. Even the shift to the left that occurred in the 1998 elections was perceived as a major and risky innovation despite the fact that the CSSD has no links with the former regime. The party was recreated after 1989, has a classical type of social-democratic program, and has repeatedly assured it refuses any kind of coalition with the communists.

At a local level, this residual anticommunism affects not only election results (i.e. the dominance of the ODS as a reforming party and the weak results of the KSCM), but it is also visible in the party coalitions which rule the cities. The biggest city in which the PDS gained a mayor seat is Hoyerswerda (Saxony), with its 61,000 inhabitants. The biggest cities in which the Communist Party has a mayor in the Czech Republic are Zabrec and Bor u Tachova. KSCM is almost nowhere associated with the ruling coalitions in the city-councils in larger cities, and has almost no deputy mayors in these cities.[30] Its position in the local political landscape is far from being "normal." Czech communists are still resented as a threat and kept as far as possible from power. However, their position has begun to change. It is slowly moving towards a broader acceptance from other parties. Especially during the second legislature, the serious work of some communist local deputies was appreciated by the other parties, but the distance is still very big and the symbolic barrier between communists and non-communist fractions remains.[31] The normalisation of the situation of the communist party and its members will certainly occur in the Czech Republic, as it did elsewhere in Central Europe, but this process is only at its beginning and it will take more time.

In Eastern Germany this process of integration of the Communist Party is completed, as the 1994 and 1998 elections have demonstrated. Not only does the PDS have mayors, but it is increasingly a normal participant in local and regional political life. It is at a local level that coalitions between SPD and PDS were first tried, before being transmitted to the *Länder* level.[32] The PDS, after being associated with power in the *Land* of Mecklenburg-Vorpommern and having a Vice-President of the Bundestag, can be considered a normal actor in political life in Germany,[33] whereas this is still unthinkable in the Czech Republic.

To explain this, we now have to look beyond mere pluralisation, and elite circulation. We have to try to investigate to what extent the political culture and practices changed among local politicians.

2. The transformation of political culture and practices

The first part of this study of the democratisation process focused on the problem of the renewal of parties and representatives. In this second section, we will consider the transformation of political culture and practices. This point is as crucial as the first. Even if a process of elite circulation has occurred at a local level, this doesn't necessarily mean that the new political elite will act in a democratic way. Democratic habits have to settle. The people who were in the opposition were socialised under the communist regime, and even if they did not practice politics or hold power positions as the old elites did, they had no concrete experience of democratic politics and were influenced too by forty years of communist rule.

The significance of local politics in the attempts at transformation of the Communist parties
Local politics are in many respects an important feature of the transformation process, for the bottom-up input they allow, the opportunity they provide to the citizen to participate and to be associated more closely with decision-making, for the diffusion of the new model and practices among the citizen; and the opportunity they offer for experimentation (new forms of politics, coalitions, co-operations etc.).

For the re-creation of a political elite, local politics were of major importance. The local level represented the breeding ground for future national elites, as well as a first experience for most of the representatives. Local politics after the revolution became an important place to learn the profession of politics. "The elective and administrative roles that have to be filled [at a local level] create opportunities for the development of new elites [...] that may gradually develop the political skills required to participate in national political life, but also the skills necessary to act as a check – a countervailing force – to a national government."[34]

This is true for all people who entered politics in 1990, but it is particularly true for communists. To them local politics meant even more. The politicians who, in the process of democratisation, had to exert the greatest effort to break with their past are of course the communist parties and their representatives. Neither the SED nor the KSC were supposed to survive long in a democratic system. Both were known as the most conservative, sick and rigid Communist parties of the Eastern block. They were precisely the ones who were the most reluctant to reform under Perestroïka and which used Stalinist methods almost till the end. In the Czech Republic as well as in Eastern Germany, transformations were not set in motion by reform-communists. Change occurred through a complete break-down of the SED and the KSC under popular pressure (demonstrations) and Moscow's new non-interventionist policy.

The disrepute of the communists among people was such in 1989[35] that a renewal could only happen through a complete break with the past and a reconstruction from the grass-roots. People who had decided to stay in the party and to continue to participate in politics under the new regime needed to regain their fellow citizens' consideration and trust, to show themselves in a new, more positive light. Local commitment was one of the best ways to carry out this change and make it visible. It made it possible to act in a less ideological way, to change the image of a party that used to be subject to rigorous party discipline, centralism, and exclusively top-down directions.

By the time that the communist era ended for good, internal party-life was democratised and a break with the old habits was possible. New life appeared at the grass-roots in the Communist parties. Local representatives used the new rights they were given in order to act independently of the leadership and to set reforms in motion. At the local level, an elite, more pragmatic, more realistic and with a less ideological profile, appeared who understood the necessity to transform the party, its political culture and the possibility local politics offered in this regard. Local politics with its immediacy to the citizen was the ideal way to prepare a political come-back. Through a new kind of commitment in city councils, through an active and positive participation, local communist representatives had a chance to leave the political ghettos to which they were confined, and to regain a reputable position on the political scene. In this certain legacies served as advantages to them, for example the know-how they had inherited from 40 years of power, their traditional ability to mobilise their supporters, the importance of grass-roots organisations, and their all-encompassing networks extending throughout the whole territory.[36] All that permitted very active politics.

The SED-PDS turned out to excel in this, going through a radical rupture with the past, pushing forward an image of diversity and of tolerance. The PDS established a very dense network of local assistance which provided help to old people for example, or provided social clubs in a period of intense changes. It managed to position itself as the continuation of the GDR (refusing a radical break with the past and asserting the existence of a specific GDR identity), and at the same time to modernise itself and to break with the communist political culture. Of course this led to numerous contradictions which often created fights inside the party among the different wings, and therefore a certain weakness, but it also constituted the great force and integration potential of the PDS.

The KSCM, despite efforts of certain of its members, did not succeed in the same way to break with its past. Just as it failed to change its name,[37] it also failed to adopt a new profile, with a modern social-democratic oriented program, or to develop active local grass-roots organisations committed to social assistance. Where the Eastern German neo-communists no longer favour a planned economy and recognise that there is no alternative to a "social market economy", Czech communists still hope for a return to the former system, which they still judge as better. Eastern German neo-communists resemble the Polish and Hungarian ones who successfully managed their conversion, as described by Mink and Szurek,[38] whereas Czech communists did not succeed in adapting to the change and failed in the process of reconstruction of their identity. They changed under constraint because they were forced to. However, in their minds, if the communist regime collapsed, this is mainly because of external factors (the withdrawal of Soviet support and Perestroïka) rather than because of internal flaws. Whereas in all other countries their fellow parties and party members "rapidly reconverted to social democracy [...] and officially admitted that, in the historical debate between communism and democratic socialism the latter had the last word"[39] as the East German communist elites did, Czech communists still believe in the superiority of communist doctrine. The attempt of the new elite of local politics to establish its influence in the party in order to use new methods and move towards social democracy failed. No bottom-up processes (initiatives coming from the grass-roots, which turned out to be crucial in the new PDS party-life), no such vitality and renewal took place in the KSCM despite some attempts to this end. The new elite coming from local politics failed to establish itself inside the KSCM, whereas it succeeded in the PDS.

Influence of the external factor in the success of the democratisation of the Communist party
To explain this success in the case of the PDS and the failure in the case of the KSCM, both external factors and historical legacies have to be taken into consideration. In the Czech Republic the crushing of the Prague Spring and the period of normalisation killed any possibility of reform in the Communist party. The legitimacy of the Czech communist leaders depended on foreign support from the initiators of normalisation: the Soviet Union. In order to explain the sclerosis of the Czech Communist Party, one must add to these legacies the influence of recent changes (the democratisation process and the economic transformation) and the way in which the political landscape emerged after 1989.

In the Czech Lands the political scene was quickly dominated by new political parties that were created or re-created after the revolution and were able to mobilise broad support with their radical reform projects. At the same time, despite their radically anti-Communist discourse, these new, independent, democratic parties showed a pragmatic attitude towards former members of the Communist party. They were ready to integrate the less compromised ones among their adherents. Former communists, who were not excluded by lustration laws,[40] and wished to participate in the new system, were able to enter a party like the ODS or CSSD or to a lesser extent the ODA or KDU-CSL.[41] Furthermore, the existence of a social-democratic party that was created after the revolution made the evolution of the communist party in this direction more difficult, especially since Milos Zeman took over the leadership in 1993 and steered his party to active opposition to Vaclav Klaus's ODS and governmental policies. CSSD membership has attracted reform communists who saw no future in the KSCM, as the CSSD offered good career perspectives, since it had few members and was in a good position to win the 1998 parliamentary elections[42] and to have much better scores at a local level in the folowing local elections in November.[43] Even though Czech Social Democrats still reject the idea of coalitions with the communists, they accept their integration within their party. The pressure communist reformers were able to exert inside their own party is therefore weak. The existence of a strong CSSD weakens the position of the reformers inside the KSCM, for the CSSD occupies this reform position.

A new reform elite emerged at a local level and developed a competent, realistic and modest profile. Yet by showing themselves more open, more modern, less dogmatic and ideological, the elites had a very difficult time in the party and were never in the position to exert power (as with the failure of the internal referendum concerning the change of the name). The people who managed to transform the party at a local level, to modernise it and to rebuild a little popular confidence did not manage to extend their influence beyond this level and use their experience centrally. The KSCM remained the only eastern party which still called itself a "communist party". It kept its very dogmatic positions and stayed monolithic within.

In the Eastern German case the situation was quite the opposite. Because the integration of former communists into other political movements was almost unthinkable and because of external pressure and Western German laws, the SED had no other chance to survive than to transform itself radically. Even though in the GDR a social-democratic party appeared too after the revolutions, it had to adopt a very strict anti-Communist attitude, in order not be accused of coalition with the old power.[44] The CDU (using the strong anti-Communist feelings of the Western Germans, and a very aggressive approach in the East,[45] which was supposed to make people forget that more than half of the CDU itself was composed of former members of the Block-CDU) pushed very strongly to create a symbolic barrier between the former communists and the other political forces.

The SPD was more or less forced to declare a one year moratorium in 1990 before integrating former SED members. After one year it was too late, and reform communists had had time to impose a renewal inside their own party. The SPD was less attractive to them (it had lost the elections[46]) and things were getting worse for Eastern Germans. The early enthusiasm for unification had given way to a certain scepticism if not outright disappointment. The PDS saw its own chances in the political contest improving, the electoral mood became increasingly favourable to them. Furthermore, because of the permanent threat of being banned, and the legal obligation of having democratic practices inside the party,[47] the pressure on the PDS towards change was strong.

The reforming elite was encouraged to exert power and to overrule for good the Stalinists at the Magdeburg congress in 1996, which was dedicated to local politics. The new elites coming from the local political scene were able to impose themselves and their reformist views and to push aside the dogmatic wing. They created a realistic stream (the "realos") inside the party. The quality of local involvement of the representatives and party organisations helped regain popular confidence. Very quickly the PDS was recognised by other political parties as well as by citizens as an important part of the local political landscape. Though its most radically reformist members had hardly a chance of being integrated into other political parties, as a party it returned to the political scene as an acceptable partner (even as a coalition partner). Increasingly influential were those people who in city councils or in *Landtage* had been active, who had been confronted with the obligation (like members from other parties) to cope with the new system of laws, to become familiar with new practices, and a more complex system that came from the west. Local politicians had to adapt to new rules of the game, and to try to become familiar with new practices. This obligation was rewarded. The local politicians had a great impact on the entire SED and on the transformation of this party from within. The obligation to act formally in a democratic way, to conform to democratic principles had a positive impact on the democratisation process as a whole, and on the transformation of people's mentality. Furthermore, the efficiency of the new system helped make the change more acceptable to the new politicians and even former communists gladly admit that they favour this new, more efficient way of governance.

This example of the transformation of communist parties shows the influence of external factors on the democratisation process and the way in which, in the end, these influences played a positive role. If the renewal of the political elite has been less deep in the GDR from a numerical point of view, if there was more "elite reproduction" than "elite circulation," it doesn't mean that the rupture hasn't been as deep in the end. Things have changed in the new *Bundesländer*, and even though there is a greater continuity in personnel and political organisations, people have converted to the new system.

The fact that despite a high degree of elite reproduction the GDR has gone through a more profound change can be demonstrated from another point of view which will be only briefly mentioned here. In the Czech Republic, the emergence of new actors didn't necessarily mean a rupture with past practices. The ODS provides a good example. ODS established itself rapidly as the main actor of Czech transformation after the 1992 elections, in which it won a broad majority[48] with its allies from the ODA and the KDS. Not only was the ODS undeniably the leading figure in parliament, and in government, but it also had hold of all major cities in the country.[49] Its tolerance of divergent opinions and opposition was not always strong. Due to its power, at a local level, it tended to overlook the existence of the citizen and develop an arrogant attitude, never consulting other political formations nor citizens about their decisions, acting sometimes like the communists did.

Because of its powerful position, it re-created a kind of party-state. People from ODS held all key positions, exactly as the communists did a few years ago. Many people entered the party because of the connections it meant, because it was a precondition for occupying certain positions. All these factors favoured the development of corruption inside the party and in the state apparatus. The same tendencies were perceivable in East Germany, in the *Länder* in which one party had an absolute majority and had hold of some of the major cities like Dresden in Saxony with the CDU and Potsdam in Brandenburg with the SPD. But the party-state remained limited to the *Land* and phenomena like corruption were not able to develop with as much impunity as in the Czech Republic. Federal institutions always remained as a possible recourse against non-democratic practices.

Concluding remarks
The transformation through "system transfer" that occurred in Eastern Germany has paradoxically not engendered a more radical break at a political

level. At first sight, it seems contradictory that such a process favoured the preservation of the former structures (parties, and personnel). This continuity is the result of unification and of the intervention of an external agent in the establishment of the new Eastern German political landscape. In the Czech Republic the transformation of the political scene was more radical, even though its establishment lasted longer. However, the imposing of already established rules and institutions from "above" favoured the process of elite conversion and party transformation in Eastern Germany. This has to be taken into account in order to measure the advancement of the democratisation process. The new system which was transferred from outside forced the emergence of a democratic political culture and democratic practices among the Eastern German elite.

The situation is quite the opposite in the Czech Republic. There, despite a seemingly profound break with the communist system, greater continuities with past practices appear. Political behaviour has changed in a more radical way in Eastern Germany, whereas this process is much slower on the Czech side, where the learning of democracy is more superficial among the new elites and the conversion of communists to the new system often non-existent.

In spite of greater difficulties, the faith and expectations towards the new system are much stronger and more positive among Czech elites than among Eastern German elites. Generally speaking, Czechs show a high degree of satisfaction with reforms.[50] The continuously strong results of the ODS are a good example of this.[51] Czechs remain very attached to the reform process in the political as well as in the economic sphere. They believe more in the democratisation process than Eastern Germans, and they tend to worry more about the continuation of these reforms in the future. They believe that democracy is a fragile and not yet well anchored system. Whereas Eastern Germans have no fears about the future, and perceive the changes that have occurred since 1989 as stable and irreversible, Czechs fear any form of destabilisation, which makes them in a sense much more conservative.

Czech and Eastern German fundamental political attitudes differ: Czechs are to a great degree in favour of liberalism, and put the emphasis on the role of the individual, while Eastern Germans favour state interventionism and stress the preservation of social equality. This is a logical consequence of the type of transformation process experienced since 1989, even though some explanations might be sought in the communist period.

Eastern Germans are more reserved towards the ability of democracy to solve their problems and more suspicious towards the new system. Because of the type of transition, which on the one hand produced a very brutal transformation and on the other hand left them in many respects powerless, they have developed a more cynical attitude towards democracy. If today's Eastern German political practices and culture are more democratic, it is nevertheless true that Eastern Germans tend to view their new political system in a cynical and negative light. As Claus Offe shows,[52] there is a serious risk that the German system transformation will produce a resigned society with elites incapable of representing and creating adherence to the new system among the people. In Eastern Germany democratic mechanisms might function better today, at least in a formal way, than in the Czech Republic. The question, though, is whether the shock of modernisation will be followed by the creation of an informal basis for collective action which will be guided by attitudes and experiences that tend towards the implementation of democracy. Compared to other Eastern European countries there has been a strong tendency in Eastern Germany to expect help only from outside and from above. Unification created high expectations and led to a mentality of "waiting for a governmental miracle," and less to a "spontaneous, self-conscious collective effort for the creation of a renovated economy".[53]

The political maturity of the Eastern Germans is greater. This is partly due to the far more traumatic experience elites had to face and to the more complex nature of the issues they had to deal with, but it is also related to a high level of disenchantment. Whereas Czech elites might still be more naïve about the changes, they have a greater confidence in democracy and its ability to solve problems. Here again, the positive Czech attitude is linked to the perception of the transformation process and the feeling of successful economic transformation and privatisation. This feeling is nevertheless fragile and has diminished a lot these last years in which economic crisis and unemployment rose. Czech self-confidence was hurt as well as their faith in democracy. The reactions that followed were very similar to the Eastern German reaction to the shock of unification. They were not as far-reaching because the shock was not as brutal as it was for Eastern Germans in 1990 but they were of the same nature.

This again is an argument showing the similarities of both processes. In the Czech case disenchantment with democracy was simply postponed because the economic crisis appeared later. But for the Czechs, there is no possible recourse to stable and consolidated institutions in order to respond to dissatisfaction. Czechs might therefore face a process of political radicalisation, which could result in a pronounced polarisation of the political scene and create instability.

Notes

[1] One can draw the comparison between Eastern Germany and the Czech Republic from 1989 on, even though the Czech Republic did not exist as such at the time. In the years in which Czechoslovakia still existed (till 1992) we will only take into consideration the Czech Lands (Bohemia and Moravia) leaving the Slovak part out. This is possible because two distinctive political landscapes emerged after 1989. A movement like the Civic Forum (OF) for example existed only in the Czech part, whereas in the Slovak part of the federation it had a counterpart called Public against violence (VPN). There were four puppet parties in the Czechoslovak National front, two Czech ones, two Slovak ones. Only the Communist party was organised throughout the whole Federation.

[2] In both countries there was only a very weak counter elite or opposition, which had no experience with politics or mobilisation and was neither organised nor prepared to take power. No movement like Polish Solidarity existed. The Communist party in both countries refused until the very end to have any contact or to negotiate with the opposition. During the revolution the political situation was very polarised.

[3] See Andreas Pickel and Helmut Wiesenthal, *The Grand Experiment* (Boulder: Westview, 1997), notably: "Introduction: Postcommunist transformation and the problem of systemic reform," pp. 1-24.

[4] This article is based on a research project that the author conducted over the course of three years in Czech and in Eastern German city-councils: Plzen, Olomouc, Kladno, Hoyerswerda, Dresden, Potsdam.

[5] See A. Offerdal, D. Hanspach, A. Kowalczyk, J. Patocka, "Elites and Parties," in: Harald Baldersheim, ed., *Local Democracy and the Process of Transformation in Eastern Europe*, Boulder: Westview, 1996, p. 106.

[6] See Michael Burton and John Higley, "Elite Settlement," *American Sociological Review*, vol. 52 (June1987), 296, and their typology of the three basic forms of elite structure in the modern world.

[7] See H. Wollmann, "Between rupture and legacies. Local government transformation in Eastern Germany," in: Gernot Grabeler, ed., *Restructuring Networks in Post-socialism: Legacies, Linkages Localities,* Oxford: Oxford University Press, 1997.

[8] H. Wollmann, op.cit., p. 5.

[9] In both countries the autumn revolutions were soon followed by free elections. In Eastern Germany this took place a little earlier than in Czechoslovakia, in March 1990 for the *Volkskammer* of the still existing GDR, followed by municipal elections in June 1990. In the Czech Lands (at that time still part of Czechoslovakia) the first free parliamentary elections were held in June 1990 and were followed by local elections in November 1990. Having a look at the calendar is important because it indicates the time that was given to parties and movements to get organised, right after the revolution, and between national and local elections. The second municipal elections were held in both cases four years later, in June 1994 in Eastern Germany (Brandenburg is an exception; there municipal elections took place in December 1993, because of a *Kommunale Neuordnung* that changed the time of legislature) and in November 1994 in the Czech Republic.

[10] The Civic Forum (OF) was the movement that was created during the revolution and led the opposition to the communists' power.

[11] In Dresden and in Hoyerswerda the CDU became the strongest fraction, in Potsdam the SPD, in Plzen, Kladno and Olomouc the OF. Everywhere the mayors were political newcomers, chosen in the strongest fraction.

[12] The Party of Democratic Socialism (PDS) is the successor Party to the SED: Sozialistische Einheitspartei Deutschlands, the Eastern German Communist Party.

[13] In both countries a facade pluralism was maintained. Other political parties than the Communist parties existed. They were united in a National Front, with other mass movements, and had no influence at all on politics. They were completely obedient to the Communist party.

[14] All these parties were in the National Front in the GDR.

[15] KSC meaning Communist party of Czechoslovakia, CSS: Czechoslovak socialist party, and CSL: Czechoslovak peoples party. These were the Czech parties that belonged to the Czechoslovak National Front.

[16] In 1990 two fractions appeared inside the OF. During its February 1991 extraordinary Congress, it got divided between its two main fractions: one which stood behind the leader V Klaus who aimed at forming a structured political party, with a well-defined hierarchy and objectives (this became the ODS), and one, the OH (citizens' movement), that refused this party-like organisation and wished to stay in the tradition of the civic movement that had appeared during the revolution. It wanted to keep a loose network, to avoid too well-defined hierarchies. This second movement was led by J. Dienstbier and was favoured by many former dissidents.

[17] This party-building process must be considered as a top-down process, imposed by the Prague centre that felt the need for a regional basis in order to settle its power in Parliament and win the elections.

[18] "Club" is the term Czechs use for their fractions inside the different parliaments.

[19] In the city councils which were studied, OH and independent candidates represented in the Czech case only 6 among 33 elected representatives in Kladno, 2/47 in Plzen, 4/45 in Olomouc. In the Eastern German case, Bündnis 90 or Independent candidates represented only 6/70 in Dresden, 1/42 in Hoyerswerda, and 3/50 in Potsdam.

[20] The *Allianz für Deutschland*, a coalition of the CDU and DSU, obtained 48.1% of the votes in the *Volkskammerwahlen* of March 1990.

[21] The Social Democratic Party already existed in the first Czechoslovak Republic. It went into exile after the communist take-over and survived there until the revolution. It was re-created in November 1989 in the Czech Lands as a continuation of the first Republic's exile movement (its first Congress took place in March 1990).

[22] The coalition Bündnis 90/Grüne obtained only 2.9% of the votes in the first parliamentary elections, and the SPD 21.9%.

[23] The eastern *Landesorganisationen* had very weak positions inside the new united parties. The same situation as in unified Germany was reproduced inside unified parties. Unification occurred through *Beitritt* of the eastern part to the western one. Thus, Eastern political parties got absorbed by the more powerful, better organized western party-organizations, in which it became extremely difficult for them to assess their specific Eastern German positions and interests. They were outnumbered by the West and were unable to acquire sufficient weight on the national political scene or in the parties. Further the fact that the GDR was divided into *Länder:* six different subjects (five *Länder* and East Berlin,) made it even more difficult for the Eastern Germans to be heard and to impose their specific interests. The absence of a specific East German elite, which lacked time to emerge and above all was often accused of Stasi collaboration did not help to solve the problem of Eastern German representation in the new Germany.

[24] KSC stands for Communist Party of Czechoslovakia. It became KSCM: Communist Party of Bohemia and Moravia in 1990.

[25] The KSCM obtained around 14% at the parliamentary elections in 1992, 13.3% at the municipal elections in 1994, 14.3% at the first round and 10.74% in the second round of the senatorial elections in 1996, 10.33% in the 1996 parliamentary elections, and 11.03% in the 1998 parliamentary elections.

[26] The KSCM won only 13.4% in the second municipal elections which is about four points less than in 1990. In Plzen, it had 16.4% votes in 1990 and 13.4% in 1994, in Olomouc 16.9% in 1990 and 15.4% in 1994, In Kladno 25% in 1990 and 19.3% in 1994.

[27] As Georges Mink and Charles Szurek ("Europe centrale: La revanche des néo-communistes," *Politique internationale*, no. 68 (1995), 157) show: in 1992 the ex-Communist Party of Lithuania won 73 of the 141 seats of the Parliament; in November 1993, the Union of the Democratic Left, (ex-communists) won 171 seats at the Polish Sejm; in May 1994 the Hungarian Socialist Party (ex-reform communists) won 209 of the 386 seats of the Hungarian Assembly.

[28] See Claus Offe, *Der Tunnel am Ende des Lichts*, Frankfurt a.M.: Campus, 1994. In chapter 3, "Die deutsche Vereinigung als 'natürliches Experiment'," Offe writes about the effects of unemployment saying that East German citizens know that help can come only from above and from outside. This dependency which is a result of the unification process creates or reinforces a mentality of awaiting help instead of a help-yourself mentality.

[29] The Slovak leader V. Meciar established a regime in which he defied the EU and the Council of Europe on several issues (privatisation, rule of law, human rights, respect of the opposition ...) which had as a result that Slovakia was not among the first wave of countries selected to start negotiations for entering the EU.

[30] In only 6 of the 30 biggest Czech cities the KSCM is associated to the executive. These cities are Karvina, Opava, Chomutov, Jablonec, Uherske Hradiste, and Znojmo.

[31] This is less true from a personal point of view. Communist representatives tend to be better accepted by their colleagues than used to be the case during the first legislature.

[32] At a regional level the first step in the direction of an integration of the PDS into normal political life was done in Sachsen-Anhalt's *Landtag* where the SPD set up a minority government with the cooperation of the PDS. A next step is in the process was in Mecklenburg-Vorpommern, where, after the 1998 October *Landtag* elections, the SPD decided to negotiate a coalition with the PDS instead of forming a great coalition with the CDU. The coalition paper was signed at the end of October 1998. This is the first time the PDS was associated with government (other than at a municipal level) since the end of the GDR.

[33] See, *Der Spiegel*, no. 43, 19.10.1998. "Der Kurze Marsch zur Macht," 38-52.

[34] H. Baldersheim and M. Illner, "Local democracy : The challenge of institutions building," in: H. Baldersheim et al., *Local Democracies and the Processes of Transformation in East-Central Europe*, Boulder: Westview, 1996, p. 4.

[35] In contrast with Poland or Hungary, the Eastern German and Czech Communist Parties could not hope to gain any positive feelings from their attitude in 1989. They could not claim, unlike the Hungarian and Polish communists that they were the ones who initiated reforms.

[36] The KSCM with its 160,000 officially reported members in 1998 is by far the largest party. It is about eight times as big as the ODS, the main party created after the revolution. The KSCM is divided in 4,500 grass-roots organisations which allows it to be present in almost all Czech cities and villages (which is impossible for other parties).

[37] In June 1993 J. Svoboda, the reformer who had led the party since October 1990, was forced to resign after his reform projects were rejected and the party refused to change its name into "Party of Democratic Socialism" in March 1990.

[38] Georges Mink and Charles Szurek, "L'ancienne élite communiste en Europe centrale: stratégies, ressources et reconstructions identitaires," *Revue française de science politique*, vol. 48, no.1 (February 1998). 3-41.

[39] Mink and Szurek (1995), p. 166.

[40] The lustration law that was adopted on October 4th 1991 excluded from all public jobs former members of the people's militia and members of the Communist party who were in leading positions.

[41] There is no prohibition concerning the admission of former members of the Communist Party in the Statutes /Bye-laws of the ODS and the CSSD, provided these people do not fall under the lustration laws. The local basis organisations are free to decide on this issue. The ODA is the only party that stated in its party statutes/bye-laws its hostility towards the admission of former communists, and has adopted a special admission procedure for them.

[42] The CSSD's election results were in constant progress since the 1992 elections. The social democrats obtained 7.67% of the votes at the 1992 Federal assembly elections, and 6.8% in the Czech Chamber, 8.1% at the Municipal elections in 1994, 26.44% at the Parliamentary elections in 1996, and finally 32.31% at the 1998 Parliamentary elections. They became the ruling party and had their leader Milos Zeman appointed Prime Minister.

[43] The ODS had about 23,000 members in 1997 whereas the CSSD had almost half less: 12,657 (*Lidove Noviny*, 29.9.1997) and therefore needs to broaden its basis.

[44] This is a legacy of the *Ostpolitik*. Right-wing parties reproached the SPD for having established relations with the SED during the existence of the GDR and for having tried to normalise relations with this non-democratic state.

[45] The "Rote Socken" campaign which was especially used during the 1994 elections against the PDS is a good example of this.

[46] SPD election results for the *Volkskammerwahlen* in March 1990 were of 21.8% and only slightly better in the December 1990 *Bundestagswahlen*: 24.3% in the East.

[47] According to the Basic Law, political parties have a role to fulfil in German society ("politische Willensbildung") and they are bound to have internally democratic structures and practices (*Parteiengesetz*, 1967).

[48] During the 1992 parliamentary elections the ODS won 33.9% of the votes at the Federal assembly, and 29.73% at the Czech National council where the ODA obtained 5.93% of the votes.

[49] Among the ten biggest Czech cities, all have ODS mayors except for Hradec Kralove which has an ODA mayor. Among the thirty most important Czech cities the proportion of ODS mayors is of the two third. Every where the ODS takes part in the ruling coalitions except in Opava, Karlovy Vary, Chomutov and Mlada Boleslav. See : *RESPEKT*, no. 51, 19-25.12.1994.

[50] See Wolfgang Seifert, "East Germany and Eastern Europe Compared," *Studies in Public Policy*, no. 233, Wissenschaftszentrum Berlin (1994).

[51] The ODS still obtained 27.74% of the votes in the last elections in June 1998, and remained the second most important party in parliament.

[52] See Offe (1994), pp. 42-56.

[53] Ibid., p. 53.

Meredith A. Heiser-Durón

PDS Success in the East German States, 1998-1999: "Colorful calling card from the Forgotten Communist Past?"

This chapter explores four different explanations for the success of the reformed East German Communist Party, the Party of Democratic Socialism (PDS), in six recent state elections. These include the milieu thesis, the "losers" of unification thesis, the representation gap thesis, and the vacuum thesis. Moreover, the chapter considers the impact of local economies, local leaders of all parties, and local coalition possibilities on electoral results. The study shows that no single explanation is sufficient to understand the success of the PDS and that the disappearance of the PDS in the next electoral period is quite unlikely.

This chapter summarizes the victories for the Party of Democratic Socialism (PDS), the reformed communist party of East Germany, in the East German states, explaining the impressive nature of the PDS's electoral results in the eighteen month period from April 1998 to October 1999. In April 1998, the PDS unofficially joined a coalition in Sachsen-Anhalt, by supporting a Social Democratic (SPD) minority government.[1] Then, six months later, it officially joined in a coalition with the SPD in Mecklenburg-Vorpommern. Finally, in 1999, it pushed the SPD out of second place in the state governments of both Thüringen and Sachsen and landed in first place in East Berlin.[2]

This paper analyzes two different trends in the academic literature concerning the PDS's future as a party as well as its fate within the electoral system. On the one hand, Laurence McFalls makes a cultural argument that the PDS is limited in the long-term, because as East Germans accept the contradictions of West Germans' capitalist culture, they no longer need a reformed communist party. According to McFalls, given a choice between modern socialism and East German identity interests, the PDS has mistakenly chosen the latter. Hence, once these "old identity" interests evaporate, so too will the PDS. McFalls also suggests that ultimately, right-wing extremist parties, such as the *Deutsche Volksunion* (DVU), will replace the passé PDS, because right-wing anti-immigrant programs are closer to conservative and xenophobic East German interests than the present party program of the PDS.[3]

Other authors, including Henry Krisch and Gero Neugebauer, have also argued the PDS will disappear. However, they base their analysis primarily on political factors, the growing number of cleavages in the party itself: the split between the younger and the older generation of members, between modernizers and traditionalists, and between socialists and regionalists.[4] From their point of view, the PDS's strategy is not necessarily at fault; it is simply impossible for the party to represent both socialism and East German interests adequately. Therefore, if the PDS wants success as a leftist socialist party in the West, it will lose the East German vote and if it focuses solely on East German interests, it won't win in the West.[5]

After reviewing both cultural and political arguments, David Patton comes to different conclusions about the PDS.[6] He argues that the party does have a long-term future. Analyzing the party's performance in a string of electoral successes, he applies four different theories as alternative ways to explain the party's success. Two theories are based on conditions in the former East Germany and are, therefore, "made in East Germany." Two others are predicated on conditions in a unified Germany and are, therefore, "made in a united Germany."

He selects a theory in the latter category, the "representation gap" theory, as the best explanation for the PDS's recent victories. In essence, he argues that *as long as other parties do not represent East German interests adequately*, the PDS has a future. From this view point, which I share, East German interests can be defined in numerous ways and are not necessarily synonymous with a nostalgic drive to return to the past.[7]

In this paper, I analyze the state level of government, in part because the PDS's gains there brought about coalition possibilities, but also because, in the German federal system, states are especially important actors. They not only allow for more creative governing combinations, but they can affect the federal government's coalition and its policy-making. State parliaments are generally closer to the people, East Germans, who are the sole constituents.[8] The new state governments offer a better test case than the *Bundestag* for the continuity and future of the PDS, because their personnel and institutions were not built entirely from scratch. Finally, the PDS politicans who have been successful at the state level tend to be more pragmatic and less ideological. This is the sort of party member most crucial to the PDS, if it does have a future.

In the following section, I discuss Patton's four theories in more detail. In later sections, I apply them to three different kinds of PDS victories at the state level in 1998 and 1999: victories in the poorer states, in the most politically and socially de-stabilized states, and in the richer states. I analyze the poorest East German states, Mecklenburg-Vorpommern and Sachsen-Anhalt, in the most detail. Although the PDS only received slightly more votes than in 1994, the PDS and SPD together received enough votes to experiment with new coalitions. Furthermore, analyzing the electoral victories and the governance of the PDS in these states, we find evidence that PDS participation in a coalition may create some pre-conditions for PDS losses.

In Berlin and Brandenburg, the states which face some of the most serious economic, political and cultural challenges associated with unification, the PDS experienced a significant increase in votes. This may suggest when western-based established parties such as the SPD and/or Christian Democratic Union (CDU) are in power for several election periods, the PDS can use the parties' poor performances coupled with social and economic uncertainty to gain votes. Ironically, the PDS received the largest *increase* in votes in the richer, more industrialized states which were once leftist strongholds, Sachsen and Thüringen. This suggests that even in the wealthier East German states, the PDS can win votes if it is viewed as more credible than the other potential opposition party, the SPD.[9]

Four Theoretical Explanations
First let's explore Patton's "milieu thesis," which forms the crux of McFalls' argument. It was "made in East Germany" and it focuses on the cultural legacy of communism, as well as other cultural variables. According to McFalls, PDS voters are those East Germans who still praise the DDR, and who are nostalgic about certain aspects of the past, such as child care or full employment. Socialism has a cultural and symbolic value for these voters who still exist in an anti-Western and anti-capitalist milieu. Of course, it is logical that this group would diminish over time. In this scenario, if the PDS could not expand to other groups, it would eventually be extinct. It would not be able to gain votes among younger East Germans, who have few memories of communist East Germany.

While McFalls' analysis of cultural developments in East Germany is certainly correct, and a complicated and modern post-capitalism is taking hold, his political analysis of East German interests and his conclusions based on these cultural developments are more suspect. The varied type of victory which the PDS experienced at the state level in 1998 and 1999 generally contradicts the milieu thesis as an overall electoral explanation.

First, while it is true that the members of the PDS come from the *nomenklatura*, the PDS has already experienced losses in voters in several of the SED past strongholds, among the East German working class, among women, as well as among communist *nomenklatura*. While 90% of PDS members were formerly SED members, only one-half of PDS voters are considered core voters, many of whom are former SED members. The other one-half are first-time voters, previous non-voters, undecided voters or former CDU/SPD/ Green party voters. The PDS has been equally popular among younger and older voters as well as poorer and wealthier voters. It has also experienced growing popularity among the middle class and entrepreneurs.[10] These developments suggest that, while the East German populace is adapting to capitalism, an ongoing anti-West resentment can not be ruled out.

Even if the milieu theory were true and the PDS could not expand to other groups, anti-Western and/or anti-capitalist feelings could be reignited to attract voters in election campaigns, even though these attributes are no longer essential to a new East German identity. The milieu argument is most applicable to areas such as East Berlin and past capitals of other states, where the vast majority of former party officials live.[11] However, why has the PDS sometimes lost votes and sometimes gained votes in its old milieu, while greatly increasing its votes in other non-milieu areas?

According to Patton's second thesis, one that is also "made in East Germany," while fewer and fewer people are nostalgic for the GDR, more and more East Germans may view themselves as "losers" of unification. This theory goes beyond cultural variables and focuses on economic as well as psychological variables. The term "loser" can be easily misunderstood as a transient category and one only applicable to individuals. While economic losers, the unemployed, have voted at a high rate for the PDS, one does not have to be an objective, material loser to identify subjectively as a relative loser. As McFalls himself points out, almost all East Germans know someone who lost a job and changed jobs, so loss does not have to be personal but can pertain to an East German's friends or larger community.[12] One does not have to experience ongoing loss to harbor bad memories of loss. This theory, in my view, suggests a role for the PDS in the near future because there will always be some aggregation of East Germans who identify with loss or can at least remember a sense of disappointment in the history of unified Germany.

Although the PDS has attracted various kinds of protest voters, which usually·would suggest a transient appeal, in the case of the PDS, when one type of protest became less pertinent, another type often emerged. The intensity of identification with the PDS by its voters also suggests that these people are not simply motivated by momentary, situational factors such as unemployment or frustration.[13] The fact the PDS has done well among wealthy, educated voters would suggest that the unification loser/protest argument is flawed. Unfortunately, it is hard for even the most sophisticated polls to account for the psychological status of voters as winners or losers.

Both of these above theses assume that the cultural and/or economic legacy of the GDR is the reason for the party's recent victories. However, Patton examines two other theories, which assume that PDS success was "made in united Germany." Such theses tend to assume a more long-term future for the PDS.

For example, the representation gap theory posits that the long-term success of the PDS depends primarily on the actions of the more established parties, which many East Germans still associate with West German interests. In short, the answer to the question, "Why are reformed communists doing so well in the former East Germany?" is "Other parties are doing so badly."[14] This theory focuses on political factors, such as institutional performance. Patton does not view the PDS as a passive recipient of good luck; he credits the PDS for its strategic response to this lack of an eastern political presence, because as of March 1994, once the PDS began to focus on East German interests, it reached new heights in its electoral results.[15]

The more strategic mistakes the other parties make, the better the electoral chances are for the PDS, no matter what the PDS adopts as a strategy. In both 1994 and 1998 the "red socks" and "red hands"[16] campaign may have worked to gain West German votes in the federal election, but caused all East Germans to feel stigmatized and misunderstood by Westerners. This campaign cost the CDU in East German state elections as well. As the reader will see in the following sections, the CDU and later the SPD made many such mistakes in the 1998-1999 round of state elections.

It is becoming more common for all Germans to view the CDU and SPD as "cartel parties," agents of the state who do not necessarily use state resources wisely or in the interest of citizens, but are more concerned with guaranteeing their own collective survival.[17] The PDS can use this adverse perception of other parties to advertise itself as a credible alternative in the East. Kohl's refusal to name names in a recent CDU party corruption scandal further convinces East Germans that political corruption was not endemic to the SED alone.

However, one defect of the representation gap theory is its institutional focus. This theory does not explain why the PDS could tap into the protest vote so much more successfully than other parties. East Germans could vote for anti-Bonn politicians no matter what their party affiliation, or for any opposition party, or for the far-right. While the latter have had episodic victories, they have had no string of victories as was the case for the PDS. This is due in part to the PDS's strong organization from the past as well as some of its charismatic leaders, especially at the federal level, and its excellent campaigns. However, the representation gap theory does not explain why the PDS has done so well in states where other leaders clearly represent East German interests, such as Manfred Stolpe (SPD) in Brandenburg or Kurt Biedenkopf (CDU) in Sachsen. This issue will be explored further in the following sections, which examine the interplay between the ruling coalitions, the minister-presidents, and the opposition in each state.

Finally, Patton develops a fourth theory, which focuses on other political factors such as party programs and party policy: "the vacuum thesis." This theory, which also stems from a united Germany, suggests that recent PDS gains are simply due to the movement of the SPD and the Greens into the political center in the 1998 federal elections. This development opened up space on the left for more radical parties. Of course if this thesis were true, long-term gains for the PDS could be based solely on the changing dynamics of the German party system. This thesis would also suggest that a vote for the PDS depends on its policies and policy results. However, the fact that many East Germans report voting for the PDS for reasons other than policy goals sheds some doubt on this thesis. Furthermore, many East Germans who now vote PDS previously voted CDU. The vacuum thesis would predict that former SPD voters would favor the PDS.

The recent state election victories suggest that the PDS has come up with a complicated but successful vote-winning strategy: a focus on regional populism, which allows the PDS to combine the diffuse "eastern interests" (made in East Germany theories) of some voters with other voters who question the fairness and corruption level of western institutions or the viability of other party programs (made in unified Germany theories). In both categories, the PDS can insist it represents outsiders against insiders: local interests v. the central government.[18] In fact, sub-regional identities have been strongly reinforced by these elections, further contradicting an overall cultural explanation.

Of course, winning elections and participating in coalition governments creates new problems for the PDS. What happens to the party appeal as it becomes part of the establishment? While the PDS may lose some protest voters as well as traditional, milieu voters, it could conceivably replace these with voters who focus on the importance of contemporary East German representation as well articulation of issues not discussed by the other established parties in a modern, post-capitalist society. Whether the PDS can actually deliver on these expectations remains to be seen.

Finally, the past can not be easily distinguished from the present. I agree with McFalls that East German identity interests are changing, but even the most modern, post-capitalist East German is affected by the past in his or her perceptions and voting behavior. Analyses of the PDS's appeal to East Germans will have to look not only at cultural factors, but also economic perceptions, political institutions, and policy-making of all parties.

Explanations for the behavior of East German voters have to emphasize the overlap between theoretical and discipline-based approaches: in the 1998/1999 state elections, some PDS voters may have been responding to poor representation and policy-making, while others were responding to nostalgia, their personal economic situation, or the status of their state economically and politically. While we may no longer have a specific set of East German interests, we can still refer to a divergence between East and West German interests. As Patton has expressed it: "Political institutions and party strategies exacerbated economic and cultural tensions between the German regions."[19] Anti-Western resentment, therefore, remains an effective way to focus East German interests.

Sachsen-Anhalt/Mecklenburg-Vorpommern: The Case of the Poor State
In Sachsen-Anhalt, a SPD-Green coalition tolerated by the PDS was replaced in 1998 by a SPD-led government, within which the PDS remained an unofficial coalition partner. Of course, this meant the PDS could not effectively lay claim to the title of a protest party, as it had spent almost four years in government with the Greens and the SPD. Six months later, the PDS joined the SPD in its first official coalition, gaining three of eight ministerial posts, in Mecklenburg-Vorpommern.[20]

In the face of large turn-outs, many had expected that the PDS could not come close to maintaining its portion of the vote.[21] In Sachsen-Anhalt, where turn-out was at 71.7%, up almost 17% from 1994, the PDS gained over 68,000 voters, but decreased its percentage of the overall vote by 0.3%. In the face of over 80% turn-out in Mecklenburg-Vorpommern, up 7.5% from 1994, the PDS gained 1.7% of the vote for an absolute count of more than 264,000 voters.[22]

Moreover, the DVU gained a large percentage of the vote in Sachsen-Anhalt, 13%, which translates to over 192,000 voters. Of course, the DVU was helped by the fact that it was the only right-wing extremist party on the ballot and the PDS, as a semi-official part of the government, was subject to suspicion as a vehicle of protest. The DVU could not get over 5% in Sachsen-Anhalt in the federal elections six months later nor in the Mecklenburg-Vorpommern state elections held on the same day as the federal elections.

To investigate the milieu thesis, let's look more closely at those people who voted for the PDS and DVU. While the PDS gained voters from all age groups, the DVU appeared to be more of a milieu party, not of older nostalgic East Germans, but of unemployed, angry, young East German men who voted for the party in droves. According to a survey conducted by the Mannheim Election Research Group, of those voters 18-24 years old, 32% percent voted for the DVU.[23] If we just looked at the youth vote in Mecklenburg-Vorpommern, the party would have received over five percent of the vote there. In contrast, in both states, the PDS received the most votes among voters 35-59 years old, with only a few percentage points variation among different age groups. In Sachsen-Anhalt, there is evidence of one other connection between the PDS and DVU voter: compared to other voters, twice as many DVU voters thought the PDS should be treated as a normal party.[24]

This would seem to substantiate McFalls' argument that the DVU is replacing the passé PDS, especially among young voters. However, there is also contradictory evidence in this regard. The DVU had no candidates on the candidate list (first vote), so DVU voters had to decide among other parties' candidates with their first vote: DVU voters placed an almost equal number of votes between the CDU, SPD, and PDS.[25] This suggests DVU voters could identify with all types of parties. Moreover, since its victory in this state election, the DVU has had trouble with turnover in its legislative delegation and with its program, which casts doubt on its future as a rival for the political protest vote.

In this author's opinion, the "losers" thesis more accurately applies to these states in both an economic and psychological sense. More people leave these states than move to them; by 1998, both had close to 25% unemployment. Citizens are very aware of their position in relationship to the other states. In a poll at the time of the election, 59% of the citizens in

Mecklenburg-Vorpommern thought their economy was worse than that of the other new states, while 52% of the citizens in Sachsen-Anhalt thought their state was worse.[26]

One problem, however, with this explanation is the case of Sachsen-Anhalt, where voters rewarded (re-elected) an administration which did not bring about economic growth. The representation gap thesis appears to explain this contradiction: in both states the CDU lost the election more than the PDS won it. In Sachsen-Anhalt, the CDU did not offer a credible alternative and so the SPD and PDS could win despite a dismal record. In the case of Mecklenburg-Vorpommern, voters did throw out an administration which had failed to bring about economic growth.[27] The SPD and PDS campaigns in each state focused on the extreme corruption and problems of earlier CDU administrations. This was the case, even though in Mecklenburg-Vorpommern, the vote was held on the same day as federal elections and such timing would normally favor the established parties as voters think less in terms of protest.

When one reviews the history of corruption and failure in these two states, the representation gap appears to be the best explanation for PDS success. In Sachsen-Anhalt, the first minister-president, Gerd Gies (CDU) had to resign during his first year in office due to rumors of a STASI (East German secret police) connection. The second West German minister-president Werner Münch (CDU) resigned along with his whole cabinet in 1993 due to alleged salary fraud.[28] The third minister-president, Christoph Bergner (CDU), who was the 1994 and 1998 candidate for minister-president, had been in office one year, when the SPD and PDS agreed on the toleration model of government to replace his grand coalition. In 1996, Bergner, who felt personally betrayed, attempted a vote of no confidence against his SPD opponent, Höppner, for mismanagement of the heavy-machine building industry. Bergner could not raise enough votes.[29] Moreover, in the 1998 election campaign in Sachsen-Anhalt, Bergner and the rest of the CDU relied heavily on Kohl's support and the CDU party headquarters almost ran the campaign in Sachsen-Anhalt.[30] Voters who wanted to see the emergence of a vibrant CDU with local talent were alienated. After the 1998 loss, Bergner resigned his federal party post, but continues, not without controversy, as leader of the CDU parliamentary group in Sachsen-Anhalt.

The CDU's federal parliamentary chair at the time, Wolfgang Schäuble, responded to the electoral results in Sachsen-Anhalt as if he was acknowledging a representation gap. Several weeks after losing that election, he admitted that the CDU had alienated East German voters. He encouraged former SED members to consider joining the CDU, nominating Angela Merkel, who was at the time head of the CDU in Mecklenburg-Vorpommern, as the first East German and the first woman to serve as General Secretary of the CDU, replacing Peter Hintze, who had been responsible for the red socks/red hands campaign.[31]

As for corruption, failure and controversy in Mecklenburg-Vorpommern, the CDU had a vote of no confidence in its original minister-president, Alfred Gomolka, in 1992, because of his unsuccessful efforts to save the ship-building industry. Berndt Seite (CDU), a West German, became minister-president and served until 1998. In 1996, after another scandal in the ship-building industry, Ringstorff made one of several attempts to create a red-red coalition. He had some federal support but he lacked the support of his own state party.[32] In the 1998 election in Mecklenburg-Vorpommern, Ringstorff got the approval of chancellor candidate Schroeder for such a coalition. The SPD hoped he could build on the moderate popularity of the unofficial coalition in Sachsen-Anhalt. However, the Mecklenburg-Vorpommern CDU could not be easily vilified as it relied much less heavily on Bonn than the Sachsen-Anhalt CDU.[33] As a result, while the CDU lost 12.4% in Sachsen-Anhalt, it only lost 7.5% in Mecklenburg-Vorpommern.

As for the vacuum thesis, it appears to apply, but in the form of a vacuum on the right. Both the PDS and SPD took votes from the CDU. Very few PDS votes came from previous SPD voters. If anything, the timing of the Mecklenburg-Vorpommern election may have caused PDS voters to favor the SPD. In Sachsen-Anhalt, one could say the SPD minority government's toleration by the PDS gave the party a way to gain votes from the SPD and the Greens without being held responsible for its own party policies. As one author phrases it, "toleration allows the achievement of government to be claimed as credits while direct responsibility for mistakes and unpopular measures can be avoided."[34] However, the PDS was held at least partially responsible, as indicated by the success of the DVU in attracting so many protest votes.

Whether East Germans wanted to see the PDS treated as a normal party or simply wanted to try out the first red-red coalition, they seem unconcerned with policy results. Most citizens surveyed prior to the elections were not happy with the party's work in parliament.[35] Only 7% of PDS followers in Mecklenburg-Vorpommern thought the party could solve the state's problems. This directly contradicts the expectations of the vacuum thesis.

The vote appears to be a response to a perceived "representation gap," a lack of official coalition participation by the PDS. However, the PDS may be held to a higher standard once it officially enters a coalition. In the 1999 communal vote in Mecklenburg-Vorpommern, the PDS lost 2.5% of its votes, while the SPD lost only 1.6%.

Moreover, the vacuum thesis is complicated by the different nature of SPD/PDS party officials and party organizations in each state. The thesis works best in Sachsen-Anhalt where the SPD minister-president, Höppner, is quite moderate. He has only reluctantly cooperated with the PDS, suggesting that he does not actually need the PDS because they cannot maintain a bloc vote as a party, and he only approved of the coalition in Mecklenburg-Vorpommern because the PDS could no longer make irresponsible appeals to populism.[36] In Mecklenburg-Vorpommern, however, Minister-President Ringstorff, holds out hope for new politics, a politics of the left or of modern socialism, and here SPD policies are less distinguishable from the policies and profile of the PDS. The two states also show that instead of pushing the SPD to the left, the PDS has become more pragmatic, agreeing to serious budget compromises in both states.[37]

Most interestingly, Petra Sitte, the leader of the PDS parliamentary group in Sachsen-Anhalt, has termed the Magdeburg model trying to "turn shit into sweets." Neither she nor her counterpart in Mecklenburg-Vorpommern, Caterina Muth, were advocates of joining a coalition with the SPD. Because both figures are responsible of their party's policy-making, they appear to prefer fundamental opposition roles for the PDS. On the other hand, Helmut Holter, the previous chair of the PDS in Mecklenburg-Vorpommern, presently Minister of Labor, Construction, and Technology, has been an advocate of PDS coalition participation and has been criticized by his own party as too much of a technocrat, as too pragmatic.[38]

This ideological/pragmatic split within the PDS suggests that in the states where it is part of a governing coalition, the PDS may have difficulty winning more ideological voters. What the PDS represents in these states has changed, and from many voters' perspective, not for the better. However, if the PDS is not seriously challenged for protest votes and can gain votes by pointing to corruption in other parties, it may still be able to overcome this split.

Brandenburg and Berlin: The Case of De-stabilized States

In the East Berlin and Brandenburg elections of 1999, we see further evidence that East Germans were disappointed in their governing parties and coalitions: the SPD in the case of Brandenburg and the CDU-SPD coalition in the case of Berlin. While this suggests that the representation gap might also be the best explanation for PDS gains, as was the case in Sachsen-Anhalt and Mecklenburg-Vorpommern, these states also provide some evidence for the milieu, losers and vacuum theses.

In East Berlin, the PDS got more votes than any other party, receiving more than double the number of votes for the SPD (39.5% vs. 17.8%). This was an increase of over 3% from 1995 for a total of 276,000 votes. Although the party got only a few votes in West Berlin (4.2%), it doubled its previous results, receiving over 40,000 votes. In Brandenburg, the PDS and CDU both had a large increase in votes (4.6% for PDS and 7.8% for the CDU), presumably from disaffected SPD voters. The overall vote for the PDS amounted to 23.3% or 257,000 votes. Voter turn-out was low in both Brandenburg, 55%, and East Berlin, 62.6%.[39]

As the previous *nomenklatura* of the SED were located in or near the capital of the GDR, East Berlin, the physical basis for the milieu argument is present in these states. However, the party faces a different kind of ideological dilemma in Berlin: how to attract West Berliners by posing as broad-minded and ecologically concerned socialists, while trying to appeal to a much more conservative audience in the East? The milieu theory is strengthened when one considers that the PDS lost the most votes among youth (18-24) and gained the most votes among the elderly (over 60) in Berlin.

However, the milieu theory does not explain why the party doubled its vote in West Berlin. This vote seems to have been based on policy choices and therefore supports the vacuum thesis – the PDS was the only party to oppose German actions in Kosovo and may well have interested disappointed SPD/Green voters. Before such a trend could be considered viable in the long-term, however, the PDS would have to make further increases in the upcoming west German state elections.[40] The milieu theory also does not explain why the PDS would lose votes in Potsdam, the capital of Brandenburg, or more importantly, why 27% of voters 18-24 reported voting for the PDS, a much larger percentage than those who voted for the DVU.[41] It was the SPD, not the PDS, that received most the votes of those over 60.

There is evidence for the loser thesis in both the economic and psychological sense in both states, but especially in Brandenburg.[42] The high youth vote for the PDS in Brandenburg may have been a protest about unemployment which hovers around 20%, while unemployment in Berlin is closer to 16%, and East Berlin unemployment remains lower than that in West Berlin.[43] The psychological sense of loss of identity is especially strong in these two states as both states benefited heavily in the past from their location and from government subsidies. As Berlin becomes the capital of the new Germany, traffic gets worse, construction increases, and there is a great nostalgia in East and West for the stability of the Cold War. The problem is exacerbated for Brandenburgers, who worry about becoming the warehouse for Berlin: many dissatisfied Berliners are moving to the suburbs, which technically belong to Brandenburg, while over 250,000 workers commute between the two states, mostly from Brandenburg to Berlin.

In 1996, all major parties, except the PDS, supported integrating these two states into one. The youth response at that time was especially negative.[44] In Brandenburg, in particular, approximately 75% of the population under 45 opposed fusion and in Berlin, over 50% of the population under 45 opposed it.[45] It may, therefore, be the youth who are most threatened by this relentless pace of change. Moreover, in Brandenburg, the poorer of the two states, citizens simply believe they would be the biggest losers of fusion, not Berliners. As the Brandenburg CDU plans to reintroduce fusion, possibly in the year 2000, the PDS probably has good electoral prospects in the next state election.[46]

Therefore, the electoral results in these states could be explained as a reaction to a representation gap, to cartel party politics as exemplified by the fusion issue. Even though fusion was approved by 2/3 of both states' parliaments and may be a good administrative solution to problems of the region, most citizens thought the government was shoving a program down their throats, delivering misleading propaganda in a campaign which cost too much (four million dollars). In particular, Minister-President Stolpe of Brandenburg, who has now been in power for nine years, took a populist approach to fusion, as he has to many other political problems, making many economic promises which he could not keep.[47] While 81% supported him as minister-president in 1994, by 1999 that number fell to 58%.[48]

The PDS and CDU victories in Brandenburg can also be explained in part by the vacuum thesis. First the PDS gained in exactly the voter group where the SPD and Greens experienced the most severe losses, the youth vote.[49] In Berlin, good results from the SPD-CDU coalition were credited to the CDU, not the SPD, and the SPD chose a minister-president candidate, Walter Momper, who was extremely unpopular even in his own party. The SPD made a further strategic mistake by implying that the grand coalition should be replaced by another one, possibly red-green, which East Berliners did not support. The Greens lost 3.6% of their vote in East Berlin, receiving 6.4%,[50] because a vote for the SPD or Greens was a vote for an established coalition partner, one which had not delivered on promises. In Brandenburg, the SPD also lost votes but here the loss was split between PDS and CDU, with the CDU gaining the most votes.

This vacuum theory is contradicted by the fact that a PDS vote did not appear to depend on policy outcomes. Only 22% of PDS sympathizers in Brandenburg thought the party had the greatest competence in economic policy. In Berlin, where the PDS controls many local governments and mayoral positions the figure is even smaller, 15%.[51]

The PDS did well in these 1999 elections, because voters, unhappy with the poor economic and political record of the SPD, wanted change. They got it: especially in Brandenburg, where the SPD will no longer govern alone (the CDU has joined the government), and the PDS is the sole opposition. The PDS may have the greatest electoral chances where it forms the sole opposition. The losers thesis and representation gap may be the best explanations for both the PDS's and DVU's victories in this state.

The PDS also has good chances when the SPD's policy-making reputation is weakened by being a long-term member of a grand coalition, and when the other opposition party, Berlin's Green Party, is tainted by past participation in a coalition. In Berlin, the PDS is becoming more popular than the Greens as an opposition party. In addition to the milieu theory, the representation gap and vacuum thesis may be the best explanations for the PDS victory in Berlin.

Thüringen and Sachsen: The Case of the Richer States
The PDS may have some of the best prospects in the states where citizens are dissatisfied with the SPD as the opposition or a potential opposition party.[52] In both Sachsen and Thüringen, the PDS did better than in any other state, coming in second after the CDU and, most importantly, pushing the SPD into third place. In such cases, the representation gap could explain why CDU voters choose the PDS and the vacuum theory could explain why SPD voters preferred the PDS. In Sachsen, the CDU is still able to rule alone. Despite

Kurt Biedenkopf's immense popularity, the CDU lost a small percentage of votes from 1994, 1.1%. Meanwhile, the SPD lost 5.9%. The PDS gained 5.7% over 1994, receiving 22.2% of the votes, more than double that of the SPD, which received 10.7%. This represents an additional 140,000 votes, a larger gain than any other party received, resulting in an absolute count of over 480,000 votes for the PDS.[53]

The Thüringen grand coalition, in which the CDU was the largest party, ended, so the CDU now rules alone. The CDU gained 8.4 % more votes than 1994, while the SPD lost 11.1% of the vote. The PDS gained 4.8%, receiving 21.4% of the vote. This represents an increase of about 12,000 voters, resulting in an absolute count of over 247,000 votes. The SPD received 18.5% of the vote. While the Thüringen SPD lost more votes than the Sachsen SPD, this may be explained by the large decrease in voter turn-out, which helped the PDS.[54]

As for the milieu argument, it is especially applicable in Sachsen, where the PDS made large gains in former SED strongholds, Chemnitz, Leipzig, and Dresden. In Thüringen, the PDS had slightly smaller gains in Erfurt, Jena, and Gera. As for the youth vote, the Mannheim survey indicated the PDS did poorly among 18-24 year olds, receiving only 5% of their vote, and very well among those older than 60, receiving 34% of their vote. In Sachsen, however, the discrepancy was not so great: the PDS received 16% of the vote among those 18-24 and 25% among those over 60.[55]

The losers thesis would appear to be weakest in these states because these voters have no objective reason to see their economies as weak. Unemployment has been decreasing in the region, hovering at 16-17% in 1999. Still the losers thesis has some merit. One must remember that even in richer eastern states, there is a sense of trying to catch up with the western states, where unemployment averages 10-12%. Without doubt, PDS voters are often those most pessimistic about the economy. While 15% of CDU voters in Sachsen thought the economy in that state was in bad shape, 37% of PDS voters thought so. While 27% of all voters in Thüringen thought the economy was bad, 39% of PDS voters thought so.[56]

The representation gap would also appear to be a weaker explanation, especially in Thüringen where the CDU gained a large amount of votes. Moreover, the CDU *Landesväter* and the CDU in both states are quite popular and have no reputation for corruption. In Thüringen, Minister-President Bernhard Vogel had an 82% approval rating before the election. In Sachsen, Minister-President Biedenkopf had an 89% approval rating.[57]

Moreover, while the Sachsen CDU lost some votes, Biedenkopf remains popular because of his importance as a symbol to the whole East German region. As Yoder has argued, although Biedenkopf is West German, "his inclusionary and localized strategy is much more likely to create positive attachments to the new system [...] than a regional identity rooted in resignation and feelings of inferiority."[58] Finally, the CDU was viewed as very competent in both states, especially in its fight against unemployment.

The vacuum theory appears to be the best explanation, especially in Thüringen, where the SPD campaigned on the possibility of a PDS-SPD coalition, similar to that of Mecklenburg-Vorpommern.[59] This made the PDS the clear choice as an opposition party. Ironically, it now shares that role with the SPD, which lost power. In Sachsen, the SPD, under the leadership of Karl-Heinz Kunkel, was more conservative. Kunkel clarified early on that his party would not participate in such a coalition and he appears to have been able to cut his party's losses as a result and the SPD remains an opposition party. However, while SPD losses were the greatest in Thüringen, the SPD in Sachsen received only half the number of votes of the PDS. This may be because it can hardly be differentiated from the CDU and, therefore, the PDS also appears to be a better alternative as an opposition party in this state. Still, PDS voters in both states have little faith in the PDS's policy-making abilities.

The case of the richer states contrasts with the case of the poorer states and the destabilized states. In the richer states, the PDS is replacing the SPD as the most reliable opposition whereas in the poorer states, the PDS is trying to cooperate with the SPD as a ruling party. In the destabilized states, the PDS is trying to discredit the governing policies of the SPD and present itself as the most reliable alternative whether in power or in opposition.

Conclusion

Diversity has become a permanent feature of the East German political landscape. Although the representation gap was a strong explanation for the first four cases covered in this paper, the PDS will continue to defy explanation through any one theoretical approach. The PDS has experienced different levels of success in different East German states, depending on its opposition status as well as the economic status of the state and the actions of the other parties. While it easy to view a vote for the PDS in state elections solely as a nostalgic return to the past, this brief review shows that such a vote must also be viewed as a response to the local economy, local leaders, and local coalition possibilities.

As is the case for regional parties in Western Europe, the PDS serves as a representative of regional identity, a concept which goes beyond the simple concept of milieu. Ironically, the PDS has managed to unite numerous milieus under one banner. In addition, the PDS, as has been true for other reformed communist parties in Eastern Europe, has greatly benefited from the fragmentation of and political mistakes of its opponents, which would be predicted by the representation gap and vacuum theories.

The PDS's promises, whether achievable or not, seem to have softened the trauma of simultaneous economic and political transition, especially for people experiencing a material or psychological sense of loss. PDS voters appear be less concerned with actual policy results, as the vacuum thesis would have predicted, and more concerned with issue articulation and representation vis-a-vis cartel parties. Still, votes for the PDS are likely to increase when the CDU is viewed as corrupt and/or ineffectual, as was the case in Sachsen-Anhalt and Mecklenburg-Vorpommern, and even more so if the SPD is so viewed, as was the case in Brandenburg and Berlin. Votes for the PDS are more likely to increase if the SPD opposition has been, or is predicted to be, ineffectual as was the case in Sachsen and Thüringen. Votes for the PDS may, however, decrease slightly when the PDS is involved, officially or unofficially, in a governing coalition. They may also decrease, when the CDU and its party elites play more integrative roles, which do not completely discount the East German past.

Based on these six case studies, PDS survival in this decade appears quite certain.[60] It is precisely the cultural and economic contradictions implied by a lengthy transition which have lengthened the life of the PDS, not shortened it. Even if the DVU could represent East German identity interests, it does not have the organization or personnel to do so. Ironically, the PDS, often viewed as a political nuisance both because it is a small party and only a semi-reformed communist party,[61] appears to be an important vehicle of integration in Germany. East German voters are not fundamentally and irrevocably alienated as many supporters of the milieu and losers theses imply. They are simply dissatisfied with their state's political leadership. To them, a vote for the PDS is still the most effective way to express this opinion.

Notes

[1] The PDS supported a SPD-Green coalition in Sachsen-Anhalt beginning in 1995 but in the 1998 elections, the Greens could not overcome the 5% barrier.

[2] Moreover, at the federal level, the PDS passed the 5% barrier in the October 1998 elections, winning twice the number of seats it had after the 1990 elections. In the summer of 1999, the PDS entered the European parliament for the first time, receiving more than 6% of the German vote. Finally, the PDS's representation was not limited to the East alone: of its 37 *Bundestag* members, 11 are from the west and it gained its first "defector" in the *Bundestag*, when a Bavarian Social Democrat decided to switch to the PDS. See "Germany's Ex-Communists Creeping Up," *The Economist*, 9 October 1999, 59.

[3] Laurence McFalls, "Eastern Germany Transformed: From Postcommunist to Late Capitalist Political Culture" *German Politics and Society*, vol.17, no.2 (Summer 1999). [**Editors' note:** McFalls himself finds his argumentation to be misrepresented here. He does not contend that the PDS is simply a milieu party which owes its allegedly dying strength to its voters' socialization in the GDR. To the contrary, in the article cited here he explicitly refutes socialization-based explanations of political culture, attitudes, and behavior. The editors have nonetheless let most of the references to McFalls stand since the author does effectively refute the milieu-thesis on PDS support even if she associates McFalls too closely with that thesis.]

[4] For an example of the latter, see the Letter from Saxony, written in mid-1996 by two PDS representatives in Dresden. They argued the party should focus on the regional issues for East Germans and give up its efforts to be a national, leftist party. The Erfurter Erklärung, written in January 1997, is an example of the former, support for a definition of socialism which includes coalition possibilities between the SPD, Greens, and PDS. For a critical evaluation of both sources, see Eckhard Jesse, "SPD and PDS Relationships," *German Politics*, vol. 6, no. 3 (December 1997), 95.

[5] Henry Krisch, "Searching for Voters: PDS Mobilisation Strategies: 1994-97," in: Peter Barker, ed., *The Party of Democratic Socialism in Germany: Modern post-communism or nostalgic Populism? (German Monitor* 42), Amsterdam: Rodopi, 1999, pp. 38-53; see also Gero Neugebauer and Richard Stöss, *Die PDS. Geschichte. Organisation. Wähler. Konkurrenten*, Opladen: Leske & Budrich, 1996.

[6] Neugeubauer and Stöss also revised some of their initial conclusions in "Nach der Bundestagswahl 1998: Die PDS in stabiler Seitenlage?" in: Oskar Niedermeyer, ed., *Die Parteien nach der Bundestagswahl* 1998, Opladen: Leske & Budrich, 1996, pp. 119-140.

[7] See his following two articles: David Patton, "Germany's Party of Democratic Socialism in Comparative Perspective," *East European Politics and Societies*, vol. 12, no. 3 (Fall 1998) and "The PDS as a Newcomer Party," unpublished manuscript presented at the

German Studies Association (Atlanta), October 1999. For an author who shares Patton's prediction on PDS success, see Jennifer A. Yoder, *From East Germans to Germans? The New Postcommunist Elites*, Durham: Duke University Press, 1999. In this book Yoder conducted interviews with East German state parliamentarians.

[8] See Yoder, 31-33.

[9] In Sachsen, both parties have been in the opposition since 1990. In Thüringen , the SPD was part of the government, but was voted out of its coalition with the CDU in 1999.

[10] See Patton, "Newcomer Party," 6 and Manfred Gerner, "Widerspruch und Stagnation in der PDS," *Zeitschrift fur Politik*, vol. 45, no. 2 (June 1998), 171-172. In general, however, Gerner would argue the PDS was made in East Germany.

[11] Neugebauer and Stöss, "Bundestagswahl 1998," 134.

[12] McFalls, 13.

[13] See Henry Kreikenbom "The Major Parties: Dealignment and Realignment in Post Cold War Germany," in: Christopher S. Allen, ed., *Transformation of the German Political Party System*, Oxford: Berghahn, 1999, 175.

[14] Patton, "Newcomers," 8-9.

[15] At the same time, reformed communist parties began to do well in Hungary and Poland.

[16] In 1994, the PDS was accused by the CDU of being a party of red-painted fascists. The CDU ran the slogan "Off into the future but not with red socks [not with the PDS]." In 1998, the CDU ran the slogan "We are ready. Look out Germany," as a parody on the SPD slogan, "We are ready [to replace Kohl]." This red hands campaign was based on the image of forced unification of the SPD and SED as symbolized by the handshake between Grotewohl and Pieck.

[17] Richard S. Katz and Peter Mair, "Changing Models of Party Organization and Party Democracy," *Party Politics*, vol. 1, no. 1 (January 1995), 5.

[18] Patton, "Comparative Perspective," 522.

[19] The Greens' party strategy is a good example of this. They were never able to overcome their roots as a western milieu party and they alienated the Alliance '90 members who joined them. While in 1994, the Greens played a large role as a negotiator between the PDS and SPD in Sachsen-Anhalt, by 1995, the PDS had gained the ear of the SPD without the Greens. See Andrei Markovits and Stephen J. Silvia, "Green Trumps Red: Political Identification and Left-Wing Politics in United Germany" in: Allen, 133-159.

[20] This red-red coalition greatly angered the CDU, which had been the more powerful coalition partner since 1991.

[21] This is based on the viewpoint that more radical and highly mobilized parties can energize their voters more easily than large parties and thus benefit from smaller turn-outs.

[22] *Wahl in Sachsen-Anhalt: Eine Analyse der Landtagswahl vom* 26. April 1998, no. 89 (Mannheim: *Forschungsgruppe Wahlen*, 1998), 7. *Landtagswahl in Mecklenburg-Vorpommern: Eine Analyse der Wahl vom* 27. September 1998, no. 92 (Mannheim: *Forschungsgruppe Wahlen*, 1998), 7.

[23] *Sachsen-Anhalt*, 16. According to the same research, only 19% of that age group chose the PDS.

[24] Ibid., 50.

[25] Ibid., 56. In Germany, a citizen's first vote is for a candidate and the second vote is for a party.

[26] *Sachsen-Anhalt*, 39 and *Mecklenburg-Vorpommern*, 36.

[27] In Schwerin, the government has a particularly difficult problem to solve. It must attract industry to the state. It has one-half the number of people employed in industry of Schleswig Holstein, the next most industry-poor state. Sachsen-Anhalt,however, also has to achieve more economic growth. It experienced zero growth in 1996 and only 0.6% in 1997. See *Mecklenburg-Vorpommern*, 36 and *Sachsen-Anhalt*, 39. See also Peter Heinacher, "Debakel," *Neues Deutschland*, 27 April 1998.

[28] See "Münch und Ex-Ministern müssen keinen Pfenning zurückzahlen?" *Magdeburger Volksstimme* (hereafter MV), 4 December 1997.

[29] "Linker Druck und roter Nebel," *Der Spiegel*, no. 49 (2 December 1996).

[30] Wolfgang Schulz, "Kohl kündigt fur Sachsen-Anhalt einen 'grossen Wahlkampf' an," MV, 27 September 1997.

[31] Robin Alexander, "Schwarze Füsse jetzt in roten socken," *tageszeitung* (hereafter *taz*), 13 October 1998. "Angela Merkel wird CDU Generalsekretärin," *Schweriner Volkszeitung*, 1 October 1998. Merkel has since replaced Schäuble in his recent position as CDU chair, because of his role in the Kohl financial scandal.

[32] In the 1994 election, Ringstorff tried to use the ship-building scandal to gain the party headquarter's approval of a red-red coalition. This was rejected by the SPD chancellor candidate at the time, Rudolf Scharping. Oskar Lafontaine replaced Scharping as SPD chair

in November 1995 and, as such, held negotiations with PDS Chair Lothar Bisky concerning cooperation.

[33] Rehberg, chair of the CDU parliamentary group in Mecklenburg-Vorpommern, ran a campaign which was relatively critical of Bonn. He is known as someone who would like to demystify the PDS and has said, "red-red is no more scary in the East than red-green in the West." See "Sauerer Apfel," *Der Spiegel*, no. 41 (5 October 1998).

[34] Jesse, "SPD and PDS Relationships," 97.

[35] *Mecklenburg-Vorpommern*, 43.

[36] Moreover, Höppner is now considered to be a strong spokesperson for East Germans. See "Abschied von der alten BRD," *Der Spiegel*, no. 46 (15 November 1999).

[37] Neugebauer agrees with this interpretation. See *Bundestagswahl 1998*, 135. The PDS is especially weak in Sachsen-Anhalt where it is only unofficially part of the coalition.

[38] Others charge Holter with being too ambitious and West German observers are often concerned that he had a successful career in the SED. Muth was so worried about being in power, she refused to play a ministerial role.

[39] See *Wahl in Berlin: Eine Analyse der Wahl zum Abgeordnetenhaus vom 10. Oktober 1999*, no. 100 (Mannheim: Forschungsgruppe Wahlen, 1999), 10 and *Wahl in Brandenburg: Eine Analyse der Landtagswahl vom 5. September 1999*, no. 97 (Mannheim: Forschungsgruppe Wahlen, 1999), 7.

[40] Another interpretation is that these ostensible West German votes came from East Berliners who have moved to West Berlin. However, we do see a growing organizational basis for the party as well as publications in parts of West Berlin such as Kreuzberg.

[41] The *DVU* unexpectedly got past the 5% barrier, receiving 5.3% of the vote in Brandenburg. See *Brandenburg*, 7.

[42] In the first half of 1999, Berlin had the least amount of economic growth of all the German states, East and West, 0.8%.

[43] In Brandenburg, 79% of those surveyed said unemployment was the state's biggest problem, where in Berlin 62% thought so. *Berlin*, 52.

[44] Brandenburg's Green Party also opposed fusion, but the Brandenburg Greens were so weak that they had no chance of joining a governing coalition. The Berlin Greens were pro-fusion and the PDS accused them of hoping to form a red-green coalition.

[45] See "Fusion gescheitert: Brandenburg sagt nein," *Berliner Zeitung*, 6 May 1996.

[46] According to the Brandenburg PDS, fusion could only happen by the year 2010 if the states could prove they can work cooperatively. "CDU will Neuanlauf zu Laenderfusion," *taz* 10 July 1998.

[47] See Yoder, 139, for more on Stolpe. I don't disagree with Yoder that Stolpe has been popular because he refused to play the role of an East German victim. However, I think Brandenburgers expected more policy results, especially economically, after nine years of his leadership.

[48] *Brandenburg*, 34-35. The cartel party image has been furthered in the formation of new grand coalitions. In Berlin, the SPD lost one ministerial seat, so a very competent Minister of Finance was sacked and replaced by a high-level party candidate. In Brandenburg, a very popular SPD minister, Regine Hildebrandt, resigned because she refused to be part of a grand coalition.

[49] Ibid., 56.

[50] *Berlin*, 10.

[51] *Berlin*, 65 and *Brandenburg*, 50.

[52] See also Neugebauer and Stöss, "Bundestagswahl 1998," 135.

[53] *Wahl in Sachsen: Eine Analyse der Landtagswahl vom 19. September 1999* (Mannheim: Forschungsgruppe Wahlen, 1999), 7.

[54] *Wahl in Thüringen: Eine Analyse der Landtagswahl vom 12. September 1999* (Mannheim: Forschungsgruppe Wahlen, 1999), 7.

[55] *Thüringen*, 12 and *Sachsen*, 12.

[56] *Thüringen*, 41 and *Sachsen*, 44.

[57] *Thüringen*, 35 and *Sachsen*, 38.

[58] Yoder, 147.

[59] Such a coalition announcement was especially unwise in Thüringen, which has a large number of independent voters.

[60] This remains the case despite Gysi's resignation in April 2000 as federal parliamentary chair. Even if the PDS party elite experiences more melt-down, other parties would have to change in order to attract PDS voters.

[61] Neugebauer and Stöss, *PDS*, 24-25. For the latter view, see in particular Patrick Moreau, *Die PDS: Profil einer anti-demokratishchen Partei*, Munich: Hanns Seidel Stiftung, 1998.

Jennifer A. Yoder

**The Regionalization of Political Culture and Identity in Eastern Germany:
A Study of State Parliamentarians in Three *Länder***

This chapter examines regional differentiation in the new states. It identifies regional particularities that existed under communism as well as the different trajectories of post-communist development in the new states. In the period since 1990, particular regional needs and challenges have emerged, particularly in the economic realm. Another dimension of regional development identified by the author concerns the different degrees of elite independence in the new states. The chapter concludes with a discussion of the possible implications of increasing elite independence for German politics and society.

> If internal unity is really to come about, it
> presupposes the equality made possible only by
> an acknowledgement of differences.
> *Wolfgang Thierse, upon being elected President
> of the Bundestag, October, 26, 1998*

Introduction

For a decade, many important domestic political debates and policy questions in unified Germany have been framed in dichotomous terms – west-east or old states-new states. It is time for a more nuanced examination of the new states of Germany. Whether the eastern states share common concerns, act together in all-German institutions and the European Union, or if they have developed different interests, culture, and identity, can all significantly shape political debates, public policy, and even affect the processes of political, cultural, and economic integration of unified Germany. It is important, therefore, to examine the trajectories of postcommunist development in the new states, to identify where differences may lie, and to recognize the emergence of particular regional needs and challenges in the transition, as well as regional strengths and potential contributions to German politics and society. This chapter considers the contours of regional differentiation in the new states.

It is important to recognize that, prior to unification, despite the efforts of the GDR regime to erase regional particularities, important regional differences were visible in the east. Of central importance was the north-south disparity in industrialization, with an industrialized, more prosperous south and a more agricultural, less-prosperous north. Following the war, the GDR regime began a building and re-building of industry phase that included an effort to overcome this north-south disparity by industrializing the northern and eastern regions of the country. This effort was not entirely unsuccessful; however, it resulted in a high regional concentration of industry, for example with shipbuilding on the Baltic coast, steel industry in Brandenburg and Frankfurt/Oder, chemical industry in the area of Halle, textile and clothing industry near the Czech border, and brown coal mining and energy production around Halle, Chemnitz and Niederlausitz southeast of Berlin. As a result of this mono-industry structure, communities rose and fell with the fortunes of one sector or factory. The strategy of industrializing the north-eastern part of the GDR also had significant consequences for migration patterns within that country. In particular, in the sparsely-populated region of what is today Mecklenburg-West Pomerania, *Übersiedler* flooded in from the Sudetenland to resettle and work in the newly-built factories. The GDR regime also transplanted workers (and party functionaries) from the more politically-conservative southern region of Saxony.

In addition, regional experiences in the transition period since 1990 have varied in terms of the speed and level of economic recovery and diversification, the political party landscape and coalition-building patterns, and the independence and national visibility of state political leadership. The constellation of factors producing these differences as well as their impact on unified Germany are discussed below. Based on research conducted during two periods over the last decade, I will offer regional profiles of three of the five *Länder*[1] and offer brief remarks on the other two and East Berlin.

Brandenburg

Brandenburg is a region with a historically continuous and identifiable past. *Brennabor* (from which Brandenburg is derived) was a fortress in the tenth century. In 1157, the 'Mark Brandenburg' was declared by Albrecht the Bear and his son Otto. Home to generations of Hohenzollerns, it eventually became a province of Prussia. Brandenburg's population is a mixture of Germanic and Slavic peoples; following World War II, it became home to many expellees from the east. It also was the home of many GDR-era functionaries and elite institutions.

Perhaps the factor that most shapes Brandenburg culture and identity today is its proximity to Berlin. This was illustrated in May 1996, when a proposal to fuse Berlin and Brandenburg into one state failed when it was put to referendum. Supporters of fusion, including the Brandenburg government of Manfred Stolpe (SPD), argued for a long-term perspective, claiming that the fusion would be more economically and administratively efficient and that pooling the two states' influence would make it more powerful at the federal level. Critics of fusion argued that Brandenburg would have to absorb too many of the high costs (and debts) of Berlin arising from the tremendous rebuilding of the city and the already vast public expenditures, and overall, Brandenburg would suffer a net loss in subsidies.[2] Other criticisms stemmed more generally from a desire to maintain Brandenburg's regional autonomy as well as a fear of being dominated by Berlin and, implicitly, by the west. In the end, the fears and uncertainties about Brandenburg's status in the fusion outweighed the potential benefits.

Moreover, the geographic reality that Brandenburg surrounds the city-state of Berlin has far-reaching implications for Brandenburg's economic and political life. Since Berlin is now the German capital and a major European center, the tremendous investment in Berlin's economy and infrastructure creates a *Speckgürtel* – a prosperity belt – for the Brandenburg communities nearest to Berlin.[3] Brandenburgers on the peripheries, however, do not reap the same socio-economic benefits, and this has been a major preoccupation of state legislators. An additional concern has been the spill-over of criminality from Berlin, particularly among the region's youth.

Brandenburg is the second-most rural state in the east, after Mecklenburg-West Pomerania. Agriculture and forestry employ 15 percent of the labor force, while 33 percent relies on the industrial sector. Industries are mainly concentrated in the Polish border region. Traditionally large industry was not typical of the sparsely populated plains of Mark Brandenburg. Small and medium-sized concerns dominated. Despite the old GDR regime's heavy-industrialization campaign, Brandenburg maintains a rural, small town character.

The economic recovery of Brandenburg has had mixed results. In general, its economic growth rate (2.7 percent in 1998)[4] and unemployment rate (18.8 percent for 1998)[5] are not nearly as troubling as those of some eastern states. However, its relationship with the metropole at its center and the sluggish and uneven rate of economic growth outside of the *Speckgürtel* inject a strong regional dimension into the state's politics.

Turning to the post-*Wende* political landscape, the most striking feature in Brandenburg in the first two legislative periods was the predominance of the Social Democratic Party (SPD) and the weakness (until 1999) of the Christian Democratic Union (CDU). The SPD has been the largest party in the Brandenburg Landtag since 1990. In 1994 it produced the only SPD majority government in the east, giving it a sense of uniqueness and independence. (The SPD lost its majority in the September 5, 1999 Landtag election and, although Stolpe remains Minister-President, his party entered into a grand coalition with the CDU.[6] The SPD losses in Brandenburg and Saarland in September 1999 were the first in a series of SPD setbacks, owing in large part to public anger over Chancellor Schröder's planned austerity measures.)

Since 1990, this region has become known for its "Brandenburger Weg." According to Hans Misselwitz, "The Brandenburg way is identified with a cooperative understanding of politics – a 'consensus in the interest of citizens' that is above party differences – and does not shut out the PDS (Party of Democratic Socialism) – will be valued more than simple opposition."[7] The "Brandenburger Weg" was symbolized in the first legislative period (1990-1994) by the three-way coalition between the SPD, Alliance 90/Greens and FDP. During the second legislative period (1994-1999), when the SPD governed without coalition partners, the party claimed it maintained a cooperative relationship with other parties in the parliament.

Residues of the prewar and GDR past may give 'red Brandenburg' a strong socialist culture. Indeed, the PDS has done well in local and state elections since 1990 and has provided a strong voice of opposition in the Brandenburg Landtag. Because of the strength of the PDS in the Brandenburg parliament, or perhaps due to the spirit of innovation and independence suggested above, the PDS is treated far more as a competent player and formidable opponent in Brandenburg than in most other states.

The development, or more accurately in the case of Brandenburg, the *reassertion*, of regional identity and political culture is reinforced by the emergence of political *Leitfiguren*. Minister President Stolpe and former cabinet member Regine Hildebrandt[8] are two examples of widely recognized political leaders with whom people identify, and who help to instill regional pride. While many personalities shape the Brandenburg SPD, Stolpe certainly stands out as someone whose "GDR biography" has been the subject of much allegation and criticism.[9] Yet, he has persevered, and many Brandenburgers have defended him and were proud of the fact that he did not walk away from politics as others have done when faced with similar allegations. Hildebrandt, the outspoken advocate of eastern interests and identity, whose fiery speeches are colored with a heavily accented local dialect, is another regional symbol of pride and self-confidence.

Brandenburg parliamentarians interviewed in the summer of 1997 reported that regional-*Land* identity had become increasingly important to their constituents. There are ubiquitous symbols of Brandenburg identity, including references to "Mark Brandenburg," "Alter Fritz," and displays of the red eagle, derived from the coat of arms of the Askanian margraves of Brandenburg dating back to 1156. In this state, the long history as a region, the relatively stable population, and the emergence of a number of strong political personalities have all contributed to the assertion of regional difference and independence. The development of a strong Brandenburg identity is also fostered by its particular economic challenges, owing in part to its proximity to Berlin and the perceived need to preserve regional interests and independence in the face of the large and powerful city-state.

Mecklenburg-West Pomerania
Mecklenburg-West Pomerania is a relatively poor, agricultural region in the north. Unlike Brandenburg, Mecklenburg-West Pomerania is an artificial creation resulting from the fusion of two distinct regions. While Mecklenburg has a long history of *Fürstentum*, principalities, and a sense of common history and identity,[10] West Pomerania has no history of its own. Today, it is the western section of Pomerania (formerly part of Prussia) and is closer culturally and geopolitically to the east, as revealed in the Slavic surnames and names of towns there. West Pomerania is more rural and less economically-developed than Mecklenburg. It has fewer people, and life has a slower pace than in the western part of the state (one hears often how "changes occur here one-hundred years later than everywhere else").

In contrast with Brandenburg, Mecklenburg-West Pomeranian regional consciousness is not as strong.[11] Interestingly, many parliamentarians interviewed for this study identified themselves first and foremost as Easterners – or as either Mecklenburgers or West Pomeranians. Although public opinion surveys were not part of this initial study, it was suggested by the parliamentarians that, among the general population, the eastern identity or even the local identity tends to be stronger than the regional, Mecklenburg-West Pomerania consciousness. One reason for this is the heterogeneity and historical discontinuity of its population. Many Mecklenburg-West Pomeranians come from other parts of the former GDR. In the 1950s and 1960s, many Saxons were relocated there to work in newly built factories, primarily in the ship-building industry. The population of West Pomerania, in particular, has been less homogeneous, as it was profoundly affected by the postwar migration of refugees from Poland and other eastern lands.[12] Now, as in the past, the "fishheads" of West Pomerania, as they are not-so-affectionately called, feel disadvantaged (primarily in economic terms) and looked down upon by their partners.

Mecklenburg-West Pomerania has no big city centers. Life during the communist era generally revolved around the agricultural collective, or LPG (*Landwirtschaftliche Produktionsgenossenschaft*). In many villages, the LPGs were the largest employers, providing people with a network of social and cultural activities and ties. In 1991, 20 percent of the labor force in this state was still employed in agriculture. In recent years, the attempts to change the laws affecting the large farms and land-ownership have framed political debates about the economic transition in Mecklenburg-West Pomerania. Legislators in the capital Schwerin are painfully aware that their farmers must now compete with other German and European farmers and that they are losing subsidies quickly.

As a coastal region, Mecklenburg-West Pomerania's other industries are ship-building and fishing. Towns on the Baltic sea-coast, like Rostock (the largest city with 253,000 inhabitants), are highly dependent on marine and fisheries activities. The loss of subsidies in these industries further contributes to economic insecurity in the state and shapes the political debate (as a controversial shipyard crisis at the Bremer-Vulkan plant did in the early 1990s, culminating in a government crisis). A related concern is the lack of employment opportunities and university places for young people. Diminishing opportunities at home have led many young and skilled members of the work-force to leave the state in search of jobs or university places. More than in Brandenburg or Thüringen, the other two states considered here, the elites in this state invariably raised the problem of the hopelessness and aggressiveness of many young people. Indeed, the frequency of incidents of right-wing violence in the state is alarming. In sum, the economic reconstruction of this state has been slower and more painful than in other eastern states. The economic growth rate in this state was only 0.8 percent in 1998,[13] and unemployment remains high, at 20.5 percent in the same year.[14]

The tourist industry is seen by many elites in Schwerin as the answer to Mecklenburg-West Pomerania's economic troubles. There was an overwhelming consensus among interviewees that the natural beauty of the state was one of its greatest assets – particularly in terms of tourism revenues. Many cautioned, however, that the state must be careful to preserve the natural environment while building a tourist infrastructure, including roads, train routes and stations, bike paths, restaurants and accommodations, parks and recreational facilities. While there was widespread agreement that the tourist industry would be an important economic sector for their state, a number pointed out that, "tourism is not enough ... [it] is only one leg of a strategy for economic development ... we are making a mistake if we let the tourist industry grow out of control like in Schleswig-Holstein" and "tourism is not the answer for employment, rather modern, environmental technologies should be our focus." Nonetheless, the state has devoted considerable resources to developing an infrastructure for tourism.

The post-*Wende* political landscape in this state has been characterized by shifting governing coalitions. Between 1990 and 1994, a CDU-FDP coalition governed. In 1994 the FDP did not make it into the Landtag, so the CDU entered into a grand coalition with the SPD. By the summer of 1997, both coalition partners, the CDU and especially the junior coalition partner, the SPD, were deeply frustrated with this model of government. The most recent state parliamentary election on September 27, 1998 produced yet a different situation; the SPD became the largest party in the Landtag with 34.3%, the CDU 30.2% and the PDS 24.4%. Initially, the SPD, led by Minister President designate Harald Ringstorff, did not rule out any coalition models. However, negotiations quickly indicated a preference for some kind of arrangement with the PDS – either a 'toleration' of a minority SPD government or a coalition with the PDS. After several weeks of further negotiation, Mecklenburg-West Pomerania became the first state to form an SPD-PDS coalition.

Rather than an air of self-confidence and regional pride, elites in this state exhibited a more reserved, even humble, political style. Several parliamentarians interviewed in Schwerin in 1997 suggested that is was important for politicians to remember where they came from and not rush to embrace the glitzy new lifestyle of the elite. Eckhardt Rehberg, leader of the CDU *Fraktion*, explained that he regularly receives members of the community at his home on Sunday afternoon for informal *Sprechstunde*, or office hours. Another parliamentarian, a member of the PDS *Fraktion*, related how he has not moved out of his old apartment in a *Plattenbau*, a communist-era settlement of concrete slabs, and still drives an 'economy-car' because it is important to be seen by the people as someone they can trust and relate to. Both politicians saw these activities as the best way to keep in touch with what really concerns their communities. In a state without a common territorial or cultural past, and where there is little optimism about the economic future of the state, the leadership is likely to feel less secure in the new order and, perhaps, in their ability to develop a strong regional profile or independent policies.

Moreover, relative to Brandenburg, Mecklenburg-West Pomerania lacks regional political *Leitfiguren*. Its minister presidents have been lackluster, and its governments have been plagued by scandal. As a result, the public has looked to the national level of politics for *Leitfiguren*, where two prominent Mecklenburg-West Pomeranians assumed cabinet positions in 1990. However, favorite son Gunther Krause (CDU) soon had to step down from his ministerial post in the Kohl government as a result of a scandal involving his family and misused funds. Angela Merkel, a minister in the federal government in Bonn from 1990 to 1998 and then General Secretary of the CDU, has been a source of regional pride for some people (although she was initially seen as too conservative for many, she may have redeemed herself by virtue of being able to last this long in national politics).

In state politics, Rehberg has come the closest to serving as a regional political hero. Thanks to him, this small state, with relatively little economic strength to bring to bear in unified Germany, has caught the attention of national political leaders. Among eastern politicians, Rehberg has taken the lead in espousing a new eastern confidence. He has publicly warned that easterners would no longer stand for the smear-campaigns directed at the eastern past or for cries of victory of one side over the other. In 1996 Rehberg and a few of his CDU colleagues produced a strategy paper in which they accused the national party leadership of "Besitzstandswahrung" – an attitude of possessiveness toward the east – and challenged the CDU leadership to rethink its tactics in the new states.[15] Rehberg insists that the point was to generate a much-needed discussion about the moral health of the country. He told this author that too many people (east and west) have focused only on the material-financial aspects of the transition and have neglected to carry through discussions started in 1989-1990 about morality, civic virtues, and the true meaning of the collapse of the GDR.[16] Rehberg's protests, however, are not on behalf of Mecklenburg-West Pomeranians in particular and, thus, do not necessarily contribute to the development of a regional consciousness.

Although regional political culture and identity are less pronounced in Mecklenburg-West Pomerania than in Brandenburg, there are nonetheless signs of growing political confidence and independence among the state's leaders. Rehberg's strategy paper and the bold SPD-PDS coalition are the most visible signs. Still, this small, economically weak state on the periphery of the New Germany has little national clout. In recent years, there has been some discussion about fusing Mecklenburg-West Pomerania with at least one nearby state (Schleswig-Holstein). Mecklenburg-West Pomeranians may be less adamant in their refusal to give up regional autonomy than were the Brandenburgers.

Thuringia

Thuringia presents a contrast in many ways to both Brandenburg and Mecklenburg-West Pomerania. Thuringia is a small state located in the center of unified Germany. As a political unit, Thuringia can only trace its existence back to 1920, when, in the restructuring following the first world war, eight princely states were fused.[17] Historically, this area was characterized by *Kleinstaaten*, minor states, and *Herzogtümer*, dukedoms. Thus a Thuringian regional consciousness would seem to be based more on cultural and geographic factors than on a shared political past. While cultural pride and tradition are glaringly obvious (Goethe seems to have left his mark on just about *every* town in the state), regional identity does not seem to play as prominent a role in state politics as it does in other eastern states, such as Brandenburg.[18]

The economic activities in this state are distributed rather differently than in the previous two states. Ten percent of the labor force is employed in agriculture, while 43 percent work in industry (the highest share after Saxony).[19] The economic growth rate in the state has been among the highest,[20] with productivity increasing by almost 80 percent between 1991 and 1996.[21] Moreover, in contrast to Mecklenburg-West Pomerania in particular, Thuringia's industry is more diverse and modern, including microelectronics, vehicle and machinery construction, in addition to more traditional sectors like mining and textile manufacturing.

The state is situated in the center of the unified Germany, making it a natural bridge between north and south, east and west. This geographic fact has the effect of opening Thuringia up to outside influence and, perhaps, muting the particularity of the state. Health resorts and cultural sites and activities draw many tourists to the state. Several interviewees in the state parliament noted with pride that Thuringia spends more on culture than most western *Länder*. This represents a huge financial responsibility and several parliamentarians mentioned the desire for more federal support of culture. In any event, cultural tourism and the geographic situation shape the region's economic development and its regional culture and identity.

Parliamentarians in this state were generally more accepting of or perhaps reconciled to the fact of western-driven economic recovery. One of the elites' major preoccupations was the building of a modern transportation infrastructure capable of handling the heavy volume of east-west and north-south traffic that passes through the state daily. All of these factors give Thuringia the air of a hub, where the pains of adjustment to a new system will pass relatively quickly and where "east" and "west" and "new" and "old" will more easily fade into merely "German."

Yet, Thuringia is not immune to the post-communist structural problems. De-industrialization has occurred here as well, symbolized by the example of mass layoffs of miners followed by protests and hunger strikes in Bischofferode in 1993. Unemployment in 1998 was 18.3 percent.[22] According to one parliamentarian, Thuringians have tended to look askance at other eastern *Länder* and look only to the west for models of economic development. When asked about their vision for the future of their state, typically parliamentarians' answers fell on either side of one issue: how closely to follow the West German model of economic development. Not surprisingly, members of the CDU-dominated governing coalition favored following the western model closely: "My vision is to have the same standard as in the old *Länder*." Among the opposition, a more common sentiment was "not to make the same mistakes as them – not to copy the models of the old *Länder*." If Thuringia has been more western-oriented than the other two states discussed, one possible explanatory factor that cannot be overlooked is its western CDU Minister-President, Bernhard Vogel, who, significantly, has been a friend of former Chancellor Kohl (unlike the CDU Minister President of Saxony). This staunchly CDU state has been and will continue to be less wary of the west's intentions and of the federal government's policy prescriptions.[23]

Relative to legislators interviewed in Potsdam and Schwerin, the Thuringian elites were much more confident about the progress made in their state's economy. Discussions with political leaders in Erfurt awell as residents of towns and villages in Thuringia reflect a general consensus that the state is on the right track. Among the three cases considered here, leaders in Thuringia were the most hopeful about the future economic development of their state. Interviewees spoke excitedly about areas for future development, including the construction industry, the energy and chemical industries, electronics, food production/processing, and the service sector, including tourism, which will require that even more attention be given to building accommodation and transportation links. Most interviewees placed the greatest hope in the further development of small and medium-sized firms and traditional craftsmen, whose businesses were already in private hands. Elites here also appeared more jubilant about the market in general and were happy to relate how much their own lifestyles had changed – for the better. In general, politicians here do not look back and tend to dismiss skeptics of the economic changes as *Jammerossis* – whiny easterners – and 'losers of unification.'

The postcommunist political situation in Thuringia between 1990 and 1998 was similar to Mecklenburg-West Pomerania in that the CDU dominated and there were shifting coalition governments: in 1990-1994 a CDU-FDP coalition governed, followed by a grand coalition in 1994-1998. Although the junior partners in the second grand coalition, the SPD, were not as vocal as the party in Mecklenburg-West Pomerania about their frustrations with the grand coalition, there was much speculation in 1997-1998 that, should the SPD win the most votes in the 1999 state parliamentary election, it too might opt to govern without the CDU, making the PDS a pivotal player in this state as well. On September 12, 1999, Thuringia held its third state parliamentary election. Following a string of upsets for the SPD in state elections in 1999, the Thuringian SPD came in third place (18.5 percent), behind the PDS (21.4 percent). For the first time, the CDU won an absolute majority (51 percent) in the state.

Among the Thuringian parliamentarians interviewed in 1997, a relatively stronger sense of *gesamtdeutsch*, or all-German, rather than eastern or even regional/*Land* identity was apparent. Compared to the other two states, members of the Landtag in Thuringia were far less insistent that an 'eastern profile' or identity was a necessary component of, or addition to, politics in their state. This attitude may be understood as a product of several factors. First, Thuringia lies at the geographic center of the new Germany. It is a small state with no long territorial-political tradition and with relatively less influence to bear on unified Germany. Therefore, it blends west and east more easily. In the transition, moreover, the economic situation in Thuringia has been stable, and the political situation has stabilized under Vogel. The sense that things are moving in the right direction reinforces an identification with national goals and identity rather than a backward-looking or inward-looking or defensive posture. Finally, no loud voice of regional particularism has emerged in state politics. The dominance of the CDU has fostered a *gesamtdeutsch* set of interests and identity rather than an eastern or particular, regional one. The fact that the Minister President is a westerner – and a popular westerner – and was close to former Chancellor Helmut Kohl, may have given the state a more positive relationship to the center.

Saxony, Saxony-Anhalt, and East Berlin

Although Saxony, Saxony-Anhalt, and East Berlin were not included in the elite study, it is possible to offer several brief observations in comparison with Brandenburg, Mecklenburg-West Pomerania and Thuringia. Saxony certainly has a long history as a region. Currently, it enjoys a strong sense of regional pride and identity.[24] Its economy has been among the strongest in the east since unification.[25] The state certainly has a regional hero in Kurt Biedenkopf and enjoys a great deal of visibility in Germany and Europe.[26]

Saxony-Anhalt is evidence that a *Land* with a rather weak tradition of statehood can, nonetheless, develop a strong sense of regional independence.[27] Saxony-Anhalt is one of the historically youngest states (it existed only briefly after the war, from 1945 to 1952), but since its revival in 1990, it has developed a relatively strong protest-oriented regional identity. Its regionalism owes, to a great extent, to its unique political development, whereby the PDS has played an important role in state politics, signaling a departure from established coalition patterns and, to some extent, resulting in the state's marginalization from the mainstream of German politics. Regional independence is also fostered by the state's SPD Minister-President, Reinhard Höppner, who is known for his outspoken defense of Saxony-Anhalt's prerogative to choose its own road to success. According to Höppner, "In the new states, we don't have to copy all the cliches and age-old political models of the West."[28] "We are listening carefully to external opinion, but we make policy for our state and in our state."[29] Finally, Saxony-Anhalt has experienced relative economic failure, which, as in the case of Brandenburg, is more a cause for protest and for rallying regional dissatisfaction in the name of change rather than a cause for resignation and anomie. Public frustration with the economic situation in the state was expressed in the 1998 state parliamentary election when the extremist party the German People's Union captured an alarming share of the vote.

While East Berlin is not a state, but rather part of a city-state, it is nonetheless relevant to our discussion of regional differentiation. Representing the same territory and population as before the *Wende*, it enjoys a more recent history and sense of continuity than the five eastern states. In the GDR, a core-periphery relationship put East Berlin in a privileged position. Today, within unified Berlin, East Berlin maintains a distinct political, economic, and socio-cultural profile. Compared to the other eastern states, however, its economic recovery has been successful. And in terms of political leadership, the strong influence of the PDS in East Berlin (40 percent of the vote in the eastern districts in the October 1999 Berlin election) gives the area an independent profile in the Berlin Senate and in unified Germany in general.

To conclude, while common interests and challenges may distinguish the eastern states from the western states, it is important to recognize that the east is not as homogenous as many analyses and commentaries once assumed. Within the east, there are different historical legacies, different degrees of territorial continuity, and, of particular importance, different experiences under communism that provide the backdrop to developments after 1990. Since 1990, developments in the economic and political realms have also varied from state to state. Finally, elite interviews suggest that elements of regional culture and identity have emerged in recent years. Regional mass culture, however, is an area that will require further research.

Increasing elite independence has also been a feature of regional development in new states. This independence can have implications for the relationship between regional political party organizations and the national party leadership, as was demonstrated by the Rehberg-led CDU appeal to the national party organization, or the Saxony-Anhalt and Mecklenburg-West Pomerania SPD organizations' decisions to work with the PDS, despite objections from the national party leadership. Divergent regional trajectories may also erode any lingering sense of eastern solidarity between the states. This, too, would have implications for German politics and governance. Political parties would feel less pressure to develop strategies for integrating eastern interests and identity (as Rehberg and others in the CDU in the east have desired, or as the SPD attempted with its "Forum-Ost"). Also, the waning of eastern solidarity and common interests is likely to affect the behavior of these states in the Bundesrat. For instance, rather than Bundesrat debates and votes on economic issues dividing along east-west lines, they may be likelier to be cast in partisan terms or in terms of poorer states versus wealthier states.

The new states have begun to cultivate their own relations with neighboring countries and provinces, other international actors, and, of course, investors. The individual states have worked hard to link themselves into global trading patterns, the information superhighway, the free movement of capital, and the routes of important transport networks. They have also begun to articulate their own interests at the European Union level. The multi-level governance of the EU may actually encourage regionalism. Indeed, Germany's own federal system provides significant room for regional diversity. For all of these reasons, regional differentiation is likely to increase in the east.

Notes

An earlier version of this article, entitled "Regional Differences and Political Leadership in the New German States," appeared in *German Politics and Society*, vol. 18, no. 1, Spring 2000, 33-65.

[1] Field research for this project was conducted in 1993-1994 and the summer of 1997 in the state capitals of Brandenburg (Potsdam), Mecklenburg-West Pomerania (Schwerin) and Thuringia (Erfurt). The data for this article derive from an interview study of over 80 state parliamentarians, as well as numerous secondary sources.

[2] For more on the 1996 referendum, see Joanna McKay, "Berlin-Brandenburg? Nein danke! The Referendum on the Proposed *Länderfusion*," *German Politics*, vol.5, no.3 (December 1996), 485-502; and Anna J. and Richard L. Merritt, "Ursus Tyrannus or Teddy Bear? Berlin and Its Neighbors," Paper delivered at the 1997 Meeting of the American Political Science Association, Washington, DC, August 1997.

[3] For example, while in 1996 Potsdam (within the *Speckgürtel*) had an unemployment rate of 12.8%, for periphery towns Cottbus and Eberswalde, unemployment was 18.7% and 20.3% respectively. Figures reported by the SPD-Fraktion in the Bundestag, "Jahresarbeitsmarkt-Bericht: Ostdeutschland 1996/1997", Bonn, May 1997.

[4] Landesamt für Datenverarbeitung und Statisktik Land Brandenburg, Statistische Berichte PI1-j/98, "Bruttoinlandsprodukt und Bruttowertschöpfung im Land Brandenburg, 1991 bis 1998," p.10. Figure is the change over the previous year in percent.

[5] Unemployment figures from the Statistisches Bundesamt Deutschland, www.statistik-bund.de/jahrbuch/jahrtab13.Htm.

[6] With only 55% of the eligible electorate turning out to vote in 1999, the SPD share was 39.3%, the CDU 26.5%, the PDS 23.3%, and the DVU 5%.

[7] Hans-J. Misselwitz, "Regionale Aspekte politischer Kultur – Was bleibt vom 'Brandenburger Weg'?," *BISS Public*, vol. 18 (1996) 65-69: 67. Translation mine.

[8] Hildebrandt stepped down from all of her political offices in October 1999 in protest at the SPD's decision to enter into a coalition with the CDU. She was vehemently opposed to coalitioning with the CDU due to the party's social policy positions which she regarded as inimical to SPD principles.

[9] Allegedly, Stolpe had numerous contacts with Stasi agents while he was an administrator for the Protestant Church in the GDR.

[10] For a detailed history of Mecklenburg, see Manfred Hamann, *Das staatliche Werden Mecklenburgs*, Cologne: Böhlau Verlag, 1962.

[11] This argument is supported by Klaus Schwabe, "Mecklenburgische und vorpommersche Identität," in: Martin Greiffenhagen, ed., *Die neuen Bundesländer*, Stuttgart: Kohlhammer, 1994, pp. 28-41, especially pp. 31-32.

[12] *Mecklenburgische und Vorpommersche Identität: Mentalitäten und Befindlichkeiten*, ed. Landeszentrale für politische Bildung Mecklenburg-Vorpommern (Schwerin, 1996).

[13] Reported by the Statistisches Landesamt Mecklenburg-Vorpommern, "Bruttoinlandsprodukt und Bruttowertschöpfung der Wirtschaftsbereiche in Mecklenburg-Vorpommern, 1991 bis 1998" (April 1999), p. 8.

[14] Unemployment figures for 1998 reported by the Statistisches Bundesamt Deutschland.

[15] *Identitätsgewinn im Aufbau Ost: Diskussionspapier zur Werte- und Strategiedebatte 'CDU 2000' in Mecklenburg-Vorpommern*, published by the CDU-Fraktion in the Mecklenburg-West Pomeranian Landtag (Schwerin, January 1996).

[16] Interview, Schwerin, June 1997.

[17] See Andreas Dornheim, "Thüringen: territorial und politisch-kulturell zersplittert," in: *Die neuen Bundesländer*, ed. Landeszentrale für politische Bildung Baden-Würtemberg (Stuttgart, 1994).

[18] Interviewees in the Thuringian state parliament were far more likely to identify themselves first and foremost as "Germans" or in "local" terms, as a citizen of a particular region in Thuringia, rather than as "Thuringians" or "eastern Germans." The opposite was true of parliamentarians interviewed in the state of Brandenburg.

[19] *Community Support Framework 1991-93 for the areas of Eastern Berlin, Mecklenburg-Vorpommern, Brandenburg, Sachsen-Anhalt, Thüringen and Sachsen, Federal Republic of Germany*, publication of the European Communities (Brussels, 1994), p. 15.

[20] Thuringia's economic growth rate in 1998 was 2.4% over the previous year. From the Thüringer Landesamt für Statistik, "Wirtschaft in Thüringen" (1999).

[21] Thuringia's 79.66% increase compares to Saxony's 60.13% and Mecklenburg-West Pomerania's 46.96%. "Jahresarbeitsmarkt-Bericht, Ostdeutschland 1996/1997," p. 18.

[22] Statistisches Bundesamt Deutschland, op.cit. See also Wolfgang Mühlfriedel, "Die thüringische Wirtschaft im Wandel," in: Karl Schmitt, ed., *Thüringen – Eine politische Landeskunde*, Weimar: Böhlau, 1996.

[23] See the interview with Minister President Vogel, "Thuringia's Economic, Political Situation Viewed," *FOCUS*, March 28, 1994, pp. 47-48 (reprinted in *FBIS-WEU*, March 31, 1994, p. 26).

[24] Manfred Artur Fellisch, "Sachsen: ein Land mit großer kultureller und wirtschaftlicher Vergangenheit," in: *Die neuen Bundesländer*, pp. 124-133.

[25] The gross domestic product of Saxony in 1998 was DM125.3 billion, compared with 77.8 for Brandenburg, 48.4 for Mecklenburg-West Pomerania, 71.4 for Saxony-Anhalt, and 66.5 for Thuringia. The unemployment rate in Saxony in 1998 was 18.8%. Figures from the Statistisches Bundesamt Deutschland.

[26] See the feature article "Die grössten Spinner," *Der Spiegel*, 32/1996, 22-33.

[27] For further historical analysis of Saxony-Anhalt, see Mathias Tullner, *Geschichte des Landes Sachsen-Anhalt*, Magdeburg: Landeszentrale für politische Bildung des Landes Sachsen-Anhalt, 1993 and Tullner "Das neueste der neuen Bundesländer: Sachsen-Anhalt," in: *Die neuen Bundesländer*, pp. 67-89.

[28] Quoted in *Sächsische Zeitung*, June 29, 1994.

[29] *Märkische Zeitung*, July 7, 1994.

Astrid Segert

Allokationsprozesse deutscher Eliten
Diskussion der Kolonialisierungsthese

To explain the underrepresentation of eastern Germans among elites in all sectors of German society, this chapter examines the mechanisms of elite recruitment in Germany. In contrast to colonisation theory, it argues that the exclusion of East Germans is the result of formalized allocation processes by which established West German criteria serve as a filter. The negative effect of this filter is, however, not only the marginalization of East German elites; alternative experiences and innovative competences acquired in East Germany are not drawn upon because of the mechanisms of elite recruitment in unified Germany.

Können Sie sich einen ostdeutschen Bundeskanzler vorstellen? Rein statistisch ist in der Politik die Wahrscheinlichkeit, einen Ostdeutschen in höchsten Elitepositionen anzutreffen, noch am höchsten. Die Chancen eines Ostdeutschen, in die Position des Präsidenten der Bundesbank oder eines Richters am Bundesverfassungsgericht zu gelangen, gehen hingegen tatsächlich gegen Null.

Es ist eine Tatsache, die Ostdeutschen sind in allen Sektoren der deutschen Elite unterrepräsentiert. In der deutschen Öffentlichkeit wird dies weithin als normal hingenommen. Größere theoretische oder politische Diskussionen dazu fehlen, sieht man einmal von speziellen ostdeutschen Teilöffentlichkeiten ab. Plausible Erklärungen scheinen auf der Hand zu liegen und Veränderungen zumindest mittelfristig absurd. Die Situation erscheint klar und erklärt. Sind weiterführende Erkenntnis und praktische Veränderungen nicht möglich, so bleibt dem Einzelnen vermeintlich nur, sich in dieser oder jener Weise persönlich wertend zu den unvermeidbaren Tatsachen zu verhalten. Ich werde hier jedoch statt einer subjektiven Bewertung quasi schicksalhafter Gegebenheiten ein objektivierbares Verständnis der Situation anbieten, das ein praktisches Eingreifen zumindest möglich macht. Da Erkenntnis erwächst, indem man scheinbar Bekanntes in Frage stellt, soll der Frage nachgegangen werden, wie es zu erklären ist, daß das Ungleichgewicht der Besetzung von deutschen Elitepositionen zwischen Menschen mit west- und ostdeutscher Herkunft auch noch zehn Jahre nach der deutschen Vereinigung reproduziert wird.

Dazu vertrete ich folgende These: Um die nachhaltige West-Ost-Ungleichheit bei der Besetzung der deutschen Funktionseliten zu verstehen, ist es notwendig, den Mechanismus der Elitenrekrutierung als eigenständige Ursache zu analysieren. Ich argumentiere, daß die relative Ausgrenzung von Ostdeutschen aus deutschen Elitepositionen nach einer durch politische Interessen bestimmten Transformationsphase nunmehr weitgehend über formalisierte Allokationsprozesse hergestellt wird, in denen allgemeine westdeutsche Zugangskriterien zur Anwendung kommen. Weder die Zugangsverfahren noch die -kriterien sind speziell auf die Benachteiligung von Ostdeutschen ausgerichtet, sondern sollen vor allem und direkt die organisatorische Stabilität der verschiedenen Elitensektoren sichern. Ausgrenzungen – nicht nur von Ostdeutschen – ergeben sich dabei eher indirekt. Der so reproduzierte ungleiche Zugang von West- und Ostdeutschen zu den deutschen Funktionseliten hat eine weitaus größere Bedeutung als die ebenfalls nicht unerheblichen Vermögens- oder Einkommensungleichheiten,[1] da er die Vertretung ostdeutscher Interessen auf gesamtgesellschaftlicher Ebene weitgehend vom Verhalten nicht unmittelbar betroffener und nicht entsprechend gruppenspezifisch integrierter Westdeutscher macht. Dadurch öffnet sich die west-ostdeutsche Schere beim Zugang zur Gesamtheit sozialer Handlungsressourcen langfristig.

Aktuelle Daten zur Elitenbeteiligung von Ostdeutschen
Auf diese These wird im folgenden genauer eingegangen. Doch zunächst zu den Fakten. Obwohl seit 1990 jährlich Surveys zu unterschiedlichsten Problemstellungen durchgeführt werden, gibt es nur wenig statistisches Material zur Verteilung der Machtverhältnisse in Deutschland, so auch zur Verteilung der West- und Ostdeutschen auf die gesamtdeutschen Elitepositionen. Es ist ein Verdienst der Elitestudie, die 1997 an der Potsdamer Universität durchgeführt wurde, daß dazu nun Daten vorliegen, die mit der westdeutschen Elitenstudie von 1981 kompatibel sind.[2] Von den insgesamt 2.341 Befragten sind 272 Ostdeutsche. Damit sind sie gemessen an ihrem Bevölkerungsanteil von etwa 20 % mit 11,6 % an den gesamtdeutschen Elitepositionen unterrepräsentiert. Diese Tendenz wird durch die regionale und die sektorale Verteilung der befragten ostdeutschen Eliten noch verstärkt.

Einerseits nehmen von den 272 Ostdeutschen nur 33 Personen eine Eliteposition in den westdeutschen Bundesländern ein. Da die deutsche Hauptstadt und damit das Regierungszentrum sowie eine große Zahl von Verbands- und Firmenzentralen zum Zeitpunkt der Befragung noch in Bonn bzw. in Westdeutschland befanden, kann man davon ausgehen, das die

Ostdeutschen in den nationalen Elitespitzen noch weitaus geringer beteiligt sind.[3] Dies entspricht auch dem Eindruck, der durch die Medienpräsenz von Ostdeutschen im Alltag vermittelt wird. Zusätzlich sind von den in der Studie erfaßten 402 Elitepositionen in Ostdeutschland 163 (40%) durch Westdeutsche besetzt, die inzwischen zum großen Teil übergesiedelt sind. Das heißt, daß bisher eine produktive Durchmischung von West- und Ostdeutschen bei den regionalen Eliten in Ostdeutschland stattgefunden hat. Sie findet sich so weder bei den regionalen Eliten in Westdeutschland noch bei den gesamtnationalen Elitepositionen. Eine Ausnahme bildet der politische Sektor, in dem Ostdeutsche auch in den Parteispitzen und in der Regierung vertreten sind. Damit zeigt sich die positive Seite der politischen Präsenz von Ostdeutschen.

Andererseits konzentrieren sich die befragten ostdeutschen Eliteträger mit 58,8% vorrangig im politischen Sektor. Das heißt, mehr als jeder zweite ostdeutsche Inhaber einer Elitenposition ist im Bereich der Politik positioniert. In anderen wichtigen gesellschaftlichen Sektoren wie Justiz und Militär hat hingegen bisher keine einzige Person mit ostdeutschem Erfahrungshintergrund eine Elitenposition erreicht. In der Wirtschaft wurde eine Person gefunden. Die ostdeutschen Eliten verteilen sich also sehr ungleich auf die gesellschaftlichen Bereiche. Ihre Quote beträgt nur im Durchschnitt 11,6%. Sie wird stark durch den überdurchschnittlichen Anteil an politischen Elitepositionen (32,1%) beeinflußt. Darüber hinaus liegt die Beteiligung von Ostdeutschen in den Medien (12,4%) und in den Gewerkschaften (11, 8%) etwa im Bereich des ostdeutschen Durchschnittes. In ganzen Sektoren geht sie jedoch gegen Null und in anderen Bereichen wie der Verwaltung (2,5%), der Wissenschaft (7,3%) und den Wirtschafts-verbänden (8,1%) liegt sie weit unter dem Durchschnitt. Fazit: In jedem gesellschaftlichen Bereich – außer in der Politik – sind Ostdeutsche gegenüber westdeutschen Eliten deutlich unterrepräsentiert. In ganzen Gesellschaftssektoren sind sie ausschließlich auf eine indirekte Vertretung durch Personen mit westdeutschem Erfahrungshintergrund angewiesen.

Erklärungsmuster des west-ostdeutschen Elitengefälles in der Diskussion
Wie werden nun die genannten Daten in der deutschen Sozialwissenschaft diskutiert? Drei Thesen sind gegenwärtig in der Diskussion. Die dominante Interpretation geht von einer spezifischen *Transformationsthese* aus. Sie besagt, daß der Umbruch von Institutionen notwendig mit einseitigen Kosten

Tabelle: Verteilung ost- und westdeutscher Positionseliten[4]

Sektor	Befragt (N)	Davon Ostdeut-sche (n)	Anteil der Ostdeutschen an den Sektoren in % (Ostquote)	Anteil der Westdeutschen an den Sektoren in % (Westquote)	Verteilung der 272 Ostdeutschen auf die Sektoren in %	Verteilung der 2069 Westdeut-schen auf die Sektoren in %
Gesamt	2.341	272	11,6	88,4	100	100
Politik	499	160	32,1	67,9	58,8	16,4
Verwaltung	474	12	2,5	97,4	4,4	22,3
Wirtschaft	249	1	0,4	99,6	0,4	12,0
Wirtschafts-verbände	173	14	8,1	91,9	5,2	7,7
Gewerk-schaft	97	12	12,4	87,6	4,4	4,1
Massen-medien	281	33	11,8	88,2	12,1	12,0
Wissen-schaft	164	12	7,3	92,7	4,4	7,3
Militär	135	0	0,0	100,0	0,0	6,5
Kultur	101	13	12,9	87,1	4,8	4,3
Sonstige	168	15	8,9	91,1	5,5	7,4
Davon: Justiz	42	0	0,0	100,0	0,0	2,0

auf seiten bestimmter sozialer Gruppen/Generationen begleitet wird[5]. Eine zweite Lesart präferiert die *Kolonialisierungsthese*, die die bewußte Zerstörung von DDR-Eliten durch westdeutsche Akteure betont[6]. Als drittes soll hier die *Interessenthese*, insbesondere die These von der Vertretungslücke genannt werden. Sie geht von der Elitenrekrutierung durch Akteure mit unterschiedlichen Interessen aus und sieht in der institutionellen Unterrepräsentation von Ostdeutschen eine wichtige Ursache für die Reproduktion ungleicher Strukturen. Ich vertrete ausgehend von der Interessenthese und in Polemik mit der Kolonialisierungsauffassung die These, daß der Elitenzugang langfristig nicht nur für Ostdeutsche über allgemeine Mechanismen wie die Anwendung von tradierten

Allokationskriterien sowie von Zugangsritualen reguliert wird (*Allokations-these*). Die kritische Analyse dieser Mechanismen kann gemeinsam mit der Analyse sich verändernder Interessenkonstellationen unterschiedlicher Akteure (Interessenthese) mögliche Wege zum Abbau des Elitengefälles in Deutschland aufzeigen.

Im einzelnen geht die *Transformationsthese* davon aus, daß Ostdeutsche deshalb nicht stärker in gesellschaftsrelevante Positionen gelangen, weil ihnen die dafür notwendigen Systemkompetenzen fehlen. Ihnen fehlt vielfach das notwendige Wissen, nach welchen subtilen Regeln und mit welchen spezifischen Akteuren bestimmte Dinge ausgehandelt und entschieden werden. Ihnen fehlen viele Kontakte und Beziehungen, um hinreichend Einfluß nehmen zu können. Kurz, ihnen fehlt häufig das Wissen, wie das Spiel gespielt wird und unter welchen Bedingungen man die eigenen Interessen durchsetzen und andere Akteure einbinden kann. Als Ursache für diesen Kompetenzmangel wird die Sozialisation in einem anderen Gesellschaftssystem angesehen. Aus dieser Sicht kann der Anteil an Ostdeutschen daher erst mit der in der Bundesrepublik aufwachsenden und ausgebildeten Generation wachsen. Bis dahin wird es gemessen an diesen objektivierbaren Elitekriterien als unabänderlich angesehen, daß Ostdeutsche auf die Vertretung durch Westdeutsche angewiesen sind.[7] Die Differenz der Wissensbestände zwischen ost- und westdeutschen Akteuren ist eine empirische Tatsache. Die daraus abzuleitenden Schlußfolgerungen für die Elitenallokation müssen diskutiert werden.

Die beschriebene Perspektive auf die ungleiche Verteilung von Eliten-positionen identifiziert elitenspezifische Handlungskompetenzen allein mit Fähigkeiten, die die Stabilität bestehender Organisationsstrukturen reproduzieren. Auf diese Weise verstellt sie den Blick auf Handlungs-kompetenzen anderer Qualität, die unter Umständen erhebliche Ent-wicklungspotentiale darstellen können. Nicht zuletzt legitimiert sie, daß solche alternativen Handlungsressourcen gesellschaftlich weitgehend ungenutzt brachliegen. Sie unterstellt weiter, daß jene Kompetenzen, die in der Vergangenheit Systemstabilität und gesellschaftliche Entwicklung gleichermaßen bedingten, auch unter den veränderten Umweltbedingungen der Gegenwart und Zukunft soziale Erfolge gerieren. Damit werden die aus der Geschichte der (alten) Bundesrepublik als erfolgreich bekannten Verhaltensmuster und Wissensbestände wie Mythen behandelt, deren historischer Kontext und aktuelle Grenzen nicht reflektiert werden. Der Blick auf neue Handlungsanforderungen und mögliche neue soziale Subjekte bleiben weitgehend verstellt. Die so verstandene Transformationsthese ignoriert sowohl die Differenz zwischen systemstabilisierenden und entwicklungsfördernden Handlungspotentialen wie auch zwischen dem historischen Handlungsanforderungen der Nachkriegszeit und der Gegenwart. Sie bedarf der Öffnung für die Normalität von Transformationen im westlichen System selbst nach dem Systemwechsel der ostdeutschen Teilgesellschaft und in Beziehung auf die Prozesse der Elitenbildung.

Jenseits der Transformationsdebatte gehört es durchaus zur Normalität, die Handlungskompetenzen der bundesdeutschen Eliten einer zum Teil prinzipiellen Kritik zu unterziehen. So konstatiert Hofer eine allgemeine Führungskrise der deutschen Eliten. Zur Unterstützung seines Standpunktes zitiert er unter anderem solche Autoritäten wie Helmut Kohl, Helmut Schmidt und Elisabeth Noelle-Neumann die sich mit solchen Charakteristiken wie "Verbonzung," "Abgeschlossenheit" bzw. "Negativismus" kritisch über die politische, wirtschaftliche bzw. intellektuelle deutsche Elite geäußert haben.[8] Field und Higley belegen, daß dies durchaus kein spezifisch deutsches Problem ist. Sie betonen, daß Eliten heute im allgemeinen durch Legitimationsprobleme in ihren Führungsaufgaben belastet werden. Die Ursache sehen sie darin, daß die Masse der Bevölkerung nicht in adäquatem Maße an den gesellschaftlichen Entwicklungsprozessen partizipiert.[9] Von ihnen wird also die kritische Sicht auf die Ausgrenzungsmechanismen beim Zugang zu Elitenpositionen auf eine Kritik der Partizipationsmöglichkeiten aller Bürger an den gesellschaftlichen Grundentscheidungen ausgedehnt. Die Einschränkungen beider Prozesse verstärken sich wechselseitig.

Die *Kolonialisierungsthese* betont im Gegensatz zur Transformationsthese das Machtgefälle zwischen den beteiligten Akteuren, das vom Beginn des Beitritts der DDR zur Bundesrepublik an bestand. Dem ist zunächst zuzustimmen. Solchen Entscheidungen wie zum Beispiel keine DDR-Diplomaten, -richter oder Generäle in Elitenpositionen des gemeinsamen Deutschlands zu übernehmen, lag ein politischer Wille zugrunde. Sie hätten auch anders getroffen werden können. Besonders deutlich wird der Einfluß politischer Interessen bei Entscheidungen, für die ausdrücklich Ausnahmeregelungen im Einigungsvertrag vorgesehen wurden. Als Beispiel kann die der Anerkennung des Anwaltsberufes gelten, während die meisten anderen Berufe im Vereinigungsvertrag zunächst nicht ausdrücklich gesichert und durch spätere Festlegungen nur eingeschränkt anerkannt wurden.

Mit der Beschreibung der machtpolitischen Ausgangsbedingungen der deutschen Einheit sind jedoch noch nicht die Ursachen für die nachhaltige

Reproduktion dieses Machtgefälles auch zehn Jahre nach der staatlichen Einheit benannt. Überlegungen dazu werden häufig nicht weiter ausgeführt. Sie können aber indirekt durch die Art der Problemdarstellung erschlossen werden. Unter Kolonialisierung wird die "Zerstörung der einheimischen Wirtschaftsstruktur, die Ausbeutung vorhandener ökonomischer Ressourcen, die soziale Liquidierung der politischen Elite und Intelligenz und die Zerstörung gewachsener Identität" verstanden. Kritikwürdig erscheint die Kolonialisierungsthese vor allem, da sie das "gravierende Dominanz-phänomen im Verhältnis von West- und Ostdeutschen"[10] als dauerhafte Ursache seiner Selbstverstärkung und damit auch für die anhaltend ungleiche Besetzung von Elitepositionen ansieht. Sie ist damit in ihrer Perspektive ergebnisorientiert. Sie erklärt im eigentlichen Sinne nicht in welchem Prozeß Elitenungleichheiten nachhaltig reproduziert werden. Kritik fordern auch jene Vertreter der Kolonialisierungsthese heraus, die mehr oder weniger indirekt ideologische Gründe wie den Antikommunismus als die entscheidende Ursache für die Reproduktion sozialer Ungleichheiten unterstellen. Eine solche Erklärung kommt einer Verschwörungsthese nahe, die den vergesellschafteten Charakter der westdeutschen Gesellschaft sowie ihre dezentralen Machtstrukturen verkennt. Die Bundesrepublik wird von dem genannten Standpunkt aus statt dessen aus dem Blickwinkel eines politisch-ideologisch zentralisierten Systems betrachtet. Mit dieser Kritik an der Kolonialisierungsthese soll nicht bestritten werden, daß Formen des Antikommunismus bei der Bewertung von ostdeutschen Bewerbern auf Elitepositionen durchaus eine Rolle spielen. Allerdings üben solche ideologisierten Zugangskriterien nicht den entscheidenden Einfluß auf die Elitenungleichheit zwischen West und Ost aus. Sie ordnen sich in allgemeinere Rekrutierungsmechanismen ein.

Mit der *Interessenthese* kann dagegen argumentiert werden, daß es in der hoch differenzierten bundesrepublikanischen Gesellschaft eben kein zentrales Subjekt, das den Elitenzugang unmittelbar im eigenen Interesse verschließt. Auch werden die Interessen der beteiligten Akteure nicht vorrangig durch ideologische Welt- und Menschenbilder geprägt. Vielmehr muß der Mechanismus der Elitenrekrutierung als ein vergesellschafteter Prozeß verstanden werden, an dem eine Vielzahl von Institutionen und Personen mit den unterschiedlichsten politischen, ökonomischen und sozialen Interessen beteiligt sind. Der Prozeß des staatlichen Zusammenschlusses der beiden deutschen Staaten wurde von daher nicht ausschließlich durch die politischen Parteien, sondern auch durch den

Lobbyismus unterschiedlichster bundesdeutscher Organisationen und Verbände beeinflußt. Wie von Wiesenthal belegt wurde, spielte dabei im Systemwechsel insbesondere das Interesse der westdeutschen politischen Klasse an der Aufrechterhaltung der politischen Strukturen und ihrer Einflußsphären eine zentrale Rolle.[11] Ausgehend von diesem selbstbezogenen politischen Interesse wurden gegenläufige Ansprüche und Akteure weitgehend abgewehrt. Dies gilt insbesondere für ostdeutsche, denen es aufgrund ihres geringeren Organisationsgrades bisher nicht gelang, eigene Macht- und Verteilungsansprüche hinreichend durchzusetzen.[12] Der Prozeß der Eliten-rekrutierung ist also zwar nicht zentral gesteuert, aber auch kein subjektloser Prozeß. Er wird vielmehr durch die interessengeleiteten Aktivitäten einer Vielzahl von Akteuren reproduziert, deren Ziele und Folgen sich überkreuzen und so zu teilweise völlig unbeabsichtigten Konsequenzen führen. Gemäß der Interessenthese müssen daher Überlegungen zum Abbau des Elitengefälles zwischen West- und Ostdeutschen an konkreten Interessen nicht nur von betroffenen Ostdeutschen sondern auch von den beteiligten bundesdeutschen Eliten sowie an deren Erfahrung unbeabsichtigter Handlungskonsequenzen ansetzen. Genauer gesagt, sind Interessen an einer stärkeren Beteiligung von Ostdeutschen gerade nicht nur bei Ostdeutschen selbst sondern auch in den etablierten bundesdeutschen Eliten zu suchen. Einen Ansatzpunkt dafür bilden deren bisherige Transformationserfahrungen.

Das entstandene Machtungleichgewicht bringt inzwischen nicht nur für Ostdeutsche negative Wirkungen wie die Umverteilung von Eigentum bzw. den Verlust von Arbeitsplätzen oder der Anerkennung von beruflichen Qualifikationen mit sich. Aufgrund der Komplexität gesellschaftlicher Prozesse in einer Zeit der Globalisierung und der wachsenden Risiken verteilen sich negative Fernwirkungen ungleichgewichteter gesellschaftlicher Entscheidungen nicht nur in Richtung einer sozialen Gruppe. In der Risikogesellschaft sind unbeabsichtigte Konsequenzen letztlich von allen Gesellschaftsmitgliedern zu tragen.[13] Speziell in Deutschland wirkt das Ungleichgewicht an Machtzugang und damit an Problemlagen zwischen West und Ost vor allem in Form einer wachsenden Finanzierungslücke für die Kosten des Sozialstaates auf alle Bürger zurück. Vor diesem Hintergrund zunehmend diffuser Rückwirkungen sozialer Ungleichgewichte sind die Anzeichen für ein inzwischen anwachsendes Interesse in bundesdeutschen Organisationen und bei westdeutschen Eliten an einer stärkeren Integration Ostdeutscher zu verstehen.[14] Wer an der stärkeren Beteiligung von Ostdeutschen an wichtigen gesellschaftlichen Entscheidungen in Deutschland interessiert ist, muß solche Interessenverschiebungen innerhalb der deutschen Eliten wahrnehmen und übergreifende handlungsfähige Interessenkoalitionen schaffen.

Die Allokationsthese und ihre Bedeutung für die Ausgrenzung von Ostdeutschen

Mit Bezug auf die so verstandene Interessenthese argumentiere ich, daß für eine erfolgreiche Verschiebung des west-ostdeutschen Machtgefälles nicht nur unterschiedliche Akteure, sondern auch die konkreten Prozeduren der Ausgrenzung beachtet werden müssen. Die Mechanismen der Ausgrenzung folgen vorrangig allgemeinen Kriterien und Routinen, die nicht speziell für Ostdeutsche erfunden wurden. Diese Auffassung nenne ich die *Allokationsthese.* Ausgehend von ihr stellt sich die Frage, auf welchem Wege veränderte Interessen unterschiedlicher Akteure erfolgreich in die ablaufenden Prozesse der Elitenrekrutierung eingreifen können.

Wenn die Änderung von Zugangskriterien zu den deutschen Eliten thematisiert werden, muß beachtet werden, daß die verschiedenen Akteure spezifische Rollen in einem historisch entstandenen Spiel wahrnehmen. Diese Rollen und Regeln sind Ausdruck der Interessenstrukturen der bundesdeutschen Nachkriegszeit. Durch die veränderte aktuelle Situation in Deutschland und Europa stehen auch sie unter einem gewissen Veränderungsdruck. Die allgemeinen Allokationsregeln haben eine jeweils spezifische Ausprägung in den einzelnen gesellschaftlichen Sektoren, deren Besonderheiten es zu beachten gilt. Erst in Addition dazu fungieren spezifische politische Kriterien für Ostdeutsche, wie die Regelanfrage an die Gauck-Behörde. Der Allokationsprozeß in allen deutschen Elitensektoren wird hingegen durch folgende fünf universelle Regeln beeinflußt. Ich werde bei ihrer Darstellung jeweils zeigen, wie diese traditionellen westdeutschen Allokationsprozeduren tenditiell ausschließend auf Ostdeutsche wirken:

1. Die allgemeinen deutschen Anforderungen an Berufsnachweise kann formuliert werden als Anforderung an eine *Akademisierung der deutschen Eliten* nach 1945. Damit ist nicht wie etwa in der französischen Tradition die Anforderung an Abschlüsse in ganz bestimmten Eliteuniversitäten gemeint. Vielmehr haben die Potsdamer Elitenstudie sowie andere empirische Untersuchungen gezeigt, daß die Bedeutung eines Universitätsabschlusses seit den 70er Jahren in Deutschland stark gewachsen ist. Zusätzlich hat jedes Bundesland bei Einstellungen in den öffentlichen Dienst eigene Festlegungen

getroffen. Es ist offensichtlich, das diese allgemeine Regel gemeinsam mit den Abwertungen vieler ostdeutscher Universitätsabschlüsse negative Konsequenzen für Ostdeutsche hat. Dort, wo beispielsweise Abschlüsse für ein Studienfach nur einiger DDR-Universitäten anerkannt werden oder wo zwar die formelle Höhe (Hochschulabschluß) nicht aber das Fach (Diplom für x; y) anerkannt wurde, sind Unsicherheiten und Grauzonen für Einstellungsentscheidungen entstanden. Dadurch wurde die Last der Entscheidung für oder gegen ostdeutsche Bewerber auf Elitepositionen entregelt und auf die Schultern der jeweiligen Verantwortungsträger verlagert. Und wer trägt schon gern eine derart personalisierte Bürde zur Entscheidung? Bekannt sind viele Einzelfälle, wo in Einstellungs-kommissionen zwar der subjektive Wille vorhanden war, ostdeutsche Bewerber einzustellen, sich jedoch die sogenannten "Sachzwänge" dann doch irgendwie durchgesetzt haben. Diese Mechanismen, die bei der Eliten-allokation insbesondere von Ostdeutschen auf Basis der indirekt entstandenen Personalisierung von Entscheidungsrisiken bestehen, schlagen sich letztlich in den oben skizzierten Elite-Statistiken nieder. Eine Veränderung solcher numerischen Tendenzen setzt also die Veränderung der sogenannten "Sachzwänge" voraus.

2. Eine zweite allgemeine Anforderung für den Aufstieg in deutschen Eliten kann als *organisationsinterne Langzeiterfahrung* formuliert werden. Sie ist aus Sicht der rekrutierenden Institutionen notwendig, um die Loyalität der Aspiranten organisationsintern hinreichend sicher prüfen zu können. Für Ostdeutsche hat diese Anforderung die simple Konsequenz, daß innerhalb jeder Generation jeweils Westdeutsche über eine längere Organisations-erfahrung verfügen. Dieses Problem wird gewissermaßen in die Zeit hinein-verschoben. Die Situation gleicht der im Märchen vom Hasen und Igel, wo letzterer immer schon am Ziel ist, so schnell der Hase auch rennen mag. Insbesondere die ältere und die mittlere Generation können diesen Vorsprung generationsintern niemals aufholen. Nur in der jüngeren Genration, die nach 1990 ihre Ausbildung begann, kann dieses Problem gelöst werden. Bei einer genaueren Sektoranalyse zeigen sich jedoch auch für diese jüngste Generation zusätzliche Hindernisse für einen Elitenzugang insbesondere im ökonomischen und juristischen Bereich. So hat Hartmann nachgewiesen, daß Eliteaspiranten im ökonomischen Sektor nicht nur über einen entsprechenden Abschluß verfügen müssen, sondern ebenfalls der Anforderung unterliegen, in einer gut situierten bürgerlichen Familie aufgewachsen zu sein. Wenn dies

gilt, so verfehlt auch die jüngste Generation von in der DDR geborenen Deutschen das Klassenziel, einfach aus Mangel an der "richtigen Familie". Die allgemeine Tendenz der sozialen Schließung der Deutschen Eliten in einigen gesellschaftlichen Bereichen ist kein kurzfristiges und keineswegs ein West-Ost-Problem, sondern ein Problem der Klassenbildung. Eine Lösung scheint hier zur Zeit völlig offen und sie kann keinesfalls im Horizont einer Generation erwartet werden.

3. Die dritte allgemeine Eltienanforderung nenne ich die *Anforderung nach lebenslanger Unterordnung aller Lebensbereiche unter den der Karriere.* Allgemein wird sie als Nachweis der lebenslangen persönlichen Belastbarkeit formuliert. Diese Anforderung korrespondiert unausgesprochen mit einem traditionellen Familienmodell, in dem ein Partner, im Regelfall der Mann, eine mehr als ausfüllende Karriere macht, während er sozial und emotional in der Familie entlastet wird. Es ist offensichtlich, daß dieses Elitenmodell Ostdeutsche, vor allem ostdeutsche Frauen ausgrenzt, da sich hier andere Geschlechterbeziehungen und Familientypen entwickelt haben. Die meisten ostdeutschen Frauen haben Kinder, alleinstehende Mütter sind keine Seltenheit. Sie haben Bedürfnisse nach flexiblen und Teilzeitlösungen, gegen deren Durchsetzung gerade in Elitepositionen in Deutschland enorme Barrieren bestehen. Auf diesem Wege verzichten viele ostdeutsche Frauen auf Karriereaufstiege, da sie die Kosten dieser sozialen Aufstiege für ihre Kinder und Familien völlig individuell tragen müßten. Zynischer weise wird ihnen dieses vorsorgliche Verhalten aus gesellschaftlicher Sicht häufig als Leistungsverweigerung angerechnet. In den Interessen an der Veränderung der Rahmenbedingungen für Aufstiege in Elitepositionen treffen sich ost- und westdeutsche Frauen gleichermaßen. Die Fähigkeit vieler gut ausgebildeter Frauen, unterschiedliche Verhaltensanforderungen differenzierter sozialer Sphären abzustimmen und zu verbinden, ist eine postmoderne Verhaltensqualität in differenzierten, unübersichtlichen, riskanten Gesellschaften. Die in Deutschland dominante Form des Instrumentalisierungsverhaltens birgt vielfältige Langzeitgefahren. Daher ist die in spezifischer Form insbesondere bei ostdeutschen (und westdeutschen) Frauen sozialisierte Fähigkeit zu nachhaltigen Problemlösungen eine Anforderung, die dringend in den aktuellen Allokationskriterien umgesetzt werden muß. Frauen sind nicht nur gut qualifiziert, sondern sie besitzen die Fähigkeit des flexiblen Perspektivenwechsels und der Anpassung an akute Problemsituationen, in denen Anforderungen unterschiedlicher Bereiche vermittelt werden müssen.

Daher scheint es dringend notwendig die Allokationskriterien für derartige
weibliche Fähigkeiten zu öffnen. Dies würde auch einen indirekten Vorteil
für Ostdeutsche (Frauen) schaffen.

4. Die vierte allgemeine Anforderung korrespondiert mit der dritten. Bezieht
sich auf die *ununterbochene Kontinuität der Karriere*. Auch hier entsteht ein
Geschlechterproblem. Zusätzlich erschwerend kommt für alle Ostdeutschen
hinzu, daß sie mit dem Systemwechsel 1990 in der überwiegenden Mehrheit
Karrierebrüche hinnehmen mußten. Faktisch sind alle Ostdeutschen aus
westdeutscher Sicht "Seiteneinsteiger", da es keine Kontinuitäten zwischen
den Eliten beider Systeme geben konnte. Die eigentliche Fähigkeit, die
innerhalb des Transformationsprozesses durch ostdeutsche Elitenaspiranten
nachgewiesen wurde, nämlich die Fähigkeit zur sozialen und beruflichen
Flexibilität wird in dem Maße im deutschen Katalog der Elitenkriterien unter
"ferner liefen" gehandelt. Hingegen steht die Anforderung kontinuierlicher
Aufstiege ganz oben. Angesichts der zunehmenden Anforderungen zur
flexiblen Bewältigung multivariater Anforderungsprofile scheint es dringend
notwendig, den Anforderungskatalog an deutsche Eliten zu erweitern,
wodurch wiederum indirekt soziale Öffnungen gegenüber Ostdeutschen
entstünden.

5. *Internalisierter "dress code"*. Dieser Punkt scheint auf den ersten Blick
nebensächlich. Doch wie bereits Bourdieu überzeugend für die französische
Gesellschaft nachwies, hat er in modernen ästhetisierten Gesellschaften einen
entscheidenden Einfluß auf die Verteilung von Machtpositionen. So meinen
beispielsweise viele Westdeutsche auch 10 Jahre nach der staatlichen Einheit
der Deutschen, daß sie auf den ersten Blick einen Westdeutschen von einem
Ostdeutschen unterscheiden können. Sicher lassen sich heute noch
tendentielle Unterschiede im Geschmack erkennen, auch wenn dies
insbesondere in der jüngeren Generation fast gegen Null geht. Dennoch, wie
meine eigenen empirischen Untersuchungen belegen, läßt gerade bei
Ostdeutschen das äußere Erscheinungsbild häufig keine Schlüsse auf die
Professionalität und Integrität der Personen zu. Im Gegenteil, die manchmal
unterbewertete Bedeutung ästhetischer codes zeugt häufig von einer
besonderen Konzentration auf fachliche Probleme und zum Teil auf
besondere Selbständigkeit bei der Lösung von Problemen. Die mit der
Einhaltung relativ enger ästhetischer Merkmale verbundene Erwartung an
Professionalität, Loyalität, Vertrauenswürdigkeit birgt unter den gegebenen

Transformationsbedingungen eine Verengung auf bestimmte personale Potentiale in sich. Wie Untersuchungen belegen werden in persönlichen Beziehungen entsprechende Vorurteile gegenüber Ostdeutschen häufig abgebaut, was sich jedoch in keiner Weise in Veränderungen der allgemeinen Zugangskriterien ausdrückt.

Nachdem diese allgemeinen Zugangskriterien zu deutschen Eliten in ihrer Wirkung auf die Ostdeutschen erklärt wurden, soll nun auch ein speziell für Ostdeutsche eingeführtes benannt werden: *Der Nachweis politischer Unbescholtenheit.* Sie hatte zwar in den ersten beiden Transformationsjahren eine große Bedeutung beim Elitenwechsel in ostdeutschen Institutionen, wurde in den vergangenen Jahren jedoch schrittweise durch andere Mechanismen überlagert. Ich denke, es ist deutlich geworden, daß auch nach der Abschaffung der Regelanfrage an die Gauck-Behörde die Ausgrenzung von Ostdeutschen aus den deutschen Eliten fortdauern wird, wenn nicht die allgemeinen Zugangskriterien in Bewegung kommen.

Spezifische Zugangskriterien zur politischen Elite – empirische Befunde
Die genannten fünf allgemeinen Zugangskriterien zu den deutschen Elitepositionen werden sektorintern spezifiziert. Dies kann an empirischen Untersuchungen in den Bereichen Politik und Wirtschaft empirisch nachgewiesen werden. Einer der konsequentesten Kritiker der politischen Elite in Deutschland ist Scheuch.[15] Er hat bereits in den 80er Jahren auf der Basis der damaligen Elitenstudie vor allem den bürokratischen Filz sowie Tendenzen der Bestechlichkeit kritisiert. Am Rande verweist er auch auf Mechanismen der Elitenrekrutierung. Herzog zeigt hingegen Rekrutierungskriterien und -mechanismen der politischen Elite in Deutschland genauer auf, durch die spezifische Zugangsbeschränkungen zur politischen Elite in Deutschland reproduziert werden. Er sieht insbesondere *Tendenzen zur Professionalisierung* politischer Tätigkeiten, die auch die Zugangskriterien und Zugangswege zur politische Elite Bestimmen. Er konnte belegen, daß die Mehrheit der Amtsinhaber spezielle Karrierewege innerhalb politischer Organisationen absolvieren mußten, die durch ununterbrochene und stetig anwachsende politische Verantwortung im allgemeinen und durch eine langfristige Inhabe einzelner Ämter im besonderen gekennzeichnet sind.[16] Auch in der Potsdamer Elitenstudie kann Wetzel derartige Tendenzen aufzeigen.[17] Gleichzeitig weist er nach, daß sich Karrierewillige während der langen Verweildauer in bestimmten Organisationen vor allem starken *organisationsinternen Kontrollmechanismen* ihres Verhalten ausgesetzt

sehen, die sie zur *Anpassung an tradiertes Organisationsverhalten* drängen.
Im Sektor Politik empfinden 57% der befragten Positionsinhaber ihre
Durchsetzungsfähigkeit sehr stark bzw. stark eingeschränkt.[18] Ähnlich
drastische Werte finden sich in den Sektoren Militär, Verwaltung,
Gewerkschaften und Wissenschaft. Hofer zitiert in diesem Zusammenhang
den Altbundespräsidenten von Weizsäcker, der kritisiert, daß auf diese Weise
in der Politik lediglich "Generalisten mit Spezialwissen, wie man den Gegner
bekämpft" befördert werden.[19]

Neben diesen Rekrutierungsmechanismen und –kriterien belegt Herzog
die zentrale Bedeutung von *Berufsverbänden als wichtige gestaltende
Subjekte* im Prozeß der Elitenrekrutierung in Deutschland. Sie fungieren als
kollektive Kontrollorgane der Eingangsvoraussetzungen und Verhaltens-
normen für Elitenanwärter. Sie erheben zum einen Anspruch auf Teilhabe an
der Definitionsmacht bei Zugangskriterien. Indem sie bestimmte formelle
Ausbildungszertifikate als notwendige Zugangskriterien zunehmend durchsetzen, nehmen sie unmittelbaren Einfluß auf den Prozeß der Professionalisierung der Politik. Sie beschränken zum anderen die Konkurrenz zwischen
Positionsinhabern innerhalb von politischen Organisationen, um diese so
nach außen hin zu stabilisieren. Auf diese Weise werden organisations-
strukturelle bzw. Policy-Innovationen zumindest verzögert.

In der Potsdamer Elitestudie wurde nachgewiesen, daß Ostdeutsche
gerade im Elitensektor Politik stärker vertreten sind als in anderen Bereichen,
ohne daß sie bisher einen adäquaten Einfluß gelten machen konnten. Dies
beweist nicht zuletzt die Zusammensetzung der neuen Regierung von SPD
und Bündnis 90/Grüne, in der eine ostdeutsche Politikerin vertreten ist. Wie
für die Frauen gilt für Ostdeutsche, dass hier ein wichtiger Anfang gemacht
wurde. Daran anknüpfend scheint es notwendig, das öffentliche Bewußtsein
für die entwicklungsfördernden Kompetenzen beider Gruppen zu öffnen.
Dadurch kann ein Bedarf nach entsprechenden Personen in Elitepositionen
erzeugt und über Wahlen durchgesetzt werden.

Spezifische Zugangskriterien zu den Wirtschaftseliten – empirische Befunde
Auch im Bereich der Wirtschaftseliten können allgemeine Rekrutierungsmechanismen und -kriterien nachgewiesen werden, die nicht speziell
ostdeutsche Kompetenzen ausgrenzen, sondern insgesamt auf ihre
Entwicklungsfreundlichkeit hin analysiert werden müssen. Von besonderer
Bedeutung sind hier die Forschungsergebnisse von Hartmann, der 1995 die
soziale Rekrutierung der deutschen Manager in den 100 größten deutschen

Unternehmen untersuchte. Er weist für diesen Elitensektor nach, daß Deutschland nicht wie Frankreich den Zugang zu seiner nationalen Wirtschaftselite bereits auf der Ebene von Eliteschulen limitiert. Vielmehr bilden spezielle Auswahlverfahren von Bewerbern sowie die Durchsetzung tradierter Karrierewege die ausschlaggebenden Mechanismen der Rekrutierung deutscher Wirtschaftseliten. Diese sichern eine ausgeprägte Anpassungstendenz des Verhaltens von Anwärtern und Positionsinhabern an vorhandene Gepflogenheiten, während nach seinen empirischen Daten davon abweichende Handlungskompetenzen kaum gefördert werden.[20] Er zieht ein ähnliches Fazit wie Wiesenthal für die Politik. Das Sicherheitsbedürfnis der Unternehmen erscheint diesen bedeutsamer als ihr ebenfalls vorhandenes Entwicklungsbedürfnis. Hartmann kann belegen, daß im Regelfall Positionsanwärter mit langjährigen *hausinternen*, mindestens aber mit *brancheninternen Karrieremustern* bevorzugt werden. Späteinsteiger sind eher selten und Quereinsteiger nur in besonderen Fällen etwa bei Positionsbesetzungen auf höchster Ebene (Aufsichtsrat u.ä.) nachzuweisen. Honoriert wird insbesondere die Zielstrebigkeit von Berufslaufbahnen, keine unvorhersehbaren Wechsel. Damit sind Elitenaspiranten zwar nicht wie in Frankreich seit ihrer Ausbildung, aber immerhin von Beginn ihres Berufseintrittes an der kontinuierlichen Kontrolle ganz bestimmter Unternehmen bzw. Branchen und ihren tradierten Elitekriterien ausgesetzt. Jede einzelne Aufstiegsstufe wird nur durch eine kontinuierliche Anpassung an diese Erwartungsmuster erreicht. Abweichende Handlungsqualifikationen können eventuell zusätzlich eingebracht werden, aber immer unter der Bedingung, dass die Grunderwartungen hinreichend erfüllt werden.

Darüber hinaus weist Hartmann nach, daß sich die Einstellungskriterien der deutschen Wirtschaftselite im Personalmanagement der großen und einflußreichen Unternehmen in den vergangenen 25 Jahren nicht verändert haben. Durch Expertenbefragungen von Personalmanagern und Managern wies er fünf solche relativ stabilen Auswahlmechanismen nach: souveränes Auftreten, gute Allgemeinbildung, angemessene Umgangsformen, optimistische Lebenshaltung, unternehmerische Einstellung. Erfahrungen in artfremden Wirtschaftsbereichen oder in anderen Gesellschaftsbereichen, komplexe Kommunikationsfähigkeiten u.ä. spielen hingegen eine deutlich nachgeordnete Rolle. Entscheidend sind nach seinen Beobachtungen solche Handlungskompetenzen, die bestimmten Milieuanforderungen gerecht werden sowie zunehmend eine akademische Ausbildung einschließen. Hartmann konstatiert zusammenfassend "letztlich sorgt der klassenspezifische Habitus für eine soziale Schließung".[21] Im Ergebnis vor allem organisationsinterner Rekrutierungswege und tradierter Rekrutierungs-kriterien reproduziert sich in Deutschland eine sozialstrukturell relativ geschlossene Wirtschaftselite mit relativ festgefügten Vorstellungen über erfolgreiche Wege der Wirtschaftsentwicklung. Zwei Drittel entstammen beispielsweise dem gehobenen Bürgertum, während der Anteil der Mittelschichten oder gar von Arbeitern seit 1970 gesunken ist.[22] Die Zeit des erfahrungsgeleiteten Unternehmertums der Nachkriegszeit ist vorbei. Die deutsche Wirtschaft wird am Ende des Jahrhunderts durch Akademiker aus vorrangig gehobenem Elternhaus dominiert. Es liegt auf der Hand, daß die Ostdeutschen diese Doppeldisposition weder gegenwärtig aufweisen, noch durch die nächste bildungswillige Akademikergeneration erringen können. Nur ein Wandel der allgemeinen Rekrutierungskriterien hin zur Aufwertung moderner Handlungskompetenzen und -erfahrungen gepaart mit solider akademischer Grundausbildung bei gleichzeitiger Abwertung der sozialen Herkunft und ganz spezifischer Abschlüsse und Karrierewege könnte auch Ostdeutschen größere Chancen bieten.

Anhand der von Hartmann vorgelegten Forschungsergebnisse, die in ihren Grundtendenzen durch die Daten der Potsdamer Elitestudie bestätigt werden, kann im Wirtschaftsbereich wie in allen anderen Elitesektoren in den vergangenen 25 Jahren von *Professionalisierungstendenzen* der Eliten und damit von einer Akademisierung gesprochen werden. Diese verhindert jedoch bisher nicht, daß der gleichzeitig zu verzeichnende Rückstand zum internationalen Trend der Einbeziehung von sogenannten Hektik-kompetenzen sowie von sozialen Kompetenzen bei der Rekrutierung deutscher Eliten fortbesteht. Aktuelle Analysen des globalen Wandels und der zu verzeichnenden Krisenerscheinungen betonen die Notwendigkeit, instrumentelle Entwicklungsvorstellungen und die ihnen entsprechenden Handlungskompetenzen durch kommunikativ integrierte Entwicklungs-konzepte und die sie fördernden subjektiven Fähigkeiten mindestens zu ergänzen.[23] Neue Zukunftsmodelle wie etwa das der "Nachhaltigen Entwicklung" kritisieren die Orientierung auf kurzfristig effektive gesellschaftliche Lösungen mit zum Teil verheerenden langfristigen Folgen. Ausgehend von ihnen wird daher von verantwortlichen Entscheidungsträgern gefordert, mittel- und langfristige Zeithorizonte als Erfolgskriterium für Konzepte einzubeziehen. Dadurch sollen nachhaltige Entwicklungen begünstigt werden, indem bewußt längere Zeiten zur Lösung von Konflikten sowie die Beteiligung vielfältiger Beteiligter und Betroffener mit sehr unterschiedlichen Interessen in Kauf genommen werden. Auch vom Standpunkt der modernen Organisationsforschung aus wird zunehmend die Notwendigkeit betont, nicht starr an der strukturellen Stabilität von Organisation durch klar definierte Umweltabgrenzungen festzuhalten. Vielmehr kann Organisationsstabilität in sich verändernden Umwelten nur über partielle strukturelle und personale Organisationsöffnungen gegenüber ihren Umwelten reproduziert werden.[24] Es geht also um die Reproduktion von Strukturen gerade durch deren Veränderung. Nicht die Anpassung von mehr oder weniger großen Gruppen von "fremden" Individuen an bestehende und bewährte Organisationsstrukturen ist das Thema, sondern die Anpassung von Organisationen selbst an veränderte Umwelten. Es geht nicht um Transformation hin zu einer gegebenen Moderne. Thematisiert wird deren Modernisierung durch Selbsttransformation.

Kritische Eliteforschungen aus diesem theoretischen Umfeld kommen zu dem Schluß, daß zum einen neuartige internationale Organisationsstrukturen für nationale, sektorale und regionalspezifische Eliten geschaffen werden müssen, um den gegenwärtigen zerstörerischen Tendenzen der globalisierten Finanz- und Informationseliten entgegenwirken zu können.[25] Zum anderen erscheint es dringend geboten, sozial und ökologisch analytische und integrierende Handlungskompetenzen in den Kanon der notwendigen subjektiven Fähigkeiten von Eliteaspiranten aufzunehmen.[26]

Schlußfolgerungen

Welche Schlußfolgerungen lassen sich aus den kritischen Befunden der Elitenrekrutierung und den konstatierten Entwicklungsanforderungen für die Überwindung des Elitengefälles zwischen West- und Ostdeutschland ziehen? Eine stärkere Integration von Ostdeutschen in die deutschen Elitepositionen durch eine etwaige Herabsetzung von Zugangskriterien ist weder entwicklungspolitisch sinnvoll noch von den Betroffenen selbst gewünscht. Wird der Zirkel der Elitenkriterien hingegen genau in die Richtung sozial analytischer und integrierender Fähigkeiten geöffnet, so empfehlen sich neben Frauen auch ein Teil der Ostdeutschen (und speciell der ostdeutschen Frauen) wie von selbst auf verantwortliche Positionen. Gerade für die sensible Analyse differierender Ansprüche und Bedingungsgefüge sowie ihre längerfristige Integration in spezifische Lösungskonzepte könnten Ostdeutsche ihre Erfahrungen und Handlungskompetenzen einbringen, die sie im Prozeß der erfolgreichen Bewältigung des Transformationsprozesses gewonnen haben.

Es muß betont werden, daß hier nicht Verhaltenskompetenzen gemeint sind, die sich auf den Umgang mit den spezifischen DDR-Bedingungen einer politisch zentralisierten Mangelwirtschaft beziehen. Vielmehr sind daran mehr oder weniger anknüpfende, aber den neuen gesellschaftlichen Bedingungen angepaßte Verhaltensmuster gemeint, durch die Ostdeutsche sich im Transformationsprozeß in die deutsche Gesellschaft eingebracht haben.

Zusammenfassend läßt sich feststellen: Die Ostdeutschen sind in den deutschen Eliten unterrepräsentiert. Diese Ungleichheit wird nach einer anfänglichen Phase besonderer politisierter Auswahlverfahren durch allgemeine Prozesse reproduziert, in denen historisch gewachsene Zugangskriterien und -regeln zu den deutschen Eliten wirksam werden. Diese reagieren völlig unzureichend auf neuartige Kompetenzen, die für moderne Eliten unversichtbar werden. Es sind dies die oben skizzierten Fähigkeiten

• zum Perspektivenwechsel und zur Verbindung unterschiedlicher fachlicher Anforderungsprofile

• zum individuellen Lernen in unüberichtlichen riskanten gesellschaftlichen Situationen

• zur kommunikativen Lösung von Problemsituationen.

Solche Kompetenzen sind sowohl bei Ost- als auch bei Westdeutschen, bei Frauen wie auch bei Männern zu finden. Die Frage ist folgerichtig nicht, wer kompetenter sei für Elitenpositionen, die einen oder die anderen. Die Frage muß vielmehr lauten, welche Verhaltenstypen und Qualifikationsfiguren sind für moderne Eliten unverzichtbar und wie können sie unter den Aspiranten aufgespürt werden.

Wie meine eigenen empirischen Untersuchungen belegen, können sich ostdeutsche Handlungspotentiale bisher in vielen Fällen nicht hinreichend gesellschaftlich entfalten. Teilweise verfallen sie auch, wenn ihre Träger die Erfahrung machen, daß sie damit anhaltend auf strukturelle Widerstände stoßen und so ihre Kräfte ohne hinreichende Ergebnisse verschlissen werden. In Folge solcher Erfahrungen erfolglos verbrauchter individueller Kräfte zieht sich gegenwärtig ein Teil der ostdeutschen Kompetenzträger wieder in eher private Handlungsnischen zurück, deren alternative Gestaltung sich nicht unmittelbar auf gesellschaftliche Strukturen auswirkt. Aus meinen eigenen empirischen Untersuchungen läßt sich ein Trend zum Verschleiß der mittleren Generation der zukunftsorientierten Ostdeutschen erkennen. Er macht die große Bedeutung der Zeit für mögliche Veränderungsprozesse in der Elitenzusammensetzung deutlich.

Anmerkungen

[1] Vgl. Walter Hanesch, *Armut in Deutschland*, Der Armutsbericht des DGB und des Paritätischen Wohlfahrtsverbands, Rowohlt: Reinbek bei Hamburg 1994; Astrid Segert and Irene Zierke, *Sozialstruktur und Milieuerfahrung, Empirische und theoretische Aspekte des alltagskulturellen Wandels in Ostdeutschland*, Westdeutscher Verlag: Opladen, 1997.

[2] Die Studie wurde von der DFG gefördert. Mitte 1995 wurden insgesamt 2341 mündliche Interviews durchgeführt. Es wurden nach dem Positionsansatz Führungskräfte aus den wichtigsten Organisationen aller gesellschaftlicher Sektoren ausgewählt.

[3] Vgl. Michael Hartmann, *Topmanager, Die Rekrutierung einer Elite*, Campus: Frankfurt a.M., 1996.

[4] Wilhelm Bürklin and Hilke Rebenstorf, 1997, *Eliten in Deutschland, Rekrutierung und Integration*, Leske und Budrich: Opladen, 1997, S. 67.

[5] Vgl. Martin Diewald and Heike Solga, "Ordnung im Umbruch? Strukturwandel, berufliche Mobilität und Stabilität im Transformationsprozeß", in: Lars Clausen, Hgb., *Gesellschaften im Umbruch*, Campus: Frankfurt a.M., 1996, pp. 259-274; Christian Wetzel, 1997, "Rekrutierung und Sozialisation der ostdeutschen Elite – Aufstieg einer deutschen Gegenelite?", in: Wilhelm Bürklin und Hilke Rebenstorf, *Eliten in Deutschland. Rekrutierung und Integration*, Leske und Budrich: Opladen, S.. 201-238.

[6] Vgl. Wolfgang Dümke and Fritz Vilmar, *Kolonialisierung der DDR: Kritische Analysen und Alternativen des Einigungsprozesses*, Agenda: Münster, 1995; Wolfgang Richter, "Kolonialisierung der DDR", in: Klaus Jürgen Scherer, Ulrich Wasmuht, *Mut zur Utopie*, Agenda: Münster, 1994.

[7] Christian Wetzel, "Rekrutierung und sozialisation der ostdeutschen Elite – Aufstieg einer deutschen Gegenelite?", in: Wilhelm Bürklin und Hilke Rebenstorf, *Eliten in Deutschland, Rekrutierung und Integration*, Leske und Budrich: Opladen, 1997, S. 201-238.

[8] Max A. Hofer, "Führungskrise der Elite. Anmerkungen zu einer Umfrage", *Forschung & Lehre*, H. 4, 1997, S. 175.

[9] G. Lowell Field, John Higley, 1983, *Elite und Liberalismus*, Westdeutscher Verlag: Opladen, 1983, S. 21.

[10] Dümke et al. 1995, S. 14.

[11] Vgl. Helmuth Wiesenthal, *Blockaden, Asymmetrien, Perfektionsmängel: Ein Vergleich der Repräsentationschancen sozialer Interessen im Transformationsprozeß*, Humboldt-Universität Berlin, 1993.

[12] Vgl. Heidrun Abromeit, "Die 'Vertretungslücke'. Probleme im neuen deutschen Bundesstaat", *Gegenwartskunde*, H. 42, 1993, S. 281-292.

[13] Ulrich Beck, *Risikogesellschaft. Auf dem Weg in eine andere Moderne*, Suhrkamp: Frankfurt a.M., 1986.

[14] Als Beispiele können die Antrittsrede des neuen Bundeskanzlers Gerhard Schröder (SPD), in der er sein ausdrückliches Verständnis gegenüber den Interessen der ostdeutschen Länder äußerte, sowie der damalige Vorschlag Wolfgang Schäubles (CDU), die CDU für ehemalige SED-Miglieder zu öffnen.

[15] Erwin Scheuch and Ute Scheuch, *Cliquen, Klüngel und Karrieren: Über den Verfall der politischen Parteien – eine Studie*, Rowohlt: Reinbek bei Hamburg, 1992.

[16] Dietrich Herzog, "Der moderne Berufspolitiker", in: Landeszentrale für politische Bildung Baden-Württemberg, ed., *Eliten in der Bundesrepublik Deutschland*, Kohlhammer: Stuttgart/Berlin/Köln, 1990, S. 37.

[17] Wetzel, 1997, S. 186.

[18] Ebda., S. 297.

[19] Vgl. Hofer, 1997, S. 176

[20] Hartmann, 1996, S. 135

[21] Michael Hartmann, 1997, "Soziale Öffnung oder soziale Schließung, Die deutsche und die französische Wirtschaftselite zwischen 1970 und 1995", *Zeitschrift für Soziologie*, H. 4, 1997,. S. 296 and 308.

[22] Hartmann, 1997, S. 303.

[23] Christopher Lasch, *The Revolt of the Elites and the Betrayal of Democracy*, Sage: London, 1995.

[24] Richard W. Scott, *Institutions and Organizations*, Sage: London, 1995.

[25] Vgl. Lester R. Brown, Christopher Flavin und Sandra Postel, 1992, *Zur Rettung des Planeten Erde. Strategien für eine ökologisch nachhaltige Weltwirtschaft*, Fischer:

Frankfurt a.M., 1992; Christopher Lasch, *The Revolt of the Elites and the Betrayal of Democracy*, Sage: London, 1995.

[26] Segert et. al, 1997, S. 239; vgl. auch Carol Hagemann-Wite, "Können Frauen die Politik verändern?" *Aus Politik und Zeitgeschichte, Beilage zur Wochenzeitschrift Das Parlament*, H. 9-10, 1987, S. 29-37; Hilke Rebenstorf, "Frauen im Bundestag – anders als die Männer", in: Landeszentrale für politische Bildung Baden-Württemberg, Hgb., *Eliten in der Bundesrepublik Deutschland*, Kohlhammer: Stuttgart/Berlin/Köln, 1990, S. 52-75.

Notes on the Contributors

Gary Bruce holds a Ph.D. in German History from McGill University. He is currently a lecturer with the Department of History at St. Thomas University in Fredericton, New Brunswick, Canada.

Randall Bytwerk is Professor of Communication Arts and Sciences at Calvin College, Grand Rapids, Michigan, USA.

Wolfgang Emmerich is Professor of Literature and Cultural Studies at the Universität Bremen, Germany. His numerous publications include the *Kleine Literaturgeschichte der DDR*.

David Harding is completing a Ph.D. in History at the University of Virginia, USA.

Meredith Heiser-Duron is Professor of Political Science at Foothill College, Los Altos Hills, California, USA. Her research, teaching, and publications focus on German unification and its consequences for party politics.

Jeffrey Kopstein is Associate Professor of Political Science at the University of Colorado at Boulder, USA. He is the author of *The Politics of Economic Decline in East Germany, 1945-1989* (1997).

Karen Kramer is the Director of Stanford University's Study Center in Berlin, Germany.

Bernd Lindner is a *Wissenschaftlicher Angestellter* of the German Federal Museum of History (Leipzig) and a *Privatdozent* in Sociology at the Universität Karlsruhe, Germany.

Laurence McFalls is Associate Professor of Political Science at the Université de Montréal, Québec, Canada, Associate Director of the Canadian Centre for German and European Studies, and President of the Eastern German Studies Association.

Catherine Perron is completing her Ph.D. in Political Science at the Institut d'études politiques de Paris, France. She is also project manager for South-Eastern Europe for the French non-profit organization Transeuropéennes.

Lothar Probst is Managing Director of the Institute for German Cultural Studies at the Universität Bremen, Germany. His research and publications focus on parties, social movements, and political culture in Germany.

Marie-Elisabeth Räkel recently completed a Ph.D. in History at the Université de Montréal, Canada, and is cultural attaché for the Québec government's delegation in Berlin.

Astrid Segert is a researcher at the Center for Contemporary History of the Universität Potsdam, Germany.

Roswitha Skare is Assistant Professor in the Department of Documentation Studies at Tromsö University, Norway.

Gerhard Wettig retired in 1999 as Director of International Relations and International Security Studies at the Federal Institute for Eastern European and International Studies in Cologne, Germany. He is currently a member of the Common German-Russian Commission on Contemporary History and co-director of a joint German-Russian research team.

Jennifer Yoder is Assistant Professor of Political Science at Colby College, Maine, USA.